KW-761-288

LEGAL THEORY IN THE CRUCIBLE OF CONSTITUTIONAL JUSTICE

For Mom and Dad

Legal Theory in the Crucible of Constitutional Justice

A study of judges and political morality in Canada, Ireland and Italy

RORY O'CONNELL
Department of Law, Lancaster University

2000

DARTMOUTH
Aldershot • Burlington USA • Singapore • Sydney

© Rory O'Connell 2000

All rights reserved. No part of this publication may be reproduced, stored in a retrieval system, or transmitted in any form or by any means, electronic, mechanical, photocopying, recording or otherwise without the prior permission of the publisher.

Published by
Dartmouth Publishing Company Limited
Ashgate Publishing Ltd
Gower House
Croft Road
Aldershot
Hants GU11 3HR
England

Ashgate Publishing Company
131 Main Street
Burlington
Vermont 05401
USA

Ashgate website: http://www.ashgate.com

British Library Cataloguing in Publication Data
O'Connell, Rory
  Legal theory in the crucible of constitutional justice : a
  study of judges and political morality in Canada, Ireland
  and Italy
  1. Constitutional law - Canada 2. Constitutional law - Italy
  3. Constitutional law - Ireland 4. Law - Canada -
  Interpretation and construction 5. Law - Ireland -
  Interpretation and construction 6. Law - Italy -
  Interpretation and construction
  I. Title
  342'.08

Library of Congress Cataloging-in-Publication Data
O'Connell, Rory.
  Legal theory in the crucible of constitutional justice : a study of judges and political
  morality in Canada, Ireland, and Italy / Rory O'Connell.
     p. cm.
  Includes bibliographical references and index.
  ISBN 0-7546-2097-2 (hb)
     1. Constitutional law--Canada. 2. Law--Canada--Philosophy. 3. Constitutional
  law--Ireland. 4. Law--Ireland--Philosopy. 5. Constitutional law--Italy. 6.
  Law--Italy--Philosophy. I. Title

K3165 .O28 2000
342--dc21   00-34253
ISBN 0 7546 2097 2

Printed in Great Britain by Antony Rowe Ltd, Chippenham, Wiltshire

Contents

Acknowledgements

An effort like this book, which lasted so long, creates many debts to which no Acknowledgements section can hope to do justice. Starting with this admission, let me thank those who helped me on this path.

I thank my Creator for what talents I possess.

I can never express sufficient gratitude to my family who have been very patient with and supportive of a - at times too single-minded - researcher and law student for far longer than a few years.

This book is based on my Ph.D. thesis completed after four years at Florence's European University Institute. I would like to thank the Irish Department of Education and the EUI for their generous support during that time.

I finished this book during my time at Lancaster University, and I would like to thank all my colleagues and students at that institution for their help and encouragement. I am especially grateful to Sol Picciotto for his advice on publishing, Michael Salter for long discussions on legal theory, and Ian Bryan for general support! I am grateful also to Carlo Casonato of the University of Trento for his advice.

I am indebted to Tom Campbell, Neil MacCormick and an anonymous reviewer for Ashgate for many helpful suggestions. Many thanks also to Sonia Hubbard, Claire Annals and all the staff at Ashgate for their help in producing the final version.

I would also like to thank the editors of the *American Journal of Law and Religion* and an anonymous reviewer for that journal for some useful comments. I am grateful to Basil Blackwell for permission to use some material from an earlier article in *Ratio Juris*.

The first comment of Massimo La Torre on my work was that it was unclear and going in far too many directions. To the extent that today this work is presentable, much credit goes to my supervisor. His comments, suggestions and support have been invaluable, and set high standards for any would-be supervisor at the European University Institute.

I also express my gratitude to my jury members who read the Ph.D. on which this book is based: Luis Diez-Picazo, Neil MacCormick and Robert Alexy. I greatly appreciate their insightful comments and assistance.

I am also particularly grateful for the first year seminars of Prof. Diez-Picazo, which stressed that constitutional law was fun. Many thanks also to Prof. Teubner, whose comments on my June Paper have never left me, though perhaps I have not taken full advantage of them.

I also thank my LL.M. supervisor, Tom Cooney of University College Dublin. I hope never to forget any of the lessons he taught me as a supervisor and teacher.

I am very indebted to the administration and academic staff of York University and the University of Toronto, who welcomed me during a very profitable stay in Toronto. I thank David Beatty, David Dyzenhaus, Allan Hutchinson, Peter Hogg for their time, their insight and their enthusiasm. I especially thank Michael Mandel and his family, whose friendliness, generosity, help and comments were far more than any wandering academic could hope for.

Without the many support services of the EUI this thesis could (literally) not have been written. In particular I express my gratitude to the members of the Library and Computer Service, and the Coffee Bar. I am also grateful to the researcher reps and bar committee members at the EUI for all their work. More globally, I am grateful to the European University Institute for giving me the four most memorable years of my life.

To more personal matters. Living in one of the most beautiful regions of the world, and studying at one of the most prestigious research institutes in Europe, were minor privileges compared to that of knowing all the people I have met in San Domenico from all over Europe and the world. I cannot hope to thank everyone who has contributed to making my stay so rewarding and enjoyable. I hope no one will feel offended if I neglect to mention their names in what follows. I am grateful to you all for all your chats, smiles, kind inquiries and empathy.

To all those who helped directly with my dissertation, in one way or another: Aileen Kavanagh, Andrew Butler, Ben Crum, Cathy Richmond, Cecile Aptel, Daniel Oakey, David O'Neill, John Paterson, Leonor Soriano, Mario Drago, Marku Kiikeri, Ruth Rubio Marin, and

Yannis Papadopoulos. I appreciate all your efforts to influence me onto the right path!

To everyone who lived in Pian di Mugnone from Sept. 1993 to Sept. 1995, an infinity of thanks, we will never see the likes of those times again.

Nothing has been more important during the past years, especially in Florence, than the friends I made along the way. For their encouragement, support, patience, honesty, and trust my heartfelt thanks to: Ad, Adrienne, Alison, Andy, Fanny, Ide, Inge, Jeroen, Julian, Kirsten, Lisa, Marion, Mikko, Patrick, and Quico.

Finally, I owe some life-long debts: to Karin for her Dutch lessons and skiing example, and to Ruth for her uncompromising friendship, honesty and loyalty.

List of Abbreviations

A.C.	Appeal Cases
A.I.R. S.C.	All India Reports Supreme Court
Am. J. Comp. L.	American Journal of Comparative Law
Buff. L. Rev.	Buffalo Law Review
c.c.	codice civile
C.C.C.	Canadian Criminal Cases
C.H.R.R.	Canadian Human Rights Reporter
C.M.L.R.	Common Market Law Reports
c.p.	codice penale
c.p.p.	codice di procedura penale
Cal. L. Rev.	California Law Review
Card. L. Rev.	Cardozo Law Review
CJ	Chief Justice
CJC	Chief Justice of Canada
CLR	Commonwealth Law Reports
Col. L. Rev.	Columbia Law Review
D.P.P.	Director of Public Prosecutions
D.R.	Decisions and Reports
D.L.R.	Dominion Law Reports
E.C.R.	European Community Reports
E.H.R.R.	European Human Rights Reports
F.Supp.	Federal Supplement
Foro It.	Foro Italiano
G.C.	Giurisprudenza Costituzionale
H.C.	High Court
H.C.R.C.L.L.Rev.	Harvard Civil Rights and Civil Liberties Law Review
I.L.R.M.	Irish Law Reports Monthly
I.L.T.	Irish Law Times
I.L.T.R.	Irish Law Times Reports
I.R.	Irish Reports

Ir. Jur.	Irish Jurist
J.	Justice
J.Phil.	Journal of Philosophy
l.	legge
l.c.	legge costituzionale
L.R.C. (Const.)	Law Reports of the Commonwealth (Constitutional Law)
Law & Cont. Prob.	Law and Contemporary Problems
Law Q. Rev.	Law Quarterly Review
McGill L. J.	McGill Law Journal
Mich. L. Rev.	Michigan Law Review
Mod. L. Rev.	Modern Law Review
Nw. U.L.Rev.	Northwestern University Law Review
Ox. J.L.S.	Oxford Journal of Legal Studies
Phil. & Pub. Aff.	Philosophy and Public Affairs
Pol. Th.	Political Theory
Proc. Aris. Soc.	Proceedings of the Aristotelian Society
Q.B.	Queen's Bench
R.	Regina
r.d.	royal decree
R.D.P.	Revue de Droit Public
Riv. Int. Fil. Dir.	Rivista Internazionale di Filosofia del Diritto
S.C.	Supreme Court
SCC	Supreme Court of Canada
SCR	Supreme Court Reports
Soc. Phil. & Pol.	Social Philosophy and Policy
T.L.H.V.	Tanner Lectures on Human Values
U. Toronto L.J.	University of Toronto Law Journal
U.S.	United States Reports
unrep.	unreported
Valparaiso L. Rev.	Valparaiso Law Review
Yale L. J.	Yale Law Journal

1 Introduction: Legal Theory in the Crucible of Constitutional Justice

Introduction

This book is about the fundamental laws of three liberal democratic states, and the role played by the highest judicial authorities of those states in interpreting the law. The interpretations given are often of great moment for the states, and frequently involve unexpected interpretations of the law. Consider three examples.

In 1992, the Supreme Court of Canada ruled that one of the leading promoters of holocaust denial literature, could not be punished for peddling his lies. Although the Canadian Charter of Fundamental Rights and Freedoms emphasises the importance of equality and multi-culturalism, the Court ruled that the relevant section of the Criminal Code was unconstitutional. It violated the right to freedom of expression.

Also in 1992, a case came before the Supreme Court of Ireland, touching on the provision of the Irish Constitution which recognises the right to life of the foetus. The chief law officer of the State sought to restrain a 14 year old rape victim from going to Britain to have an abortion. By a majority vote, the Court recognised for the first time in Irish legal history, a (very) limited right to abortion - and rooted this right in the very article which was adopted in 1983 to *prohibit* abortion.

In 1989 the Italian Constitutional Court took a long hard look at various constitutional provisions - including a special provision on the Catholic Church. On the basis of this examination, the Court declared a new 'supreme principle of the Constitution' - the principle of laicity.

These cases are typical examples of 'constitutional justice' in modern liberal democracies. These are cases at the intersection of legality, legitimacy and legitimation - here questions of law intermingle with questions of power and of right. These cases resurrect the natural law tradition of studying law not merely as it is but also as to how it ought to be. 'Law' (*Recht, diritto, droit*) takes on nuances not merely of law, but of 'right', as was typical in natural law thinking.

The Argument

In this work I study the interrelation between constitutional interpretation and political morality, referring both to the work of constitutional judges and to the work of theoretical writers. My basic argument is the following:

> Constitutional judges, in the task of constitutional interpretation, try to *reconstruct* the legal materials before them, to provide the most acceptable reconstruction of the legal system from the viewpoint of political morality. In doing this they rely on *(legalised) criteria of political morality* to judge the correctness of the interpretation. Their reconstruction is a contribution to the *public debate* on the legitimacy of the legal order.

Traditional debates about the concept of law centred on a dispute between 'positivists' who rejected a conceptual link between law and morality, and 'natural lawyers', who asserted such a link. This book tries to steer a 'third way' between the conventional understandings of positivism and natural law.[1] It regards constitutional justice as an important feature of modern liberal democracies and sees constitutional interpretation as one of the principle paths for the third way of law.

In this introduction, I wish to do four things. First, I will explain some of the terms I will be using. Second, I look at the relevance of this topic in today's world. Third, I explain what is noteworthy about the approach in this book. Finally, I outline the structure of the argument.

Terms Used

First, this book deals with cases in liberal democracies, specifically Canada, Ireland and Italy, with references to cases in other such democracies. By liberal democracy I refer simply to those states which (1) have a basically democratic structure (universal suffrage, regular free elections to governing bodies, etc.); (2) recognise at least some basic rights and freedoms (free expression, equality, etc.); (3) embrace the concept of the *rule of law* (*état de droit, Rechtsstaat, stato di diritto*) in some sense (e.g. that state action should not be arbitrary, and that the law should be upheld by independent courts, etc.); and (4) generally rely on peaceful means to secure social change, transformation, etc. Of course, these concepts are themselves vague. Each state may have a different conception of these general concepts.[2] Indeed this book is precisely about those differing and competing conceptions of democracy, rights and the rule of law.

Secondly, this book is about the constitutions of these liberal democracies. I use this term in its material sense - the body of fundamental rules which organise the state, establish official bodies, regulate their powers and provide restrictions on those powers.[3] In the three case studies the constitutions are all written ones - Ireland's 1937 Constitution, Italy's 1947 one - and the set of documents that make up the Canadian Constitution, especially the 1982 Charter of Rights and Freedoms. However, this work is also about constitutions in a larger sense, for constitutions are richer than the sum of their written parts. The three case studies all demonstrate that a state's constitution may extend far beyond the ink on parchment. There is a constitutional morality or spirit for the written rules must be interpreted in the light of other concepts, such as custom and morality.

So, this book concentrates on constitutional interpretation. It looks at how meaning is ascribed to the words of the written text. In this sense every time we read a text we are interpreting it.[4] However, the process of interpretation is only obvious when the text we look at is ambiguous in some way, i.e. more than one meaning can be fairly attributed to it. This book argues that we should decide the meaning of the words of the constitutional text by testing competing interpretations for their conformity to the criteria of legalised political morality. These criteria do not necessarily provide a sure path to a single correct answer to legal questions. Rather they provide criteria by which we can orient our thinking in constitutional matters.

The criteria which I propose for constitutional courts are drawn from the sphere of political morality. The definitions of these concepts ('morality' and 'political') involve large debates of which I fear to treat. A 'morality' I understand as a set of normative rules, principles or goals, which purport to set standards of right and wrong, of virtue and vice, good and bad, just and unjust. Morality is thus an aspect of 'practical reason', it concerns fundamentally the question 'what to do?'. I use it, unless clearly indicated otherwise, in the sense of a critical, not conventional, morality. That is, I am not concerned with what *is* the moral system of a given agent or society (this is an empirical question), but rather with questions of what *ought* to be the moral rules (a normative inquiry). But I am not concerned with the interconnection primarily between law and morality, but between law and *political* morality, those set of moralities which purport to decide how the common life of many people is to be organised, and in particular when it is appropriate to use power and force in such relationships. Political moralities may be either free-standing or else embedded in broader moral theories. I also do not limit myself necessarily to consciously systematised political moralities, but also look at latent political moralities.

These concerns are all brought into sharp focus by looking at the organs of constitutional justice, those judicial or quasi-judicial bodies entrusted with interpreting the constitution, and deciding the constitutional validity of other legal acts. I concentrate on the 'highest judicial interpreter but not the final interpreter of the higher law'[5] - the Supreme Court. More specifically I look at the decisions of the Supreme Courts of Ireland and Canada, and of the Constitutional Court of Italy (to avoid repetition, I use phrases like 'constitutional court' and 'constitutional tribunal' to refer also to the Supreme Courts which exercise the power of constitutional review). Of course, these bodies are not the only organs of constitutional justice - all judicial bodies interpret and apply the constitution in cases before them. However, as far as the supreme moment of constitutional justice is concerned - whether an enactment of the Parliament goes beyond what the constitution permits - these are the courts with the judicial final word.

These themes unite in what might be described as a 'modern natural law' or 'post positivist' approach to legal work.6 Traditionally 'natural law' theories have been opposed to 'positivist' conceptions of law, with the main point of contention being the 'separation thesis': is law *conceptually* separate from morality? Both camps are host to many different theories, which at the fringes tend to merge, to form a third way of legal thinking - 'post-positivism' or 'modern natural law'- a third way typified by the writings of members of both camps.7 This book argues for an intimate connection between constitutional law and political morality.

Why Study the Topic of Constitutional Justice?

This topic is interesting for six general reasons. Constitutional justice is a wide-spread phenomenon, with the constitution serving as the supreme law of all modern states. The constitution is not merely the supreme law, it also serves as a guiding light in enacting and interpreting other legal acts. From the viewpoint of political science, constitutional courts serve many political purposes, operating as either facilitators of reform, or logjams. From the viewpoint of morality, constitutional law is the normative lynchpin of the entire legal system. Finally, despite the importance of constitutional justice there is still no agreement on the correct criteria of a valid constitutional interpretation.

The origins of modern constitutionalism are found in the US and French Revolutions, ('in which the ancient European structures of authority and legitimacy were irreparably fractured'8) the philosophical debate and political evolutions which preceded them and the new states which emerged in their wake. Whilst I cannot survey this large topic here, I just note some ironies. Both these revolutions claimed justification on the basis of natural law ideology, and were closely associated with versions of that ideology. The birth of these new states coincided with the demise of the great schools of natural law - the positivist approach to law soon emerged dominant. The ideas of natural law led, in the case of one of those revolutions, to influencing the creation of constitutional justice and judicial review of legislation; whilst in the other, it lead to a complete rejection of judicial review. Finally, the views of two of those natural law thinkers (Rousseau and Kant) are often interpreted as leading to two different elements of modern constitutionalism - democracy and fundamental rights. Modern political philosophy is still trying to reconcile these two,[9] while constitutional justice is continually buffeted around in the tempest of their apparently conflicting demands.

Constitutional justice was born in the young United States (despite some antecedents[10]) with the celebrated decision of *Marbury* v. *Madison*, in 1803.[11] Marshall C.J. defended judicial review of statutes as being required by the very idea of a written Constitution which sets limits on the government: the Constitution expresses the permanent will of the sovereign people; statutes are but the creation of an authority constituted under the Constitution; if a law enacted by Congress violates the higher law, then it 'is emphatically the province and duty of the judicial department to say what the law is'; in discharging this task, the judges must give priority to the Constitution, or else defy the very point of having a written Constitution with checks on governmental power.

With such crisp reasoning Marshall C.J. became midwife to a remarkable feature of modern democracies: the power of judicial authorities to set aside the will of popularly elected legislatures, for defying the will of the people (as expressed in the constitution and interpreted by the judges, naturally).

The seeds of this argument had already been set during the debate on the ratification of the Constitution in the period 1787-1788. In commenting on the need for an independent judiciary, an erstwhile defender of the new republic asserted that judicial independence was especially necessary in a 'limited Constitution':

> ... one which contains certain specified exceptions to the legislative authority; such, for instance, as that it shall pass no bills of attainder, no *ex post facto* laws, and the like.

In the event of conflict between the law of Congress and the law of the people, the latter should prevail for there:

> ... is no position which depends on clearer principles than that every act of a delegated authority, contrary to the tenor of the commission under which it is exercised, is void.

It is for the judiciary to reconcile these conflicts, for the 'interpretation of the laws is the proper and peculiar function of the courts'. There is no danger in entrusting these powers to the judiciary for the judges form the 'least dangerous branch of government', wielding neither sword nor purse strings, and so pose the lesser danger to the political rights of the Constitution.[12]

For the first century of its youth, constitutional justice did not travel far beyond the American shores,[13] though it enjoyed a turbulent enough youth there.

Most European states were slow to follow the US lead. For a variety of reasons they were reluctant to entrust the ordinary courts with the power to control the validity of statutes. Partially this was because of the dominant ideology of the day, which stressed the 'regne de la loi', i.e. the supremacy of the statute-law, and the legislature.[14] The statute expressed the legislature's will, the 'general will' of the sovereign people. This general will was uncriticisable and could do no wrong.[15] Therefore, clearly there could be no review of the content of the statute.

Also, there was a great reluctance to politicise the judiciary.[16] Writers stressed the essence of an impartial, apolitical judicial branch to the importance of the liberal theory of the state and the separation of powers. Carl Schmitt (criticising the Austrian model to which I turn in a moment) noted that, in the legalisation of politics, 'politics has nothing to gain, and law has everything to lose'.[17]

The most important European initiative came in 1920 when Austria adopted the proposal of the legal philosopher Hans Kelsen, and created a special tribunal to hear cases involving claims that the Constitution had been violated. The creation of a special tribunal was defended by Kelsen as essential to ensure the protection of the legal hierarchy of norms. Each legal norm frames a range of legitimate action for an inferior legal authority to take. As one descends the legal scale, the scope for creativity diminishes. The judicial decision leaves little room for the executive to exercise discretion; the statute of Parliament accords a larger scope for discretion to the judge, but still binds her. The Constitution on the other hand, imposes relatively few limits on the legislator - but it imposes limits none the less. For the normativity of law to be ensured, each legal act must be based on a higher legal norm, but this then requires a means to ensure that the statutes do not violate the Constitution. For this an independent quasi-judicial body was required - obviously Parliament could not be trusted to police itself. This

Constitutional Court would exercise a mélange of judicial and legislative power. It would have the power to invalidate statutes - clearly a legislative power, if only the negative one of veto. However it would also be an independent body, staffed by jurists, a body whose acts would be absolutely determined by the Constitution, and would mainly involve the legal questions of the proper interpretation of the text.[18]

Kelsen offered some very pertinent observations on the interpretation of human rights guarantees and other vague references to justice, equality, and equity. For Kelsen, it was the task of the legislator to give substance to these guarantees, not the Constitutional Court. By themselves, the human rights guarantees added nothing to the real state of the law. Indeed they posed such a serious risk of causing a conflict between the assembly of the people, and the Constitutional Court, that drafters of Constitutions should either not refer to such matters or should use very precise language if they did. Kelsen's parting advice was that constitution makers should avoid such phrases.[19]

The late Nineteenth and early Twentieth Centuries saw an expansion of the institution of constitutional justice - in Latin America, Greece, Austria, Ireland and Germany the practice began, and in the US the practice increased greatly. However, the period prior to 1945 was not a happy one for either constitutional justice or democracy. Judicial power did nothing to halt the spread of the dictatorships. Often judicial decisions ranged on the side of conservative interest groups - in particular in the US conservative judges inhibited progressive social and racial reform in such cases as the *Civil Rights cases*,[20] *Plessy* v. *Ferguson*,[21] *Lochner* v. *New York*,[22] etc. Only the famous 'switch in time that saved nine' allowed legislative reform to go ahead.[23] In Canada and Australia, judges also delayed reform measures in controversial decisions.[24] In Ireland, the courts upheld an extraordinary series of statutes creating military courts to try and execute suspected terrorists in peace time.[25] During the Second World War courts in the non-Axis countries did little to restrain arbitrary exercise of powers, looking the other way while their governments interned many persons, and executed some without a fair trial.[26] One can expand without difficulty the sorry list of regrettable judicial decisions. Most seriously, Neumann lays part of the blame for the collapse of the Weimar Republic on the expansion of judicial power in the 1920s, which lead to an erosion of legality and the rule of law.[27]

Viewing this bleak period, it seems somewhat strange that after the cataclysm, constitutional drafters should look to judges as one possible bulwark against oppression. Yet drafters in Germany, Italy, Austria, Japan and India all (re-)created constitutional tribunals, to safeguard the constitution against the supposed threats of the legislatures. The 50 years since then have been remarkable for three more aspects of this phenomenon - the increase world wide in the number of courts acting as constitutional tribunals, the upsurge in judicial activism, and the theoretical debate on the function and legitimacy of constitutional justice.[28]

The number of constitutional tribunals world wide is now little short of staggering. Following the collapse of right wing dictatorships in Europe and Latin America (Spain, Portugal, Greece), the fall of communist regimes (Russia, Poland, Hungary, Albania, Czech Republic, Latvia), the ending of colonial or racist regimes (South Africa, Bangladesh, Pakistan, Papua New Guinea) many states have decided either to create a special constitutional court, or to entrust the task of constitutional justice to the ordinary courts (the countries listed are merely examples and by no means exhaustive lists). To these national organs of constitutional justice should also be added various international tribunals such as the World Court, the European Court of Justice, the European Court of Human Rights, which police the boundaries of the higher law. Nor should one forget that even in those countries without the formal trappings of constitutional justice, the practice still exists in some ways (in the Netherlands for instance the courts may not invalidate a law as unconstitutional - but they may ignore one that violates the European Convention on Human Rights[29]). And even in states with no written constitution, no constitutional review of statutes, and no incorporated international human rights treaty, questions remarkably similar to the ones dealt with by constitutional courts often appear.[30] Finally, even those states whose legal culture was most opposed to the idea of constitutional justice have moved to embrace the institution.[31]

Even more astounding has been the explosion in judicial activism over the past 50 years. Judges have been deciding more cases, in important areas of social interest, claiming greater power, invoking more imaginative doctrines, and sometimes even defying the will of the other branches of government. The Indian Supreme Court delayed the enactment of much property reform legislation in the 1950s, 1960s and 1970s - today it acts as the main engine for social reform.[32] In the 1970s, it developed its remarkable 'basic features' doctrine, holding that some parts of the Constitution were unamendable and immutable.[33] In 1971 the French Constitutional Council decided that not merely could it control the validity of a legislative bill by reference to the text of the 1958 Constitution, but also by reference to the Preamble, and, through it, the 1946 Preamble and the 1789 Declaration of Rights.[34] The German Federal Constitutional Court has also adopted a case law on 'superpositive rights' that cannot be amended under the Constitution.[35] It has twice intervened in the sensitive debate on abortion.[36] More recently, it has handed down important decisions on questions one might be forgiven for thinking were intensely political: participation of German soldiers in UN operations,[37] and membership of a single European currency.[38] In the United States the courts have acted as the motor of egalitarian reforms in the 1960s and 1970s, and, more recently stand in the front line of the Reaganite counter-revolution. In 1992, the High Court of Australia astonished many by reading the right to free expression into the Constitution as an implied right.[39] The South African Constitutional Court more or less began its career by throwing out parts of the draft Constitution of the new republic.[40] The power of the constitutional tribunals in Canada, Ireland and Italy will become clear in later Chapters. Particularly noticeable in all these cases is the importance of rather vaguely formulated human rights guarantees, a feature unforeseen by Hamilton and criticised by Kelsen.

Such power has given rise to vigorous debate - among citizens, constitutional lawyers, legal philosophers, politicians, and journalists - on the 'mysterious'[41] justification and proper scope of constitutional justice. In this debate, all political shades can be found on all sides. I cannot here canvas the different positions that have been defended by writers. They range from those who oppose constitutional justice on the grounds that the democratic will of Parliament should have decisive sway in a democracy, to those who argue that constitutional justice is the only way to protect individual and minority rights. There are opponents of constitutional justice who see it as a radical left-wing threat to social values; others oppose it because it serves merely to re-inforce a conservative status quo. Advocates of constitutional justice include some who see it as the surest protection of fundamental rights, and others who see it as a bulwark against socialism. Among people who accept constitutional justice are those who believe courts should be timid in the exercise of their great powers, while others enthuse about judicial activism. Some argue for a mixed approach with judges actively defending certain values, but leaving others to fend for themselves in the political market place. All these debates must each be considered in the light of a particular state's constitution, political practices, history, economy and social *mores*. This book is not concerned (directly) either to defend constitutional justice or to attack it. Constitutional justice exists in legal texts, and jurists must seek to understand it, describe how it works, and prescribe how it ought to work (though as we shall see, the legitimacy of the institution plays a role within this task).

The extent and activity of constitutional justice justifies theoretical and empirical work done in relation to it. This is particularly so since constitutions (and constitutional justice) play essential legal, political and moral roles in modern societies.

From the viewpoint of lawyers, a constitution serves as the supreme law of the land. It forms the legal basis for inferior bodies and norms. The constitution is thus superior to these other norms, and the institution of constitutional justice rests on the basis that there should be some way of recognising that superiority. In the event of conflict the constitutional law must take priority. However, the method of institutionalising that superiority is not uncontroversial. The choice of a constitutional tribunal is not the only one - many would argue that Parliament or a special parliamentary commission is a more important and more appropriate watchdog.

Constitutional justice rests on the superiority of constitutional law over ordinary law. This central premise of supremacy is open to challenge. Some argue that certain moral norms override constitutional ones; others believe that democratic majorities ought to be able to loose the binds of the constitution without using the formal amending powers. Some point to the complicated relationship between national and international law. Most intriguingly, there can be conflicts about the respective value of constitutional law and supranational law, such as that typified by European Union law. Some of these disputes go beyond the boundaries of the inquiry in this book. It should be noted that, whatever the answer to them, they are still disputes within the realm of constitutional theory. Here there are conflicts over the meaning of the material constitution, and indeed over what constitutes a constitution. However for most cases, it is an unproblematic assertion that constitutional law takes priority over lesser laws. Constitutional tribunals play the key role in upholding the supremacy of the constitution.

However, it is only in a very small number of cases that a statute is invalidated. Indeed the number of cases which even involve the question of a statute's validity is small enough. Most cases turn on questions of interpretation of statutes, regulations and case law, the determination of the facts, and the application of the law to the facts in the case. So the role of the constitutional courts as 'negative legislator' / 'guardian of constitutional supremacy', might seem to be of limited importance. Actually, the constitution (and constitutional interpretation) is in action not only when a statute is invalidated, but in many other cases as well, in the hands of judges, politicians, administrators and the people.

For instance, the Italian Constitutional Court has relied on certain constitutional values in interpreting Italy's bewildering array of statutes. The fundamental values of the protection of health, and environmental protection have been guiding themes in dealing with many statutes in a coherent manner.[42] The Irish courts have relied on the Constitution to remodel criminal procedure and administrative law in ways more favourable to the criminal accused and the individual challenging administrative decisions. Constitutional law also influences decisions in the private law field - see the German courts' use of constitutional doctrines in areas such as family law, labour law, tort law and indeed contract law.[43]

Acts of constitutional interpretation do not influence merely judicial activities. Politicians also take their cue from judicial pronouncements. In Canada, the entire process for considering refugee requests has been modified to take account of judicial interpretations of the right to a fair process. The *Corte costituzionale*'s extensive case law on freedom of expression and fairness in the media has been the framework within which Italy's media industry is regulated.[44]

Therefore, the importance of constitutional justice stretches far beyond those cases where statutes are invalidated. The influence reaches into many aspects of judicial decision-making and political policy-making.

Constitutional justice is not merely important and influential from the legal point of view, it also serves as the focus for very basic political and moral concerns. Constitutional justice can also serve to reform or consolidate certain public policies, bringing them more into harmony with fundamental principles and so defusing tensions. Bobbio has rightly stressed the capacity for non-violent reform as one of the great merits of democracy,[45] and constitutional courts have played their role in this. Of course it is a two-edged sword - courts have facilitated (even encouraged) some reforms, but have also delayed others, or even caused catastrophes. The US Supreme Court has been accused of indirectly causing the Civil War, the racial strife of the 1960s, and the abortion wars of more recent times. More positively, the Italian *Corte costituzionale* can claim credit for consolidating Italy's democracy by pruning the legal code of fascist legislation, and (more recently) confirming its status as a secular republic.[46]

Looking at the legal system from the viewpoint of morality, another important aspect of constitutional law becomes apparent. In today's world, questions of justification, of legitimacy play a major role. Political questions are not limited to merely prudential ones; often questions are raised as the Government's very right to decide certain matters, or to decide for certain people. Why should Ireland's nomadic community accept decisions made by the Irish Parliament about them? By what right can the Canadian state legislate for (or against) abortion? More prosaically, why should people obey laws which take some of their property from them by way of taxation? Why accept laws which require planning permission to build something on one's own land? The answers to these questions do not depend just on the examination of the particular topic (planning laws, taxation, abortion, minorities, etc.). They are also related to the wider political system, the decision-making process which enacts such measures. Questions of legitimacy look also to the use of correct procedures, fair political processes, respect for fundamental rights and fundamental values. These issues are those of political morality - but they are also the issues which constitutional law determines in a specific state. Looking at states from the moral point of view, constitutional law often expresses their claim to legitimacy.

This brief survey of the importance of constitutional justice from the legal, political science, and moral viewpoints shows the importance of decisions of these tribunals, which brings us to the final reason for this book. There are many questions about these bodies - one is 'what are the appropriate criteria to use when interpreting the Constitution?'. This is a question which judges must ask themselves, but which we may also ask as jurists critiquing their work, politicians concerned about the implications of constitutional justice, and citizens, not quite sure why we entrust these unelected officers with the power to check the elected branches of government.

The criteria of validity of interpretation are important because constitutional justice itself is important, and more specifically because it is controversial. It is controversial because of the 'counter-majoritarian difficulty' as US scholars like to put it.[47] In a democracy there is something faintly embarrassing about an organ of constitutional justice. The dissatisfaction is easily identified: democratic politics is all about the will of the people, expressed through specified political channels. Generally the people elect a Parliament (and / or President) to determine public policy. After a political debate the public policy is enacted in law. The faintly embarrassing bit is that most democratic states now operate with some sort of constitutional court, i.e. a body which is not legitimated through popular elections, and yet which is authorised to override the will of the elected legislature. For many, this smacks of platonic guardianship rather than democratic politics.[48] Those who defend constitutional courts must try to legitimate them within a democratic theory of some sort. There are various ways to legitimate them: for instance in most states the appointment of constitutional judges is very much a political matter with the executive and legislature playing a major role in the appointment. Another tactic is to limit the court's powers procedurally. A third approach is to develop mechanisms whereby the elected branches can respond to unpopular judicial decisions (see Canada's 'override' procedure). A fourth approach is to insist that the decisions of the courts be justified, that the interpretations comply with appropriate standards of validity. Through its examination of the practice of constitutional justice this book seeks to discern the criteria of validity appropriate to this subject matter in liberal democracies.

How does this argument differ from others?

I have already indicated that there are several writers who have very heavily influenced this book, and indeed whose work provides the basic plan, structure and much of the material for it. The shadows of writers like Alexy, Dworkin, Habermas, Rawls, Nino, Dyzenhaus and Ackerman pass over most pages. To them I owe the insights that (constitutional) law and (political) morality are linked in some way; that judicial interpretation relies on political morality; that judges contribute to public debate on law and politics. However, there are also differences in the brush strokes at least.

First, I approach the issue of constitutional justice from the legal, not the political or moral, viewpoint. I am not primarily concerned with why morality leads to law,[49] nor with what role a just political theory assigns law courts,[50] nor yet with what role the political self-understanding of a historically constituted nation accords its tribunals.[51] I start off from the perspective of the legal practitioner, the jurist trying to understand and interpret the constitutional scheme. That legal starting point leads however to political morality (in the context of constitutional justice which is a special, though not an aberrant case of law).

Second, I want to study this connection through a thorough immersion in the waters of constitutional justice - waters that are rarely clear and seldom calm and often flow in opposing currents. Whilst all of these writers use legal decisions for illustration, several of them rarely engage in a thorough legal discussion of legal doctrines. The lawyers among them do try to engage fully with 'law in the courts' as opposed to 'law in the (political theory) lecture hall', but even they seem to remain within the legal theory lecture hall.

Third, I wish to move away from the examples typically used by these writers. Usually they see their theories as applying to more than just one country; often they seem to extend their principles to cover those countries that are characterised as 'liberal democratic' (or perhaps 'would be liberal democratic'?) regimes. Yet, most of their writings concentrate on the United States and Germany.[52] I wish to broaden the scope of this type of research, and extend it to more countries within the liberal democratic family, rather than limit it to these two (perhaps aberrant) examples.

Fourth, in discussing the connection between (constitutional) law and (political) morality I wish to lay out specific criteria of legalised political morality. These writers do not always specify what criteria judges should use when reading constitutional texts in the light of political morality. Dworkin in particular advocates that judges should interpret laws to make them as attractive as possible from the viewpoint of political morality, but unfortunately does not explain how we determine this.[53] The criteria I propose are similar to Alexy's.[54]

A fifth feature is more latent. There are, I believe, many points of convergence between three different themes in liberal democracies as diverse as Germany and the US, Canada and India, Italy and Ireland, Argentina and South Africa. I think there are many similarities in recent moral and political thought in these countries - see for instance the recent exchange between Habermas and Rawls, where Habermas describes their differences as being a family dispute.[55] See also Nino's impressive analysis of moral constructivism in *The Ethics of Human Rights* where he gathers together these different writers. Second, legal thinkers also seem to be drawing more on each other and becoming aware of their shared traditions, concepts and problems. Writers such as Peczenick, Aarnio and Alexy have much to offer their Anglophone brethren and writers such as MacCormick and Dworkin can certainly return the favour.[56] And third, there is growing awareness of the importance of comparative law, and particularly comparative constitutional law, rooted in the realisation by judges, law professors and citizens that constitutional principles do speak to universal (or at any rate, trans-contextual) values and needs.[57] We have much to learn from our foreign colleagues.

The Approach

I make this argument relying on studies from three disciplines: political moral theory, constitutional law and legal theory. Chapter Two discusses one of the most common debates in legal theory: the separation thesis. In that Chapter, I consider the standard arguments for positivism in favour of the separation thesis, that law and (political) morality are conceptually distinct. I look at the weaknesses in these arguments, and explain why the normativity of law requires a connection between the legal and moral spheres, albeit not an identity of law and (political) morality.

Chapter Three starts with a discussion of the appropriate criteria of argument in political morality. It tries to establish that some element of rational argumentation exists when discussing matters of political morality. This is important for one of the chief objections to intermingling of law and morality is that such a mixture degrades the certainty of law. Furthermore, Chapter Three will introduce the reader to the criteria which will emerge repeatedly in later Chapters.

Having identified these criteria, I then turn to three detailed case studies of constitutional debates in liberal democracies. The detail is necessary for any discussion of constitutional argument must be rooted in a full understanding of constitutional practice.

I have selected Canada, Ireland and Italy for my studies. This I have done for several reasons. First, they are all within the liberal democratic group of states, sharing features already mentioned with other states in Europe, North America and other parts of the globe. Second, the debate on constitutional justice (/ constitutional politics / legal theory) has tended to concentrate on a handful of major states. The massive amount of work done on the United States and Germany is fascinating and important, but constitutional theory should not be limited to just a few states, at least if it purports to deal with phenomena common to a group of states. Further, all three states have institutions of constitutional justice and rather activist ones at that. So they offer rich ground for the legal scholar.

However, the states are also different from each other in many ways. Italy of course is a civil law jurisdiction, whereas Ireland is a very traditional common law country, while Canada is influenced by both traditions (Quebec is a civil law jurisdiction while the other provinces follow the common law lead). Italy has adopted the Kelsenian constitutional court, while Ireland and Canada rely on the ordinary courts to exercise the power of constitutional review. From the viewpoint of society and politics, Ireland is notably more conservative than the other two (though conservative interest groups exist there also). Italian politics is noticeably more charged and radical than in the other two states.

In each state the constitutional court has pronounced on several political controversies, and I study one controversy in each state in depth. I have selected three different topics for several reasons. First, I am not studying a particular constitutional doctrine (e.g. free expression) but constitutional practice and interpretation more generally. Second, I wanted to select controversies that were in a sense typical of the court's role in the politics of the country concerned. In each state, certain political controversies cannot be discussed without discussing the case law of the courts in them. There were many such topics (e.g. criminal law reform in Ireland, labour relations in Canada, media regulation in Italy), but I have selected three in particular having regard to their relatively major importance for the type of society in which the court is working. Canada takes very seriously its commitment to equality of gender and of race, and this sometimes leads to conflict with the value it puts on free expression, and so I have selected cases on hate propaganda and pornography for Chapter Three, 'The Politics of Equality'. Ireland's conservatism in matters sexual is renowned and has been at or near the centre of political and social debate for most of the last 25 years, and so in 'The Private is Political' I look at the charged issues of contraception, homosexuality and abortion. Italy has had a long (and troubled) relation with the Catholic Church, and the religious controversy of 'The Two Romes' is the focus of my fifth Chapter.

In these Chapters, there are common themes. First I look at the reasoning of the judges in the cases before them, and show how the reasoning only becomes fully justified if one observes certain 'jumps' in the chain of reasoning, jumps which rely on political moral beliefs. These political moral beliefs play a significant role in the reasoning, but usually it is an unacknowledged one. I wish to make it more transparent. Second I try to show how these judicial pronouncements interact with the wider political system, how other political actors and citizens pick up on what has been said and use them in their own political arguments. There are multiple dialogues going on over time.

Chapter Seven brings these different threads together. Constitutional judges interpret the Constitution by offering a reconstruction of the legal materials before them. The aim of the reconstruction is to present the legal system as the most legitimate that it can be, i.e. they seek to provide a claim to legitimacy. In choosing between different interpretations the courts rely on the criteria of political moral argument suitably legalised. I refer to instances where this was done in the case studies, and also to instances where the courts failed to follow these criteria. In this Chapter, I also try to show how these criteria may need to be adapted in a legal context.

Notes

1   Mackie, 'The Third Theory of Law', (1977) *Phil. & Pub. Aff.* 3. See also Lyons, 'Reconstructing Legal Theory' 16 *Phil. & Pub. Aff.* 379, p. 379 where he comments 'But positivism is not Dworkin's target, nor natural law his aim'.

2   See Gallie's celebrated distinction between concepts and conceptions: 'Essential Contestable Concepts', (1956) *Proc. Aris. Soc.* 203.

3   See Guastini, *Le fonti del diritto e l'interpretazione*, p. 67 et seq. He notes that 'constitution' refers to the group of fundamental norms which identify a legal system, and which may include norms regulating the State's organisation, its relations with its citizens, expressing fundamental values, regulating the creation of laws, etc. See also Kelsen 'La Garantie Juridictionnelle de la Constitution' 45 R.D.P. 197, 204, where he identifies the core idea of the Constitution as being a supreme principle which determines the State's entire order and the essence of the community which is constituted by that order. More specifically it regulates the creation of the legal norms essential for the State, and determines the fundamental organs and procedures for the creation of law.

4   Guastini, 'Interprétation et Description de Normes' in Amselek ed. *Interprétation et Droit*, p.89 et seq. Wroblewski also identifies different sense of 'interpretation' ranging from 'understanding of any cultural object' to 'removing the doubts' over the 'direct meaning' of a piece of text, *The Judicial Application of Law*, pp. 88 -90.

5   Rawls, *Political Liberalism*, p. 231.

6   Cappelletti describes the late Twentieth Century as: '... *the* epoch of natural law. More accurately, however, I would say that modern constitutionalism is the attempt to overcome the plurimilinary contrast between natural and positive law .....' (emphasis in original) *The Judicial Process in Comparative Perspective*, p. 210.

7   J. Raz, N. MacCormick, O. Weinberger, L. Fuller, J. Finnis, R. Dworkin, R. Alexy, C. Nino are writers who cover this spectrum of thought.

8   Kelly, *A Short History of Western Legal Theory*, p. 244.
9   See Habermas, *Between Facts and Norms*, and Rawls, *Political Liberalism*.
10   See Cappelletti, *The Judicial Process in Comparative Perspective*, 'Judicial
        Review in Perspective' pp. 120 - 132; Kelly *A Short History of Western Legal
        Theory*, pp. 277 - 282.
11   Cranch, 137. For the dispute on the origin of judicial review see Beard, *The
        Supreme Court and the Constitution*, with the Introduction by A. Westin in the
        1962 edition. The US operates the 'American model' of judicial review. This
        means that when any court finds itself in confrontation with a law it judges
        unconstitutional, it refuses to apply that law *in that case*. At the level of the US
        federal Supreme Court, such a decision has the effect of ruling the statute invalid
        for all purposes (through the doctrine of precedent).
12   Hamilton, *The Federalist Papers*, Paper no. 78, pp. 464 - 467.
13   The Mexican Constitution created this power in Art. 25 of its 1847 Act of
        Reform; the Argentinean Supreme Court recognised this power in 1887;
        Colombia adopted a law on this also in 1887. Brazil followed suit in the 1890s.
        See Brewer-Carías, *Judicial Review in Comparative Law*.
14   See Redor, *De L'État Légal a L'État de Droit*, studying the development of
        French public law thinking from 1879 to 1914. Deleperee quotes from a
        decision of the Belgian *Cour de Cassation* of 23 July 1849: '... il n'appartient
        pas au pouvoir judiciaire de vérifier si t'elle disposition légal est ou non en
        harmonie avec la Constitution' in 'Crise du Juge et Contentieux Constitutionnel
        en Droit Belge', Lenoble, ed. *La Crise du Juge*, p. 47.
15   Kant, *The Metaphysics of Morals*, p. 316.
16   Redor, *De L'État Légal a L'État de Droit*, p. 223.
17   *Il Custode della Costituzione*, p. 60 (quoting Guizot). Schmitt's position is of
        course rather more complicated and controversial than this brief quote indicates.
18   'La garantie juridictionnelle de la Constitution' (1928) *R.D.P.* 197, 224 - 227.
        See also 'Chi dev'essere il custode della costituzione?'.
        The 'Austrian' or 'Kelsenian' model of judicial review, differs from the
        American model. First, only a special tribunal hears such constitutional disputes
        - review is concentrated, not diffuse. Second, the decisions of the special
        tribunal have general effect, they do not apply just to the particular case before
        it. For a discussion of this model, see Eisenmann, *La Justice Constitutionnelle et
        la Haute Cour Constitutionnelle d'Autriche*.
19   'La garantie juridictionnelle de la Constitution' (1928) *R.D.P.* 197, 241 - 242.
20   109 U.S. 3 (1882). This case invalidated an early civil rights statute.
21   163 U.S. 537 (1886). This is the infamous 'separate but equal' case.
22   198 U.S. 45 (1906). Here the Supreme Court invalidated a New York maximum
        work hours statute.
23   *West Coast Hotel* v. *Parish* 300 U.S. 379 (1937). See Schwartz *A History of the
        Supreme Court*, Ch. 10.
24   Mandel describes the 'judicial slaughter' of legislation in Canada during the
        Depression: *The Charter of Rights and the Legalization of Politics*, pp. 10 - 12.
25   *Att. Gen.* v. *M'Bride*, [1928] I.R. 451; *State (Ryan)* v. *Lennon*, [1935] I.R. 170.

26   US examples of this include: *Ex parte Quirin*, 317 U.S 1 (1942) sanctioning a
      military execution of German spies; and *Korematsu* v. *US*, 323 U.S. 214 (1944)
      permitting the internment of 112,000 US citizens of Japanese origin. In the UK
      Liversidge v. *Anderson* [1942] A.C. 206 gave a generous interpretation to
      internment powers. Irish courts upheld the legality of a military court, from
      which there was no appeal, and which could inflict only one type of punishment
      - death: *In re M'Grath and Harte* [1941] I.R. 68; *State (Walsh)* v. *Lennon*,
      [1942] I.R. 112.

27   Neumann, *Behemoth*, p. 364.

28   See Symposium 'Judicial Review in Comparative Perspective' (1990) 19 *Policy
      Studies Journal* 76; Symposium, 'Constitutional Judicial Review of
      Legislation' (1983) 56 *Temple Law Quarterly* 287-583; Epp, *The Rights
      Revolution*; Beatty, *Human Rights and Judicial Review: A Comparative
      Perspective*; Brewer-Carias, *Judicial Review in Comparative Perspective*;
      Cappelletti, *The Judicial Process in Comparative Perspective*; Favoreau, *Cours
      Constitutionnelles Europeenes et Droits Fondamentaux*; Landfried,
      Constitutional Review and Legislation, (Baden-Baden: Nomos, 1988);
      Roermund, *Constitutional Review: theoretical and comparative perspectives*;
      Stone Sweet, *Governing with Judges: Constitutional Politics in Western
      Europe*; Tate, and Vallinder, *The Global Expansion of Judicial Power*;
      Volcansek, *Judicial Politics and Policy Making in Western Europe*;
      Symposium, 'The New Constitutional Politics of Europe', (1994) 26
      Comparative Political Studies (4) 397; Kenny, *Constitutional Dialogues in
      Comparative Perspective*.

29   Art. 94, Dutch Constitution.

30   See MacCormick's discussion of the *Anisminic* v. *Foreign Compensation
      Commission*, [1969] A.C. 197 in *Legal Reasoning and Legal Theory*, pp. 143,
      195.

31   The last few decades have seen the emaciation of the French doctrine of
      'souveraineté de la loi', notably due to the work of the *Conseil constitutionnel*.
      In the UK the adoption of the 1998 Human Rights Act, and, more importantly,
      the acceptance of European supremacy have dealt serious blows to the concept
      of parliamentary supremacy.

32   For a typical case preventing property reform see *R.C.Cooper* v. *India*, [1970]
      A.I.R. 564 S.C. For cases promoting socio-economic reform see: *Khatri* v.
      Bihar, [1981] A.I.R. 928 S.C.; *Mukti Mocha v. India*, [1984] A.I.R. 802 S.C.

33   *Kesavananda* v. *Kerala*, [1973] A.I.R. 1461 S.C. See R. O'Connell, 'Guardians
      of the Constitution: Unconstitutional Constitutional Norms', 4 (1999) *Journal of
      Civil Liberties* 48.

34   Decision of the 16th July 1971.

35   *Art 117 case*, 3 BVerfGE 225; *Southwest State*, 1 BVerfGE 14; *Klass*, 30
      BVerfGE 1 (1970).

36   *Abortion decision*, BVerfGE 39, 1 (1976), *Second Abortion Decision*, BVerfGE
      88, 283 (1993). See P. Quint, *The Imperfect Union*, Ch. 12.

37   *Soldiers Serving Abroad*, BVerfGE 90, 286 (1994).

38   Decision of March 31, 1998.

39   *Australia Capital Television* v. *Commonwealth*, (1992) 177 C.L.R. 106. The US Supreme Court had already discovered unenumerated rights in *Griswold* v. *Connecticut* 381 U.S. 479 (1965), as had the Irish High Court in *Ryan* v. *Ireland* [1965] I.R. 294. See also Bhagwati J. in *Gandhi* v. *India*, [1978] A.I.R. 597 S.C.

40   *Certification of the Constitution of South Africa*, CCT 23/96 6 Sept. 1996.

41   Nino, 'A Philosophical Reconstruction of Judicial Review', (1993) *Card. L. Rev.* 799, 799.

42   Modugno, *I 'nuovi diritti' nella giurisprudenza costituzionale*, p. 40 - 49; p. 55 - 58. See also Pizzorusso, 'L'influence de la constitution italienne sur le droit judiciaire' (1983) *Rev. int. droit comparé* 7.

43   See P. Quint, 'Free Speech and Private Law in German Constitutional Theory' 48 (1989) *Maryland Law Review* 247; G. Weick, 'Challenges to the Law of Contract' in Wilson and Rogowski, *Challenges to European Legal Scholarship*; B. Markesinis, *German Law of Obligations*, Vol. 2, pp. 27 - 31.

44   Similarly, see the case law of the French *Conseil constitutionnel* on nationalisations and monopolies: Stone *The Birth of Judicial Politics in France*.

45   *Il futuro della democrazia*, p. 29, citing Popper.

46   See Chapter Six.

47   The term originates with Bickel, *The Least Dangerous Branch*.

48   Among the more persuasive of these critiques, note: Dahrendorf, 'A Confusion of Powers: Politics and the Rule of Law' 40 M.L.R. 1 (1977); Walzer, 'Philosophy and Democracy', (1981) *Pol. Th.* 379; Waldron, 'A Right-Based Critique of Constitutional Rights', 13 *Ox. J.L.S.* 18 (1993).

49   See Habermas and Alexy.

50   As is Rawls.

51   As I understand Ackerman's approach in *We, the People*.

52   Dyzenhaus and Nino are exceptions.

53   *Law's Empire*.

54   *A Theory of Legal Argumentation*.

55   'Reconciliation through the Public Use of Reason' (1995) *J. Phil. 109*.

56   Richards argues for the similarities in the work of Alexy and Dworkin in a book review of Alexy's *A Theory of Legal Argumentation*, (1989) 2 *Ratio Juris* 304. Lenoble and Berten have written on the fundamental links between Habermas and Dworkin, Kantian critical theory and hermeneutics in 'Jugement juridique et jugement practique', (1990) 95 *Rev. de Metaphys. et de Mor.* 337.

57   See Beatty, *Human Rights and Judicial Review: A Comparative Perspective*.

2 Going Back to Basic (Norm)s

Introduction

In this Chapter, I begin a contribution to legal theory based on the nature of constitutional justice. I suggest that the positivist paradigm of the separation of law and political morality is not an adequate description of our legal experience. I argue that there are gains for our concept of law if we incorporate a notion of constitutional justice into it, rather than leaving it out in the cold.

The main point of this work is that there is a conceptual link between law and political morality: the criteria of validity in constitutional legal argument mirror the criteria of validity in political moral argument (discussed in Chapters Three and Seven). This is not surprising since the issue of justification lies at the heart of both law and political morality. Only by assuming this centrality of political moral argument to law, can key questions about the interpretation of law, the argumentative nature of law, the foundations of law, be answered.

Someone might object to my project that it is looking at an (unimportant?) fringe of legal experience, a fringe so far out as to fall into the lap of politics, not that of law. To the extent that this is a definitional dispute (you say law, I say politics) it is not very interesting. However, there are two reasons to pursue this matter. The first is a practical one. The argument is often made that law is law, (and constitutional law is still law), and must be argued about in terms of 'neutral' principles.[1] Only by exposing the moral debate at the core of law, can this formalism be avoided. Second, this topic stains the purity of law generally even outside the exotic realm of constitutional law. It is the political moral debate which provides the lynchpin of the legal enterprise, and particularly its claim to authority.

The Path to Constitutional Justice as a Concept of Law

What justifies this revision of the classic paradigm of law of the Twentieth Century? Our concept of law must be rooted in our experience of law. The experience of modern law is radically different from that which formed the legal experience of Hans Kelsen, HLA Hart, Neil MacCormick, Alf Ross, Joseph Raz. Taking their own legal experience as the central case of law, they interpret the legal systems of such states in accordance with those systems. I think that they missed something. Perhaps we can add to their achievements if we reverse the procedure and interpret the concept of law in the light of those states which embrace constitutional justice and then applying it to those states which do not.

I do not advocate philosophical absolutism. Legal positivists have contributed greatly to our understanding of law. The notions of law as a union of secondary and primary rules, the legal hierarchy of norms and institutions, law as an institutional fact, legal reasons as 'protected reasons', and many of the other doctrines put forward by positivist writers are crucial contributions to our comprehension of law. They have powerfully defended the thesis that law and morality are not identical. In this work I do not wish to reject all this valuable work, nor devise a comprehensive theory of law. Rather I wish to draw attention to certain features of our modern experience of law, in an age of constitutional justice.

Before returning to the debate with the positivists, I just wish to note the extent of constitutional justice. Constitutional courts are a firmly entrenched part of the legal world - from Latin America to Eastern Europe. There are countries where the institution does not exist, or exists only in an attenuated form (Scandinavia, Japan). However, even those countries traditionally hostile to constitutional justice have begun to adopt such institutions (the UK with its Human Rights Act, France with its Constitutional Council). There are more countries where the organ of constitutional justice wields its power with a degree of frequency - Spain, Portugal, Belgium, Austria, the countries of Eastern Europe, the Republic of South Africa. Finally there are countries where the role of the constitutional tribunal is extremely prominent - and even provokes accusations of a 'government of judges': Hungary, Australia, Germany, Greece, the United States, India, and not least, Canada, Ireland, and Italy.

In other words, constitutional justice is no longer a legal lost uncle, but an important member of the family.

This book argues that judges in constitutional cases must use certain criteria - those of political moral argument, as outlined in Chapters Three and Seven.[2] This is due to the nature of a constitution which plays a particular role within the concept of law, by securing its normativity.

The key issue is that of law's 'normativity' and its claim to issue binding rules. Most writers in both the positivist and anti-positivist camps agree that legal systems are composed of norms, which claim to be binding. The two great Twentieth Century positivists, Kelsen and Hart, emphasise that law is about norms, not facts. Norm statements are 'ought' statements; they do not explain what 'is' the case, but what 'ought' to be the case. There are different types of norms, (or rules). There are moral norms, linguistic rules, customs of etiquette, rules of a game, legal rules, religious rules, the edicts of terrorist groups and robber bands, and so on.

Law is about what people *ought to do*; not about what they, in fact, do. Indeed law seems to claim a very strong type of normativity. It is not merely normative in the sense that the rules of a game are normative. Raz identifies as a key feature of law that it claims legitimate authority.[3] This is also a fundamental feature of anti-positivist (natural law if you prefer) writings.[4] Finnis indicates that the 'central case of the legal viewpoint' is that in which 'legal *obligation* is treated as at least presumptively a moral *obligation*'.[5] The disagreement is over how to understand this normativity of law.

The law's normativity seems to involve a notion of *obligation*, similar to the normativity claimed by morality. When we break the law, other people (and the State) tend to invoke this defiance as a good reason to do nasty things to us. Our transgression of a norm is cited as a reason to justify punishment, or criticism, at least presumptively. This makes the law's normativity seem very like morality. Both normative spheres have rules, and obligations and rights and duties. Both normative spheres often regulate the same matters. It might be thought that the two are identical.

Legal positivism has many different interpretations,[6] however its one fundamental stance is that it rejects the theory that law and morality are identical. This is well and good - and absolutely correct. Law and morality clearly are not identical. It is not the case that a rule is a legal rule simply because it is a moral rule, nor the case that a rule is not a legal rule simply because it is immoral, nor yet the case that because a rule is legal it is also moral.

However legal positivism has generally gone further and put forward the strict separation thesis: at a conceptual level, law and morality are strictly distinct:

> Their [i.e. positivists] is that the moral value of law (both of a particular law and of a whole legal system) or the moral merit it has is a contingent matter dependent on the content of the law and the circumstances of the society to which it applies.

> [The strong social thesis states that a] jurisprudential theory is acceptable only if its tests for identifying the content of the law and determining its existence depend exclusively on facts of human behaviour capable of being described in value neutral terms, and applied without resort to moral argument.[7]

This argument means that one can 'do law', 'follow law', without relying on moral considerations. To study law one does not need to study morality - though of course one should as a human being. Positivists will quickly add that an actor should not ignore moral considerations. Indeed, many positivists will say that moral considerations override legal and other considerations. However they play no role in the arguments about the validity and interpretation of law; they come into play only where law runs out, so to speak. To 'do law' one does not need to 'do morality'. This position I do not accept, and in this Chapter, I will outline why the standard positivist arguments for a strict separation are flawed.

Positivists recognise the importance of the constitution. In Kelsen, it is the most important posited norm. In Hart, it provides many of the rules of recognition, change and adjudication without which the legal system would be a primitive one. But what is it that makes a constitutional order law? What is the connection between legal validity, constitutional order and political morality? The constitution plays an essential role in securing the normativity of law. However the constitution is not normative simply because it says it is.

> Obviously such a constitution cannot lift itself unaided into legality; it cannot be law simply because it says it is.[8]

Why is it normative then? Kelsen would say because it is recognised by a hypothetical Basic Norm (a hypothetical norm that we must presuppose if our practice of law is to have any sense). Hart would say that the 'rule of recognition', used by the legal officials to recognise what is valid law, conveys legal status on the constitution. I do not accept these two interpretations. The implication of a hypothetical norm is only acceptable if there is no other way to explain law's normativity. Hart's rule of recognition approach seems doubly unsatisfactory to me. First, it seems to rest normative validity on a fact (which cannot be done). Second, it is not clear to me that one can identify a simple (or even a complex) rule of recognition in legal systems. In Chapters Four, Five and Six we shall see that constitutional case law is better described as centring on an on-going public debate, than on any Basic Norm or rule of recognition. It is a debate which involves practical reason in its moral exercise. That debate is all about the constitution as a legitimate reconstruction of the legal order.[9]

This point is strongly made by Carlos Nino. He argues that a constitution is not 'a social practice or a document resulting from such a practice under a descriptive concept'. Rather the constitution must be conceived as 'the expression of those moral principles which grant legitimacy to the laws or legal norms of lower hierarchy'.[10] Only such an 'ideal Constitution' can secure the normativity of law, explain how law can make a claim to be obeyed. Thus, a constitution plays a crucial role in the legal system. It is the focus of Dworkin's concept of law: the law decides when force may be used, in terms of the rights and responsibilities which flow from political decisions about when force is to be used.[11] The law represents a moral position (albeit that it may be moral or immoral of course).

We should see law as involving a public discourse of justification between various parties on the use of state power. In this discourse of justification constitutional law plays a particular role, because it concerns the procedures through which norms are enacted and the limits on the law making power - those fundamental rights which in traditional secular natural law theory are the conditions of legitimacy for the exercise of state power.[12] This discourse of justification is bound up in the activities of a judge - determining the validity of legal rules, interpreting legal rules, and applying them to fact situations (validity, interpretation, application). When considering questions of legal validity, interpretation, application, a judge (lawyer, legislator, citizen) must consider that function in the light of the need for justification. In this work, I emphasise the interpretation of the constitution, and so also the question of the validity of laws (statutes inferior in status to the constitution). There are many other questions I avoid, or deal with only peripherally - the validity of an entire legal order, the process of application, the interpretation of statutes and court decisions.

I note however that anti-positivist writers must avoid an even worse flaw. Anti-positivist writers argue that there is a necessary conceptual link between law and morality. However, they must not fall into the trap of *identifying* the two normative spheres. Nor must they draw too strong a link between law and morality. It may well be a weakness of anti-positivist accounts of law that it requires one to accept as sound morality a 'legally codified' immoral system.[13] Anti-positivists must explain the link between law and morality without conferring an unimpeachable legitimacy on law.

The approach I have outlined is opposed to traditional positivist theories of law. In the next section, I want to expose some of the weaknesses in the positivist arguments for the separation thesis.

Assessing the Positivist Arguments

I believe that legal argument involves a significant amount of political moral argument. I argue that this role ought to be explicit and will argue that it ought to be conducted using certain criteria (Chapters Three and Seven). Positivists argue that this element of legal experience must be kept distinct from our concept of law. Political morality and law are sharply distinct. I do not agree - if we do make this distinction then I fear that this element of law will be sidelined, even though most positivist writers would not wish to sideline it. Further, I fear we lose a full understanding of the legal experience, and particularly one of its most troubling features, its claim to be obeyed. The political moral argument which I see as the heart of the concept of law, not the *Grundnorm* or Rule of Recognition, is the most obvious way to make some sense of this claim, without conferring an unimpeachable legitimacy on the legal system. In Chapters Four, Five and Six I will demonstrate the role played by political moral argument in the legal process of three liberal democratic countries. In this Chapter, I explain why the separation thesis is not invincible.

But There are Unjust Laws!

This is the first and readiest of the positivist attacks on connections between law and morality. Hart and Kelsen say that the traditional cry of Natural Law, that an unjust law is no law, is a self-contradiction.[14] There clearly are unjust laws, and so justice cannot be a criterion of the validity of law: 'The problem is not that viciously oppressive laws do not exist, but that they do.'[15]

This first and readiest of criticisms is flimsy. It only deals with a very simplistic form of Natural Law, which it is by no means clear that anyone has ever defended.[16] The form of Natural Law which it attacks is one which asserts the *identity* of law and morality. That thesis, of identity, is an untenable one. However, it is not the thesis of this work, which is that law and (political) morality are intimately connected, but not identical. It is compatible with a thesis of connection for unjust laws to exist.[17]

One of the judicial tasks is to interpret the law in accordance with a justified notion of the legal order. This involves a political moral reconstruction of that order. This reconstruction is particularly evident in the area of constitutional justice. However the reconstruction does not ignore the terms of the laws, but rather interprets them. The legal order may well contain unjust laws, and this may lead to a less than ideal theory of political morality. It may lead to a theory of political morality which is a very weak one and which citizens should not obey. However, the judge in interpreting the law, in determining the validity of laws, in deciding the applicability of laws, is not in the same situation as ordinary citizens who decide what an appropriate theory of political morality is. The judge is guided by the materials before her, by the sources of law, - the private individual is not so limited by the public norms (unless the private citizen is purporting to interpret the law). Each of them is bound by the appropriate criteria of argument.

In using those criteria the judge may be compelled to accept that the justification of the legal order is a second best one, as the range of materials before her is only compatible with such a second best one. The statutes or case law may be the product of persons with moral conceptions very different from the judge, the citizenry, even from the legislators of today. The task of legal interpretation is to reconstruct a justification of the laws, making those laws into the best that they may be. The judge balances the terms of the laws and the criteria of political moral argument in considering the validity, the interpretation and the applicability of laws.

In trying to make the laws the best they may be, the judge runs into certain limits however. The text of a law, even when given an interpretation in the light of the criteria of political moral argument, may seem seriously lacking. For instance, there is little ambiguity in a poll tax law which reads 'Every householder shall pay a 100 pound tax annually'. There is no scope to give this a reading more in accordance with ideals of material equality. The question must then be asked whether this law is valid, within the reconstructed meaning of the constitutional order - that is does it violate the constitution, and if so does the Court have the power to invalidate it, or ignore it, or refer it to a constitutional court?

At this stage, the court dealing with the question of validity must contrast the terms of the law with the terms of the constitution, interpreted according to the criteria of political moral argument. A variety of conclusions are possible of which the two most obvious are that 1) the law is invalid and void, and the court will declare it so and 2) the law is valid and the court will recognise that validity.

Assume that the norm is compatible with the reconstructed understanding of the Constitution. That may not resolve the issue of its validity, though in the vast majority of cases it will. There is a possibility that the law is compatible with the constitutional order, but only because the constitutional order itself is seriously flawed. I anticipate here the next chapter. The criteria of political moral argument suggested in the next chapter are generally not to be interpreted in an all or nothing manner. That is, a theory, or norm, may comply with them more or less. However, there are certain theories which are not merely only poorly compatible with those criteria, but are indeed totally incompatible. A libertarian theory of justice may be seen as inadequate when contrasted with a liberal, socialist or communitarian conception. Nevertheless it may clear the basic hurdle of the criteria of argument. A Nazi theory however so bluntly rejects the criteria of argument that it is not possible to see it as even a potential justification. In this case, the legal order cannot even make a claim to any sort of authority, but only the authority of fear and terror.[18]

Law Involves Coercion, Morality Does Not

One of Kelsen's claims is that law and morality must be considered distinct because law is essentially a coercive order, whereas morality is not.[19] One of the key features of law is that it *uses* coercion as an instrument. Indeed Kelsen goes so far as to say that since the theory of Natural Law regards moral facts as self-evidently obvious, there is no need for the use of force to secure compliance - everyone immediately recognises what is a true moral statement.

This argument raises the spectre of the problem of law's relation to coercion, force, violence. This is a difficult issue and Kelsen's position, that law is essentially a coercive order, is a much disputed one - it is not accepted by HLA Hart for instance. However, Kelsen's treatment of morality is also dubious. And in particular it does not apply too well to political morality. Morality and political morality do not use coercion as an instrument in the way law does (according to Kelsen), but they are not unrelated to coercion.

Coercion comes in, in two ways. First, the rules of morality stipulate when violence, coercion etc. is acceptable, and when it is forbidden. 'Do not kill an innocent person' is clearly a rule regulating the use of violence. The implied term 'One may kill a guilty person in certain cases' is also a rule regulating the use of coercion. The rules of political morality often concern violence, force in this manner. Kelsen would accept this, since he comments that law and morality often have the same content, e.g. the prohibition of wrongful killing.[20]

Moral theories lay down what it is right or wrong to do. Some people have argued that morality leads to law - a coercive order - in order to ensure that its demands are enforced.[21] I am not so sure this is true of morality as such. However, with the exception of anarchism, it seems to me to be a feature of political morality. It seems that morality (understanding it in the broad sense) does not have enforcement or coercive apparatuses. It is basically a personal attitude to right living, or good behaviour or whatever. Political morality deals with moral issues when the coercive (and other non-coercive) activities of certain public bodies are involved - the state, legal officers, etc. Political morality does not *use* such instruments directly, but it does require that they be used.

Kelsen seems to feel that morality cannot involve coercion, for any natural law with which he is familiar insists that the moral code is something self-evidently recognisable. If this were so then everyone would recognise without difficulty what was in accord with right reason, and so there would be no need for coercion to require him or her to comply with it. This seems to me to be an overly optimistic view of the potentials of moral theory. If we do accept a cognitivist approach (that is, morality is something which one recognises, not creates) then we may still recognise that some people either fail to recognise morally valid norms, or that there may be a failure of their will to follow the moral norms, or even a decision of their will to violate those moral norms. I do not see why it is inconsistent for a theory of political morality to prescribe the use of coercion to remedy - or at least counter act - these faults.

So it cannot really be argued that law involves coercion and morality does not. Indeed Kelsen seems to admit this himself, when, in his discussion of the relative nature of morality, he notes that some moral codes glorify the use of violence.[22]

A Moral Approach to Law is a Legitimation Strategy

Kelsen's most potent argument for separation is one rooted in historical reality. A legal theorist once quipped that the purpose of the Natural Law theories was always either to actualise the ideal, or idealise the actual. Down through history, Kelsen notes, those people who have argued for a connection between law and morality have usually been more concerned to glorify the actual state of the law rather than reject evil laws or somehow improve the legal system. Always the point was to provide a justification for whatever the content of the law was. In Kelsen's eyes this was an act of straightforward political ideology - a legitimation strategy to glorify the law as the emanation of practical or moral reasoning.[23]

The law and political morality are not identical. The law is a debate about the justification of authority in a particular legal order. Those participating in the debate should use the criteria of political moral argument outlined in the next chapter. It is a public debate on political morality with several parties. Nevertheless, this does not mean that whatever answer is reached by a country's Supreme Court, even if using the criteria outlined in the next chapter, is an ideal view of political morality. It is a reconstruction of the legal system's view of political morality, of the legal system's claim to authority. The judges (or anyone else engaged in legal interpretation) are tied to the sources of law. They may require an unacceptable theory of justification, at least when viewed from the stance of persons not bound by the legal sources. It is always for those persons (in effect everyone) to evaluate the system's theory of political morality in the light of their own.

This approach to law - seeing it as a public debate on the justification of the use of power - does not serve merely to legitimate the actual law, whatever it may be. It is not a legitimation strategy. Rather it puts the question of legitimation at the heart of legal practice, without endangering its invocation to hold the legal system or specific legal rules illegitimate.

Separation is Essential to Clarity

A key argument offered by Hart justifying separation is that this is conducive to clarity of discussion - law is one thing, morality another. It is one thing to discuss whether something is a valid law, and another to discuss whether something is a just law. The question of validity is entirely separate from the question of justice.[24]

Clearly I agree that something may be a valid law and yet be unjust. However I do not think that the issues of validity and political morality are unconnected. The connection comes in this way. A judge must decide upon the interpretation and validity of laws. The legal system is seen as a discourse of justification. The judge takes the legal sources and weaves them into the most convincing possible justification of the legal system. In doing this she must rely upon the criteria of political moral argument. So the issues of interpretation and validity are not entirely distinct from that of justice. Yet this does not mean that a valid law is a just law. It is always possible to criticise the reconstructed justification of the legal system, and so criticise the law as being unjust.

It is true that this picture is not so neat as that offered by Hart - it is one thing to discuss the validity and interpretation of laws, and another to discuss their justice. However, Hart's picture is just too neat. The legal system works with a degree of moral argument running through it. In a sense, law is one very special case of a political moral argument. It is one where authorities and sources play a much greater role than is usual. For this reason, wrong or inadequate answers (from the viewpoint of unrestricted political morality) may be given, as judges are constrained by the sources before them. Nevertheless, it is an answer to a question posed in political morality.

Separation is Essential to the Integrity of Moral Choice

This is no doubt the most worrying of the positivists' arguments. Those people who argue for a moralistic approach to law are generally concerned to take morality or political morality as a serious worthwhile institution. Here the positivists argue that they do not, that they demean the nature of moral choice and responsibility.

The argument is this: each individual must always be prepared to decide whether to obey the dictates of law or the demands of conscience. The moralistic approach obscures this moral position, by confounding, or worse identifying law and morality. The moralist says that a law necessarily satisfies certain standards of morality, that it is moral. This, says the positivist robs the individual of the power of moral choice - once it is clear that a certain command is lawful, it assumes that it is moral and so the individual cannot assess its moral validity and then answer for herself the question 'Should I obey this law?'. The positivist approach leaves the issue of moral choice starkly open - 'This is law; but that says nothing about its morality. I must still decide whether I should obey it'.

The positivist argument makes two powerful points here. The first is that when discussing the concept of law, the sphere of legal norms, we must not treat the moral sphere as not existing. We must not isolate law from all the other social phenomena we know. Secondly, within the moral sphere there is one important feature which stands out - the individual must decide whether something is right or wrong, whether to obey a law, ignore it or defy it. The sovereignty of moral choice must not be fettered by a moralistic concept of law.[25]

These are two extremely important points, though perhaps controversial. I agree with both points. I agree that we cannot, in our analysis of legal life, simply ignore other social phenomena. I also agree with the sovereignty of individual moral choice (I do not interpret this as meaning that whatever the individual decides is right, but rather that each individual must decide and accept the responsibility for deciding). I do not accept that these two facts provide a ground to deny a connection between law and political morality.

I believe that judges should mould the legal structure in the form of a coercive order which is justified according to a particular theory of political morality, but this is the law's theory of political morality (the state's theory of political morality) and not that of every single person. It is moulded with a view to critical political morality, but it is not critical political morality.

Normative orders can be divided according to their concern and their subject - that is an order concerns a particular topic, and particular people. For instance, Habermas divides the concerns of what is broadly called 'morality' into morality and ethics - the former concerns inter-personal disputes, the latter notions of one's own good life.26 Similarly, one can also speak of Habermas' morality, German society's morality, and the morality of German law. The approach of this book concerns the judicial development of the law's political morality, through interpretation. The law has its theory of political morality, just as other people or groups have theories of political morality, and also of personal morality.27 A judge should try to justify the legal norm and legal order as furthering a particular ideal of political morality, but this *does not* impair the sovereignty of individual decision. It is still for the individual to decide whether the justified legal order is sufficiently close to her own morality, or political morality to permit obedience or compliance. To the judge who asserts 'This legal order is justified because I have given it an interpretation in accord with its most appealing claim of political morality', the defendant may always respond 'I reject this legal order, and its political morality'.

Positivists have perhaps been unfairly accused of ignoring the importance of the moral decision to obey the law or not. However, the positivist counter attack that arguing for a connection between law and political morality also undermines moral decision making is not convincing. It is always open to the individual to deny the validity of a proposed political morality.

This relates back to the point made above that a judicial justification of the legal order may well accept the validity of unjust laws, or involve the use of a less than adequate theory of political morality. The questions of the interpretation of laws, of the validity of laws, of the applicability of laws are not identical to the question of obedience to law, though they are related. In determining the validity, interpretation and application of laws, judges must reconstruct a justification of that legal order, and so must indirectly provide an answer to the question, why should one obey the law. However in providing this justification they are limited by the (admittedly somewhat flexible) terms of the law itself. So the law's reconstructed answer to the question why to obey, may not be a very convincing one. Indeed it may be so unconvincing that it does not amount to an answer and so that we feel justified in calling it 'an abuse of law', a 'perversion' of law, a peripheral case of law, or even a robber gang without law.

To put this in another way. Each individual in making her decision about the validity or otherwise of a legal order or a legal rule, is engaging in the exercise of practical reason, the most important part of which is the moral argument. The individual tries to put forward a moral position. So does the judge in a case. The individual's exercise of practical reason is unrestricted - autonomous if you like.[28] The judicial exercise of practical reason is basically limited in a way that the individual exercise is not. As we shall see in the next chapter, one may make use of firmly held judgements when justifying moral beliefs in a reflective equilibrium. An individual has the possibility to reject as many of her own firmly held judgements as she pleases. She may reject all of them. The judge does not, but is bound by the committed judgements expressed in the legal order, i.e. in statutes, constitutional law texts and (depending on the legal system) precedents and custom. Even with these there is room for manoeuvre, through interpretation and declarations of invalidity. Nevertheless the power to (re-)interpret and deem certain norms invalid is not of the same order as the individual power to do so. As Habermas well puts it, the judicial task is a reconstructive rather than constructive one.[29] The judicial exercise is an exercise in practical reason but it is restricted. Since it is restricted it does not invalidate the individual's exercise of practical reason. So a judicial reconstruction cannot be used to negate the moral right of disobedience.

This view of the role of law has similarities to Rawls' notion of an overlapping consensus. There is a political conception of justice (if you like the state's or the legal system's) which tries to gain the support of the various reasonable conceptions of justice held by different actors in the society. The points of similarity are these: first, there is a conception of political morality which stands by itself; second, the conceptions of political morality held by other parties may agree or disagree with the conception of the legal system - but that is a decision each of those actors must make.

There Is No Moral Obligation to Obey Law

This is the most interesting of the positivist challenges to a connection between law and morality. Raz avoids the difficulties other writers have of explaining law's claim to obedience through the simple expedient of denying that it has any. The concept of law nowhere touches the concept of morality and so no claim to obedience can be grounded.[30]

Yet this neat solution of the Gordian knot goes against our convictions. If a judge sentences a person to prison, she has no doubt but that the executive authority will imprison that person, and that it is right that that person be imprisoned. The legal enterprise, and particularly judging, is a *practical* exercise. Whilst there are theoretical elements to it, the legal enterprise is always one with a view to action. The judge who makes a decision expects it to be implemented; the plaintiff who makes her case expects, if successful, that the benefits will be accorded to her. That practical consequences flow from the legal arguments cannot be ignored.

The legal rules are not like the rules of a game or linguistic rules. If I refuse to play a game, or to speak a language, then the degree of social criticism and pressure brought to bear on me is not the same (usually) as when I defy a law. The legal 'game' is one I cannot simply choose not to play. The legal order does not accept the voluntary removal from its sphere of authority, which it claims pre-empts every other normative sphere. The legal order attaches serious consequences to infringements of its rules. It requires obedience, and practically speaking, can enforce its rules.

These consequences the legal actor must be prepared to justify. A judge who says 'You are to go to jail, even though it is not even conceivably justifiable that you should go to jail' or 'You should go to jail because of a technical requirement of the law, leaving aside all questions of morality' is not perceived as the best of judges. To wield the wide range of powers, including coercive and violent powers open to the legal system, a legal actor must be ready with a good reason to justify the use.

Furthermore, when faced with defiance the court (legal system) does not regard this as a legitimate option. Defiance is not expected, it is not perceived as legitimate, it is a ground for punishment itself. The judge does not say 'If you want to behave in a legal manner, you must act in such a way'. The judicial announcement leaves no scope for the discretion of the actor.

Hart himself puts it thus:

> For ... [participants in a legal system] the violation of a rule is not merely a basis for the prediction that a hostile reaction will follow but a *reason* for hostility.[31]

The violation of a legal rule is seen as something justifying punishment. If we do not ask why this is so, then we are forsaking the internal point of view entirely, which is a methodological loss we cannot accept. The appropriate point of view is not that of a purely external observer, nor perhaps that of someone completely immersed in a legal system, accepting all its values, but it must at least be that of someone who appreciates that insiders do accept the legal rules, and do regard them as reasons for criticism (indeed coercive response) in cases of deviance, which only makes sense if we assign some meaning to the notion of legal obligation, at least in a *prima facie* sense.[32]

Raz takes an important point throughout his work, most recently in *Ethics in the Public Domain*, when he notes that the law claims legitimate authority.[33] Law always claims legitimate authority, even though 'a legal system may not have legitimate authority, or though its legitimate authority may not be as extensive as it claims'. To understand law from the insider's perspective (without necessarily fully endorsing everything about a legal system and its values) we must give some meaning to how the law can make a claim to *legitimate* authority. This poses, for insiders, the tension between law's positivity and normativity, 'between facts and norms' as Habermas puts it. It is a tension between the particularity of the legal order and the universality of the claim to legitimacy. It poses also the dilemma between affording too much legitimacy to law, and none at all. An anti-positivist approach acknowledges that law does make this claim to legitimacy, a claim most importantly seen in the area of constitutional law. In making this claim, critical morality is not allowed unrestricted sway, but nor is it altogether excluded. Traditional legal sources as used in the particular legal system are not jettisoned in the pursuit of an 'ideal constitution', but nor are they the exclusive content of law. Legal actors, particularly judges, must mediate between the particularity of a legal system and the universality of critical morality, when interpreting and confirming the validity of legal sources. Traditional legal sources are thus treated as the 'provisional fixed points' of a reflective equilibrium. In this way the law's claim to obedience makes sense.

From the internal point of view we cannot ignore the law's claim to *legitimate* authority. What is it that makes an exercise of power legitimate? If it is not that the legal norm is right in and of itself (which it may be or may not; it may be morally neutral, or morality may be ambivalent), then it is only the constitutional democratic system which produces it which authorises the claim of legitimacy. Nino sums this up:

> A judge can not justify a statute enacted by the legislature by relying on that statute if she does not assume either, explicitly or implicitly, judgements on the moral legitimacy of the authority of the legislator and on the fact that the fundamental rights which condition that authority have not been violated by the enactment.[34]

In saying that a claim to a right to obedience is part of our experience of law, this is not saying that it is always a justified claim, that everyone should always accept it. The law does make that claim. It makes that claim because the law is all about providing a reconstructed claim to legitimacy of the use of power in a given legal order. Yet the claim may be flawed, unacceptable for some reason, when viewed from outside the limits of legal discourse. As legal actors we mediate between the specifications of law, and the requirements of critical morality. As human persons we stand by the dictates of critical morality. This preserves the integrity of conscience, without denying that the legal order makes the claim it seems to make. The nature of critical moral argument is one to which I turn in the next chapter.

Conclusion: Law and Political Moral Argument

In this Chapter I have tried, by referring to well known legal theories to weaken the positivist argument that there is no necessary link between (political) morality and (in particular constitutional) law.

My understanding of law is that it includes an attempt to answer the question of justification, of legitimacy, which is necessarily posed by the coercive activity of law, by its claim to obedience. This attempts to steer a path between two extremes - the extreme which insists that whatever is law is moral, and the extreme which insists that between law and morality there is no link.

The latter theory runs into severe difficulties in the area of constitutional justice. The classic positivist theories of Hart and Kelsen tend to leave participants in the discourse of constitutional justice without any guidelines when it comes to interpretation. Furthermore, their approach does not reflect adequately the inherently argumentative, more precisely, publicly argumentative nature of constitutional law. We will see in Chapters Four, Five and Six, how constitutional law acts as a public debate on the justification of state power, with judges, legislators, ministers, and citizens acting as interlocutors. Yet this argumentative nature does not come across readily in classic positivist writings. Furthermore, the separation thesis does not answer the foundational question of law - what is really at the heart of law that explains these phenomena? In Hart and Kelsen, it is a norm (of different types); in my opinion, it is a debate over legitimacy.

Seeing law as involving a discourse of justification at its core confers a meaning on law's claim to obedience. It does so in a way that is more satisfactory than classical positivist work. Hart's theory requires the legal system to be based on an empirical basis, the rule of recognition which is accepted as an empirical matter by the legal officials of a country. Kelsen's theory requires a presupposed, unposited, hypothetical norm to confer normative validity on a legal system. He makes the powerful point that we must try to understand our social practice of law as normative. Normativity can only be grounded in norms not facts. The only way to make sense of law is to presuppose the Basic Norm. This presupposition would only be acceptable if there was no other way to confer meaning on our social practice of law including law's normativity. Kelsen's obsession with the non-identity of law and morality, and his consequent insistence on the strict separation of law and morality, precluded using a moral concept to guarantee law's normativity.

Furthermore, in this Chapter, I have tried to show the weakness of the classic arguments in favour of the separation thesis. The connection thesis does not necessarily lead to either confusion, or automatic legitimation of legal norms. Rather the connection is that legal practitioners must, when considering questions of validity, interpretation, application, also consider questions of justification. They must try to, from within the constraints of law, provide a justification of the law. This is not a reason to assert that the law is always moral, or politically acceptable. Judged from the viewpoint of the political morality of an individual, it may well be found lacking. All that law can say on its behalf, is that the justification is the best that can be offered.

However there is the worrying claim, raised by various writers, that morality is such an indeterminate flux of assertions and thoughts, that it can provide no guidance to the more secure, certain discourses of law. With this objection in mind, I turn, in the next chapter to consider whether there can be any criteria for rational intersubjective political moral argument. If there are not then this book is meaningless. If there are then they can be used in the legal argument where the question of political moral justification is paramount, and so provide criteria for argument that positivists insist are none of the legal theorist's business.

Notes

1   Bork, *The Tempting of America*, Ch. 7; Weschler, 'Towards Neutral Principles of Constitutional Law' (1959) 73 *Harv. L. Rev.* 1.

2   This approach is similar to ideology of 'legal and rational judicial decision-making': Wroblewski, *The Judicial Application of Law*, Chs. 10, 14. See Peczenick, *On Law and Reason*, Ch. 5; at p. 241 he notes that 'legal interpretation is creative and value-laden' it accomplishes an 'improvement of the law, its adaptation to critical morality'. See also Aarnio, *The Rational as Reasonable*, pp. 189 - 190.

3   *The Authority of Law*, p. 30.

4   Dworkin describes the concept of law as 'the concept of the standards that provide for the *rights* and *duties* that a government has a *duty* to recognise and enforce', *Taking Rights Seriously*, p. 47 (emphasis added). See also *Law's Empire*, p. 93.

5   *Natural Law and Natural Rights*, p. 14 (emphasis added).

6   For discussions of different legal positivisms, see: Hart 'Positivism, Law and Morals', *Essays in Jurisprudence and Philosophy*, at p. 57; Grzegorczyk, Michaud, Troper (eds.) *Le Positivisme Juridique;* Raz, *The Authority of Law*, pp. 37 - 57; Nino, 'Dworkin and Legal Positivism', (1980) 89 *Mind* 519, 519 - 520.

7   Raz, *The Authority of Law*, p. 37 and p. 39.

8   Fuller, 'Positivism and Fidelity to Law: A Reply to Prof. Hart', 71 *Harv. L. R.*, 630, 642.

9   See Raz, *Ethics in the Public Domain*, p. 318.

10   'A Philosophical Reconstruction of Judicial Review' (1993) *Card. L Rev.* 799, 815. Compare this with Kant, *The Metaphysics of Morals*, p. 123, sect. 43 (311).

11   *Law's Empire*, p. 93.

12   See Locke, *Two Treatises on Civil Government*; Paine, *The Rights of Man*.

13   Dyzenhaus gives as an example a 'Dworkinian' judge in the former apartheid regime of South Africa, 'Law and Public Reason', (1993) 38 *McGill Law J.* 366, 389.

14   Kelsen, *The Pure Theory of Law*, p. 66.

15   MacCormick, *An Institutional Theory of Law*, p. 127.

16   Finnis, *Natural Law and Natural Rights*, pp. 24 - 29.

17   Both Dworkin and Finnis acknowledge this possibility. See *Law's Empire* p. 103; *Natural Law and Natural Rights*, Ch. 12.

18   See Peczenick, *On Law and Reason*, pp. 248 - 249, where he argues that an extremely immoral normative system does not create valid law. See also Dworkin, *Law's Empire*, pp. 103 - 104.

19   *The Pure Theory of Law*, pp. 27, 34, 35, 38, 48, 54, 62.

20   *The Pure Theory of Law*, pp. 61, 62.

21   Habermas says 'The complementing of morality by coercive law can itself be morally justified'. 'Law and Morality' (1988) 8 *Tanner Lectures on Human Values*, p. 217 at p. 245; *Between Facts and Norms*, Ch. 3, pp. 114 - 116.
        See Finnis, *Natural Law and Natural Rights*, pp. 28 - 29, commenting on Aquinas.

22   *Pure Theory of Law*, p. 64.

23   *Pure Theory of Law*, pp. 69, 106, 282, 285; 'Law, State and Justice in the Pure Theory of Law', in Kelsen, *What is Justice?*, p. 297. According to Kelsen, the law is not, in any way, naturally moral, and so can be subject to extra-legal moral criticism. It is the very positivity of the Pure Theory that permits one to criticise - or justify - legal rules (p. 67).

24   *The Concept of Law*, pp. 202 - 207.

25   Hart, *The Concept of Law*, pp. 206 - 207; MacCormick, *An Institutional Theory of Law*, p. 139 et seq.; MacCormick, 'A Moralistic Case for A-Moralistic Law' 20 *Valparaiso Law Review* 1. See Soper's critique in 'Choosing a Legal Theory on Moral Grounds' 4 *Soc. Phil. & Pol.* 31.

26   *Justification and Application*, pp. 1 - 19; *Between Facts and Norms*, pp. 96 - 97.

27   In saying that 'the law has a theory of political morality' I am using that phrase as a shorthand metaphorical way of saying that the legal practices and norms of a legal order can be constructed and seen as being justified by a theory of political morality - a theory of political morality can be ascribed to it. The 'Law' is not an independent actor, it is the set of norms and practices of certain actors, such as judges, legislators, lawyers, and ordinary citizens when engaged in legal activity.

28   MacCormick, 'The Concept of Law and 'The Concept of Law'' (1994) *Ox. J. Leg. St.* 1, 4.

29   *Between Facts and Norms*, p. 192.

30   Raz, *The Authority of Law*, pp. 137, 233 - 260; Raz, *Ethics in the Public Domain*, p. 326. Compare Coleman, 'On the Relationship between Law and

Morality' (1989) *Ratio Juris* 66; Peczenick, *On Law and Reason*, pp. 246 et seq. This section is based on Nino, 'A Philosophical Reconstruction of Judicial Review' (1993) *Card. L Rev.* 799. A related argument from the claim to correctness is found in Alexy, 'On Necessary Relations Between Law and Morality' (1989) *Ratio Juris* 167, 177.

31 *The Concept of Law*, p. 88.
32 *The Concept of Law*, p. 87.
33 At pp. 199 et seq.
34 'A Philosophical Reconstruction of Judicial Review' (1993) *Card. L. Rev.* 799, 815.

3 Political Argument: Intersubjectivism

Introduction

Arguments about political morality play a considerable role in (constitutional) legal argument. Legal decisions rely, implicitly or explicitly, on claims rooted in political morality. Claims of political morality provide the links in the chains of legal argument. This intermingling of law and political morality we shall see in the three following chapters.

Furthermore, I argue that this link is not just observable in practice, but that it is also unavoidable: law and political morality are intimately linked at the conceptual level. This claim is controversial in legal circles and indeed forms the focus of the perennial debate between natural lawyers and positivists. Positivist legal writers argue that the two normative spheres, law and political morality, are conceptually rigidly separate. I disagree with this understanding of law. The normativity of law rests on the claim that it has been made, from the viewpoint of political morality, the best it can be. All legal practitioners should make clear and explicit these political normative commitments, and argue them out. Legal discourse cannot expunge political moral discourse.

Later chapters will demonstrate the intimate links between law and political morality in practice, and make an argument for their conceptual link. Before exploring those issues, this chapter will outline my approach to issues of political moral argument. As well as providing the framework for examining the constitutional doctrines, it will answer another objection. This is the objection, directed not at the link between law and political morality, but rather at the concept of political morality itself. It might be said that there is no point to introducing talk of political morality into legal discourse because political morality is too indeterminate and too controversial. The argument says that

> There is no way of deciding which view in a political argument is 'correct'. All that you will succeed in doing is adding another factor of indeterminacy. Having shown the frayed edges of the open texture of law, you suggest that we solve it by relying on a discipline, which offers shapeless apparitions and no hard cores at all! Further, you will simply make savage an already bitter debate. It is one thing for a judge to say that someone or something is (un)lawful. It is much more serious to say that someone or something is (un)just.

So political morality is too unstable a compound to introduce into the stable relations of law.[1]

Political moral argument is a territory which lawyers, for better or worse, occupy without always intelligently discussing. We give implicit answers to moral issues in our legal arguments, yet those answers may not be very good ones, since we do not consciously deal with them. I believe we should try to answer intelligently the questions we implicitly answer. Occupation of the moral territory implies a responsibility to argue intelligently. Fortunately the question of moral argument is one oft treaded by many thinkers and writers. In trying to map out the path of moral argument, we can rely on those who have gone before us.

In this chapter, I try to outline one particular way of dealing with the argument about indeterminacy and controversy of political morality. My approach simply draws out the trends implicit in the works of several recent moral and political thinkers. I wish to clarify the grounds on which we may adjudicate between contested political moral claims, rather than propose a particular political morality. The project is a 'second-order' one - I am talking about how we argue about political morality rather than arguing for a political morality.[2]

My approach has three stages. First, I explain the basic idea and explain why I find it preferable to other general approaches. Second, I enumerate the requirements of this approach. Third, I defend it against certain common criticisms.

How should the reader assess this proposal? As regards the indeterminacy of morality, I suggest that the aim of the proposal should be to provide guidelines by which to assess the adequacy of different theories of political morality, and which serve to disqualify plainly inadequate theories. I do not claim that I can provide a proposal which identifies one clear winner, and leaves the rest straggling well down the field. Indeed, I wish to leave areas of indeterminacy, to be resolved by active participants in a debate. I simply suggest the criteria by which they should judge a political moral claim to be acceptable or otherwise. It is one of the strengths of this approach that it does not decide everything in advance. At the level of generality at which we are discussing, little else is possible.

We are talking about political morality, that is an exercise of practical reason. Practical reason, as distinct from theoretical reason, is fundamentally oriented towards the question of what one should do. Should I buy this dress? Should he tell that lie? Should the State raise taxes? Practical reason covers many different fields. It covers straightforward 'technical' or 'means - end' reasoning: if I want to make a model aircraft, I should buy the requisite parts, etc. Practical reason may be addressed to self- interest in the short term ('I am hungry so I shall find out where the nearest pizzeria is'), and self-interest in the long term ('I wish to be a successful pianist, so I shall not spend so much time playing sports or watching television, but practising'). Practical reason also addresses itself to the claims of morality, i.e. the claims about what is the *good life* to lead, what is *the right thing* to do. Leaving aside the questions of satisfying one's wants, desires and needs, what ought one to aim for in life?[3] Therefore, we are interested in the moral sphere of practical reason. More precisely we are interested in questions of political (public) morality, that is questions of the good and the right when political action is at stake. There is a distinction between questions of the good and the right in the private sphere and in the public sphere. I have certain opinions on what I ought to do as a person, but they are not necessarily identical to my opinion on what political actors (the State, judges, administrators, local councils, etc.) ought to do.

How should we adjudicate between competing moral claims? I assume that if there is no disagreement over a practical evaluation or course of action, then there is no need for a theory to adjudicate between claims. So we are centred in a dispute, which is appropriate given that the overall topic of this work is legal interpretation. The focus is on competing claims about how one should behave. Where there is such a conflict how do we decide which view we ought to adopt (i.e. which is valid)?4

My basic idea, which is found in much recent German and American philosophy, is that the validity of moral claims must be grounded on a reason that one can offer to the other party to accept the claim. Or, in other words, one may reasonably expect someone to accept certain types of reasons which justify the claim. This is a notion of *intersubjective* validity. It is intersubjective in that it rests on a debate between different people. Such an approach has also been called *constructivist* - we attempt through argument and debate to construct rules and judgements.5 Morality is not something given to us, or found by us - we constructively establish valid moral norms. With apologies to Sartre, we might say that there is no moral essence which precedes our reasoning.

Intersubjectivism

Competing Conceptions of Validity in Morality

I have an intersubjective conception of validity in moral matters. What exactly does this mean? I shall try to explain by outlining competing conceptions of validity.

Some people adopt a sceptical position that argues that no moral claim is ever valid. Others may adopt a subjectivist approach - moral claims may be valid for the person holding them but no one else. Another approach is also relativist, arguing that some moral claims may be valid in certain groups or communities, but there can be no valid trans-communal validity. A closely related stance is the hermeneutic claim that certain moral positions are valid because they express the development of a particular tradition, or self-understanding. A final claim might be that validity means that a claim is 'objectively' right. Let us just briefly see what each view might claim, and note the valuable and problematic elements associated with each.

The thoroughly sceptical view is an unusual one to encounter. Few people say that it is not possible to ascribe validity to any moral claim. I do not say that no one believes that rape, murder and torture are on a par with charity, cooking and sport. Nor do I assert that no one exists who, facing a death squad, would not cry 'I do not want this, but you do no wrong in your course of action'. However, this is an extreme position, and one likely to involve the sceptic in practical self-contradiction.[6] The other form of sceptic is the self-assured philosophy lecturer, who gently chides the less mature:

> We do what we can to make things better, or more pleasant, but of course our beliefs have no 'real' validity. We do them, and why not; but they are not *actually really* valid in any sense.

Such scepticism indicates some important features about moral validity. Most importantly, that it differs from the sort of validity that we tend, in everyday life, to associate with scientific or logical validity. The validity of propositions such as 'murder is wrong' is different from the validity of propositions such as '2+2=4', or 'water consists of two atoms of hydrogen to one of oxygen'. The notion of validity in the moral sphere seems not so certain as validity in these other spheres. However that the notion of validity in moral matters does not seem to be the same as in other matters does not mean that no concept of validity is possible. It just means that a slightly different concept is required.

The subjectivist vests the criteria of validity in the decision or beliefs or emotions of the individual, though in two very different ways. Such a person may proclaim that his or her decision determines the validity of moral claims for everyone, or alternatively only for him or her self. The first is the stance of dictators, obsessed with their own importance for humanity. The second, is the claim of many people who flee to subjectivism from fear of intolerance. Anxious not to condemn people unreasonably, they hold that no claim is valid for anyone except the person holding it.

There are different varieties of the modest subjectivist. She or he may subscribe to emotivism, prescriptivism, or decisionism. Thus, an emotivist says 'moral claims reflect my passions'. They are valid in that they are the genuine emotions of the person concerned. Or they may be more complexly described as the attitudes of the subject.[7] The prescriptivist (also imperativist) does not express her attitudes, but more precisely *prescribes* what ought to be done. The decisionist may be an existentialist of sorts. Once I decide my belief, I should stick to it, just as others should stick to theirs. I violate a subjectively valid norm when I fail to implement my decisions.

Subjectivists, like sceptics, emphasise the difficulties in different people reaching agreement on moral matters. Further, they emphasise that there is something profoundly individualistic about moral decisions and attitudes.

The common problem with subjectivist approaches is that they make no real sense of moral disagreement and reasoning.[8] That you and I have different attitudes, prescriptions, etc., indicates a difference. Subjectivists do not find this disagreement radically different from 'You like chocolate and I like vanilla ice cream'. More importantly, such subjectivist approaches do not provide a way to reason about these different beliefs.

A very common position is the relativist one, which is not identical with the sceptical position, though sometimes confounded with it. Here someone says that a particular community has certain values, which are valid for all its members. However, other communities have a different scale of values, which are just as valid for their members. This approach is a response to certain features of the world. We realise that there are many different moral beliefs actually held by different people in different communities, i.e. there are many different *conventional* moralities.[9] We are reluctant to criticise any one conventional morality simply because it differs from our own. A relativist draws the conclusion that each is valid, only for its own members. This type of person could ban crucifixes and turbans from French classrooms, but rush to defend the policies of the parochial Irish Catholic society of the 1950s. Or, more sophisticatedly, could tell us that our bourgeois liberal institutions are as valid for us as the project of ethnic cleansing for others - but we still ought, in fidelity to our *mores*, to seek to eliminate the latter.[10]

The hermeneutic approach is often so closely tied to the relativist approach, as to make the two indistinguishable. However the hermeneuticist need not be bound to an identifiable community (she may concentrate on the individual or humanity as a whole), nor need the relativist adopt a hermeneutic approach. The hermeneuticist claims validity for those moral claims which evolve in the unfolding narrative of the moral actor (and its members, if appropriate).[11] We are born to, live out, interact with certain moral beliefs, and the ever-developing beliefs are valid, as they are rooted in our lived experience.

The approaches to validity mentioned above all make claims that are in some sense weaker than the intersubjectivist claim. The objectivist makes a claim stronger than does the intersubjectivist. Moral claims are valid not because they might gain the consent of others, or could gain the consent of others, but because they are rooted in some objective reality, say, nature or divine will. Objectivists may identify goodness or rightness as a property, either natural or non-natural, simple or complex of various actions or situations, which we somehow see, sense, or grasp. An objectivist can accommodate variations according to space and time, notwithstanding Cicero's memorable cry that the natural law is timeless, unchanging, unalterable and knows no boundaries. Many natural law theories claim that the specific requirements of the natural law vary with time.

Traditionally natural law theories have been associated with objectivist approaches to moral validity. One of the most powerful objectivist arguments of recent years is John Finnis' defence of the natural law, a set of basic principles of reasonable human behaviour, which hold true through the ages, as do the 'mathematical principles of accounting'.[12] Finnis insists that there are a range of basic goods (approximately eight) and a list of principles of practical reasoning (approximately nine) which anyone who thinks about such matters will identify as self-evidently good and right, that is they will accept them without the need for any argument.[13]

Objectivist theories have been very popular, since they seem to give sense to our belief that we are saying something in a sense *real*, or at any rate, non-trivial, when we say something is good or evil, right or wrong. Furthermore, objectivist theories suggest that it is possible for people to have a reasoned discussion as to moral matters. Objectivist theories generally fall down in explaining though just how people identify and talk about moral propositions.

Some order may be imposed on the above by considering them as answering different questions. Are there criteria of validity for moral norms? If so, how are norms deemed valid (by decision, nature, argument, consensus, tradition, or some other method)? What is the role played by reason in moral deliberation (none, balancing of reasons, interpreting of traditions, instrumental means-end assessment)? If moral norms are valid, then for whom are they valid (the individual, community, humanity, all rational beings, everything)?

The Intersubjectivist Conception of Validity

An intersubjectivist approach tries to borrow the valuable elements from these different approaches. The intersubjectivist accepts that there are criteria for the validity of moral norms, i.e. she rejects moral scepticism. However she rejects the idea that morality is something objective, self-evident, given by nature. Moral scepticism asserts too little in favour of moral validity, objectivism too much. A middle position is appropriate:

> We have found, indeed, that although we had purposed to build for ourselves a tower which should reach to Heaven, the supply of materials sufficed merely for a habitation, which was spacious enough for all terrestrial purposes and high enough to enable us to survey the level plain of experience, but that the bold undertaking designed necessarily failed for want of materials.[14]

The intersubjectivist does not seek to build a tower which will claim objective validity, nor does she renounce the project in favour of anarchy. Rather she seeks to discuss claims of moral validity for all terrestrial purposes: what should we do here and now. The intersubjectivist starts by seeing what can be accomplished in the moral sphere by reasoning rather than making grand claims about objectivity or nihilism.[15] This she does by assessing moral claims about practical action to see if they can be backed up by reasons which others could accept, and then determining what are the criteria of validity for such reasons. The basis for validity is not found in tradition, or individual decision, or emotion, but rather in rational intersubjective argumentation.

The answer to the question for whom are moral norms valid, is more problematic. The outcome of a rational argument aimed at consensus is valid for the participants. However, the participants may also have to recognise its validity for others, where this is entailed by the arguments put forward. Of course these others may then, not unreasonably, insist on joining the argument; once they do, they too are bound. However, someone committed to rational intersubjective argument need not claim that specific requirements are valid for everyone. For instance, one may conclude that a proposition is legitimate if everyone in the area affected consents to it. There would then be no inconsistency in supposing that two propositions which would be incompatible on the same territory could be valid for different territories, each sustained as valid under the same less specific criteria, valid for all.

Another complexity in the intersubjective approach then becomes clear. That is there are layers of rational argument. Thus, we might hold that certain criteria govern rational argument generally. We may decide that the criteria need to be modified when applied to practical rather than theoretical questions. Further, the criteria applied to prudential or technical questions may differ from those appropriate to decide questions of the right and the good (morality). In the sphere of political morality, rational criteria of argument produce a more specific set of criteria. That these political criteria of argument produce more specific still criteria of argument for different types of society, or that they produce different theories for different societies, or that they produce different applications of the same theory for different groups, or different stages in economic development.

This complexity will (I trust) become less daunting as the chapter develops this approach. However, I also signal that, although variability is inherent in the approach, it is not an infinite versatility. Intersubjectivism is not moralistic plastic, mouldable to any outcome whatsoever.

The Foundation of Rational Intersubjective Argument

The basic idea is that for a moral claim to be valid, the person proposing it must be able to give a reason that any other person involved could accept as right.[16]

The immediate objection posed is: why should I consider the validity of my moral claims to rest on whether they are such that other people could accept them as right? Why should one enter into rational intersubjective moral argument? There seem to be two ways of answering this. The first is to identify such moral reasoning as being an aspect of reasoning as such. The second is to note the rather serious consequences of rejecting rational intersubjective moral argument.

The argument that moral reasoning is based on reasoning as such runs as follows.[17] Claims about truth and validity make an intersubjective appeal to other persons. That is, one claims that all other persons should accept the truth or validity of the claim.[18] One's claims must not merely be backed up by reasons, that is must not merely be argued for. They must be argued for to other persons, for the claim is that those other persons should accept the validity or truth of the claim. This process of reasoning (argumentation or deliberation) in any field (scientific, moral or otherwise) presupposes intersubjectivism.[19] Anyone who reasons, i.e. takes part in deliberation (or even merely deliberates within her own mind, weighing differing points of view), must presuppose certain criteria which the people with whom she is deliberating, and herself, are bound to apply.[20]

The decision to enter into rational intersubjective argument is itself a foundational choice. That is, it is the basic starting point for argument.[21] There is nothing beyond or behind it on which to base a decision about it. I cannot give any reason to you to accept it. For if I could give you a reason that you could accept, then it would mean we had *already* accepted the notion. This is the bottom line. Anyone who tries to make an argument or any validity or truth claim must accept the criteria of a rational intersubjective argument. You cannot argue without accepting the need to give reasons that can be accepted by another. As Habermas notes, anyone who refuses to do so, must refuse to argue, to make any claims at all. Such a person faces serious difficulties. Such a withdrawal from argumentation is possible only through 'suicide or serious mental illness'.[22]

In determining the criteria of rational intersubjective moral argument we are simply applying the notion of a rational intersubjective argument to one particular sphere, that of practical reason, and specifically morality. In so far as we are rational we engage in interpersonal argumentation. We should try to see what can be accomplished by interpersonal argumentation in the sphere of morality. The alternatives to this are rather stark.

Suppose we reject the idea that validity of normative political arguments hinges on whether one can give a reason to someone else to accept them. What is wrong with such a rejection? Well then, how would we solve our differences? Reject this and there is no option left but force, or perhaps a *modus vivendi*, a grudging compromise on how to live, rooted in self-interest. To reject the requirement that moral claims be justified by intersubjective argumentation, is to choose might over reason, the sword over the pen. I do not give you a reason to resolve a conflict; you do not give me a reason to solve a conflict. Absent a requirement for such reasons, what is left? If the requirement is rejected, then nothing remains between persons who disagree on this question, but to pick up the cudgels and fight it out, each invoking their own divine inner light. The person who refuses to give a reason to another to justify the assertion that his conduct is wrong, cannot expect that other to heed her. She can give no reason for the other not to resist her (or enslave her), using force.

When the dust of battle settles, what is left? If the opponents of rational moral argument lose, and they are lucky, their opponents will be tolerant.[23] If those who select reason are a lucky minority, they will not pose such a threat as to provoke suppression. Faced with this dilemma, the choice cannot be made by armchair sceptics.

Further, if one rejects the notion of rational intersubjective argument then one cannot expect others to accept as valid one's own beliefs. No theory of obligation (in a normative sense) is possible if this duty is rejected. One cannot expect others to accept a theory which cannot be rationally justified to them. That is, one cannot say 'You do wrong in disagreeing with me, even though there is no reason for you not to disagree with me'. For if we give no reason, there is no warrant for the assertion; it may be dismissed. And if we do give a reason to the other person, then we must play the game of rational intersubjective moral argument.

In conclusion the decision to enter rational intersubjective argumentation, with a view to giving someone reasons to follow a certain course of action, is itself the foundational choice.

The Requirements of Rational Intersubjective Argument

The proponents of a political theory must provide reasons for it, which another party can accept to regulate a dispute. What criteria do we use to decide whether another person could accept such reasons? I argue here for nine such criteria. A claim that fails to meet any one of them should not be regarded as an acceptable reason. Further, a theory should strive to fulfil these criteria as well as possible. There is no way though of closing the debate on the acceptability of a political morality, which exceeds the threshold requirements. Its acceptability can only be judged by comparing its compatibility with the criteria with the degree of compatibility offered by other theories. It is always possible that someone else may propose a new theory, and the argument would once again have to take place. Or someone may try to explain why a previously discarded theory responds better to the criteria than more recent ones. There is no way of closing the debate on the adequacy of a theory of political morality.

Further, it must be a debate. The basic idea with which I start presupposes a disagreement between parties over a practical course of action. So, subject to three riders, this proposal does not receive its best implementation unless there is an actual disagreement.

The first rider is that there is nothing inherently objectionable about someone trying to mimic such a dispute by herself, to clarify her ideas and positions. In particular, in the absence of any genuine conflict, she may use them to develop a moral position. Where conflict or disagreement does emerge, she must give reasons. She must not say that she has considered all theories according to these criteria, and has rejected all except her own, so her own is correct! She must be prepared to defend her theory with reasons when others disagree.[24]

However, this leads to the second rider. Although one must be prepared to defend with reasons, one does not need to accept the consensus of everyone else on the validity of particular reasons. One must always be able to offer reasons of one's own, but one must always exercise for oneself the power of judgement over which reasons best comply with these criteria. In this sense, the subjectivists are correct in identifying the individualistic nature of morality.

The third rider is that the disagreement need not involve the actual parties involved in the disputed problem, placed in the actual situation. It is not the case that only the inhabitants of the former illegal regime of South Africa could adopt a moral position on the acts of racism there. The disagreement must be genuine, not real. We can debate the legitimacy of the death penalty, even though the death penalty may not be a practical possibility in our lives. We can debate the value of blood sports, even though neither of us attend blood sports, provided we disagree on a practical attitude towards them.

Theories of political morality should be judged according to the following criteria: they should be justified by reasons, consistent, non-individualising, general, capable of solving problems, factually accurate, explicable, held by a reflective equilibrium, and universalisable. Some of these criteria are relatively non-problematic, and indeed some are rather trivia. Others however are more demanding and open to dispute. I shall demonstrate these criteria, by discussing a debate with a racist, and demonstrating how racism is a theory which fails these criteria.[25] Please note that I am considering racism as a supposed 'moral' theory. Can a racist give someone a reason that she can accept to follow a racist ideology?

Giving Reasons

The first element of a rational intersubjective argument is that one be prepared to back up claims with reasons.[26] When challenged about a claim, the person asserting it must offer a reason to justify it. If the person refuses to offer a reason, then clearly she has not offered a reason at all, never mind one which another person could accept. This is a refusal to enter into rational intersubjective argument at all.

The process of giving reasons is an inherently argumentative one. One person offers a claim, which another person then challenges. The first person offers a reason for the claim. To this the challenger responds with a counter-reason against the claim. This highlights the multi-level nature of deliberation. To adjudicate between different reasons, we need a second order level of reasons, about which we can also argue and seek justifications, counter-arguments, etc.

Imagine that our racist lives in a state where there is an ethnic itinerant minority; call them 'Voyagers'. He proposes measures which discriminate against them. When asked for a reason, he replies 'I approve of these measures'. Now there are various counter-reasons. The most simple is to say 'Well so what - I disapprove of these measures'. A different answer would be that 'But these measures hurt people'. This second answer appeals to a second order level of reasoning where the challenger apparently believes there are reasons to give greater weight to considerations of hurt and injury rather than 'mere' approval or disapproval. The parties to the argument may now graduate to this second level to consider whether there is such a hierarchy.

There can of course be several such layers of argument. At one stage or another - if carried far enough - they will shade from ethical to meta-ethical concerns. If the parties to the argument go far enough they will end up debating the different meta-ethical positions discussed earlier in this chapter, and consider the merits and demerits of rational intersubjective argument itself. The process of reasoning - giving reasons and counter-reasons extends to this level as well. Intersubjectivism tries to avoid, as far as possible, cutting off arguments by referring to 'self-evidence' or 'brute decisionism' or 'subjective taste'. Arguments can also be levelled against and in defence of the criteria of rational argument themselves. I think however most of the criteria I discuss here are supported by reasons, though I am open to counter-arguments. What cannot be argued against is the notion of rational intersubjective argument itself. How would one go about giving a reason not to accept reasoning?

Consistency

One of the least decisive of these criteria is that of consistency. One must not utter norms or reasons which are contradictory.27

Outraged by the perfidiousness of the Voyagers, our racist adversary protests publicly against them. He declares that all Voyagers ought to be subject to arbitrary police searches. Then a few minutes later, he insists that no Voyager ought to be subject to such searches. His listeners query this, asking him to explain how he can wish something both to be the case, and not to be the case. He has uttered a self-contradiction; one cannot affirm and negate at the same time. The uttering of self-contradictory advice cancels the advice - he has failed to give a reason that one can accept.

This is the simplest form of inconsistency - the self-contradictory affirmation both of something and its negation.

The racist now explains that he erred in his second statement. He meant to say that no one ought to be subject to arbitrary police searches - such violates the rights of citizens he affirms. Yet here we have another inconsistency - if no one should be subject to such searches, then neither can Voyagers, yet he has said that Voyagers should be so subject. Although not a self-contradictory affirmation both of a norm and its negation, this new stance is still inconsistent. To follow the more general norm would mean that no one at all should be subject to arbitrary searches; to follow the more specific norm would mean that some people should be so subject. It is not possible to obey both norms at the same time.

Our racist now recasts his opinion. As a general principle, people ought not to be subject to arbitrary police searches. This is a principle, more abstract than the concrete rules mentioned earlier. A principle is a type of rule which does not have an absolute character. A principle is a norm to be considered, it is not a rule to be followed. Strictly speaking there is no inconsistency between a norm 'In general no one ought to be subject to arbitrary police searches' and a norm 'Voyagers ought to be subject to arbitrary police searches'. It is possible to implement both norms, since the former allows for exceptions. There is no self-contradiction.[28]

Note that the criterion of consistency does not set a particularly onerous requirement. Many particularly wicked theories comply with them. There is no obvious inconsistency about a doctrine of universal hatred. However, without the standard of consistency, it is not possible to give a reason for a norm, which other people can accept. Indeed, in the case of self-contradiction, one fails even to state a norm, never mind a reason for it.

It might be argued that the notion of consistency is very much rooted in one particular culture, and is not universally valid. I do not find it credible that anyone could utter an inconsistent set of statements and still be taken seriously (as regards those statements). Either he is mistaken, or he has failed to explain fully his statements, or there are other statements which will clarify the apparent inconsistency.

Non-Individualising

Our racist decides upon a perfect method to avoid the problem of consistency. He need simply avoid any general norms and announce only non-contradicting individual norms. An individual norm (or particular norm) refers to an identified person (or other actor or situation). It is contrasted with a universal norm which does not refer to identities. For instance, in a court case, the disposition of the concrete case involves an individual norm (e.g. 'Ms. Robertson should go to jail for two years'). By contrast the rules in the civil code, statute book, common law precedents, etc. are universal (e.g. 'Everyone who commits tax evasion should go to jail for two years').

Suppose our racist acquaintance claims that some Voyagers, Mr. Le Pen, and Ms. Keegstra, and their families, should not be allowed to receive any services in any shop offering services to the public. He then lists every one else in the town, by name, and specifies that they are not to be so victimised. Clearly there is nothing self-contradictory about any of these norms. One can ostracise Ms. Keegstra and not ostracise Mr. Brown.

Those singled out for this special attention object to this. Now what kind of reason could be given to them that they could accept to resolve the dispute? The racist could explain that 'It is a rule that Mr. Le Pen, and Ms. Keegstra and their families should be so boycotted.' Here he claims to provide a reason to justify the course of conduct he favours. This is in no sense a reason justifying the boycott. The Voyagers would respond 'Yes we know that you want us to be boycotted. What we want to know is what reason you can give for this.' The individual rule which the racist offers is simply a restatement of the racist's original proposition, not a justification of it.

I am not saying that individual norms play no role in moral argument. Certainly they play a role, but they cannot provide a reason for themselves. Individual norms cannot be used as justifying reasons.[29] Consider the effect if they were permitted. Persons could be singled out for treatment 'Y should be murdered' 'X should be released' 'Z should be rewarded' even though there is no discernible difference between any of them other than their identity. The mere fact of not being identical with someone else is not a reason for treatment, and recognising it as such would permit arbitrary discrimination. Indeed, it would permit any treatment at all - which is no way to resolve a dispute.

Singer makes the point that a moral claim turning on someone's identity is not capable of providing a reason. It can be invoked by each and every person because anyone can also make a claim rooted in her identity. To enunciate a rule that 'I, with my name and identity, should receive special treatment even to the extent of ignoring other's wishes' cannot resolve any dispute. *Everyone* can say 'I, with my name and identity, should receive special treatment even to the extent of ignoring other's wishes'. Singer considers that such claims involve a contradiction. The person claims, because of her identity that her case should be exceptional. Yet everyone could claim that because of her identity her case is exceptional. This results in all cases being exceptional, which is counter-intuitive.[30]

Someone may object that we rely on such individualising norms always. 'Máire ought to love her spouse Seán', 'Luis ought to return Massimo's book', 'John ought not to have deceived Mary'. Of course I am not saying that one should never use such individualising norms. Simply that they do not themselves function as reasons to resolve a dispute. Presumably in all these cases there is a universal norm behind the individual one. 'Persons ought to love their spouses (except in cases of ill treatment, marital breakdown, etc.)', 'People ought to return borrowed property', 'One ought not to deceive another'. The identity of the parties should not make a difference.

Some people have argued that such individual norms can function as reasons - they provide reasons for more general ones, which are no more than extrapolations from the individual ones.[31] One could draw a legal analogy from the common law doctrine of precedent. Courts reach individual decisions (e.g. 'Mr. Stevenson ought to pay $25 to Ms. Robinson for negligently damaging her property') and later a non-individual principle or rule emerges from the accretion of individual decisions ('Persons ought to compensate others for damage negligently inflicted'). However, I do not think this proves the claim for individual norms as the reason for general or universal ones. If the day after *Robinson* v. *Stevenson*, a case with identical facts, except for the identity of the parties were to present itself, then no court would consider the difference of identities relevant. Each individual decision presupposes a non-individual reason, though it may not be explicit, and may only become clear after many cases. (This argument involves also the notion of formal equality, which I discuss later.)

What role do individual norms play in moral argument? Certainly, they will often be the conclusion of the argument. That is we face a particular problem (e.g. 'Should I, Rory, lie to my friend') and try to resolve it by rational intersubjective argument. The result will be something like 'In this particular situation, I, Rory, should (not) lie to my friend'. Also individual norms play a 'prompting' role. That is, I may believe that 'My partner should not lie to me'. Such a norm should prompt me to consider what non-individualising general rule have I implicitly adopted as regards lying. In this way, individual norms play a role in the consideration of a reflective equilibrium.

General

Now turn to a related matter. A morally acceptable reason cannot be such as to apply to designated individuals by name, or other indications of individual identity. That is the reason must apply universally. It must have the potential to apply to persons other than the individuals involved in the dispute. Suppose our racist now explains that the reason for the policy of boycotting he advocates is that 'People who live in caravans with red and blue colours, who have two or three children each, who live in a small town of less than 1500 inhabitants, where that town contains people with a settled life style ...'. It becomes evident that he intends to include just about every detail of the particular case, in his statement of the reason. So, the reason applies irrespective of identity, but it is highly specific. It is a universal rule, but it is not a general rule.[32] Whilst highly specific norms play a role in moral discourse, they must be justified by reference to more general reasons.

Such a highly specific norm once again fails to give a reason, since it essentially applies only to this one case. The racist says that the Voyagers should be boycotted, because they should be boycotted. To resolve the dispute, the racist should refer to a reason which transcends the particularity of their situation. The one he gives attempts to smuggle in an individualising norm as a justification.

Many theorists dispute this requirement of generality. They argue that any moral position must be tied into the minute details of the particular situation. There is nothing in it which can be used in other situations, no matter how similar, nor can any other situation, or any reason applying to more than one situation be relevant. Any reason for a moral position (if it is possible for there to be a reason) must specify all the details of the situation.

This approach seems flawed for at least two reasons. First, it is not the case that every single detail of a case is morally relevant. Second, the situationalist approach poses serious pragmatic difficulties.[33]

I do not believe that we consider every single detail to be relevant in any moral dilemma. For instance, if I tell a friend that I am planning to lie to my partner by saying that I love her mother, and my friend counsels that such would be immoral. Many details would not usually be taken into consideration, e.g. the type of clothes my partner wears, our favourite foods, her and my political beliefs, and so on. Indeed, it would not be unthinkable for my friend to disclaim the relevance of any fact at all, except that I plan to lie.[34] Such a completely general reason is clearly a reason, though I may not accept it, and may propose a different reason which takes account of more of the details. However a 'reason' which simply repeats every single detail is no reason.

Consider another example. Supposing after the acquittal of the police officers who maltreated Rodney King, I express my outrage at what they had done.[35] My friend cautions me not to pass judgement, as I am not familiar with all the facts. We only know that the police officers attacked Mr. King, causing him serious injury; that Mr. King had not provoked them; that Mr. King presented no threat to anyone. What other details might be relevant to decide on the morality of the action? (Indeed, someone might make the point that not even all four of those facts are relevant.) If any other details are relevant, they cannot be many in number. If told 'He tortured an innocent person' we do not normally inquire 'Yes, but tell us all the facts, so that we may decide whether it was wrong'. (Again, someone might well argue that the fact that the victim was innocent, or even the fact that the victim was a person as opposed to an animal, was irrelevant.)

So reasons will not always comprise entirely of highly specific descriptions of facts, embodying all the details. The reason may be very general, and refer to only a small number of details.

I do not suggest that we should not carefully examine all the elements of a given problem. Of course we should. However, it is not the case that every single detail is relevant to this case and only to this case. Consider the sort of case that often comes up in family law: the child of a separated couple lives with other relatives for a number of years. The relations between the child, her mother and father, and her custodians, and their relationships with each other, will no doubt be very complex. Even so, we look at those specifics, in terms of more general norms. We ensure that we do not give the child to someone who will maltreat her, we look to give some sort of say over her future to her parents, to see who will pay most attention to the child, to make sure that the child receives the emotional, moral and material education she needs, and so on. These are all rather general norms which we apply in the instant more complex case.

There are serious pragmatic difficulties with a situationalist approach. First, one could well argue that it is impossible to describe all the details of any situation. We have some grasp on reality, but we cannot list off *all* the elements of any situation - we have to resort to some conventions or designations, which mask some of the details.

A second pragmatic difficulty with the situationalist approach is that it would be very difficult to discuss, teach, or pass on moral beliefs. If one cannot discuss them, then communication, and any form of rational discussion, is impossible. Yet, our practice (and the practice of many moral systems) seems to accept the possibility of discussing, and certainly teaching and passing on moral beliefs. At the very least, we want to be able to pass on certain precepts, be they very general like 'do not cause unnecessary suffering', or more specific like 'never call a person a nigger'.

Capable of Resolving Problems

Our racist acquaintance now announces that the Voyager families should be boycotted because of the fundamental norm '5 = 2 + 3'. Whilst no one disputes the accuracy of the statement, most people are at a loss to see how it can solve the dilemma before them. Regrettably for the segregationist efforts of our character, it is an important requirement that a reason be capable of resolving the relevant dispute.[36]

The basic idea with which we started was that a norm is valid if supported by a reason that another person could accept *to resolve a dispute*. This last element imposes certain requirements that globally can be termed the ability to resolve problems. Moral argument is always a matter of practical reason; that is, it always deals with the question: what should I (or we) do? However, the legal context is, if anything, even more thoroughly practical. This criterion is particularly important because our main concern is not with moral argument, but with moral argument in legal cases. That is moral argument in the context of a disagreement, usually over a practical course of conduct, either actually, or hypothetically involved in the disagreement.[37] Our jaunt through moral theory is pointless if we ignore the importance of this.

The mathematical equation offered provides no guidance as to a solution - it is irrelevant, and can be invoked by all the parties, in equal support of all the ideas. The claim that the sky is blue, does not usually help any one side in a dispute more so than the other. It is a neutral irrelevant factor which provides no guidance.[38]

So for a reason to be useful in problem solving, it must not be equally invokable on all sides. The criteria must be relevant. This is not to say that it is invalid, inaccurate or morally irrelevant, just that it provides no help in resolving the dispute.

So our racist turns to a different tactic - the Voyagers should be boycotted, he explains because, 'Good ought to be done, and evil avoided'. Whilst one has to agree with the sentiment, it provides no guidance on this matter. It is much too general. Of course we should do what is good and avoid what is evil, but the question we need to decide is what is good, or evil in this case. The reason gives us as much guidance as if a judge were told 'Do what is lawful, do not do what is unlawful'. What we need are criteria to determine what is lawful or not, moral or not, (or a procedure to determine the same). The reason the racist must give us must refer to such features of the situation as to enable us to see how it resolves the matter. Such a totally general, vague norm is of no help in this case.

Suppose our racist gives as a reason, 'threats to public health should not be tolerated'. This reason is more specific, and may be capable of giving us guidance, provided we know either one or both of two more matters. First, 'threat to public health' is still somewhat unclear - what kind of threat is important, and what level of danger justifies repressive action? We need more criteria to determine precisely when something does constitute such a threat. There is secondly, the problem of a procedure to determine whether the criteria are met. The procedure suggested must provide a viable method of resolving the dispute which the other parties can be expected to accept.

Avoidance of intractable disputes is another element of problem solving.[39] At some stage in a moral argument, someone may suggest turning a dispute over to a procedural method for resolution (e.g. democratic vote of the people). That procedure should allow a chance for a decision to be made, not merely an opportunity for endless debate. Someone who argues that no norm is valid unless approved by everyone in existence (or even everyone dead, or unborn), must explain how such an idea could be useful in practical situations. It is not likely that we could consult even every living person, never mind persons dead or unborn. Even if we could consult everyone, there is no certainty that everyone would concur. Or a party to an argument may propose delegating some decision to an administrative procedure renowned for its inefficiency and waste, in the hope of postponing a decision indefinitely. So someone putting forward such a procedure must be prepared to explain how it could be used to arrive at a decision. This she might do by specifying that only people involved in the particular dispute need be consulted, and that they may arrive at a decision by a majority or supermajority vote. If the procedure is one which is particularly difficult then we are justified in asking for a reason for the procedure in question.

To sum up, reasons must be capable of solving problems - they must not be vague, unclear, or irrelevant. If procedural solutions are suggested, then they must not be unnecessarily unwieldy.

Factually Accurate

Our racist interlocutor now offers another reason for anti-Voyager actions: 'Voyagers are habitual criminals, they ought to be ostracised'. If this is to function as a reason, then the fact asserted must be accurate (true). So the racist must be prepared to adduce evidence demonstrating the accuracy of the statement. One cannot be expected to act on the basis of a false factual statement!

However, this is not all. All the criteria tend to interrelate, and so in running down one avenue of debate, the others emerge. This example shows how this happens.

The racist's statement is more complex than it looks. There is a distinction between facts and norms. More correctly he should say that 'Voyagers are habitual criminals. It is right that habitual criminals should be ostracised. So Voyagers should be ostracised'. The correctness of the course of conduct he proposes depends on two elements - the correctness (validity) of the general norm that habitual criminals should be ostracised, and the accuracy (truth) of the factual assertion that Voyagers are habitual criminals. If the factual assertion is inaccurate, then the criteria for the application of the norm have not been fulfilled, and the ultimate assertion fails.

Suppose that the racist now offers as evidence that one out of every ten Voyagers has been convicted of a crime. This proves, says he, that they are habitual criminals, and so the general norm applies. Supposing that someone now points out that one out of ten members of the non-Voyager community has been convicted of a crime. Consistency requires the racist to call for the ostracism of the non-Voyager community as well (which seems to mean that everyone should be ostracised)! Otherwise, the racist would be saying that 'Communities, ten percent of whose members have been convicted of a crime, should be ostracised' and 'Communities, ten percent of whose members have been convicted of a crime, should not be ostracised'. The requirements of consistency, generality and factual accuracy thus serve as a control on the reasoning.

Of course, this is a simple example; however the process of reasoning - consider the interrelated criteria of consistency, accuracy, generality, etc., - should hold even in more complicated cases.

Explicability: Publicity, Teachability, Transparency

This is one of the more demanding of the criteria presented. The reasons given by a party to a dispute, must be explicable. By this term, I understand what others have variously called 'publicity',[40] 'teachability',[41] even 'universality'.[42] That is, they must be such that they can be explained to another person. If it is not possible for another person to understand a reason, then she cannot be expected to accept it. If there is no way another person could understand a 'reason', then probably it is no reason at all. Reasons might be inexplicable because they are secret, or need to be secret, self-frustrating, illogical (in a strict sense), irrelevant, or opaque.

That reasons not be secret is covered by the first criterion I discussed - that of giving reasons itself. The entire point of rational intersubjective argument is about submitting reasons to public examination. A secret reason is one which has not been offered in rational intersubjective argument. A further requirement of this is that all stages of the argument must be transparent, or if not, a reason must be given for this. Consider for instance the racist's argument that Voyagers should be isolated because they are a threat to public health. Here there are links in the argument which have simply been left out - why do Voyagers form such a threat? All the stages in the reasoning process must be exposed, for otherwise the conclusion simply does not follow from the basic premise.

Secondly, reasons that need to be secret to be effective are impermissible (unless a public reason is offered to justify the secrecy). For instance if the racist offers the reason that he dislikes Voyagers and believes that anyone he dislikes should be victimised, such a reason is not acceptable. For as soon as it would be made public knowledge everyone would oppose it. Similarly the reason 'You should support me in my argument against Voyagers because I will make you rich for doing so, or harm you if you do not', is likely only to be successful if it is given behind closed doors without anyone knowing about it.

A further variant on this is the class of self-frustrating reasons, i.e. reasons whose 'purpose is frustrated as soon as everybody acts on them, if they have a point only when a good many people act on the opposite principle'.[43] The most obvious example of this is the motto of the free-rider that one should take whatever public benefits are available without trying to contribute anything. Obviously if many people acted on this motto, there would be no public benefits. Therefore, such a reason must be kept secret.

Some reasons are inexplicable because they contain a logical error and so do not actually explain anything. There has been great debate over what is meant by 'logical'. Some people give it a very narrow scope - e.g. the rule of non-contradiction. Others expand it to cover all reasons for action that anyone might give. For instance, you will no doubt have heard someone say that 'To give all your wealth to the poor is not logical'. One could only make this statement if one accepted a very broad notion of logic. From the narrow point of view there is nothing either logical or illogical about it. I am giving 'logic' a limited meaning here, as part of a scheme of more substantive logic or reasoning. (I do not make the claim that some writers have wrongly made, that reasons based on narrow rules of formal logic are in a sense better than other reasons.[44])

In the previous section I took the example of the racist who says that 'Voyagers are habitual criminals, habitual criminals should be ostracised'. I assumed that the racist was referring to a general norm that habitual criminals ought to be ostracised. However suppose that this is not the case. Seeing the trap in effect laid for him in that section, he asserts that there is no intervening norm, not even implicitly, between the two statements. So his proposed norm cannot be slain on the twin peaks of consistency and factual accuracy. Rather, he bluntly asserts the fact and a conclusion and so falls into a logical fallacy. This is an example of the naturalistic fallacy; one cannot jump from a factual statement (an 'is') to a normative statement (an 'ought'). We cannot deduce any normative conclusion from the fact that people have certain hair colour, certain needs, certain features, etc. Supposing someone argues that 'People live; no one should kill herself'. It would be as valid to argue that 'People die; so everyone should kill himself or herself!' Both arguments are invalid unless an intervening norm is understood. For instance 'People live, and life is a gift from God, and *we ought not to reject God's gift,* so no one should kill herself'. Here a norm supplies the link between the facts and another norm.

It may be objected that we do make such jumps all the time 'Aulis robbed a bank, Aulis should be punished'. 'Ota agreed to a contract, Ota ought to perform the contract', 'Ronald made a promise, Ronald ought to perform it'[45] 'God created man, man ought to worship God'. Do not all these involve a move from a factual to a normative statement? Yes, but there is no immediate jump. All of these statements presuppose an implicit norm 'One ought to be punished for robbing banks', 'One ought to keep promises and perform contracts', and 'One ought to worship one's creator.' Only these implicit norms guarantee the correctness of the normative conclusion, given the factual scenario. If the intervening norm were left out, the conclusion could not be reached. By illogical I mean therefore such logical fallacies.

Logic also requires a formal notion of universality or formal equality.[46] If I suggest that we treat two things differently, there must be some reason for this, i.e. that they are relevantly different. Imagine that the racist simply says that 'Voyagers should be ostracised, but no one else.' When asked what is the difference between Voyagers and other people, he responds 'None'. Then we are confused as to why he wishes to treat them differently. He should give some reason, indicating that the two groups are different in some respect. This requirement is formal; once a reason is suggested, the criterion is satisfied.[47] That reason may be very trivial or even obnoxious. As has often been noted, the Nazi regime could well have complied with this requirement.

An argument may be inexplicable because it involves consideration of irrelevant factors, or fails to consider all relevant factors. A claim which asserts the importance of irrelevant features, or denies the significance of relevant features, is one which fails to explicate its basis.

Irrelevance is something already encountered. I said earlier that an irrelevant reason cannot help to resolve a dispute. It is also an inexplicable reason. Suppose that our racist explains that Voyagers ought to be removed from the town because they are of shorter stature than other people. It is not immediately apparent why their height should have any relevance to the issue of whether they should be allowed to stay. One is entitled to ask for an explanation of the relevance. Height becomes relevant if the racist claims there is a valid norm that shorter people should not receive equal consideration.

As well as avoiding irrelevant matters, the participants in an argument must advert to any relevant consideration. It is not the case that every single detail is relevant to the resolution of the dispute (see the section on generality). However an argument is flawed if it ignores, without reason, relevant considerations. Suppose that the racist claims that the wishes of the Voyagers at issue do not count at all, they are irrelevant to the argument. He can be challenged to explain the irrelevance of their wishes. He may do this by referring to a norm which says that their wishes are irrelevant. Of course this takes him into disputes on other criteria. Saying that Voyagers' wishes are irrelevant because of a norm that they are irrelevant, is simply restating the first clause of the sentence. Generality requires a norm more general.

The reasons given must not be opaque.[48] They must be transparent so that others can understand them, and so perhaps accept them. For instance, I may claim that I have received a divine command from God to ensure the separation of the races. Other people cannot be expected to accept this as a reason, unless they can verify that there was a divine command, that it did come from God, and that it specified the content claimed by the racist. (There are of course, other elements to be considered, but these are the ones as to transparency. For instance, why should one obey God?)

Another example of opaqueness might be the claim that, as the only expert in phrenology (a pseudo-science that claimed to permit one to determine someone's characteristics from the shape of their head), a science which no one else can understand, one has determined the moral worthlessness of Voyagers. As well as the obvious problem of the relevance of bumps on the head to morality, there is the problem of opaqueness - no one else can verify the observations even according to the rules of phrenology.

No doubt there are times when we are entitled to rely upon a private reason which is not comprehensible to others. However, the reason we use in public disputes must be a reason capable of being generally understood, or else it is disguised domination.[49] The reasoning in public disputes is 'meant for everyone'.[50]

Reflective Equilibrium of Considered Judgements

This requirement is quite controversial, and has been bitterly assailed by Richard Hare, for instance. This requirement assumes that we do not start our argument from an abstract plane vacuumed clean of all belief. Rather we enter argument complete with a whole host of beliefs, on many different matters (e.g., what constitutes rationality, what is immoral) and at many different levels of generality (e.g. life is a human good, the death penalty is wrong). Argument involves acting on, and debating these beliefs.51

Reflective equilibrium requires that the specific judgements and reasons in dispute be considered in the light of other uncontested reasons and firmly held judgements. It is a reason in favour of the contested judgements that they are consistent and coherent with those other beliefs. A party to an argument first tries to place her claim and supporting reasons within her own reflective equilibrium. This is presenting a subjective conception of reflective equilibrium. She may then point out to other parties that her reconstruction of beliefs corresponds closely to the uncontested beliefs held by others, and that since her claim fits within it, they should accept it or alter their own notion of a coherent set of beliefs, or propose a more appealing set. This is a move to a more intersubjectivist conception of reflective equilibrium.52

However bear in mind that this is a *reflective* equilibrium of *considered* beliefs. The beliefs on which we rely must not be immune to re-examination.53 We may decide to reject (or continue with) them. More particularly, we may decide to reject them in the light of other criteria of moral argument. Just as I cannot endorse a thorough going rationalisation which rejects the need for these beliefs, I cannot endorse an approach which gives them a privileged, unreviewable position. It may be a part of our considered beliefs that 'Women ought to bear children, because they are capable of bearing children'. As explained above, this claim involves a logical fallacy, it fails to explain anything. It cannot be relied upon in reflective equilibrium. Previously held beliefs can be used to answer our questions - but they must also be open to being questioned. If found wanting when considered in the light of other criteria, then they must be rejected. This is the difference between what Dworkin terms 'constructivist' and 'naturalistic' conceptions of reflective equilibrium. The naturalist assumes that our considered beliefs somehow reflect moral truths which we are trying to explicate. They cannot be jettisoned. A constructivist approach is willing to drop those considered beliefs when they conflict with the criteria of rational intersubjective argument, or when they no longer fit into a coherent reflective equilibrium.54

This requirement is also one of *equilibrium*. This requires notions of consistency between beliefs of varying levels of generality. We can accept or reject any belief, but those we do have should be free of contradiction. It also requires a certain level of coherence. Coherence is different from consistency. Two norms may be incoherent, without contradicting each other. For instance, we may hold that violent rapists generally ought to be severely punished, but nevertheless sanction the early release of a seriously ill rapist. In such cases, we should look to see whether there is some deeper coherence which explains the attitudes. In this particular example we might argue that our beliefs about human beings include notions of empathy and respect for everyone, respect for their ability to choose their own faith, empathy for the severe suffering they may face. We may see our reflective equilibrium of considered beliefs as trying to balance the two sides of respect and empathy as well as possible.[55] Such does not seem incoherent, particularly when compared with other examples (e.g. where large scale tax offenders are systematically not charged with their crimes - how does one explain the coherence of having tax evasion as a crime, yet not punishing the criminals?).

A blunt objection to this requirement of reflective equilibrium might be: 'What is the point of relying on considered beliefs? If people share beliefs, then there is no argument! It is precisely when beliefs are different that we actually need rational argument!' It is true that we enter rational intersubjective argument precisely when we disagree over practical courses of action - we can hardly expect to resolve the dispute by referring to an agreement on the dispute!

However, it may be possible to find zones of agreement elsewhere. Our racist may note that whatever about the issue of ostracism, there is a shared belief that public health or security must be protected. He may then argue that these general principles cannot be adequately respected without ostracism of Voyagers. Or he may turn to someone and ask whether she would marry, or accept a family member marrying a Voyager. If many people would not accept intermarriage, he may argue from that highly specific belief, that it is commonly accepted that Voyagers are a threat to a public interest (health or security), and that ostracism is a perfectly coherent element in the set of beliefs so shared. (Of course I would argue that that specific belief cannot be selected as a considered judgement for the purpose of finding a reflective equilibrium - it violates other criteria of rational intersubjective argument.)

The impact of reflective equilibrium in moral argument also explains certain aspects of moral debate.[56] Many societies have very different political moralities, which they take seriously. The moral relativist rightly suggests that each is entitled to some respect, even though those moralities may be contradictory. An intersubjectivist approach allows for an explanation without sacrificing the possibility of trans-contextual debate and criticism. Though different societies may have very different conventional moralities, it may be the case that they are each compatible with critical morality. How so? The criteria of rational intersubjective argument interact with considered and firmly held judgements. They act as a sieve to remove moral impurities. In each society there may be different shared beliefs, each compatible with the criteria of argument here discussed, yet each requiring different solutions. For instance, imagine that after rational intersubjective argument, we conclude that a political moral theory stating that all socially valued goods should be equally divided among all members of society. Obviously what is socially valued may differ from society to society. In a materialist society it will be wealth; in a society emphasising social welfare, it may be education, health etc. In a society stressing political life, it will be political power and influence.

Any belief, no matter how commonly held, may be disqualified if it fails to obey the threshold requirements of rational intersubjective moral argument. In that case it may not be put forward as a reason that other people could accept, and cannot be used to support a reflective equilibrium.

Universalisability as Equal Respect

The final criteria to employ in rational intersubjective argument is that of universalisability. This is a very controversial notion that has been given both very formal (and basically empty) interpretations and very material ones.[57]

Suppose our racist friend caps all his arguments by straightforwardly claiming that Voyagers are simply inferior to other people, and being of lesser worth their desires and interests should not count. He finds that only by such a prescription can he provide a consistent, general, non-individualising, etc. It does not pose any factual issue since it is a naked prescription, and it may well be conforming to the dominant reflective equilibrium (indeed we can even envision circumstances in which the Voyagers themselves accepted this belief). Even if it does qualify under every other criteria it should be rejected as being non-universalisable. One cannot say that another person can accept a reason to resolve a dispute in a particular way, if that reason simply asserts the inferiority of the other party. Note that this requirement may well be the only one that applies even in the absence of a dispute.

The very act of entering the process of giving reasons in a rational intersubjective argument presupposes a minimum amount of respect. This idea can be variously expressed:[58] treating someone 'as an equal',[59] or in a more famous formulation:

> Act in such a way that you always treat humanity whether in your own person, or in the person of any other, never simply as a means, but always at the same time as an end.[60]

Assertions of simple inferiority are not permitted by the criterion of universalisability.

There have been many different and controversial interpretations of the universalisability requirement.[61] Some do not establish a criterion which rules out many positions. Others are much more robust. Richard Hare gives a formalist understanding: if we say that something has a certain quality, then we are committed to saying that everything relevantly similar, also has that quality.[62] This involves nothing more than what I have already suggested under the requirements of consistency and generality and explicability. If someone states that a particular situation is relevantly identical to another, so we should react to it differently, then there is a gap somewhere in her statement - if there is nothing different, then why act differently? The parties must discuss what is the feature relevant in both cases, i.e. refer to a more general rule or idea.

However, Hare then goes a step further. He introduces the concept of reversibility: a person must be willing to prescribe universally a moral rule, even though he looks at it from every viewpoint.[63] This still leaves Hare accepting the idea of a morally sincere Nazi - there may be someone who says that Jews should be exterminated, and insists that he does not mind being exterminated if it turns out that he is a Jew.[64] I do not regard such a person as making a valid argument, if all he offers is a claim (prescription, belief, whatever) that certain people are simply irrelevant, that they are inferior. The entry into rational intersubjective argument presupposes that one takes seriously the idea of offering arguments which another person could accept. How could anyone accept a basic assertion of inferiority? The racist in my example is leaving the realm of moral argument and opting for the power of the sword. So my criterion of universalisability is stronger than Hare's.

Singer offers an alternative, the Generalization Argument, which he relates to one particular interpretation of Kant's universality principle.[65] The Generalization Principle states that:

> If the consequences of every member of K's doing x in certain circumstances would be undesirable, while the consequence of no member of K's doing x (in those circumstances) would not be undesirable, then no member of K has the right to do x (in such circumstances) without a special reason.[66]

This is obviously a stronger idea of universalisability than the one I have offered. It may be an appropriate approach for participants in a rational intersubjective argument to adopt; it is not a criterion which defines the argument. The parties to an argument are trying to identify what is undesirable; they cannot rely on that notion beforehand (except where it is a shared belief, held in reflective equilibrium). Further, a person could accept a rule which only a few could act on. Singer's principle cannot be a criterion in our scheme.

Rawls also incorporates this notion of universalisability as equal respect into his conception of the Veil of Ignorance, which is a heuristic device to help us make decisions excluding from consideration such irrelevant criteria as wealth, race, sex.[67] There are differences however - the Veil of Ignorance only applies at certain levels of moral reasoning whereas universalisability as equal respect always applies. Further, although the Veil of Ignorance is a powerful device to conceive the notion of equal respect, that notion does not require such thorough-going ignorance of facts. It simply requires that reasons not refer to beliefs about the inferiority or superiority of persons.

One of the most famous formulations of the universalisability criterion is Habermas'. His criterion of universalisability goes thus:

> All affected can accept the consequences and the side effects its general observance can be anticipated to have for the satisfaction of everyone's interests (and these consequences are preferred to those of known alternative possibilities for regulation).[68]

In so far as this expresses the requirements of a rational intersubjective argument, and more particular the idea of equal respect, i.e. that claims of inferiority and superiority are ruled out, then I accept it.

A claim of inferiority might involve a claim that the other party is not entitled to engage in argument or in a certain procedure. To take up an example from earlier on, if I say that 'Threats to public health should be banned, and I am the sole judge of what is a threat to public health', then the other party may reject this, unless some guarantee of impartiality is given. The sort of procedures which might be acceptable, include delegation to an expert, decision by an independent body, or a body representing everyone's interests, unanimous decision by all the parties involved, decision by reference to highly specific criteria which leave little room for discretion.

There is a difference between a claim of inferiority and one of incompetence. A claim of incompetence might be justified, by referring to the age or mental capacities of the party. A claim of inferiority can never be acceptable. The point is that an unjustified claim of incompetence amounts to a claim of inferiority. And a claim of inferiority is ruled out of bounds in rational intersubjective argument.

It is important to note that I do not in any way, purport to derive this principle of universalisability from any weaker formal notion of universality or formal equality. Such cannot be done.[69] Instead, it derives from the notion of giving arguments that another person could accept. The goal of a political theory is to appeal to other persons as a rational argument. I consider that this is not possible unless the theory reflects in some sense the notion that all persons are equal. I cannot say 'You ought to accept this, and you have a reason to accept this, because you are inferior to me'. I must be able to justify my assertion by referring to something other than a simple commitment to inequality.

The Status of These Criteria, and Some Objections

The criteria that I have presented do not form a comprehensive, or even embryonic, political morality. Rather they are criteria by which actual debaters can consider the acceptability of political theories. They are elements of meta-political theory rather than any political theory.

So these criteria are at a very general level, the level of political moral argument. Actual political theories, whether substantive or procedural, must be debated under the terms of these criteria. These criteria do not purport to provide a comprehensive or concrete solution. They refer to notions that we must presuppose when debating comprehensive or concrete solutions within the framework of rational intersubjective argument. I do not propose to say which theory or solution ought to be adopted by anyone.

Certain of the criteria (e.g. consistency, formal equality, and generality) are compatible with just about any substantive position, provided it is properly framed. Others deliberately leave open the possibility of regional, communal, etc. differences. This is particularly the case with the criterion of reflective equilibrium. So we should not be surprised to find that different societies have different ideas of what is morally acceptable. I stress that this does not mean that a social norm may be maintained, unexamined and uncriticised, simply because it conforms to a reflective equilibrium. In particular, the criteria of explicability and universalisability must be complied with.

This variability is important and reassuring, given that our overall concern is with legal systems. It is a notorious fact that legal systems also differ according to the society in which they are embedded. We find that there exist different institutions, procedures, solutions, laws, etc. in different legal systems. This fact is often used to make the argument that since law is particular, tied to its social roots, and morality is universal, there must needs be a distinction between the two spheres. However, an intersubjectivist approach to moral argument demonstrates that morality, like law, is not a purely universal matter; context is also relevant here.

Are these criteria themselves beyond argument? Is it impossible to question them? Rejecting the criteria of rational intersubjective argument implies rejecting the effort to offer reasons to resolve a dispute that another could accept. The criteria cannot simply be rejected. They can however be questioned. They are open to dispute. The previous pages have been an attempt to justify the adoption of these criteria. At any stage anyone may question the validity (acceptability, correctness) of any of these criteria. What cannot be left aside is the notion of offering reasons that another person could accept.

The Whole Thing is Imaginary

Certain writers have lambasted what they perceive as imaginary pseudo-dialogues in which a theory is set up precisely so that it can be knocked down.[70] They may accuse me of setting up this unsympathetic racist on the edge of an artificially crafted precipice, so to tumble him into a philosophical abyss.

My racist interlocutor has been imaginary certainly (though many of his comments are based on typical statements of such people). And certainly, he was never going to 'win' the argument. However, it would be rather strange if a racist were to succeed in moral argument! When I started this chapter I indicated two criteria for determining the success of these criteria for argument - do they provide guidelines, and do they eliminate certain unacceptable theories? Racism is clearly such an unacceptable theory, so much so that even its advocates are reluctant to call it by its name. That it is ruled out of the debate by the criteria is not unfair or imaginary.

Further, bear in mind that what I am trying to do is to provide a set of criteria for many different political arguments. A certain degree of abstraction is inevitable. Nevertheless, the examples are not unreal. Moral arguments are made in all walks of life, from the court room to the pool room. To the extent that they suffer from the flaws described in these criteria they can and should be challenged.

Third, these criteria are not unchallengeable. They do not purport to resolve once and for all a debate. They are themselves a contribution to a real debate. I am here presenting my beliefs for debate. I cannot establish their validity by conquering any hypothetical opponent. I can only establish their validity by presenting them to you the reader, and letting you judge whether the reasons I offer are acceptable. I give examples and use dialogues to draw out all the levels of my reasoning, so that you can better judge it. If you find the reasons insufficient or contrived, then so argue. It is open to anyone to challenge them, and incumbent upon me to defend them against anyone's challenge.

The Criteria are Unfair

Another objection is that although I purport to offer certain bases on which to judge the acceptability of political arguments, I do so unfairly, because my criteria contain a hidden preference for certain political philosophies.

It is true that the criteria will tend to support some theories rather than others. Indeed one of the standards by which to judge the adequacy of these criteria is that they do precisely that. If they did not, then I would be accused of providing totally indeterminate criteria which serve no use.

However, the criteria do not serve to completely determine the argument. The outcome depends on the beliefs and arguments, and factual observances that people bring to argument. In a debate between a fascist and a libertarian,[71] I suspect the latter would have the better arguments according to these criteria. If a communist were to join the debate, then she may well have better arguments than the libertarian. And if a communitarian joins.... So the criteria provide certain directions to the participants, without deciding the exact path or destination.

To show that the criteria are not unfair I propose to show that a certain theory which some people might suspect is simply ruled out arbitrarily, is not actually ruled out. It can be proposed and defended in argument, and might (or might not) succeed.

Rational Intersubjective Argument: The Communitarian Example

There will be those who argue that this notion of rational intersubjective argument is hopelessly prejudiced in favour of certain theories. Specifically they may suspect that a theory which shares assumptions about the possibility of rational argument in moral matters will fare better than others. They see such theories in the tradition of Kant as being flawed. However, to prove this objection, one must show that these criteria unfairly eliminate other theories from the realm of argument. In this section, I demonstrate how a theory which is not in the Kantian tradition, communitarianism, *might* satisfy these requirements. Please note that at this stage, I am concerned with these criteria as *minimum threshold* requirements.

Communitarians disagree with the Kantian conception of the self (the individual) and society.[72] According to them, Kantian tradition sees the self as abstract and isolated, apart from any historical, social condition. A Kantian society is an anaemic mockery of a full-blooded society. They argue that the self is always situated in society and is constituted by the ends, the goals, of that society. That is, there are some social ends which are intrinsic to our identity. Can communitarianism fit into this framework of moral argumentation? I shall take Sandel's *Liberalism and the Limits of Justice* as a classic example of a communitarian argument.

The first requirement is that of consistency between norms both of the same level and across different levels. There is no reason why any communitarian theory must be contradictory. Sandel's *Liberalism and the Limits of Justice* is an attempt to expose inconsistencies in liberal argument, inconsistencies which only disappear in a communitarian framework.

Furthermore, a communitarian theory can be formulated to provide practical guidance. It can provide rules stipulating which communal practices the State should enforce, or stipulating rules about how to determine those practices. In the 'Procedural Republic', Sandel argues for decentralisation and a return to democratic participation.[73]

Communitarian theories can be general. Such thinkers do not just assert the moral duty to follow communal practices. They justify this obligation on the basis of conceptions of the person and of the community, whereby a person cannot be fulfilled without community. One must work with the idea of a self constituted by communal ends. Why? Because to do otherwise would be to 'imagine a person wholly without character, without moral depth'.[74]

Communitarian theories can also be non-individualising. They need not invoke the names or identities of specific persons, although they may put stress on the need to consider all situations considering all the facts. Thus, for instance Sandel's view of the person as being constituted by social ends applies to all persons.

I do not impose an insuperable burden on communitarian thought by insisting that it be factually sound. If one element of a communitarian theory is that persons are unhappy unless located within a community, then the communitarian must demonstrate some evidence for this. So Sande proposes his ideal family scenario.[75] He contrasts a communitarian anti-individualist vision with a 'Rawlsian' vision of the family, where every individual demands and accords justice.

The criterion of explicability is not *per se* incompatible with communitarianism. After all communitarian thinkers do publish their works and claim that persons should be persuaded by their arguments. Accordingly, they must claim that persons find those arguments comprehensible and persuasive. This is so at least at the more abstract levels of their arguments. At the concrete level, communitarians may reject the criterion of explicability, arguing that only someone embedded in a society can decide its values.

Given the communitarian thesis, I would have thought that the criterion of reflective equilibrium is one which communitarians accept willingly. This after all, requires consideration of the actual judgements of a given group of persons. The entire point of Sandel's critique of Dworkin's affirmative action thesis, for instance, is that Dworkin fails to explain convincingly why our instincts about competition for educational places are wrong.[76] Furthermore, only communitarian beliefs (according to Sandel) can explain notions of moral self-discovery and altruism.[77]

Finally the criterion of universalisability. Can a communitarian theory be put into such a form that everyone is regarded as an equal in some sense? Consider the following as a communitarian ethic: 'Everyone, to be fulfilled, must live within a constitutive community, a community which guides their lives. Therefore, communitarianism provides for all persons the constitutive community without which they would lead an atomistic existence.' Prima facie at any rate, everyone can assent to such a formulation.

Communitarianism is not therefore ruled out by the criteria designated. It might be possible to state a theory in such a form as to satisfy them. I do not claim that all communitarian thinkers satisfy these criteria (or even that Sandel's comprehensive theory does), but merely that communitarian assumptions are not unfairly ruled out by this argument.

Conclusion: Political Moral Argument

This jaunt through moral theory has not bored the legally inclined reader, I hope. I have tried to develop a set of criteria, drawn from much recent political thought, by which we can judge the acceptability or otherwise of political claims. I have not sought to argue that any one political theory is 'right' universally and forever. I have left open many areas for concrete debate and resolution, according to some more developed, less abstract political theory, or ideal. To the extent that judges, or anyone, engage in political moral argument, then they must use these criteria.

Of course, I do not claim that just any conclusion can be reached using these criteria. Certain beliefs, or ideas are ruled out of contention. They may be expressed, but they cannot be accepted under its terms. Also certain approaches are more or less likely to be accepted or rejected than certain other approaches. Rational intersubjective moral argument is not moral plastic.

The political moral debate is not a closed one under these criteria. Any matter is always open to re-examination, including the criteria themselves.

In the next three chapters, we shall see that judges are regularly involved in political moral debate when they engage in constitutional interpretation. We shall see them putting forward norms which are political moral norms and using arguments that have a decided resemblance to the types of arguments presented in this chapter.

Notes

1   See Ely, *Democracy and Distrust,* Ch. 3; Bork, The Tempting of America, p. 227; Kelsen, *The Pure Theory of Law,* pp. 18, 22, 63 - 69; Kelsen, *General Theory of Law and State,* pp. 6, 8, 13: 'justice is an ideal inaccessible to human cognition'. See also 'Law, State and Justice in the Pure Theory of Law', in Kelsen, *What is Justice?,* pp. 295 - 301; Ross, *On Law and Justice,* 'Like a harlot, natural law is at the disposal of everyone', p. 261.

2   The difference is that between ethics and meta-ethics. In ethics, I say how people should live. Meta-ethics involves consideration of how people go about debating, talking ethics. Of course, my meta-ethical stance has very definite effects on the ethical stance I would endorse.

3   Some writers, notably Rawls and Habermas, draw a distinction between these two questions of morality, labelling them the good and the right, ethics and morality. On the good and the right, see Rawls, *A Theory of Justice,* pp. 30 - 33, 446 - 452. See Habermas, *Between Facts and Norms,* pp. 95 - 99, 255 - 259 on ethical and moral discourses. Many writers dispute the distinction. I do not think it necessary for this book to get involved in this dispute. Morality, broadly conceived includes questions both about the good life and the right action. Any theory of morality can probably accommodate complementary theories of both (compare Rawls, *Political Liberalism,* pp. 173, 175). That it may draw a

distinction between one and the other is probably a matter for the clarity or content of the particular theory and not a matter of a meta-ethical position.

4   As a preliminary it may be objected that my starting point, with its notion of a conflict is too narrow (The notion of a conflict is often attributed to Hume - see Rawls, *A Theory of Justice*, p. 127; Richards, *A Theory of Reasons for Actions*, pp. 108 et seq.). It might be objected that political morality has a role to play even in the absence of a conflict. I agree - political morality may well involve the growth of a uniform consciousness, where there is no disagreement. However, the terms of my enquiry are decided by its starting point in a judicial arena, which is largely concerned with disputes. It is with the element of disagreement over practical action that I must start. Nor can we really ignore what writers refer to as the fact of pluralism in our world. See Rawls and Habermas again, *Political Liberalism*, p. 36; *Between Facts and Norms*, p. 97. See also MacIntyre, *After Virtue*, Ch. 2.

A slightly different preliminary objection is not that political morality includes non-conflictual elements, but that it includes no conflictual elements. That is, it might be objected that notion of conflict betrays a particular world-view, either male, or European, or modernist, that has no place in a true political morality. I refer again to my starting point - the problem of choosing among competing ideas. The blistering response may come that this is illegitimate - that I am referring to an ethnocentric institution within an ethnocentric political world-view, to justify an ethnocentric starting point. Perhaps this is true, but it simply underscores that there *is* a conflict, at the very least between the conflictual ethnocentric and the non-conflictual non-ethnocentric (?) viewpoint. My task is to discuss how we can choose between such moralities.

5   See Rawls, *Political Liberalism* pp. 89 - 129 on 'Political Constructivism'; Nino, *The Ethics of Human Rights*, pp. 63 - 83 on 'Moral Constructivism'.

6   This suggests another minor point, directed against those who claim that there can be no discussion of the rational validity of moral claims. Even if logically, there is no contradiction in moral scepticism, in practice there is. If the self-professed sceptic persists it must be pointed out to her that she herself attaches some importance to elementary moral principles which belie her alleged scepticism. If the theoretical sceptic is self-consistent, the practical one may often be a 'walking self-contradiction'. Of course the sceptical rejoinder may be simple. If the sceptic rejects conventional notions of rationality, then the inconsistency will not trouble her. However the rejection of rationality, argumentation and deliberation would place the sceptic in an even worse position practically, she could not live. See Scheffler, 'Moral Scepticism and the Ideals of a Person' 62 *Monist* 288; Habermas 'Discourse Ethics: Notes' p. 100.

7   Stevenson, *Ethics and Language*. The purpose of moral language is to express our attitudes about certain things, not genuine claims about right and wrong. We use reason and persuasion to recommend our attitudes to others.

8   See Toulmin, *The Place of Reason in Ethics*, pp. 29 - 60 on 'The Subjective Approach' and 'The Imperative Approach'.

9   The actual moral beliefs of any actor are that actor's *conventional* morality, as opposed to a *critical* morality. Baier draws the distinction between 'moralities'

and 'morality'; between someone's morality and morality as such. See *The Moral Point of View*, p. 181 et seq; pp. 112 - 115 (2nd ed.).

10 Rorty, 'Human Rights, Rationality and Sentimentality', in *Amnesty Lectures on Human Rights*.

11 The writings of communitarian writers often display a hermeneuticist slant. Thus MacIntyre says 'The unity of a human life is the unity of a narrative quest'. p. 203 in *After Virtue*, 'Virtues, Unity of Life and Concept of a Tradition'.

12 *Natural Law and Natural Rights*, p. 24.

13 *Natural Law and Natural Rights*, Chs. 3, 4, 5; *Fundamentals of Ethics*, Chs. 1, 2, 3.

14 Kant, *Critique of Pure Reason*, p. 397, 'Introduction to the Transcendental Doctrine of Method' Meiklejohn ed. See the comment on this by O'Neill, 'Vindicating Reason' in Guyer ed., *The Cambridge Companion to Kant*. This work refers to theoretical, rather than practical reason, but the approach is analogous.

15 Alexy notes how such an approach offers an alternative to what he identifies as 'Hobbesian', 'Aristotelian', or 'Nietzschean' approaches to practical reason; see 'A Discourse-Theoretical Conception of Practical Reason' (1992) 5 *Ratio Juris* 231, 233.

16 This notion finds its roots in parts of Kant's philosophy, and the philosophy of those writers influenced by him. See the *Groundwork of the Metaphysics of Morals*, but also *The Metaphysics of Morals, The Critique of Judgement, The Critique of Pure Reason, On the Common Saying: This may be true in theory, but does it apply in practice?, Religion within the Limits of Reason Alone*. See O'Neill, 'Kantian Politics. 1. The Public Use of Reason', (1986) 14 *Pol. Th.* 523; 'Vindicating Reason' in Guyer ed., *The Cambridge Companion to Kant*.

Writers who build on the Kantian notions include: Baier, *The Moral Point of View*; Singer, *Generalization in Ethics*, Rawls, *A Theory of Justice, Political Liberalism*; Gewirth, *Human Rights*; Ackerman, *Social Justice in a Liberal State;* Dworkin, *Taking Rights Seriously, A Matter of Principle*, 'In Defence of Equality'; Hare, *The Language of Morals, Freedom and Reason*; Richards, *A Theory of Reasons for Actions*; Larmore, *Patterns of Moral Complexity;* Toulmin, *The Place of Reason in Ethics*; Nagel, *Equality and Partiality*; Nino, *The Ethics of Human Rights*; Waldron, *Liberal Rights*; Apel, *Towards a Transformation of Philosophy;* Benhabib, *Situating the Self*; Habermas, *Moral Consciousness and Communicative Action, Justification and Application, Between Facts and Norms*; Alexy, *A Theory of Legal Argumentation*; Günther, *The Sense of Appropriateness;* Arendt, *Lectures on Kant's Political Philosophy*. Arendt's concept of communicative power is related to this and is fundamental for Habermas' concept of discourse ethics; see *Crises of the Republic*. This chapter borrows liberally from these writers.

17 See Toulmin, *The Place of Reason in Ethics*; Apel, *Towards a Transformation of Philosophy*, 'The a priori of the communication community and the foundations of ethics'; Habermas, *Moral Consciousness and Communicative Action*, 'Discourse Ethics: Notes on a Program of Philosophical Justification', pp. 78 - 86, 98 - 109; *Justification and Application* pp. 20 - 35.

18   As Kant says, speaking of aesthetic judgements in the *Critique of Judgement*: 'Cognitions and judgements must, together with their attendant conviction, admit of being universally communicated.' (p. 83, sect. 21)
        See also *The Critique of Pure Reason*: 'This privilege [free criticism] forms part of the native rights of human reason, which recognises no other judge than the universal reason of humanity.' (p. 422, Meiklejohn ed.)

19   Apel, *Towards a Transformation of Philosophy*, p. 260: 'Arguments ... must always be understood simultaneously as meaning and validity claims that can only be explicated and decided upon in an interpersonal dialogue.' See also p. 280.

20   Habermas says, in his 'Discourse Ethics: Notes': 'In taking part in the process of reasoning, even the consistent fallibilist has already accepted as valid a minimum number of unavoidable rules of criticism.' (p. 81)

21   Dworkin discusses the notion of a foundational concept. He believes that his 'right to equal concern and respect' is a foundational concept. See 'In Defence of Equality' 1 *Soc. Phil. & Pol.* 1.

22   'Discourse Ethics: Notes' p. 100.

23   See Rawls' discussion of the treatment of intolerant minorities, by liberal majorities. *A Theory of Justice*, pp. 216 - 221.

24   Nino sees *epistemic* constructivism as a compromise between epistemic individualism and epistemic collectivism, 'A Philosophical Reconstruction of Judicial Review', (1993) *Card. L. Rev.* 799, 822. Kant stresses the importance of communication to the process of thought: *What is Orientation in Thinking?*, p. 247.

25   Compare Hare's discussion of a rational Nazi, in *Freedom and Reason*, Chs. 6, 9.

26   Alexy, *A Theory of Legal Argumentation*, pp. 196 - 197; Ackerman, *Social Justice in a Liberal State*, p. 4, 37. See Ch. 2 in Baier, *The Moral Point of View*, on 'reasons'. See Toulmin, *The Uses of Argument*, for an account of reasoning. Toulmin develops an analogy between reasoning and judicial trials (*ibid.*, p. 7), echoing Kant's reference to the tribunal of reason (*Critique of Pure Reason*, 'The Discipline of Pure Reason with respect to its Polemical Usage').

27   Alexy, *A Theory of Legal Argumentation*, p. 188; Ackerman, *Social Justice in the Liberal State*, p. 7.

28   On the notion of rules and principles, see Alexy, 'Rights, Legal Reasoning and Rational Discourse' (1992) *Ratio Juris* 143; Dworkin, *Taking Rights Seriously*, p. 71 - 80; Habermas, *Between Facts and Norms*, pp. 71 - 72.

29   See Rawls, *A Theory of Justice*, pp. 131 - 132 on generality and universality; Richards, *A Theory of Reasons for Actions*, p. 26.

30   Singer, *Generalization in Ethics*, p. 20 et seq.

31   Perry, *Morality, Law and Politics*, Ch. 2.

32   See Hare, *Freedom and Reason*, p. 37 et seq. on the difference between a general and a universal norm. See also Richards, *A Theory of Reasons for Actions*, pp. 25 - 26.

33   Some forms of situationalist ethics bring out the difference between the criteria of non-individualising and generality. Consider Sartre's famous dictum that

when a person chooses in a moral situation, she chooses for all humanity. One interpretation of this is that the person choosing is asserting that all persons, in an identical situation, would make the same choice. Whilst all persons would do so, there is no norm because the decision is limited to that very specific situation. See *L'existentialisme est un humanisme*, p. 70.

34   See Kant, *Groundwork of the Metaphysics of Morals*, pp. 67 - 68 (pp. 402 - 403).

35   Rodney King was an innocent Afro-American, who was seriously beaten by four white policemen in Los Angeles some years ago, without any reason.

36   As Singer explains, moral theory must be relevant in solving moral problems, though it need not provide automatic solutions - *Generalization in Ethics*, p. 7. Alexy, *A Theory of Legal Argumentation*, p. 205.

37   I say hypothetically as sometimes jurisdictions provide for a question to be considered in abstraction from any particular dispute, as a reference case. Such is possible in Canada, Ireland, Italy, Germany, France, Spain, to name only a small number.

38   Ackerman gives this example: *Social Justice in a Liberal State*, p. 40.

39   Ackerman, *Social Justice in a Liberal State*, p. 35.

40   See Kant, *Theory and Practice*, pp. 125, 126; *Critique of Judgement*, Sect. 21, p. 83; Nino, *Ethics of Human Rights*, p. 72; Rawls, *A Theory of Justice*, p. 132; *Political Liberalism*, pp. 69 - 70.

41   Baier, *The Moral Point of View*, pp. 101 et seq. (2nd ed.).

42   Rawls, *A Theory of Justice*, p. 132.

43   Baier, *The Moral Point of View*, p. 101 (2nd ed.).

44   Toulmin explores the errors of this formalist approach in *The Uses of Argument*. See also Perelman, *Ethique et Droit*.

45   See Searle, *Speech Acts*.

46   Alexy, *A Theory of Legal Argumentation*, pp. 188, 190, 196. Hare, *Freedom and Reason*, p. 10 et seq. This, coupled with the rule of non-individualisation, also seems to be the core of Singer's generalization principle: 'What is right for one person must be right for any *similar person* in similar circumstances.' *Generalization in Ethics*, p. 14, (emphasis in original). The notion of consistency is very similar to the principle of universality or formal equality.

47   Many interpreters of universality in Kant's *Groundwork of the Metaphysics of Morals,* accuse Kant of having a purely formal notion.

48   This is similar to Rawls' notion of publicity. See also Baier, *The Moral Point of View*, p. 196.

49   Kant, *Religion Within the Limits of Reason Alone*, pp. 151 - 155.

50   Baier, *The Moral Point of View*, p. 101 (2nd ed.).

51   Richards, *A Theory of Reasons for Action*, p. 8: 'The task of the philosopher is to provide a theoretical account of normative concepts which, given peoples' nature and predilections, naturally and readily explains the normative judgements which people do make.'
See also Singer, *Generalization in Ethics*, p. 8: our moral beliefs provide the 'data and starting point for ethical theory'. See Rawls, *A Theory of Justice*, pp. 19 - 21, p. 47; *Political Liberalism*, pp. 28, 91 - 99; Dworkin, *Taking Rights*

Seriously, pp. 159 - 164; Nino, *Ethics of Human Rights*, p. 76; Larmore, *Patterns of Moral Complexity*, p. 29 on 'contextualism'.

52 Arguably, this is a development in Rawls thought between *A Theory of Justice* and *Political Liberalism*. There seems to be a greater emphasis on producing not just a coherent consistent set of beliefs but on producing such a set of beliefs which is 'the one most reasonable *for us*' (*Political Liberalism*, p. 28, italics added).

53 Richards, *A Theory of Reasons for Action*, p. 226: '... a filter which we may use in cleaning our moral beliefs of the extraneous particles which have become patched together with the pure element in the process of moral education and development.'

54 Dworkin, *Taking Rights Seriously*, pp. 159 - 164.

55 I do not endorse a reductivist conception of coherence, such as criticised by Raz, which obsessively pursues one single master principle, see *Ethics in the Public Domain*, Ch. 12 'The Relevance of Coherence'.

56 See Richards, *A Theory of Reasons for Action*, p. 90; Baier, *The Moral Point of View*, p. 255.

57 Formalist notions basically express the notions covered by the idea of universality or formal equality: 'If it is admitted that someone may justify his actions or attitudes on the basis of a principle which applies to his case, anyone else in similar circumstances, as defined by the principle itself, is also allowed to justify his conduct by appealing to it.' Nino, *Ethics of Human Rights*, p. 72.

58 Larmore, *Patterns of Moral Complexity*, pp. 61 - 62.

59 Dworkin, *Taking Rights Seriously*, pp. 179 - 183; *A Matter of Principle*, pp. 190 - 191.

60 Kant, *Groundwork of the Metaphysics of Morals*, p. 429. The notion also resembles Rawls' idea in *Political Liberalism* that all persons should be perceived as self-authenticating sources of claims, p. 32.

61 Alexy summarises the rules of Hare, Habermas and Baier thus: '(5.1.1) Everyone must be able to accept the consequences of the rule - presupposed in his normative statements - regarding the satisfaction of the interests of each individual person even for the hypothetical case in which he finds himself in the situation of this person.
(5.1.2) The consequences of every rule for the satisfaction of the interests of each and every individual must be capable of being accepted by all.
(5.1.3) Every rule must be openly and universally teachable.'
See also Ackerman, *Social Justice in the Liberal State*, pp. 11, 43, on 'neutrality'; Kant, *Groundwork of the Metaphysics of Morals*, pp. 67, 84 (para. 402, 421); Hare, *Freedom and Reason*, p. 8, p. 90; Rawls, *Theory of Justice*, p. 132; Habermas, *Moral Consciousness and Communicative Action*, pp. 58 *et seq.* Benhabib, *Situating the Self*; Dworkin, 'In Defence of Equality'; Kymlicka, *Liberalism, Community and Culture*, pp. 21 - 40; Finnis, Boyle, Grisez, *Nuclear Deterrence, Morality and Realism*, pp. 264 - 267; Nagel, 'Moral Conflict and Political Legitimacy', 16 *Phil. & Pub. Aff.* 215.

62 *Freedom and Reason*, pp. 10 - 16.

63   *Freedom and Reason*, pp. 108 et seq. Baier comments that 'behaviour in question must be acceptable to a person whether he is at the 'giving' or 'receiving' end of it'. *The Moral Point of View*, p. 108, (2nd ed.).

64   *Freedom and Reason*, pp. 110, 159 et seq.

65   Singer defines the Kantian principle thus: '... if, as a consequence of everyone's acting or trying to act in a certain way, no one would be able to, then no one has the right to act in that way - without a reason.' *Generalization in Ethics*, p. 275.

66   *Generalization in Ethics*, p. 73.

67   *A Theory of Justice*, pp. 18 - 19.

68   'Discourse Ethics: Notes', p. 65. This he distinguishes from the discourse principle which states that: 'Only those norms can claim to be valid that meet (or could meet) with the approval of all affected in their capacity as participants in a practical discourse.' (p. 66)

69   Nielson argues that one cannot move from the principle of formal universalisability to the principle of impartiality. See 'Universalisability and the Commitment to Impartiality' in Timmons, Potter, *Morality and Universality.*

70   Walzer, 'A Critique of Philosophical Conversation' in Kelly ed., *Hermeneutics and Critical Theory in Ethics and Politics.* See Warnke's reply to Walzer in the same volume.

71   I use 'libertarian' to designate beliefs similar to Nozick's: individual freedom, free uncontrolled market, anti-welfare state. See *Anarchy, State and Utopia.*

72   Standard works in the communitarian canon are MacIntyre, *After Virtue*; Walzer, *Spheres of Justice* and Sandel, *Liberalism and the Limits of Justice.* See the essays on the Kantian / Communitarian debate in Avineri and De-Shalit, *Communitarianism and Individualism*; Kelly, *Hermeneutics and Critical Theory in Ethics and Politics*; Rasmussen, *Universalism vs. Communitarianism*; Horton and Mendus, eds., *After MacIntyre.*

73   12 *Pol. Th.* 81, (1984).

74   Sandel, *Liberalism and the Limits of Justice*, p. 179.

75   Sandel, note 74, p. 33.

76   Sandel, note 74, pp. 135 *et seq.* and especially pp. 141 - 2.

77   Sandel, note 74, pp. 179 - 183.

4   The Politics of Equality

Introduction

In this and the two following chapters I look at constitutional doctrines in three liberal democratic states, and the interplay of political morality and legal reasoning in the judicial decisions of those states. I seek to show how political moral arguments provide links in the reasoning, which contribute to a public debate on the legitimacy.

The first of the three countries which I examine is Canada. I have decided to study a series of cases which bring into conflict two core values of liberal democracy: free expression and the right to equality. May the liberal democratic state punish certain obnoxious forms of expression, such as hate speech, holocaust denial, pornography? If so, to what extent, and why?

This topic is particularly important for Canadians, for whom of course free expression is a fundamental value. Moreover, few countries are as proud of their commitment to equality and diversity. As ably brought out in an exchange between Canadian and US free expression experts, Canada strives to protect equality through multi-culturalism rather than assimilation; its self-metaphor is a mosaic, not a melting-pot.[1] The maintenance of equal respect between different groups is held to justify restrictions on extremist expression.

In this Chapter, I first outline the basic features of the Canadian political and legal system. Then, I provide an introduction to Canadian constitutional law, looking at the role of the Charter, the doctrine of constitutional interpretation, the theory of free expression, and the limiting clause of the Charter. The bulk of the Chapter involves an examination of four cases raising difficult legal and political problems.

Political System

Canada is caught between two pairs of legal traditions. First, Quebec is in the civilian tradition, whilst the other provinces are in the common law tradition. Second, Canada is influenced by both the US and UK models of law. This can be seen in the legal revolution wrought by the 1982 Charter of Rights and Freedoms. Before this innovation case law was marked by the traditional English model of deference to the sovereign legislature. Opportunities for constitutional review of legislation were limited. After the enactment of the Charter a more activist judicial style appeared. Although Canadian public debate, like US public debate, is now much more 'rights-centred', Canadians give fundamental rights a more 'pro-State' interpretation than their southern neighbours, welcoming state intervention to protect fundamental rights and social values.

Canada is a federal parliamentary monarchy, based on the 1867 British North America Act, (now called the Constitution Act) and the 1982 Constitution Act, which contains the Charter of Rights.

The Head of State is the British monarch, who is represented by the Governor General. Parliament consists of the Queen, a House of Commons and a Senate. The House of Commons is elected by universal adult suffrage. It sits for five years, unless dissolved by the Governor General, who follows the wishes of the Prime Minister. The members of the Senate are nominated by the Governor General, that is, the Cabinet. Senators hold their posts until the age of 75. Although, formally, the Senate disposes of powers almost equal to those of the House, it rarely opposes the elected chamber.

The Cabinet is elected by the House of Commons, and is presided over by the Prime Minister. It is responsible only to the House of Commons.

Under the Canadian doctrine of federalism, the provinces exercise only enumerated powers, but the federal Parliament exercises all residual powers.

The Canadian Constitution is a rigid one, which can be enforced by judicial action (S. 52 of the 1982 Constitution Act). The Constitution can be amended by one of five procedures established by Part V of the 1982 Act, depending on the nature of the change.

The apex of the Canadian judicial system is the Federal Supreme Court of Canada. The Supreme Court of Canada (SCC) has nine judges, three of whom must come from Quebec. Each judge may deliver a separate opinion, dissenting or concurring, in any case in which he or she sat. To be appointed, one must be a judge of a superior court, or a lawyer of 10 years standing. The Supreme Court of Canada is competent to hear any type of case, be it based on federal, provincial or common law. Most civil appeals require leave to appeal, granted either by the Supreme Court of Canada, the Federal Court of Canada, or a provincial court of appeal. In criminal matters there is a right to appeal, if the lower court was split in its opinion on a point of law. The Supreme Court also has advisory functions. The Governor in Council (i.e. the federal government) may refer certain important legal questions to Court. There is also a Federal Court of Canada, with trial and appellate branches. Provincial courts have jurisdiction in all causes, including constitutional.

The Federal Government appoints the members of the Supreme Court and the superior federal and provincial courts. They may only be removed by parliamentary impeachment for misbehaviour. Judges of the Supreme Court must retire at 75 years of age.

Constitutional Law and the Charter

The motor of Canadian constitutional development in recent years has been the Canadian Charter of Rights and Freedoms.[2] The 1982 Charter was introduced for quite special reasons, as a survey of its provisions indicate. Although a better defence of fundamental rights was no doubt intended, the crucial motivating factor was a desire to promote 'national unity' in the context of a federal state facing a serious secessionist threat and linguistic cultural disharmony. This explains the great care lavished upon the linguistic rights provisions of the Charter, and also the mobility and education rights. All these rights (like the political participation rights, but not such mundane ones as the rights to life or expression) are immune from derogation under section 33.[3] The Charter has not succeeded in assuring national unity, and its achievements in protecting fundamental rights are also controversial. The judicial enforcement of the Charter has been criticised both for its excessive activism and its shabby deference![4]

The Charter has 34 sections. Section 2 protects the standard fundamental freedoms of conscience, expression, assembly and association. Sections 7 to 14 provide guarantees of procedural due process. Political rights are dealt with in sections 3 to 5. Section 6 assures the mobility rights of citizens and permanent residents. Section 15 comprises a comprehensive guarantee to equality, complete with a clause protecting affirmative action programmes. The right to use either French or English is secured by sections 16 to 22 and section 23 deals with language rights in education. Section 28 expressly assures equality of the sexes. Section 27 stresses the importance of Canada's multi-cultural inheritance.

Two particularly interesting features are sections 33 and 1. Section 33 permits any legislature to include an 'override' clause in any piece of legislation, providing that the statute shall be valid notwithstanding anything in section 2 or sections 7 to 15. Such a clause has effect for five years, and may be renewed. Section 1 states that all rights and freedoms are guaranteed 'subject only to such reasonable limits prescribed by law as can be demonstrably justified in a free and democratic society'.

Constitutional Interpretation

From the beginning of Charter jurisprudence, the Supreme Court has emphasised that rights and freedoms must be interpreted in a purposive, broad and liberal manner. The Court has rejected the traditional techniques of statutory interpretation in Charter cases. Dickson J. bluntly observed that the meaning of Charter phrases such as 'unreasonable'

> ... cannot be determined by recourse to a dictionary nor for that matter, by reference to the rules of statutory construction.[5]

A Charter, unlike a statute, created a 'continuing framework for the legitimate exercise of governmental power' rather than specifying rights and duties in a detailed and easily altered statute. Accordingly, it must be capable of development. Judges must adapt its meaning to resolve situations that the constituent authority never considered (p. 649). The 'fine adjustment process' of interpretation must be 'modulated by a sense of the unknown of the future'.[6]

In *R.* v. *Big M Drug Mart Ltd.*, the accused pleaded that Sunday closing legislation was invalid, as it infringed freedom of religion.[7]

Dickson C.J.C., speaking for the Court, agreed that the law was for an unacceptable purpose and so was invalid. He emphasised that a Charter right must be interpreted so as to implement its purpose. The purpose is to be determined:

> ... by reference to the character and the larger objects of the Charter itself, to the language chosen to articulate the specific right or freedom, to the historical origins of the concept enshrined, and where applicable, to the meaning and purpose of the other specific rights and freedoms with which it is associated within the text of the Charter. The interpretation should be ... a generous rather than a legalistic one, aimed at fulfilling the purpose of the guarantee and securing for individuals the full benefit of the Charter's protection. ... [The right must] be placed in its proper linguistic, philosophic and historical contexts.[8]

In *R. v. Oakes* legislation, partially reversing the onus of proof in drug trafficking cases was invalidated. Dickson C.J.C. directed judges to consider the words 'free and democratic society' in section 1.[9] The courts must consider the values underpinning such a society, which he listed as human dignity, 'social justice and equality', pluralism, 'respect for cultural and group identity', and democratic institutions promoting participation in society (p. 225).

The Court has emphasised that attention must be given to the constitutional traditions of Canada in determining the scope of rights. 'The [constitutional] tree is rooted in past and present institutions but must be capable of growth to meet the future'.[10] However, rights are not limited by past understandings.[11]

Canadian courts have also been willing to look to Canada's international obligations, international and comparative law generally, in interpreting the Charter. Thus in the *Public Service Employee Relations Act Reference*, Dickson C.J.C. referred to UK, US and various international law documents in considering the scope of freedom of association.[12] He considered that Charter guarantees should be interpreted to guarantee rights to at least the same extent as in international treaties which Canada had ratified (p. 185). Several judges are also willing to rely on works of legal and political theory.[13] Judges and jurists regular quote Mill and Milton in freedom of expression cases.[14]

Some jurists are not so enchanted by an overly liberal and expansive approach. In *Morgentaler* the Supreme Court had to decide whether a doctor could be punished for performing an abortion without following the requisite, cumbersome and time-consuming procedures.[15] The majority struck down the burdensome statutory provisions. McIntyre J. protested in dissent:

> The Court must consider not what is, in its view, the best solution to the problems posed, its role is confined to deciding whether the solution enacted by Parliament offends the Charter. (p. 465)

Dickson C.J.C., although holding that the provision was unconstitutional, also asserted that the courts should not attempt to solve all problems (p. 393).

One element in Charter interpretation is the growing emphasis on 'context'. This view has so far been most powerfully and consistently expressed by Madame Justice Wilson and Madame Justice L'Heureux-Dubé, in minority and dissenting opinions, but it plays a major role in several of the cases to be examined in depth. The most elaborate treatment of the contextual approach is found in *Edmonton Journal* v. *Attorney General for Alberta*.[16] The Supreme Court invalidated s.30(1), (2) of the 1980 Judicature Act, which prevented publication of information concerning a marriage dispute in court. Wilson J.'s concurring opinion outlined the problems with the abstract approach used by the other judges in the case. Both the contextual and abstract approaches involved identifying the value justifying the relevant right, and determining the legislative purpose of the impugned statute. However, the approaches diverged in their use of section 1. I shall return to this in the section on that clause.

Freedom of Expression

The Supreme Court has articulated a particular approach to freedom of expression cases. Section 2(b) states that

> Everyone has the following fundamental freedoms: ... (b) freedom of thought, belief, opinion and expression, including freedom of the press and other media of communication.

The values underpinning free expression were identified by the Supreme Court in *Ford* v. *Quebec*[17] when it invalidated section 58 of the Charter of the French Language. Section 58 had required public signs to be exclusively in French. The Supreme Court rejected pre-Charter case law, which would have limited free expression to free political expression. The Court, relying on two academic articles,[18] identified three purposes of free expression: the maintenance of democratic institutions, the pursuit of truth, and the self-fulfilment of the agent (participation, truth, self-fulfilment).

The Canadian courts have adopted a broad approach in deciding what is protected by s. 2(b). In *Attorney General of Quebec* v. *Irwin Toy*, the validity of s. 248 of the 1978 Consumer Protection Act was at issue.[19] The section prohibited, subject to regulation, advertisement aimed at persons under the age of 13. The Court upheld the provision. The majority dealt with the issue of what fell under the scope of 'expression'. The Court observed that expression has two elements, content and form. No activity could be deprived of s. 2(b) protection because of its content, i.e. meaning (p. 606). Thus anything which could have meaning was, in principle, expression. Even activity which normally conveys no meaning, may acquire it for the purposes of s. 2(b), on occasion (p. 607). However, the form of some activity, may be such as to exclude it from s. 2(b) protection. Although the judges declined to list all of the excluded forms, they specified that violence was not covered by s. 2(b). Commercial expression was therefore covered by s. 2(b).

Once the court determined that the expression was so covered, the next step was to decide whether public action had restricted freedom of expression. This it could do either by its purpose or its effect.[20] If the state was trying to prevent particular messages being broadcast, or to control access to messages, or to control the influence a message may have, then its purpose was considered to be the restriction of expression. If however, the public action was directed only to the 'direct physical result of the activity', then its purpose was not to restrict. In this last case, the person impugning the validity of the statute had to demonstrate that the statute had the effect of limiting expression. She had to show that her expression served one of the three values of free expression.[21] If the purpose or effect was to restrict free expression, then the statute violated s. 2(b) and could only be saved by section 1 (or section 33).

Section One

This section declares that the Charter rights are guaranteed 'subject only to such reasonable limits prescribed by law as can be demonstrably justified in a free and democratic society'. This section is a limiting clause, such as does not exist in the US Bill of Rights. It is open-ended in its list of justifiable restrictions, unlike the European Convention, which designates specific exceptions to each right.

The standard test under section one is found in *R. v. Oakes*.[22] Any acceptable limitation on a right must be prescribed by law, have a legitimate purpose, and be proportional. A provision is not 'prescribed by law' if it is: 'so obscure as to be incapable of interpretation with any degree of precision'.[23] However 'absolute precision' is not required, merely an 'intelligible standard'.[24]

For the purpose to be legitimate, it

> ... is necessary, at a minimum, that an objective relate to concerns which are pressing and substantial in a free and democratic society. (*Oakes*, p. 227)

On only three occasions has the Supreme Court held a legislative purpose to be illegitimate.[25]

There are three elements to the proportionality wing.

> First, the measures adopted must be carefully designed to achieve the objective in question. They must not be arbitrary, unfair or based on irrational considerations. In short they must be rationally connected to the objective. Second, the means, even if rationally connected to the objective in this first sense, should 'as little as possible' the right or freedom in question. ... [Third] The effects must not be too severely deleterious. (p. 227)

This test is called the *Oakes* test. The apparent severity of this test has been much modified by case law.

In *Edmonton Journal*, Wilson J. discussed 'abstract' and 'contextual' approaches to section one.[26] She argued that an abstract approach considered the values underpinning rights in an 'at large' manner. That is, judges concentrated on expression as a contribution to truth, participation, self-fulfilment, without considering the specific claim in the instant case (p. 582). Using a contextual approach, values had to be considered as they operate in the particular case. According to Wilson J., this allowed one to decide what importance to attach to the particular claim, as the value of the right could change depending on context. Thus expression might be of more importance in a political context, than when reporting on a family dispute.[27]

This emphasis on context has led to greater flexibility in section one analysis. The flexibility of section one has been emphasised particularly where legislative choices on redistribution, or the assessment of competing claims has been at issue. Where this is the case the rational connection and minimum impairment wings of the *Oakes* test are weakened, the courts accepting a less than perfect fit, or measures that are not necessarily the least intrusive.[28] This has been justified by the roles of democratic institutions as a form of collective self-government.[29]

> When it comes to choosing between divergent if not contrary interests or to allocating resources that are scarce or at least often in decline, provincial legislatures and Parliament must have a margin of free manoeuvre when the constitutional validity of legislative measures is assessed.

So explained La Bel J.A., of the Quebec Court of Appeal upholding limitations on tobacco advertising.[30] La Bel J.A. held that section 1 was satisfied if the state could adduce evidence establishing a 'reasonable foundation' for the statute (p. 319). The flexible approach provoked a blistering dissent from Brossard J.A. who felt that it was a betrayal of the Charter (p. 389).

The courts have also explained that the legislature will be allowed a greater latitude when it is protecting vulnerable groups, as well as where it is deciding between different claims of different groups. As Wilson J. explained such deference is justified 'where something less than a straightforward denial of a right is involved' or when there are competing constitutional claims.[31]

This development of the section one test has been accompanied by reminders that freedom of expression is not absolute,[32] and that some forms of expression may merit less protection than others.[33]

Comment

In the next four sections, I examine four free expression cases decided by the Supreme Court. My point is simply this: that the reasoning leading from the constitutional provisions in sections 1 and 2(b) of the Charter is incomplete unless one assumes certain commitments of political morality.

Such commitments have already been apparent in discussing the broad scope of s. 2(b). The idea that every content and almost every form of expression is entitled to *prima facie* protection is clearly a liberal idea. The mere fact that someone wishes to express a meaning is enough to give prima facie constitutional protection to it (unless expressed through violence), and switch the burden to the State. Those who embrace communitarian or perfectionist, even liberal perfectionist ideas, would see no need to protect all types of expression. Despite the broad wording of s. 2(b) such a broad approach was not required (or prohibited) by the specific words of the section.

However, it is in the s. 1 analysis that political commitments are most apparent. Whilst judges have emphasised that s. 2(b) is not tied to any one theory of expression, the actual application of section one in this regard, indicates that some judges interpret the section in the light of a liberal perfectionist, others a neutral liberal, and yet others a more conservative theory. Thus, the test is differently applied depending on the type of expression. The notion of core forms of free expression indicates a political belief which attaches importance to political development, artistic expression, personal development, rather than commercial or sexual expression. More specifically expression embodying anti-egalitarian ideas is of very low value.

The Politics of Hate: Keegstra

The traditional controversies about freedom of expression have, in the main disappeared in liberal democratic states. Few believe that the state is in the business of tearing pages out of *Lady Chatterley's Lover*. However new problems have arisen which divide public and legal opinion. In a series of cases, Canadian courts have confronted some of the more intractable controversies in the area of free expression. Must a free and democratic society, in the name of toleration, permit the vilification of groups traditionally subject to vicious discrimination? May racists tell deliberate lies in the pursuit of fascist dreams? Can the state punish, or severely regulate, the deliberate degradation of women for economic motives?

The Canadian Parliament has taken a clear stance on all these matters, though sometimes the political authorities have wavered in individual instances. It has maintained in force the old laws on obscenity, and the spreading of false news, though giving those laws an interpretation more appropriate to modern times when the values of equality and multi-culturalism seem more important than conventional sexual morality and protection of royal sentiments. It regards prostitution as a dubious social practice which requires strict regulation. Most importantly, it has taken a conscious decision to suppress the most obnoxious form of expression - incitement to racial hatred. The Supreme Court of Canada has reviewed these legislative choices and has upheld some of those which it sees as motivated by equality concerns.

In *Keegstra*,[34] the Supreme Court considered section 319 (2) of the Criminal Code which punished anyone who 'by communicating statements other than in private conversation, wilfully promotes hatred against any identifiable group'.[35] In *Zundel*, the validity of section 181 of the Criminal Code was at issue. The section proscribed the wilful spreading of news known to be false and likely to harm a public interest. I will consider *Zundel* later. This section concentrates on *Keegstra*.

The facts and lower court decisions

Keegstra was the mayor of a small town and a secondary level teacher, who described Jews as 'treacherous', 'subversive', 'child killers', 'power hungry' and so on.[36] He expected his students to regurgitate this rubbish, or else suffer in their examinations. He was convicted of wilfully promoting hatred against an identifiable group, contrary to s. 319(2) of the Criminal Code.

The original trial took place in the Alberta Court of Queen's Bench.[37] Quigley J. held that freedom of expression was to be interpreted in accordance with four values mentioned in the preamble to the 1961 Bill of Rights: the supremacy of God, human dignity, respect for moral and spiritual virtues and the rule of law. These values were confirmed by s. 15 and s. 27 of the Charter. Considering this, he held that s. 319(2) was a safeguard of free expression, ensuring that members of minorities would not be unfairly excluded from public debate by reason of hatred which attacked their dignity. The speech at issue did not fall under the protection of s. 2(b). However, the trial judge continued, if s. 2(b) did cover the expression, then it was justifiable under section 1, as it prevented the infliction of psychological and physical harm.

Keegstra appealed. The Alberta Court of Appeal invalidated s. 319(2).[38] Kerans J.A. explained that s. 2(b) protected erroneous and imprudent beliefs, (though not lies). The aim of preventing psychological harm to minorities was legitimate, but the measure was invalid because it criminalised *attempts* to stir up hatred, and not merely the stirring up of hatred. The provision was overbroad, catching both of these activities.

The Supreme Court of Canada

From this opinion the state appealed.[39] The case was heard by Dickson C.J., Wilson, La Forest, L'Heureux-Dubé, Sopinka, Gonthier and McLachlin JJ. The Chief Justice delivered the majority opinion. Sopinka, La Forest, McLachlin JJ. dissented, with McLachlin J. delivering the dissent.[40]

Dickson C.J. reviewed group defamation style offences in Canadian law (p. 722), such as the spreading of false news likely to injure a public interest (section 181) and seditious libel (section 59). Courts had interpreted both provisions as applying only to statements which incited violence, public disorder or disobedience.[41] Section 319 was enacted as a consequence of the 1966 Report on Hate Propaganda (p. 725), which advocated the balancing of free expression and egalitarian interests.

Dickson C.J.C. then considered the value of free expression (p. 726). He reiterated the values underpinning s. 2(b): the pursuit of truth, social and political participation, and self-fulfilment and flourishing in a 'tolerant and welcoming environment' (p. 728).

Dickson C.J.C. held that the expression was covered by section 2(b). The activity at issue was clearly expressive, and its 'invidious and obnoxious' nature was irrelevant for the purposes of s. 2(b) (p. 730). Also, clearly the purpose of the s. 319 (2) was to restrict expression (p. 730).

Dickson C.J.C. dismissed two arguments that would deny s. 2(b) protection to this type of expression. First, hate propaganda was not itself physical violence, and so did not fall within the *Irwin Toy* exception regarding violent forms of communication (p. 732). The second argument was that s. 2(b) must be interpreted so as not to conflict with Canada's international obligations, s. 15 or s. 27 of the Charter (p. 733). The Chief Justice believed that these issues were more appropriate for consideration in a contextual analysis under s. 1 of the Charter (p. 734). Having concluded that s. 2(b) was violated, Dickson C.J.C. moved on to s. 1.

Section 1 must not be seen as a:

> ... rigid and technical provision, offering nothing more than a last chance for the state to justify incursions into the realm of fundamental rights. (p. 735)

Dickson C.J.C. noted that s. 1 tied the guarantee of rights into their restriction, uniting each principle in the concept of a free and democratic society (p. 736). Section one permitted the protection of values beyond those enumerated in the Charter. Furthermore, an analysis under s. 1 must be a contextual one which respected the 'synergetic relation' between Charter values and the facts of the case (p. 737).

Dickson C.J.C. exhaustively reviewed the US case law relating to hate propaganda (pp. 738 - 744). He warned judges not to be too eager to follow the US case law for three reasons (p. 741). First, the exact status of hate propaganda in the US was problematic. Second, US courts had not rigorously applied the content neutral standard, on which opposition to hate propaganda laws rested. Third, s. 1 of the Charter requires an analytic framework distinct from that existing in the US.

Was the objective a substantial and pressing one? Dickson C.J.C. noted that there was an appreciable amount of hate propaganda in Canada, which was on the increase, and that Canada had been used as a supplier to European hate-mongers (pp. 745 - 746). Hate propaganda provoked humiliation and degradation in the victims (p. 746). Such propaganda could discourage minorities from participating in public life, or exercising their right to be different. Further, society could be harmed by such expression, as individuals might be seduced by the message. Dickson C.J.C. considered that the effects of modern advertising and subtle propaganda might delude some individuals (p. 747). The eventual result could be violence and discrimination. These harms justified restrictions.

The importance of suppressing hate propaganda was also emphasised in international law. Art. 4 of the Racial Discrimination Convention and Art. 19 of the International Covenant on Civil and Political Rights required suppression (p. 752). Such suppression was also permitted by Art. 10, Art. 14 and Art. 17 of the European Convention (p. 753).

Also of consideration in determining the importance of the aim were s. 15 and s. 27 of the Charter, with their 'strong commitment to the values of equality and multi-culturalism' (p. 755). The Chief Justice believed that the state had a duty to promote equality and multi-culturalism. The elimination of expression harmful to notions of tolerance and mutual respect was one facet of that duty (p. 756). In view of all this, s. 319(2) had a pressing and substantial purpose (p. 758).

Was the measure proportional? Dickson C.J.C. stressed the importance of a contextual approach:

> While we must guard carefully against judging expression according to its popularity, it is equally destructive of free expression values, as well as the other values which underlie a free and democratic society, to treat all expression as equally crucial to those principles at the core of s. 2(b). (p. 760)

Some expression could be suppressed more easily than others. This depended on the relevance of the expression to s. 2(b) values, the interests of the audience, whether the measure protects vulnerable groups and so on.[42] Considering these factors, Dickson C.J.C. continued:

> [The expression] is deeply offensive, hurtful and damaging to target group members, misleading to his listeners, and antithetical to the furtherance of tolerance and understanding in society. (p. 761 - 2)

The Chief Justice argued that not all censorship offends the value of free expression (p. 765), and that hate speech degraded all three values of s. 2(b).

The message of hate-mongers was unlikely to be true or valid, and therefore could not be said to be essential to the pursuit of truth. An unregulated marketplace of ideas did not necessarily assist in the pursuit of truth (p. 763). Second, whilst the section limited the self-fulfilment of a small minority, it prevented that minority from attacking 'with inordinate vitriol' the self-fulfilment of others, who sought development in their particular ethnic or religious group (p. 763). Finally, although s. 319(2) restricted the participation of hate-mongers, again its purpose was to prevent expression which was inimical to the foundations of democracy. The public condemnation of hate propaganda furthered the value of democratic participation (p. 764). Considering these factors, hate propaganda should not be considered too weighty an interest under s. 1 (p. 765).

Dickson C.J.C. considered there to be a rational connection between the section and the aim (pp. 767 - 771). He rejects several arguments which denied this. Whilst criminal trials might attract publicity for hate mongers, the process of a criminal trial was a public reaffirmation of equality, and 'comforts' many Canadians (p. 769). Secondly, such punishment in no way dignified the criminals. As the Chief Justice said 'pornography is not dignified by its suppression' nor are defamatory remarks (p. 769). Third, there was the argument that hate propaganda laws in Weimar Germany failed to prevent the rise of Nazism. This argument failed as it compared two historically dissimilar situations (p. 770). Finally, he noted that many states (England, New Zealand, Sweden, Netherlands and India) do not regard such laws as ineffective (p. 770). Accordingly, there was a rational connection.

Did the section impair the right to free expression as little as possible? The section only captured communication which was wilful in its intent to provoke hatred (pp. 773 - 775).

Dickson C.J.C. rejected the Court of Appeal's argument, that only the actual promotion of hatred could be punished, and not merely the attempt to promote hatred. There would be two problems with such an approach. First, it did not take seriously the psychological harm inflicted by hate speech. Second, it ignored the evidential difficulties in proving causation. The state could 'prevent the risk of serious harms' using criminal laws (p. 776).

The accused also alleged that 'hatred' was an unacceptably vague and subjective term. The Chief Justice said that 'hatred' indicated a particularly narrow range of the most intense and unreasonable emotions (pp. 777 - 778).

The effect of s. 319(2) was also controlled by various limits. Section 319(2) covered all communication in a public place, but not private communication. Dickson C.J.C. believed this to be an unnecessary compromise (p. 773). The defences offered the opportunity to the accused to show that he acted in good faith, or to demonstrate that what he said was true (p. 779). Dickson C.J.C. considered that there was no obligation under the Charter to provide an exception for statements that the accused could show to be true (p. 781). Nor was the section overbroad simply because it did not provide that negligent or innocent error as to fact is a defence (p. 782). Neither of those factors would alter the essential nature of the offence, the promotion of hatred. Nor could the fact that some administrative officials had been overzealous in applying the section, affect its constitutionality (p. 783).

Keegstra objected that the state could use other, non-coercive methods. Dickson C.J.C. replied that the state was not obliged to renounce the use of the criminal law, if it served a non-redundant purpose, and achieved its objective more effectively than other methods (p. 785).

Finally, Dickson C.J.C. concluded that the restriction at issue, affecting as it did a type of expression 'only tenuously connected with the values underlying the guarantee of freedom of speech' was not an excessive restriction, given the 'enormous importance of the objective fuelling s. 319(2)' (p. 787).

Dissenting Opinion

McLachlin J. delivered a dissenting opinion with which La Forest and Sopinka JJ. agreed, as regards freedom of expression.

McLachlin J. reviewed the different philosophical basis of free expression (free expression as the linchpin of political democracy; as essential to protect other rights; as necessary for the pursuit of truth, in a 'free marketplace of ideas';[43] as an end in itself and finally the argument that no government can be trusted with the power of censorship, for that will put it in the position of judging for itself (pp. 802 - 805).

McLachlin J. accepted an 'eclectic approach' to s. 2(b), arguing that its broad scope did not permit the adoption of any one rationale (p. 807). Rather all of these rationales might play a role in different factual circumstances. The proper place for considering which rationale was more important was section one (p. 806). Despite the importance of these values, free expression was not an absolute. Certain acts of expression endangered Charter values (defamation, sedition, incitement to violence or hatred). In some cases, the balancing exercise under s. 1 could require expression to be limited. However, all expression was prima facie protected by s. 2(b) (p. 807).

McLachlin J. reviewed freedom of expression in Canada, both before and after the Charter (pp. 808 - 811), noting that post-Charter jurisprudence extended freedom of expression to non-political expression, and even to commercial expression.[44]

She then considered the status of hate propaganda. It challenged the very basis of society: tolerance, dignity, equality (p. 811):

> The evil of hate propaganda is beyond doubt. It inflicts pain and indignity upon individuals who are members of the group in question. In so far as it may persuade others to the same point of view, it may threaten social stability. (p. 812)

How should this evil be dealt with under s. 2(b)?

McLachlin J. reviewed the US case law on the topic (pp. 812 - 820). She noted the initial reluctance of the courts to protect unpopular speech, and the original defence of free expression in dissenting opinions of Holmes and Brandeis JJ.[45] Shortly after the nadir of First Amendment jurisprudence during the McCarthyite era, the US Supreme Court upheld a statute which prohibited hate propaganda: *Beauharnais* v. *Illinois*.[46] However the validity of that decision had been undermined by a strengthening of free speech jurisprudence.[47] McLachlin J. identified several useful US doctrines, such as the concepts of content, viewpoint, and 'time, place and manner' regulations, overbreadth and vagueness (p. 819).[48]

McLachlin J. thought that the European Convention (which clearly permitted proscription of hate speech) was of limited relevance to the discussion because of its 'lukewarm' defence of expression values in cases like *Handyside*[49] (p. 820). She referred to the Racial Discrimination Convention, Art. 4 and the International Covenant on Civil and Political Rights, Arts. 19 and 20, which required the suppression of hate propaganda. Indeed the UN Human Rights Committee had rejected a challenge to Canada's anti-hate propaganda laws.[50] She considered that both the US and international approaches allowed for restrictions on expression, but that the US one was more exacting in its requirements (p. 822).

Was hate propaganda entitled to s. 2(b) protection? The case law affirmed that all non-violent expressive activity was protected (p. 827). Specifically, nothing could be excluded on the basis of its content. McLachlin J. dismissed three arguments which disputed this protection of hate propaganda. First, McLachlin J. explained hate speech was not the same as violence (p. 829). Violence prevented the free choosing of ideas or behaviour. However hate propaganda did not. It did not prevent the democratic process taking its path, though it might heighten emotions (p. 831). Nor could it be argued that it restricted the right of others to be believed; the right of free expression:

> ... guarantees the right to loose one's ideas on the world; it does not guarantee the right to be listened to or to be believed. (pp. 831 - 832)

The second argument was that s. 2(b) ought to be limited by s. 15 and s. 27 of the Charter and international obligations. McLachlin J. notes that, regarding the Charter provisions there is no direct conflict between the scope of the rights guaranteed, there is a conflict 'between philosophies' (p. 833). McLachlin J. held that any conflict between the s. 2(b) and other Charter provisions had to be resolved under s. 1, in a contextual analysis (pp. 833 - 836). Furthermore, the essence of multi-culturalism involved the notion of tolerance (p. 836). Concerning international law, the judge observed that the treaties had an approach different from the Charter's, in that they expressly permitted the proscription of hate propaganda (p. 837). Furthermore, those treaties left a certain margin of manoeuvre as to the method used by the state. The third argument was that hate propaganda was utterly evil and without any redeeming value, and should be denied s. 2(b) protection (pp. 839 - 842). This argument was that the framers never intended to increase the scope of free expression so far beyond that obtaining in pre-Charter times. However, such a history oriented approach had never been acceptable in Charter jurisprudence. Finally, the state claimed that expression which failed to further any of the values identified in *Irwin Toy* did not merit protection. That approach had never been used by the courts:

> Attempts to confine the guarantee of free expression only to content which is judged to possess redeeming value or to accord with the accepted values strike at the very essence of the value of the freedom, reducing the realm of the protected discussion to that which is comfortable and compatible with current conceptions. (p. 842)

Section 2(b) was violated, and s. 319(2) must be justified under section 1.

McLachlin J. explained that s. 1 involved a contextual balancing exercise.

> ... requiring the judge to make value judgements. In this task logic and precedent are but of limited assistance. What must be determinative in the end is the court's judgement, based on an understanding of the values our society is built on and the interests at stake in the particular case. (p. 845)

McLachlin J. considered that the objective of the legislation, the protection of social harmony and human dignity, was an important one (p. 847).

Was the method used proportional? McLachlin J. emphasised that one must not over concentrate on the offensive nature of the speech, as all expression was entitled to protection.[51] She noted that free expression was unique among fundamental rights for two reasons. First, it was essential to the protection of other rights, and second, restrictions on expression tended to have a 'chilling' effect even on those who were not the target of the regulation (p. 850).

McLachlin J. found that there was no rational connection between the means and the aim of the provision. Although some deference must be paid to the legislative branch, this could not be done if the measure failed to promote, or actually worked against the aim in question. First, persons prosecuted under this and similar provisions received publicity as a consequence. Second, the public trial could confer martyr status on the accused. Third, since the argument for s. 319(2) rested on the belief in human gullibility, then it was just as reasonable to believe that people will believe the message of hate-mongers simply because the state prosecuted them (p. 853). All this was confirmed by the failure of anti-hatred laws in Weimar Germany to prevent the rise of Nazism. Accordingly the rational connection was not clearly demonstrable.

Furthermore, the method did not impair as minimally as necessary the right to free expression. First, s. 319(2) was overbroad in its impact (pp. 855 - 860). 'Hatred' was a vague term. It was for the judge and jury to determine what exactly counted as hatred. The requirement of 'wilful promotion' did not limit the scope of the provision, as the contribution to a valid debate might be accompanied by knowledge that hatred will ensue (p. 857).[52] Also, the statutory defences did not provide adequate protection for the accused; it was up to the accused himself to prove the defence of truth, and in any case many allegations might not be capable of being judged true or false. The defences of public interest and reasonableness turned the issue over to the judge and jury, and left too much scope to them. Furthermore all forms of communication, except private communication were caught. The overbreadth of the section could be gauged from the various publications threatened with prosecution: a film on Nelson Mandela, Uris' *The Haj*, Rushdie's *Satanic Verses*, pamphlets saying 'Yankee go home' (p. 859). The chilling effect of s. 319(2) might reach as far as *The Merchant of Venice*.

Furthermore, methods were available to the state, other than criminalising expression (pp. 861 - 863). Discrimination could be banned, and human rights legislation used to encourage people to accept egalitarian principles.

The section also violated the third wing of the proportionality test, that the restriction not be too severe (pp. 863 - 865). The section criminalised expression on the basis of its viewpoint and content. It covered all possible domains and areas of communication (except the private), works of art, words of momentary anger. The expression at issue was more important than the 'right to turn a profit'. It might be important to the political process and individual self-fulfilment. And, despite the importance of s. 319(2)'s aim, it was not clear that the section actually achieves it. In conclusion, s. 319(2) failed all three wings of the proportionality test.

Analysis

I am concerned with the links between political morality and law. Considerations of the former play a role in legal adjudication, and this is legitimate, for law and political morality are each forms of public dialogue centring on the issue of justification. From a legal viewpoint one can say that adjudication is a process of giving reasons for decisions, for developing normative standards and applying them to concrete situations. Among the legal reasons which one can give to justify decisions are reasons concerning political morality.

In this case, the Supreme Court reviewed Canada's hate propaganda law, enacted by Parliament to limit certain forms of expression in the interest of maintaining the principle of equality on which democratic society is based. Equality is not merely a value to be left to struggle in the marketplace of ideas; the State must affirm it and root out viewpoints violently opposed to it. The majority judgement in this case concurred with this assessment, or at least agreed that it is one that Parliament could reasonably make.

Consider the two judgements in this case. Both of the judges agreed that the expressive activity at issue was covered by s. 2(b). Further, the aim invoked by the state to justify its restriction, was agreed by both to be a pressing and substantial reason. However, Dickson C.J.C. and McLachlin J. disagreed on the proportionality of the means used to achieve that end. McLachlin J. applied a much more rigorous version of the *Oakes* test than did Dickson C.J.C.

McLachlin J. required the state to show that hate propaganda laws would not backfire, that they would not dignify such speech, or attract publicity for hate mongers' cause, and that would not mislead people into believing that the state was censoring something worthwhile. The Chief Justice believed that none of these dangers were real, and that s. 319(2) was valuable as an expression of society's hatred of hate speech. Furthermore, Dickson C.J.C. regarded the measure as narrowly drawn, capturing only wilful, public speech attempting to incite hatred. McLachlin J. saw every one of the section's elements as introducing an unacceptable level of vagueness and subjectivity. The Chief Justice thought the statutory defences were more generous than required by the Charter; McLachlin J. disagreed. Finally, the judges disagreed on whether the effects of the provision were too severe, given the nature of the aim.

One judge applied a particularly rigorous approach to s. 1, the other a more relaxed approach. Now why should this be so? I think the reason is clear. The majority regarded the expressive activity as being obnoxious and of limited constitutional value. The dissenters saw the expression as obnoxious, but nevertheless of constitutional value.

Why, according to the majority, was the expression of little value? Hate propaganda limited the rights of minorities. It advocated a message opposed to the guarantees of equality and multi-culturalism found in s. 15 and s. 27 of the Charter, as well as in international treaties. The expression was 'obnoxious' and attacked the values underpinning s. 2(b). It involved statements unlikely to be true, and it limited the self-fulfilment and participation rights of others.

McLachlin J., though expressing her contempt for hate speech, disagreed on the issue of its constitutional value. Speech inciting hatred might play a role in the political process, and in the process of individual self-fulfilment. This possibility was unlikely, considering the actual example of the speech, but it still merited constitutional protection. The majority viewpoint violated the principle of content neutrality emphasised by both judges in their s. 2(b) analysis.

The conflict was not between legal doctrines but between 'conflicting (political) philosophies'. Dickson C.J.C. applied a lower level of protection to the expression at issue for the very good reason that it urged the violation of some of the core principles of liberal democracy. The core issue was: in what circumstances may speech be denied protection because of its content and why? The Charter did not explicitly answer this question; only a reconstruction of the Charter could do so.

That some speech may be undeserving of the full protection of the Charter is evident from earlier cases. However, this principle had been limited to a particular category of expression, commercial expression. In *Keegstra*, this principle was extended to arguably political speech having a particular content. McLachlin J. insisted that any restriction on expression be closely and precisely tailored to the aim of protecting minorities. Dickson C.J.C., because of the particular viewpoint expressed, did not insist on the close, narrow, specification of the restriction.

The difference is between two variants of liberalism, which I briefly designate as perfectionist liberal and liberalism as neutrality. Both versions agree with the central tenets of liberalism, such as equality, autonomy, toleration, pluralism, etc. but they derive different injunctions from them.

Perfectionist liberals argue that the state must protect the rights of individuals, that it must encourage the creation of a liberal society, and foster liberal virtues.[53] The good life a life which one leads autonomously, in a spirit of toleration.[54] The state must encourage people to lead this life. In certain instances it must prohibit people from failing to lead such a life, for the 'ideal of autonomy requires only the availability of morally acceptable [liberal] options'.[55] Such a theory, although perfectionist, is strongly committed to pluralism. A very wide range of lifestyles may be chosen in the perfectionist liberal state. Pluralism must be consciously defended, not merely left to the marketplace of ideas. This political theory has been defended by at least one Canadian scholar referring to the *Keegstra* decision.[56]

Liberals who adopt the notion of neutrality believe that the state must not discriminate between different conceptions of the good.[57] It must provide a framework in which each person has an equal opportunity to pursue his or her conception of the good life, without interfering with each other's pursuit. In certain instances this may require the use of coercion, e.g. to prevent violence against the person, or to raise taxes to fund a welfare state. However, the choice of the good, the selection of a lifestyle must be left to the 'marketplace of ideas'. All choices in this marketplace must be available and not eliminated by the state. The very notion of the marketplace includes the notion of expressing and arguing for the different lifestyle choices, and so puts a premium on free expression, irrespective of content or viewpoint.

In many instances, adherents of the two versions will agree. Both will denounce laws which discriminate against people because of race, gender, sexual orientation, religion and so on. Both will support traffic regulation laws, and, probably, laws which regulate the market. However, on certain contentious issues they will differ. Should the state ensure a particular form of education for everyone? May the state fund third level education? How does the state deal with expression which abominates the liberal principles of equality, autonomy, toleration, pluralism?

A liberal who agrees with the notion of neutrality might agree to the suppression of such expression, but only where the restriction was narrowly tailored and clearly necessary to prevent imminent harm. She could not agree to reducing the standard of protection simply because the message communicated expressed contempt for liberal values. She might well adopt something approaching the US Supreme Court's clear and pressing danger test, though she would apply it more consistently, not excluding obscene words from its protection. For the perfectionist liberal, however, people must lead a liberal life. This allows a wide range of freedom to choose a particular lifestyle. But it excludes those lifestyles predicated on contempt for the core values of liberal society. Such a person could accept reducing the protection of free expression because of the content of the message.

McLachlin J. was motivated by a political philosophy broadly similar to those liberal approaches which embrace neutrality. She would not apply anything other than a stringent test to laws which limit a type of political speech, no matter how repugnant that speech was to core liberal beliefs. She interpreted the sections of the Charter in the light of this peculiarly US style 'liberalism as neutrality'. She saw this philosophy as animating the text of the Charter, filling in the interpretative gaps. However there was, in McLachlin J.'s words, a tension between 'competing philosophies' in the Charter - there was a free expression centred philosophy and an equality centred one. McLachlin J. solved this tension by giving decisive weight to the former.

Dickson C.J.C. was motivated by a more perfectionist, some might say, realistic, vision of liberalism. He saw the Charter as emphasising equality and pluralism, and the role of the political authorities was to uphold those values. His interpretation did not see such a clear cut schism between different Charter philosophies. Both the freedom and the equality concerns were based on a coherent notion of egalitarianism - the equal right to free speech, within a marketplace of ideas regulated according to the value of equality. Toleration, pluralism, free expression were of overriding value, and those messages which deny their value were themselves valueless and could be restricted.

Lying About the Holocaust

The defendant, Zundel, had published assertions, invoking alleged new evidence, that there was no Holocaust, no Final Solution, that there was merely a plan to remove European Jews to Madagascar. The Holocaust was a myth, fabricated by a Jewish conspiracy to undermine the 'Anglo-Saxon' world. He claimed that the death camps were work camps, that the *Diary of Anne Frank* was fictitious, that all evidence of the crime of crimes was forged. He invoked a fragment of Goebbels' diary to justify the assertion that there was no campaign of genocide. He stated that 'to exterminate' meant 'to deport'.58

A Toronto Jewish group brought a charge against him under s. 181 of the criminal code. Section 181 punished the publication of false statements, known by the publisher to be false, which harmed, or were likely to harm a public interest.59 Four elements of the offence had to be proved: that the publication was wilful; that it concerned a matter of fact, not opinion; that the accused knew it to be false; and that the falsehood was likely to injure a public interest. The section provided for a jail sentence of up to two years.

The trial judge indicated to the jury that it was not open to them to decide that there was no mass murder of Jews during the Second World War. However the accused was allowed to plead that the systematic, calculated, racially motivated abomination known as the 'Holocaust' never took place.

The prosecution demonstrated the falsity of each of the factual allegations. It also introduced testimony that Zundel was aware of the falsity of the allegations for at least ten years. The prosecution explained that the fomenting of hatred against Jews violated a public interest. Zundel's defence was that the pamphlet was a matter of opinion, but if it was adjudged to be an assertion of fact, then it was accurate. Finally, he asserted that s. 181 was invalid. The jury convicted him.

Zundel appealed to the Ontario Court of Appeal. The Court of Appeal held that the accused's pamphlet did not fall within the scope of s. 2(b) of the Charter, but even if it did, s. 181 was justifiable under s. 1. However the Court found technical errors in the decision and ordered a retrial.60 The defendant was again convicted, and again he appealed. This second appeal was rejected in its entirety.61 Zundel then appealed to the Supreme Court of Canada, arguing that s. 181 was invalid.

Majority Judgement

Surprisingly, in view of the *Keegstra* decision, the Court invalidated s. 181.62 McLachlin J. delivered the majority judgement, with La Forest, L'Heureux-Dubé, and Sopinka JJ. concurring. Cory, Iacobucci, and Gonthier JJ. dissented.

McLachlin J. commenced by noting the differences between this provision and s. 319(2). This provision was broader in scope, covering all false statements, known to be false, and injurious to a public interest. The legislation in *Keegstra* concerned hate speech, targeted to harm certain minorities (p. 253).

McLachlin J. found that s. 2(b) covered these statements. After noting that the values underpinning the section were 'promoting truth, political or social participation, and self-fulfilment', she summarised the views of Holmes J.:[63]

> Thus the guarantee of freedom of expression serves to protect the right of the minority to express its view, however unpopular it may be; adapted to this context, it serves to preclude the majority's perception of 'truth' or 'public interest' from smothering the minority's perception. The view of the majority has no need of protection; it is tolerated in any event. (p. 260)

She rejected two arguments that would deny s. 2(b) protection to Zundel's fabrication. The first argument was that deliberate lies were a 'form' of expression left unprotected, like violence. She dismissed this argument, citing *Keegstra* and *Irwin Toy* (p. 261).

The second argument was that deliberate lies did not further expression values. McLachlin J. rejected this for two reasons. First, exaggeration and falsehood might indeed further social values. She cited some examples - the doctor who exaggerated the dangers of a plague to stir up public concern, the use of satire and caricature - to justify this assertion (p. 262).

Second, we may have difficulty in identifying the meaning of a statement, and we may have difficulty in deciding whether it is false:

> A given expression may offer many meanings, some which may seem false, others, of a metaphorical or allegorical nature, which may possess some validity. Moreover, meaning is not a datum so much as an interactive process, depending on the listener as well as the speaker. Different people may draw from the same statement different meanings at different times. The guarantee of freedom of expression seeks to protect not only the meaning intended to be communicated by the publisher, but also the meaning or meanings understood by the reader. (p. 263)

She suggested different possible meanings of the defendant's pamphlet: that one should be reluctant to accept conventional interpretations, or that there is value in all 'unimpeded communication'. Furthermore, it might be difficult to determine what was true or false. She stressed that the issue of falsity in this case was much more serious than in normal defamation cases where the allegations concerned a living person, and where there was no need to investigate 'complex social and historical facts' (p. 264).

The statements were protected by s. 2(b) and the legislation had as its purpose and effect the restriction of expression. McLachlin J. moved to an inquiry under s. 1.

According to McLachlin J., the section had no counterparts anywhere in the world (pp. 270 - 271). She noted its origins in a thirteenth century statute (*De Scandalis Magnatum*) to protect the rich and powerful from abuse (p. 255). She strongly objected to the attempt by the dissenters to assign a specific purpose to the provision, in the light of modern beliefs.

McLachlin J. said that no valid pressing and substantial interest can be assigned to the section. The goal of protecting the public interest was much too general. No more specific purpose could be shown. The section was a survival from earlier times and there had been no parliamentary debate as to its purpose. One Commission had even recommended its abolition, as it served no discernible specific purpose (p. 269). McLachlin J. objected to the 'outright redefinition' of the section's aims by the dissenters which went far beyond a shift in emphasis (p. 266). She accused them of usurping the legislative function (p. 274). The provision failed even the valid objective wing of the *Oakes* test.

It also failed the proportionality wing. The section covered a substantial amount of expression, not merely those of no value (p. 276), and it punished falsehood, known to be false, and injurious to a public interest. From the beginning of the judgement, she emphasised the 'not inconsiderable epistemological and factual problems [which] are left for resolution by the jury under the rubric of 'fact'' (p. 257). These problems were not the standard fare for jurors. They turned on whether the statements were allegations of fact as distinct from opinion, the meanings of the statements, whether the statements were false, and whether the accused knew them to be false. These were to be decided by a jury. Therefore, it was possible that inconsistency with conventional accounts of history might become the actual test of falsehood and the test for determining whether the accused knew that the statements were false (p. 272). Finally, the majority community might give a wide variety of interpretations to the public interest (p. 273). In conclusion:

> Its danger, however lies in the fact that by its broad reach it criminalises a vast penumbra of other statements merely because they might be thought to constitute a mischief to some public interest, however successive prosecutors and courts may wish to define those terms. The danger is magnified because the prohibition affects not only those caught and prosecuted, but those who may refrain from saying what they would like to because of the fear that they will be caught. (p. 274)

Dissenting Opinion

Cory and Iacobucci JJ. issued a lengthy dissent, with which Gonthier J. agreed.

The dissenters considered the history of s. 181, which began with the Statute of Westminster, 1275, 3 Edward 1 c. 34 (pp. 217 - 223). The section had been invoked only rarely. In 1907 an American who implied that US citizens were not welcome in Canada, was prosecuted.[64] In *R. v. Carrier*, the accused had protested the maltreatment of Jehovah's Witnesses.[65] In *R. v. Kirby*, a political satirist was acquitted.[66]

The dissenters determined, without any difficulty, that s. 2(b) covered the statements at issue, even though on the 'extreme periphery' of the right (p. 224). Could the limitation be saved by section one?

First, the dissenters dealt with the void for vagueness argument. They noted that indefinite words such as 'undue', 'deceit', 'indecent', 'immoral', 'scurrilous', were common in legislation, and that it was the judicial role to give a more precise meaning to such words (pp. 225 - 226). Indeed the term 'public interest' was regularly used in statutes (p. 226; they do not mention whether those statutes all involve limitations on a fundamental freedom). The courts had to interpret the provision, having an eye on Charter principles. They continued:

> A 'public interest' likely to be harmed as a result of contravention of s. 181 is the public interest in a free and democratic society that is subject to the rule of law. A free society is one built upon

reasoned debate in which all its members are entitled to participate.
... A democratic society capable of giving effect to the Charter's
guarantees is one which strives toward creating a community
committed to equality, liberty and human dignity. (p. 226)

One had to consider ss. 7, 15, 27 when deciding upon a public interest.
The deliberate publication of lies which denied s. 15's right to equality
'tears at the very fabric of Canadian society' (p. 227). Section 181 only
caught deliberate fabrication which harmed Charter values. Accordingly,
it was not too vague.

The protection of the groups designated in s. 15 was a pressing
and substantial objective. *Keegstra* was authority for the claim that
minority groups can suffer from statements directed against them (p.
227).[67] They listed the harms flowing from Holocaust denial: it made 'the
concept of multi-culturalism in a true democracy impossible to attain'; it
offended Canadians who suffered at the hands of the Nazi regime; it
denied the reality of the tragedy which the victims of the Holocaust
experienced (p. 228). They noted also that Jewish people had often been
the victims of false stories and incitement to hatred. According to the
dissenters, s. 181 expressed the 'repugnance of Canadian society' at the
publication of racist lies. They commented that the Charter should not be
used to strike down legislation protecting a minority (p. 229).[68]

The pressing importance of this aim was confirmed by
international law, comparative law and the Charter. The dissenters cited
the International Covenant on Civil and Political Rights Art. 20(2), Art.
27; the Convention on the Elimination of All Forms of Racial
Discrimination, preamble, Art. 4; article 656 of the Italian Criminal Code;
s. 140 and s. 266(b) of the Danish Criminal Code; articles 130, 131, 185,
194(1) of the German Criminal Code; and ss. 15, 27 of the Charter (p. 230
- 236). They commented, relating to s. 15:

Democratic pluralism assumes that members of society will not
simply organize around single interests of race, class or gender but
will explore and discern their commonalities, coming together
around certain issues and diverging on others in constantly
changing configurations. Deliberate lies which deny these
commonalities divide groups which might otherwise organize
around mutual interests, and instead forge loyalties based on
artificial and reified racial identifications that do not permit society
to perceive and pursue its various goals. ... By prohibiting

calculated falsehoods which undermine the equality of target group members, s. 181 enhances the goal of s. 15 of the Charter. (p. 232 - 233)

Cory and Iacobucci JJ. emphasised the role of s. 27 of the Charter, which seeks to assure everyone the right to dignity, the right to be proud of one's background, ethnicity or other status (p. 235).

The dissenters argued that the purpose assigned to s. 181 was a 'permissible shift in emphasis' (p. 236). The section was intended to protect persons from abuse, and the contemporary reading was no greater a change than that in the pornography case of *Butler*.

The dissenters then moved to the proportionality wing of the *Oakes* test. They argued that the expression at issue did not merit the strict protection of the *Oakes* test (p. 242). Free speech values required the proscription of lies which stir up racial hatred (p. 239). They noted that liberals insist:

> ... that the state does not exist to designate and impose a single vision of the good life but to provide a forum in which opposing interests can engage in peaceful and reasoned struggle to articulate social and individual projects. (p. 239 - 40)

They explained that expression was protected as it was:

> ... an essential feature of humanity to reason and to choose and in order to allow our knowledge and our vision of the good to evolve. (p. 240)

They accepted these principles and the need to protect expression, but:

> .. where there is no possibility that speech may be true because even its source has knowledge of its falsity, the arguments against state intervention weaken. When such false speech can be positively demonstrated to undermine democratic values, these arguments fade into oblivion. (p. 240)

The dissenters made a telling point about free speech, that minorities tend more often to be the victims of virulent propaganda, rather than its propagators. In a free marketplace of ideas, minorities might be left with nothing, crowded out by the rampant appeal to base consumerism of racial hatred (pp. 240 - 241). Again, they rely on *Keegstra*. They noted that, as in *Keegstra*, the statements at issue were not core issues of free expression (p. 241). These deliberate lies inhibited the search for truth.[69] Furthermore,

> Self-fulfilment and human flourishing can never be achieved by the publication of statements known to be false. (p. 242)

Concerning the third value of free expression, democratic values could only be undermined by the spreading of anti-egalitarian hatred.

The legislation was rationally related to the objective. Parliament was trying to make equality 'not merely a slogan but a manifest reality' (p. 243).

Now turn to the minimal impairment test. The dissenters argued that s. 181 was narrow in its import. It only restricted the 'right to lie' when one deliberately lied in public, harming (or likely to harm) a public (Charter) interest (p. 245). This deserved no more consideration than fraud, forgery, perjury, or libel.

The dissenters rejected the argument that statements of fact could not be distinguished from statements of opinion. The difference was in the criteria of specificity of terms, verifiability (or falsifiability), linguistic and social context (pp. 245 - 246). The distinction of opinion from fact, and of truth from falsity, were ones which every jury in a defamation case had to make. The dissenters rejected the assertion that all history is interpretation:

> However, the appellant seeks to draw complex epistemological theory to the defence of what is really only, at best, the shoddiest of 'scholarship' and, at worst pure charlatanism. (p. 247)

Bluntly, 'racism with footnotes and chapter headings' was still racism (p. 250).[70] The accused's pamphlets did not resemble the work done by minority history scholars:

> ... the appellant has not adopted a novel perspective, unearthed non-traditional sources or re-interpreted traditional materials. He has lied. (p. 248)

Analysis

To recapitulate: judges rely on political moral arguments to provide links in the chain of legal reasoning. Judicial reasoning is not full and transparent unless these links are brought to the foreground, explained and justified.

I start with the judgement of McLachlin J. One of the more striking elements of her decision was the emphasis on the 'not inconsiderable epistemological and factual problems' engendered by this type of case. Remember that here we are talking about the documented Holocaust of the Jews in German occupied Europe. The evidence about it is overwhelming. Yet she continually emphasised these difficulties. She noted that there were problems in deciding the meaning of a particular communication, and problems in knowing whether the communication transmitted falsehoods. She identified a range of meanings possible in interpreting the plaintiff's pamphlet, invoking the interactive nature of communication to justify her position. I do not see why the difficulties involved in such a case are more acute than in the other cases where meaning must be decided, from statutory interpretation to libel cases.

She also stressed the difficulty of deciding whether the allegations were true or false. Again it must be said that what is at issue is the well-documented historical phenomenon known as the Holocaust. Again I fail to see why the issue is necessarily any more difficult than in countless cases which come before the courts. Any difficulties as to determining the truth would, because of the standard of proof in criminal cases, be to the accused's benefit. Despite all these objections, McLachlin J.'s insistence on indeterminacy and scepticism, was an important aspect of her judgement.

Now these sceptical beliefs are a core part of one unusual version of liberal theory. It may be called the sceptical argument for neutrality, or tolerance. At its simplest, it runs as follows: to justify using coercion to control expression, one must be sure to have a weighty reason, i.e. that the expression is false. However, if it is impossible to determine exactly what is meant by a particular piece of expression, and if it is impossible to determine whether it is true, then it makes no sense to persecute it. One of the most famous exponents of this view was Bertrand Russell, who explained that scepticism deterred people from action with grave consequences. It makes no sense to kill someone because you believe he or she has violated the will of God, if it is impossible to know the will of God, or even if there is a God.[71]

McLachlin J. was also sceptical of jury trials, and standards of 'truth' and 'public interest'. Again these phrases posed difficulties of knowing the meaning and truth of such standards. She believed that this left open the possibility for a jury (or judge or prosecutor) to smuggle in majoritarian standards, and thus use s. 181 to oppress a minority.

This suspicious approach assumes that persons cannot be relied upon to act impartially. They have interests of their own, interests which they may be inclined to further, if given any opportunity. One opportunity is available to the majority in a community when it is applying vague standards such as 'public interest'. Accordingly, in at least some cases, the courts must insist that the legislature limit discretion by defining words precisely. They must do that in cases where the limitation of rights is at issue. This vision is based on a very cynical and suspicious view of human nature and human government. Neither private persons (sitting as jurors) nor state officials can be trusted to act with impartiality; they must be constrained by extremely precise statutory provisions. This belief is nowhere required in the text of the Charter. Whilst it is true that s. 1 says that limits must be 'prescribed by law' this does not, of itself mean that all aspects of such limits must be defined with sufficient precision as to eliminate discretion, and so prevent abuse.

McLachlin J. objected to the assignation of a particular purpose by the dissenters to the statute. She insisted that the purpose which is alleged to be legitimate under s. 1, must have been present at the time of enactment. The courts of today cannot simply assign a purpose to an otherwise vague statute, if that purpose would not have occurred to the legislators who enacted it. There is nothing in the Charter itself which requires that the legislator consciously have a particular purpose. Why insist on it when a reasonable, specific purpose can be assigned to it? The purpose of a legislative provision will often determine its meaning, its concrete effect. Whoever decides upon its purpose decides its effect. This suggests a particular attachment to democratic legitimacy, that it is for the democratically elected Parliament to decide upon legislative purpose, and no other.

There are other problems. First, there are well-known difficulties involved in the investigation of legislative intent, difficulties of both interpretation and legitimacy, which make her approach suspect. Indeed, in Charter jurisprudence such a history oriented approach is usually rejected, as McLachlin J. herself does in this case. Second, she does not adequately explain the difference between *Zundel,* and *Butler*, where an old obscenity statute is assigned a modern egalitarian purpose. If that could be done in *Butler*, then why not here? Third, McLachlin J.'s approach seems inconsistent with her own emphasis on the interactive nature of meaning.

To summarise McLachlin J.'s position: we cannot know for certain the meaning or truth of all statements. Therefore they must be given, in principle protection under s. 2(b). However, the wording of s. 1 makes it clear that some exceptions are justified. To be justified, a restriction must be for a specific purpose, and must be specified with sufficient precision to avoid discretion and overbreadth. In a democracy, the democratically accountable assembly must decide upon the purpose and scope of a legislative provision. It must respect minorities by limiting the discretion in a statute restricting freedom of expression. Allowing non-legislative bodies to determine the 'public interest' is a failure of the democratic process.

The reasoning of McLachlin J.'s opinion is different in *Keegstra* and *Zundel*. In both cases, she votes to strike down legislation inhibiting free expression. In both cases, she emphasises problems of indeterminacy and vagueness. However in *Keegstra*, her opinion seemed to be that in a liberal state all messages were equally entitled to protection and could only be restricted for the most limited of reasons and by the most precise of statutes. Vagueness is important only because it is a threat to this liberal position. In *Zundel* she adopts a view which defends obnoxious speech not on the (implied) ground of equal respect, but rather on the sceptical ground of indeterminacy. Perhaps she believed that such a shift of emphasis was necessary to accommodate the two decisions.

I do not believe that she succeeds, or that a sceptical defence of liberalism is an acceptable one. The scepticism she advocates is an epistemological and not a moral one, but the opinion may nevertheless excessively rely on it. Her opinion is riddled with outrageous statements and contradictions. Her quotations from Holmes J. imply a similarity between the peddling of pro-Nazi lies and the espousal of pacifist, anarchist or Marxist philosophy. She claims that questions of fact and opinion, truth and falsity are too difficult for juries to resolve, even though juries do so all the time in defamation cases, where the evidence is usually not so overwhelming. She regards the meaning of a statute's enactors as prevailing, but rejects such historical interpretations of the Charter. Her cynical and suspicious attitude towards government is totally out of line with the bulk of Canadian jurisprudence. She says that it is very difficult to determine the meaning of the defendant's publications, but seems to have no difficulty in determining the meaning of statutes and the Charter. She invokes the contextual approach to Charter cases, but in words only; her analysis completely ignores the social context of the harms of holocaust denial.

The dissenting opinion also rested on beliefs of political morality, which resemble the majority arguments in *Keegstra*. Indeed, strengthened by the majority opinion in *Keegstra*, the dissenters here argued for a more explicit concept of liberal perfectionism, democratic pluralism.

They defended the legitimacy of judicial interpretation of vague provisions such as 'undue', 'scurrilous' and so on. The legislature need not give exact definitions. Rather it can allow the judges to give full effect to Charter values by interpreting such provisions. Those values are of such importance as to outweigh normal considerations of legal certainty.

What value was at stake? The dissenters identified the goal of the Charter as the creation of a 'community committed to equality, liberty and human dignity'. They noted that Holocaust denial offends survivors of the Hitlerite regime and was part of a racist programme. Such lies promoted factionalism, and prevented pluralist societies developing. There could be no protection for deliberate falsehood which undermined pluralism, democracy and genuine self-fulfilment.

Now this view is the liberal perfectionist vision. It is the vision of liberalism argued for by such as Joseph Raz and Philip Macedo often in opposition to those supporting a liberalism as neutrality thesis. Often the dissenting opinion closely echoes the writings of Raz.

For both the judicial and academic writers, the liberal state is dedicated to the goal of democratic pluralism, which fosters respect for the equal dignity of all. Accordingly, the state must respect diversity of opinion, as must the state in a liberal neutrality thesis. Both states may, perhaps, promote diversity and mutual respect. However, the perfectionist liberal state may go further. It values 'democratic pluralism' the process by which groups both recognise and respect their differences, but also recognise and seek out their commonalties on various topics, forming and sundering coalitions in a never ending process of political self-government. The perfectionist liberal state may limit the expression of opinion which threatens to undermine the democratic pluralist vision, because it may persuade other people of the flaws of democratic pluralism, and the values of its antithesis.

Perfectionist liberalism looks to the end, democratic pluralism; it seeks to make equality a 'manifest reality'. Liberalism as neutrality, whilst perhaps embracing the goal of equality, looks always to the means first, and restriction of expression is not an acceptable means, except in rare cases. Whilst one can certainly find support in different provisions of the Charter for some liberal vision, it is not clear whether the state may restrict the opinion of those who object to the liberal basis of the state (or even go further and perpetrate the Holocaust denial lie). It is not clear from the Charter that the state may express 'repugnance' at the expression of certain, racist, views. If Cory, Iacobucci, Gonthier JJ. opt for the perfectionist theory, it is not because of textual evidence requiring it. There are reasons favouring a liberal perfectionist reading of the Charter: it is the reading endorsed by *Keegstra*; it is the reading the Parliament apparently accepts; and to some it appears to be a more adequate theory of liberalism than the neutrality thesis.

This perfectionist approach is particularly evident when the dissenters explain that this form of expression falls outside the core area of free expression. The accused was making comments on a historical phenomenon, to further a particular political goal to which he was strongly attached. Such expression is deeply repugnant, but one cannot say that it is unrelated to the values of free expression, (participation, truth, self-fulfilment), without forsaking the principle of content neutrality endorsed in an s. 2(b) analysis. To argue that the *Oakes* test is reduced when a non-core example of expression is involved, is to covertly modify the content neutrality standard. In saying that participation, truth and self-fulfilment are of such a nature as that Holocaust denial is not promoted by them, is to adopt a particular version of each and of free expression. People must not use their rights to attack truth, pluralistic democratic participation, and self-fulfilment. This is especially clear regarding the blunt assertion that what is at issue is not genuine self-fulfilment. The dissenters deny the legitimacy of the accused's beliefs, and then restrict his expression on that ground. That is liberal perfectionism.

Prostitution: Self-Expression or Slavery?

The legal problems associated with the sale of sexual favours poses difficult choices for legislators, since the root issue of the character of prostitution is unsettled. To some it is a harmless, almost private activity; to others, simply business. It can be seen as a moral plague, or as a public health threat. Or:

> The various expressions of this [male] dominance include a concept of women as property and the belief that the sexual needs of men are the only sexual desires to be given serious consideration. Prostitution is a symptom of the victimisation and subordination of women ....[72]

Given the ambivalent nature of attitudes to prostitution it is no surprise that the legal response is often a compromise.

In Canada, the regulation of prostitution is for the federal Parliament.[73] Prostitution itself is legal, but most of the activities associated with it are illegal. Sections 193 and 195.1(c) of the Criminal Code prohibit the keeping of a brothel ('common bawdy house'), and the communication or attempt to communicate in a public place for the purposes of engaging a prostitute or offering services as a prostitute. The Lieutenant Governor in Council of Manitoba referred the issue of the validity of these sections to the Court of Appeal.

The Court of Appeal upheld the measures.[74] The Court believed that the Charter did not protect public solicitation for the purposes of prostitution, as it was not the expression of an idea or information concerning an idea. From this decision, there was an appeal to the Supreme Court of Canada.

Opinions in favour of validity

Dickson C.J.C., Lamer, Wilson, La Forest, L'Heureux-Dubé and Sopinka JJ heard the case.[75] Dickson C.J.C. wrote the plurality opinion, with La

Forest and Sopinka JJ. concurring. Lamer J. delivered a concurring opinion. Wilson and L'Heureux-Dubé JJ. dissented.

The Chief Justice agreed with Wilson J. that s. 195.1(c) (prohibition on communication) violated s. 2(b), but that the prohibition on brothels did not (p. 1134). Therefore, s. 195.1(c) had to be justified under s. 1 of the Charter.

The Chief Justice believed that the purpose of the section was to indicate that public solicitation for prostitution was intolerable. He found that this purpose, which protected the 'concerns of home-owners, businesses, and the residents' by preventing overcrowding, harassment and 'general detrimental effects' was a legitimate aim (p. 1135).

Dickson C.J.C. thought that the restriction was rationally related to the aim. Did the measure impair as little as possible the right guaranteed by the Charter? He noted that the section directly interfered with a right of fundamental importance. He continued, however:

> It can hardly be said that communications regarding an economic transaction of sex for money lie at, or even near, the core of the guarantee of freedom of expression. (p. 1136)

He gave no reason for this comment.

He dismissed the argument that the provision was not closely tailored to deal with incidents where congestion was likely to occur. Parliament could legislate for the particular instance to prevent the cumulative harm (p. 1136). Furthermore the ban on all communication aimed at solicitation was not too broad, because courts could be relied upon to recognise which forms of activity constituted a communication to sell or buy sex. He believed that if the measure was aimed simply at nuisance, then it would indeed be too broad, but since it was aimed at suppressing the 'visible solicitation' of sex, the measure was proportionate (p. 1137). Given the history of difficulties in dealing with prostitution, the court would not demand a 'perfect' solution, but only one that was appropriate and carefully tailored (p. 1138). Finally the benefits conferred by the measure were not outweighed by the effects on the targets of the measure (p. 1139). Section 195.1(c) passed s. 1 scrutiny.

Lamer J. concurred. He noted that s. 2(b) protected most expressive activity (p. 1185). Section 195.1(c) had as its purpose the restriction of expression (p. 1188). The measure was content specific, and no mere regulation of time, place or manner.

Did the measure satisfy s. 1? According to Lamer J. s. 195.1(c) had the purpose of eliminating the evils associated with prostitution. Prostitution was connected with other criminal behaviour and was 'a form of slavery' (p. 1193). Lamer J. thought the section aimed at removing the sight of degrading, anti-woman activity and drug-related prostitution from the streets, and preventing such nuisances as the harassment of passers-by (p. 1194). These purposes were pressing and substantial.

The section was rationally linked to the purpose. He rejected the argument that punishing individual acts was illogical since one was aiming at cumulative harm (i.e. the gathering of prostitutes). Prohibiting even individual acts was one way to prevent the cumulative harm. As for the minimal impairment requirement, Lamer J. considered that courts must not 'second guess the wisdom of policy choices' (p. 1199). The limitation chosen by Parliament after consideration, was only a partial one, was limited as to place (public forum) and content (messages offering to buy or sell sex) (p. 1197). The measure was not overly intrusive. In conclusion, there was proportionality as regards the benefits of the law compared with the minimal infringement of a right (p. 1200).

Dissenting Opinion

Wilson and L'Heureux-Dubé JJ. dissented, with Wilson J. giving the opinion. The measure was an indirect attempt to control prostitution. Section 195.1(c) did not require proof of a causal link between the expressive act and the resultant harm (p. 1206). Given the wide interpretation of s. 2(b) the measure violated the Charter, which protected commercial communication whether it concerned the sale of sex or the sale of art (p. 1206). So the measure had to be justified under section 1.

Wilson J. identified three possible purposes of the section: the maintenance of unobstructed streets, the prevention of specific harms associated with public solicitation (including trespass, traffic congestion, reduced property values, noise, harassment of women, etc.), and finally the prevention of a wide range of harms associated with prostitution (including violence, drugs, crime, child prostitution) (pp. 1207 - 1209). Although Wilson J. agreed with Lamer J. that prostitution lacked social value, she did not assign this third objective to the statute (p. 1210). The purpose was the second one, the elimination of the 'social nuisance' associated with street solicitation (p. 1211), which included causing offence to other people. The prevention of this nuisance was a legitimate aim. Furthermore, the measure was rationally related to this aim.

Was the measure proportional? The section captured solicitation in any place to where the public had access as of right or by invitation (p. 1214). This definition covered many places where there would be no danger of overcrowding or causing offence. According to Wilson J. the State could not prohibit all communication of a certain type simply because sometime, somewhere, it might cause harm. Furthermore, the section covered any type of communication, no matter how unobtrusive or even silent (Wilson J. suggested that someone hailing a taxi might be arrested under the section). There was no requirement that the expressive act punished be one which had caused or was likely to cause harm. This made the section particularly unreasonable given that prostitution itself was legal (p. 1215). In conclusion, s. 195.1(c) violated s. 1 of the Charter.

Analysis

The judgements in this case again display commitments to different political moralities. Consider the decision of the Chief Justice. He said that the measure was a proportionate response to the problems of public solicitation. He attached marginal importance to expression concerning prostitution. This lack of value is crucial in permitting a less than rigorous analysis of the proportionality wing of the *Oakes* test. If he had judged the expressive activity to be more important, then the proportionality test would have had more bite. However, he did not explain why such expression had lesser value, (leaving aside the implied reference to commercial expression). Was it because prostitution was a harmful activity, or because it was distasteful? Dickson C.J.C. failed to address this issue, unlike Lamer and Wilson JJ. both of whom affirmed that prostitution is a social phenomenon with many evils attached to it, including the enslavement of women.

The legitimate purposes identified by the Chief Justice included the prevention of harassment, over-crowding and the expression of the unacceptability of public solicitation. These harms were not as serious as those specified by Lamer J. Indeed the third purpose suggested that public solicitation was seen as 'distasteful', which was not so serious as seeing it as part of a social evil. Furthermore, most of those purposes could be achieved by measures which did not deal *only with solicitation for the purposes of prostitution*. He suggested that the visible solicitation of sex, unlike mere nuisance, justified the otherwise excessive nature of the measure.

Dickson C.J.C.'s opinion is perhaps the most conservative in this chapter. He accepted a lax application of the proportionality test because (apparently) of the nature of prostitution. This can only be explained by a perfectionist belief that prostitution is not a worthy way of life and people are entitled to insist that it not be publicly apparent anywhere. Given the unlimited nature of the prohibition regarding place and manner, only a perfectionist explanation is possible. (A liberal neutralist might argue for regulation, but never a ban.)[76]

Lamer J. identified a very serious purpose behind s. 195.1(c): the elimination of various harms associated with prostitution, including drug abuse, crime and the degradation of women. Certainly, such serious harms would justify restrictions even for a believer in liberalism as neutrality. However Lamer J. ignored two points. First, the causal link between prostitution and these evils was not proved. Was it not possible that the association was simply the product of prejudice? It is remarkable that Lamer J. cited the fact that the sections target specific content of expression as a factor favouring their validity. Normally content specific regulations heighten suspicions of constitutional infirmity! This should particularly be the case where the content concerns matters condemned traditionally by 'general' 'non-fundamental' conventional morality.[77] Second, the legislative response did not punish prostitution itself, merely the public solicitation of it. Does it not seem then that the purpose of the legislation was not to eliminate the evils of prostitution, but *rather to prevent the display of something that was publicly unacceptable?*

Furthermore, the scope of the legislation covered much expression that might not cause the harms, or even public outrage at the sight of solicitation. Its sheer scope suggested some perfectionist or communitarian condemnation of pornography. Lamer J.'s suggestion that the measure was limited in scope is not credible. Would we consider that a provision prohibiting people from communicating to others about membership in a political party, in any public place, or place to which the public had access, even if only by implied invitation, to be a *limited* measure?

Wilson J. is more consistent in her expression of liberal beliefs. Whilst agreeing that there are harms associated with prostitution and solicitation with which the legislature may deal, Wilson J. insisted that the means be legitimate. She did not allow her assessment of the value of prostitution to dilute the stringency of the *Oakes* test. She did not say that the activity was distasteful to the public and so could be suppressed (communitarianism), or that it had no value because no self-respecting person would engage in it (perfectionism). She did not judge its value, but only the proportionality of the measure to the ends desired. She concluded that the measures used were excessive. The prohibition was not closely tailored to the specific circumstances in which harm could ensue, but covered all possible cases of public solicitation. Indeed, this suggested that the main purpose was to prevent the public display of something offensive to conventional morality, which would not be a legitimate purpose. However, none of the judges suggested this.

Obscenity: Erotica or Incitement to Rape?

Mention of obscenity laws used to provoke certain images: the heavy handed banning of Joyce, Lawrence, and Steinbeck. Obscenity was a call to arms for liberals and feminists, often in self-defence. Now however obscenity laws allegedly have a different purpose. Pornography is perceived by many as a threat to gender equality, a multi-billion pound industry which commercialises the bodies of women.[78] What is at issue is the deliberate dehumanisation of women:

> They [women] are exploited, portrayed as desiring pleasure from pain, by being humiliated and treated only as an object of male domination sexually, or in cruel and violent bondage. Women are portrayed in these films as pining away their lives waiting for a huge male penis to come along, ... supposedly to transport them to complete sexual ecstasy. Or even more false and degrading one is led to believe ... that they secretly desire to be forcefully taken by a male.[79]

It is a problem which has split old alliances, with feminists joining with conservative movements, and liberals berating feminists for failing to respect justice. The Supreme Court of Canada has dealt with this issue in several cases, most notably *R. v. Butler*.[80]

Butler

The accused was charged under s. 163 of the criminal code, which punishes obscenity.[81] Obscenity is defined as covering 'any publication a dominant characteristic of which is the undue exploitation of sex, or of sex and any one or more of the following subjects, namely, crime, horror, cruelty and violence'. Section 163 was the most recent in a line of provisions criminalising obscenity.

The accused operated a shop where he sold hard core videos, magazines and sexual materials. The store had signs at the entrance which indicated its nature and advised non-members, persons offended by sexual materials and persons under 18 not to enter.

The trial took place before Wright J.[82] He considered the submission that s. 163 was invalid. Applying *Irwin Toy*, he found that s. 2(b) covered the materials in question. He then addressed section one. He stated that only a specific, as opposed to a general purpose, could be invoked under s. 1. Sex scenes involving violence, cruelty, lack of consent, or other dehumanising treatment could be proscribed, but nothing else. Accordingly sexual devices and the portrayal of scenes involving masturbation, group sex, homosexuality and incest could not be banned under the Charter. Rather than striking down s. 163 because of its overbroad nature, Wright J. simply refused to convict in respect of the second category of materials, and convicted only on the basis of the first category. The Crown appealed the 242 acquittals, and the accused appealed the eight convictions.

The Manitoba Court of Appeal criticised the trial judge.[83] Husband J.A., speaking for the majority, held that the materials did not fall within the scope of s. 2(b) of the Charter. They were 'purely physical' activity, and hence not expression. The majority also held that the *form* of expression was not protected by s. 2(b), as it involved undue exploitation. The majority accepted the Crown's appeal, but dismissed the accused's.

Two judges dissented. Twaddle J. held that the prohibition on the undue exploitation of sex was invalid as its purpose, the maintenance of moral standards, was illegitimate. However, the prohibition on sex coupled with violence and so on, was valid, as it was directed to the prevention of harm. He rejected both appeals. Helper J.A. held that the aim of s. 163, the maintenance of morality in the sense of respect for the dignity of all human beings, was legitimate. However, she found the measure excessively vague: Parliament had effectively 'abdicated' its responsibility to provide standards.

Majority Opinion

The appeal reached the Supreme Court of Canada.[84] Sopinka J. delivered the majority opinion, with Lamer C.J.C., La Forest, Cory, McLachlin, Stevenson and Iacobucci JJ. concurring. Gonthier J. delivered a minority judgement, generally agreeing with Sopinka J. L'Heureux-Dubé J. agreed with Gonthier J.

Sopinka J. charted the history of s. 163. The purpose of the original law was the protection of morals.[85] Recent cases had changed the nature of obscenity law.[86] Sopinka J. explained that the courts developed a number of tests to provide an objective standard under s. 163. These tests were those of community standards, degradation, and 'internal necessities'.

The community standards test rested on a principle stated in the New Zealand case *R. v. Close*:

> There does exist in any community at all times - however the standard may vary from time to time - a general instinctive sense of what is decent and what is indecent, of what is clean and what is dirty ....[87]

This standard was to be determined by a jury. The cases made it clear that the standard was that of the entire community, not just a segment of it (p. 464). The standard was one of 'tolerance, not taste', i.e. the finder of fact must determine what Canadians, as a nation, would tolerate others watching, not what they themselves would wish to see.[88]

The second standard was that of dehumanisation or degradation (p. 466). Sexually explicit materials which degrade and dehumanise the participants were banned because they injured social values, and were a threat to women. According to Sopinka J.:

> It would be reasonable to conclude that there is an appreciable risk
> of harm to society in the portrayal of such material. (p. 467)

Material may fail this test even though Canadian society would tolerate it.

Finally, material would not be considered obscene if 'required for the serious treatment of a theme', especially an artistic theme (p. 469). This was the 'internal necessities' exception.

Sopinka J. then summarised the tests. Pornography could be divided into three categories, sex with violence, sex coupled with degradation or dehumanisation, sex without violence, degradation or dehumanisation (p. 470). The first category was most likely to involve harm to society, the last was the least likely. How to decide when society was harmed?

> Because this is not a matter that is susceptible of proof in the
> traditional way and because we do not wish to leave it to the
> individual tastes of judges, we must have a norm that will serve as
> an arbiter in determining what amounts to an undue exploitation of
> sex. That arbiter is the community as a whole. (p. 470)

What was harm?

> Harm in this context, means that it predisposes persons to act in an
> antisocial manner as, for example, the physical or mental
> mistreatment of women by men .... Antisocial conduct for this
> purpose is conduct which society formally recognises as
> incompatible with its proper functioning. (pp. 470 - 1)

Sopinka J. noted that the first category of pornography will usually be caught by this test, the second would be if the risk was substantial, and the third would rarely be caught, unless it involved child pornography (p. 471).

If material is obscene, the court must then decide whether, in its context, it would be tolerated by the community as being essential to an artistic work (p. 471).

Sopinka J. then considered whether s. 163 infringed s. 2(b) of the Charter. He criticised the Court of Appeal majority. 'Physical' activity would not be covered by s. 2(b) only if there was no expressive content. Physical activity might well have an expressive purpose; the argument that films are inherently less expressive than books was rejected (p. 474).

These materials did have expressive content (p. 472). Second, the Court of Appeal misunderstood the idea of 'form' of a communication. 'Form' referred only to the medium of communication, about which there is nothing violent (p. 473). Section 163 sought to restrict expression; it had to pass section one scrutiny.

Sopinka J. considered the vagueness argument. He recognised that many imprecise terms form a part of the law, out of necessity (p. 475). Judges had to provide an 'intelligible standard' by which to use them, and the case law on obscenity had provided such a standard.

Was the legislative objective of sufficient importance to satisfy s. 1? Could expression be limited on the basis of morality? Sopinka J. identified two categories of morality. The traditional notion of 'legal moralism' involved the state enforcing a particular conception of the good life. This was the original purpose of obscenity law, and it was now an illegitimate purpose:

> To impose a certain standard of public and sexual morality, solely because it reflects the conventions of a given community, is inimical to the exercise and enjoyment of individual freedoms, which form the basis of our social contract. (p. 476)

However, that does not conclude the matter for Parliament had:

> ... the right to legislate on the basis of some fundamental conception of morality for the purposes of safeguarding the values which are integral to a free and democratic society. (p. 476)

So the expression of such 'moral disapprobation' was valid.[89]

Despite this, Sopinka J. identified the main aim of s. 163 to be the prevention of harm, not the banning of expression inconsistent with a 'fundamental conception of morality' (p. 477). Pornography reinforced stereotypes and normalised hierarchy (p. 477). Sopinka J. rejected the argument that this involved altering the purpose of s. 163, for two reasons. First, the prevention of moral corruption, which was an aim of the legislature, and the prevention of harm, were related (p. 477). Secondly, there was evidence that Parliament believed that pornography harmed its consumers, and therefore harmed society. Its aim was 'the protection of society from harms caused by the exposure to obscene materials' (p. 478). This aim was legitimate.

Was the measure proportional? Sopinka J. noted that the expression at issue was the least valued kind, sexual exploitation for money (pp. 481 - 482).[90] The measure was rationally connected to the legitimate objective. As in *Keegstra*,[91] and *Irwin Toy*,[92] the State must be allowed a margin of appreciation when the evidence is inconclusive; there was no need for rigorous demonstration of a link (p. 483).[93] He concluded:

> ... there is a sufficiently rational link between the criminal sanction, which demonstrates our community's disapproval of the dissemination of materials which potentially victimize women and which restricts the negative influence which such materials have on changes in attitudes and objectives, and the behaviour. (p. 484)

He then considered the minimal impairment part of the *Oakes* test. He thought that s. 163 would probably only catch portrayals of sex with violence, or degrading treatment, i.e. scenes which Parliament could reasonably believe to harm society. Furthermore, materials which raised even a reasonable doubt about whether they had scientific, artistic or literary value were not banned (p. 485). Third, s. 163 was the culmination of efforts by Parliament to define obscenity precisely; no greater precision was possible (p. 485). Fourthly, private viewing was not covered (p. 486). Finally, although other methods to combat violence against women were available, none of them discharged the role of s. 163 in banning the publications which lead to violence (p. 487).

In conclusion, this expression, of minimal value, could be suppressed by Parliament to protect society from harm. Sopinka J. ordered a new trial.

Concurring Opinion

Gonthier J. delivered an opinion in which he generally agreed with Sopinka J. Gonthier J. identified the harm at which s. 163 is directed:

> Obscene materials ... convey a distorted image of human sexuality, by making public and open elements of the human nature which are usually hidden behind a veil of modesty and privacy. (p. 490)

Obscenity transformed sexuality into 'animality' (p. 490). Such images might influence the conduct of others, causing harm to others.[94]

Concerning the three part division of pornography suggested by Sopinka J., Gonthier J. commented that depictions falling into the third category - sex without violence or degradation - might still be adjudged obscene:

> The manner of representation, of public suggestion, can greatly contribute to the deformation of sexuality, through the loss of its humanity. (p. 493)

The manner of representation might make something obscene; sex in a book was different from sex on a billboard (p. 494).

Gonthier J. observed about 'tolerance':

> It seems that tolerance is for taste the conceptual equivalent of the reasonable person to the actual plaintiff; an abstraction, an average perhaps. Tolerance would be some form of enlightened, altruistic taste, which would factor in and sum up the tastes of the whole population. (p. 495)

Gonthier J. believed that 'morality' was a basis for the restriction of rights,[95] but he distinguished between two conceptions of morality - 'general' and 'fundamental' (pp. 497 - 498).[96] The state could legislate on the basis of the latter, not the former. The fundamental conception of morality was distinguished from the former by two traits. First, it was grounded:

> [It] must involve concrete problems such as life, harm, well-being to name a few, and not merely differences of opinion or of taste. (p. 498)

Second, it had to be supported by a wide consensus among society:

> In a pluralistic society such as ours, many different conceptions of the good are held by various segments of the population. The guarantees of s. 2 of the Charter protect this pluralistic diversity. However, if the holders of these different conceptions agree that some conduct is not good, then the respect for pluralism that

underlies s. 2 of the Charter becomes less insurmountable an objection to state action 97

He then claimed that most people would regard the changes in behaviour and attitudes, and the harm caused by pornography, as evils to be combated.

Analysis

What role is played by political moral argument in this case? Sopinka J. held that all expression fell under the scope of s. 2(b) of the Charter. Accordingly, s. 163 must be justified under s. 1. He identified three possible purposes for which the section might have been enacted: the maintenance of moral standards, the protection of a fundamental conception of morality, and the prevention of harm to others. The difference between 'general' and 'fundamental' morality was not clearly indicated. It could refer to the difference between a conventional and a critical theory of morality. Alternatively, it could refer to the difference between a teleological and a deontological theory of morality. I think Sopinka J. had the former division in mind.

He rejected the 'general' morality purpose. The commonly accepted *mores* of society cannot be the sole basis for the restriction of expression. Sopinka J. therefore rejected any communitarian or conservative interpretation of the Charter. However, Sopinka J. accepted that the state could express 'moral disapprobation' of certain ideas, to safeguard certain values in a democratic society. In general, this would not indicate whether he supported a state which embraced liberal neutrality or liberal perfectionism. However, in this case he supports the restriction of a fundamental freedom, thus making it clear that some sort of perfectionist values animated his approach. His opinion echoes Raz's writing in the *Morality of Freedom*, stressing that states must act on moral principles (p. 157), and may do so, so that people may not use rights to do wrongs (p. 380).

Sopinka J. then stated that the main purpose of the legislation was the prevention of harm to society. Either version of liberalism could accept such a restriction based on such an aim, provided the evidence of harm was sufficiently compelling. However, Sopinka J. waived the requirement for a strict proof, as the evidence was inconclusive.

Accordingly, Parliament must be left an area of discretion to decide whether pornography caused harm or not.

At this point, two inconsistencies appear in the judgement. First, he argued that Parliament's purpose in enacting the section was the prevention of harm to society. A legislative body, operating on that basis in the 1950s, almost certainly meant that pornography harmed the moral standards of those who indulged in it. That suggests that the aim of Parliament was the maintenance of a certain conventional moral standard, and not the prevention of harm, or the disapproval of views incompatible with a fundamental conception of morality.

The second inconsistency is this: the harm caused by the material is to be judged on the community tolerance test. It is the community as a whole which acts as the 'arbiter' of what is undue (harmful). This is certainly a second manner in which a general conventional notion of morality might be upheld by the statute, rather than a critical morality, or a harm-based principle.

Sopinka J. recognised that the harm to women was a potential one, and that it lay in the disputed influence pornography had on other people's attitudes and beliefs. On the basis of this, the section was rationally related to the prevention of harm. Yet this seems like little more than the expression of disapproval, justified on feminist or perfectionist liberal reasoning. In certain cases, where the evidence conflicts, Parliament may restrict expression without satisfying the *Oakes* test, provided that it has some reasonable evidence to believe that harm will result if people come to believe the message which it wishes to censure.

Gonthier J. also seems to invoke a form of perfectionist reasoning in his judgement. He injected an element of pluralist communitarianism into the approach. Canadian society was a pluralist one, which must respect diversity. However when there was a wide consensus among different elements of society that certain conduct was beyond the pale, then that conduct might not be entitled to the full protection of s. 2(b), provided that the judgement was a considered one involving serious issues, rather than just one of taste. The approach is slightly reminiscent of that of Rawls in *Political Liberalism,* and his notion of an 'overlapping consensus' endorsed by reasonable people.[98]

In this case, Gonthier J. seemed to believe that there was a consensus condemning the transformation of human sexuality into mere 'animality'. When Parliament was restricting such material, the *Oakes* test does not apply in full rigour.

In brief, the judgements are motivated by a form of perfectionist beliefs which make some allowance for the community's conception of morality to restrict expression.

Conclusion

In this Chapter, I have looked at four cases decided by the Supreme Court of Canada, which involved quite difficult issues of legal and political theory. The Court had to decide whether freedom of expression could be limited to protect minorities from hate speech; to prevent the spreading of falsehood likely to injure a public interest; to prevent the harms associated with public solicitation; and to curtail obscenity. In *Keegstra,* the Court upheld the restriction on freedom of expression in the interests of equality, as it did in *Butler* (obscenity). In the *Prostitution Reference*, the Court upheld restrictions on the public activities of prostitutes. And finally, in *Zundel*, the Court decided that the State could not punish someone who lied about the fact of the Holocaust (at least using that particular statute).

In this ongoing constitutional debate, the unexpressed beliefs of the judges concerning the most appealing political reconstruction of the legal order were crucial. These beliefs explain the difference between the majority and the dissenters in *Keegstra, Zundel* and the *Prostitution Reference.*

What is gained by looking at legal reasoning with an eye for political justification? First, we see how the cases fit into a public debate on the legitimacy of power,[99] and also form a debate between judges. Second, we can judge the clarity of the arguments of the judges more easily. We can understand more of the steps in their reasoning and compare the coherence of an approach in one case with that in another. Third, we can assess the success of the case as a claim to provide a justification of the state.

In the 1960s the Canadian Parliament decided that the need to assure equality in material terms demanded the restriction of certain expression, specifically incitement to hatred against particular minorities. In 1982, Canada adopted its Charter of Rights and Freedoms, largely to attain an elusive national unity. It embodied in a written constitutional document, Canada's fundamental political values, including free expression, equality and multi-culturalism. And it gave the courts a prominent role in the political debate on these fundamental values. It did not settle any arguments by its own terms but rather provided ambiguous points of reference for debates about public legitimacy, ambiguous points which Canadian judges had to concretise and perhaps develop.

The Parliamentary balance between expression and equality came to be reviewed by the courts. In *Keegstra*, the two opinions set out two different ways to understand the claims to legitimacy of the Canadian state. McLachlin J. proposed that the Charter be read in the light of a moral position strongly defended by US judges and political writers, the notion of liberalism as neutrality. If this was the most appealing interpretation of the Charter, then the hate speech laws were of dubious validity. However the majority of the Court found a more compelling interpretation of the Charter, one which also embraced Parliament's understanding, and took more seriously the Charter's impressive commitment to equality and multi-culturalism. Such a liberal perfectionist approach permits certain anti-pluralist, anti-egalitarian expression to be regarded as of limited worth, so permitting Parliament to prohibit it. In *Butler*, the Supreme Court re-endorsed this legislative understanding of the Charter, powerfully asserting that the State may prohibit expression either on the ground of the harm to society that it causes, or on the ground that it attacks certain fundamental moral principles on which the State is based. In some respects, such cases can be seen as promoting the value of universalisability as equal respect.

In *Zundel*, the dissenters articulated this understanding even more explicitly than in *Keegstra* or *Butler*. Their understanding of the Charter as a model of democratic pluralism seems a particularly powerful interpretation of Canadian practice and law, especially after *Keegstra*. Alternative visions to this particular understanding continued to be articulated however. The majority in *Zundel* relied on some very strange arguments to strike down the false news law. The convictions on which they relied can only be seen as unworkable, and deeply incompatible with the *Keegstra* reading of the Charter.

There is a similar relationship between the *Butler* and *Prostitution Reference* cases. *Butler* interpreted the Charter to allow the State to legislate on the basis of some 'fundamental' morality, not society's conventional conception of the good. This was still a perfectionist way of reasoning, but one very different from traditional justifications of censorship. The *Prostitution Reference* case though involved a much more relaxed attitude towards this issue. The plurality opinion simply accepted the stigmatisation of prostitution, and so had no difficulty in upholding a law restricting expression. There was an almost casual acceptance of conventional morality, radically at odds with *Keegstra* and *Butler*. The dissenting opinion stressed that this was no longer an acceptable justification of the Canadian state.

By seeing these arguments as a type of political argument we can judge the clarity and coherence of these arguments, according to the standards of political moral argument.[100] Consider for instance McLachlin J.'s position in *Zundel*. Such scepticism as she suggests poses a double challenge to the very institution of judicial review, an institution which she must be prepared to defend. First, if there is indeed such widespread difficulty in determining meaning and truth, then why not simply trust legislative findings? Certainly judges cannot claim any greater insight than legislators. Second, if there are such indeterminacies, then how are legal interpretation and adjudication possible? Interpretation and adjudication are all about determining meanings and facts. Such nihilistic indeterminacy would leave the legal field in a state of anarchy, making the legal process impossible. McLachlin J. should have tried to resolve these inconsistencies (this after all was one of the less demanding criteria we discussed in Chapter Three).

There is a third possible incoherence in her argument. If we cannot trust our judgements about interpretation and truth of factual matters, then how can we trust our judgements of moral claims? Whilst it is true that some people have sought to rest a defence of liberalism, and more particularly free expression, on moral scepticism, this approach seems doomed to failure. For free expression is a claim of moral right. If we embrace scepticism, then we have no more reason to protect free expression, than to suppress it. Certainly, if we look at McLachlin's J. opinion in this political light, these inconsistencies make it much less credible than the perfectionist one argued for by her colleagues.

Any legal decision involves a confrontation between legal rules (norms) and concrete facts. In the process of applying the rules to the facts, judges must engage in one or two processes. They must certainly engage in the process of adjudication, the concrete decision that this particular factual situation falls under a certain rule. They also engage in interpretation, that is deciding the scope or meaning of the norm. When engaging in either process judges (are expected to) have reasons. In the cases examined, political reasons play a role in this process.

Consider, for instance, the decisions that hate speech and obscenity belong to a category of expression which is of limited value, and therefore not entitled to the strict protection of the *Oakes* test. There is nothing specific in the Charter which would mandate the adoption of a less rigorous test in such cases. As McLachlin's J. opinion in *Keegstra* demonstrates, it is possible to apply the same level of stringency regardless of the value of the content.

Furthermore, even if we accept the specification of the norm, valueless speech is entitled to less stringent protection, why should hate speech, obscenity, or solicitation for prostitution, be subsumed under such a norm? I do not deny that they (certainly the first, and probably the second) may be valueless in the eyes of any acceptable moral or political theory, but that is the point. They can only be so judged according to some such theory.

The examination of the role of political morality in these judgements serves to highlight their claims to moral justifiability. There are few who deny the need to evaluate the justice or morality of legal decisions. To so evaluate, it is necessary to decide what is the moral or political import of a decision, and it is precisely that which I argue. Is perfectionist liberalism an acceptable form of public life? Or should liberal neutrality be preferred? Are either (liberal?) scepticism, or some communitarian approach, justifiable basis for running a political entity?

In constitutional jurisprudence, the state's very claim to legitimacy is being debated. The judges are not simply reading texts, nor writing their own philosophies into them. Nor are they trying to implement a non-moral rule of recognition or Basic Norm. They are arguing over what is the most appropriate reconstruction of the legal order. What reconstruction makes the legal order the most legitimate that it can be? This reconstruction is necessary for two reasons - to give the legal order a claim to legitimacy, and to help decide the instant case at hand. Does the Charter allow the state to ban hate speech? The Charter does not make any explicit provision for this. So, the judges must interpret it. This is a process by which judges refer both to conventional legal sources but also political reasons. The Charter is clearly a liberal document, but this is not enough to resolve the instant dispute. What type of liberalism, compatible with the Charter, provides the best justification of it? In these cases, some judges invoke democratic pluralism (liberal perfectionism) as the most appealing justification, others rely on liberalism as neutrality. The choice between these must be made according to the criteria of rational moral argument. And then one can decide the instant case, at the same time publicly clarifying for the citizenry and political authorities the different possibilities for offering a legitimate reconstruction of the legal order.

Notes

1   'Language as Violence v. Freedom of Expression' Discussion, 37 *Buff. L. Rev.* 337 (1988/89), with Borovoy, Mahoney, Brown, Cameron, Goldberger, Matsuda.

2   For an introduction to the law of the Charter, see Hogg, *Constitutional Law of Canada;* Beatty, *The Canadian Production of Constitutional Review: Talking Heads and the Supremes*; Beatty, *Constitutional Law in Theory and Practice*; Beaudoin, Ratushny, *Charte Canadienne des Droits et Libertes*, Bryden, Davis, Russell, *Protecting Rights and Freedoms*; Knopff, Morton, *Charter Politics*; Mandel, *The Charter of Rights and the Legalization of Politics in Canada*; Manfredi, *Judicial Power and the Charter: Canada and the Paradox of Liberal Constitutionalism*; Monahan, *Politics and the Constitution: The Charter: Federalism and the Supreme Court of Canada*; Trakman, *Reasoning with the Charter*; Anderson, *Rights and Democracy.*

3   See Russell, 'The Political Purposes of the Canadian Charter of Rights and Freedoms' (1983) 61 *Can.Bar Rev.* 30; Mandel, *The Charter of Rights and the Legalization of Politics in Canada* Ch. 1.

4   See Beatty, 'The Canadian Charter of Rights: Lessons and Laments' (1997) 60 *Modern Law Review* 481 and Ison 'A Constitutional Bill of Rights - the Candian Experience' (1997) 60 *Modern Law Review* 499 for (conflicting) critical views. For a more favourable opinion see Hogg and Bushell, 'The Charter Dialogue between Courts and Legislatures' (1997) 35 *Osgoode Hall Law Journal* 75. See also the essays in Anderson, *Rights and Democracy.*

5   *Hunter et al.* v. *Southam Inc.* 11 D.L.R. 4th 641 (1984) at p. 649. Note his reference to Freund. See also *Thomson Newspapers* v. *Director of Investigation*, 67 D.L.R. 4th 161 (1990) at p. 192, per Wilson J. dissenting. However see L'Heureux-Dube J. in *Thomson Newspapers* at p. 270.

6   *Law Society of Upper Canada* v. *Skapinker*, 9 D.L.R. 4th 161 (1984) at p. 168, per Estey J. See also *Thomson Newspapers* v. *Director of Investigation*, 67 D.L.R. 4th 161 (1990) at p. 192, per Wilson J. dissenting. See also the Privy

Council decision in *Edwards* v. *Attorney General of Canada*, 1 D.L.R. 98 (1930), [1930] A.C. 124. (The Privy Council used to hear appeals from the Supreme Court of Canada.)

7 18 D.L.R. 4th 321 (1985).

8 P. 360. See also *Hunter* v. *Southam Inc.*, 11 D.L.R. 4th 641, 650; *Public Service Employee Relations Act* ,38 D.L.R. 4th 161, 217 (1987), per McIntyre J.; *Thomson Newspapers* v. *Director of Investigation*, 67 D.L.R. 4th 161, 243 (1990), per La Forest J.

9 26 D.L.R. 4th 200 (1986).

10 *Ref. re Electoral Boundaries Commission Act*, 81 D.L.R. 4th 16, 33 (1991), per McLachlin J. See Wilson J. in *M'Kinney* v. *Board of Governors of the University of Guelph*, 76 D.L.R. 4th 545, 572 - 581 (1990).

11 *Reference re Public Service Employee Relations Act, Labour Relations Act, Police Officers Collective Bargaining Act*, 38 D.L.R. 4th 161, 193 (1987).

12 38 D.L.R. 4th 161, 174 - 185 (1987).

13 Wilson J., dissenting, relied on Dworkin's *Law's Empire* in her condemnation of a 'checkerboard' solution as unprincipled, *Edward Books* v. *R..*, 35 D.L.R. 4th 1, 61.

14 See McLachlin J. in *Keegstra*, [1990] 3 S.C.R. 697, 803.

15 *Morgentaler* v. *R.*, 44 D.L.R. 4th 385 (1988). See also *Public Service Employee Relations Act*, 38 D.L.R. 4th 161, 217 (1987).

16 64 D.L.R. 4th 577 (1989). See also *Symes* v. *R.* 110 D.L.R. 4th 470, 482 - 297 (1993).

17 54 D.L.R. 4th 577 (1988).

18 Emerson, 'Toward a General Theory of the First Amendment' (1963) 72 *Yale L.J.* 877; Sharpe, 'Commercial Expression and the Charter' (1987) 37 *U. Toronto L.J.* 229.

19 58 D.L.R. 4th 577 (1989).

20 *Irwin Toy*, 58 D.L.R. 4th 577, 608 - 609. See also *Big M Drug Mart*, 18 D.L.R. 350.

21 See 58 D.L.R. 577, 608 - 612. The judges relied on Scanlon, 'A Theory of Freedom of Expression' in Dworkin ed., *The Philosophy of Law*.

22 26 D.L.R. 4th 200 (1986).

23 *Osborne* v. *Canada*, 82 D.L.R. 4th 321, 339.

24 *Irwin Toy*, 58 D.L.R. 4th 577, 617 (1989).

25 *Big M Drug Mart*, 18 D.L.R. 4th 321; *Committee for the Commonwealth of Canada* v. *Canada*, 77 D.L.R. 4th 385; *Zundel*, 95 D.L.R. 4th 202, 269.

26 64 D.L.R. 4th 577, 581 (1989). The case concerned the right to print information about marital and family life which emerged in a trial.

27 At pp. 583 - 584. See also L'Heureux-Dubé J. in *Committee for the Commonwealth* v. *Canada* 77 D.L.R. 4th 385, 422 (1991).

28 *USA* v. *Costroni*, 48 C.C.C. 3d 193 (1989); *Prostitution Reference*, 56 C.C.C. 3d 65 (1990); *M'Kinney* v. *University of Guelph*, 76 D.L.R. 4th 545 (1990).

29 *Irwin Toy*, 58 D.L.R. 4th 577, 625 (1989).

30	*R.J.R. MacDonald* v. *Canada*, 102 D.L.R. 4th 289, 313 (1993).
31	*M'Kinney*, 76 D.L.R. 4th 545, 615 - 617 (1990).
32	*Frasier* v. *Canada*, 23 D.L.R. 4th 122 (1985) per Dickson C.J.C.; *Police Services Union* v. *Port Moody Police Board*, 78 D.L.R. 4th 79, 87 (1991), per Lambert J.A. of the British Colombia Court of Appeal.
33	*Rocket* v. *Royal College of Dental Surgeons of Ontario*, 71 D.L.R. 4th 68, 79 (1990) observing that restrictions on economic expression, may 'be easier to justify than other infringements'.
34	61 C.C.C. 3d 1, [1990] 3 S.C.R. 697; 1 C.R. 4th 129; [1991] L.R.C. (Const.) 333. There was a companion case, *R.* v. *Andrews*, 77 D.L.R. 4th 128 (1990). See Mertl, Ward, *Keegstra: The Issues, The Trial, The Consequences* for a discussion of this case.
35	See also *Taylor* v. *Human Rights Commission* 75 D.L.R. 577 4th; [1991] L.R.C. (Const.) 445.
36	[1990] 3 S.C.R. 697. Page references in brackets are to this report.
37	(1984) 19 C.C.C. 3d 254.
38	(1988) 43 C.C.C. 3d 150.
39	Section 319(3)(a) was also in issue. This provided that the accused could invoke the defence of truth, but he would have to prove truth on the balance of probabilities. This infringed the presumption of innocence (s. 11(d) of the Charter). The Court of Appeal held that it was not justifiable under s. 1. The Supreme Court upheld the provision, McLachlin and La Forest JJ. dissenting.
40	In 1999, Madam Justice McLachlin was elevated to the Chief Justiceship.
41	*R.* v. *Carrier*, (1951) 104 C.C.C. 75; *Boucher* v. *The King*, [1951] S.C.R. 265.
42	*Irwin Toy*, 58 D.L.R. 4th 577 (1989); *Rocket*, 71 D.L.R. 4th 68 (1990).
43	Referring to Milton's *Areopagitica*, and Holmes J. in *Abrams* v. *US*, 250 U.S. 616 (1919).
44	*Cherneskey* v. *Armadale Publishers Ltd.*, [1979] 1 S.C.R. 1067; *RWDSU* v. *Dolphin Delivery*, [1986] 2 S.C.R. 573; *Irwin Toy*, 58 D.L.R. 4th 577 (1989); *Ford* v. *Quebec*, 54 D.L.R. 4th 577 (1988).
45	*Abrams* v. *US*, 250 U.S. 616 (1919); *Whitney* v. *Calif.*, 274 U.S. 357 (1927).
46	343 U.S. 250 (1952).
47	*New York Times* v. *Sullivan*, 376 U.S. 254 (1964); *Brandenburg* v. *Ohio*, 395 U.S. 444 (1969); *Anti-Defamation League* v. *F.C.C.*, 403 F.2d 169 (1968); *Collin* v. *Smith*, 578 F.2d 1197 (1978); *American Booksellers* v. *Hudnut*, 771 F.Supp. 852 (1989).
48	Viewpoint based regulations (e.g. 'speech criticising the white race is banned') will usually be prohibited. Content based regulations (e.g. 'speech criticising members of any race is banned') will only survive if narrowly drawn, and necessary to achieve a compelling end. Reasonable 'time, place and manner' regulations (e.g. 'no loud demonstrations between 1 and 6 o'clock in the morning') will be upheld. The US approach is a 'categorical' approach. Any measure restricting expression falling into the first two categories is likely to be struck down, whereas any 'time, place and manner' regulation has a good chance of surviving.

A law is overbroad if it unjustifiably touches constitutionally protected conduct, as well as other conduct. One can challenge the validity of an overbroad statute even though the conduct of which one is accused is not itself constitutionally protected. A statute is vague if it fails to indicate clearly what is required of the accused. One can challenge the constitutionality of a vague statute irrespective of whether it touches constitutionally protected activity, but the vagueness must concern the activity of which the defendant is accused. Such statutes are invalid because of their 'chilling' effect on speech.

49   7/12/ 1976, Ser. A., no. 24.

50   *Taylor v. Canada*, 38 U.N. G.A.O.R. Supp. No. 40 A/38/40 231 (1983); 5 C.H.R.R. D/2097.

51   P. 849. This of course means she was cutting back on the contextual approach which emphasises the specific expression at issue.

52   McLachlin J. rejected the Court of Appeal's argument that only the actual promotion of hatred could justify the restriction of free expression. In her view, that failed to give adequate attention to the harm done to minorities.

53   See Raz, *The Morality of Freedom, Ethics in the Public Domain* and Macedo, *Liberal Virtues*.

54   Raz, *The Morality of Freedom*, Chs. 14 and 15.

55   Raz, *The Morality of Freedom*, p. 381.

56   Dyzenhaus, 'Pornography and Public Reason' 7 *Can. J. of L. Juris.* 261 (1994).

57   This controversial argument has been defended by Rawls, *Theory of Justice, Political Liberalism*; Dworkin, *A Matter of Principle*.

58   See Lipstadt, *Denying the Holocaust*, and Mandel, *The Charter of Rights and the Legalisation of Politics*, pp. 369 - 376.

59   The section was at one stage s. 177, but I shall refer to it only as s. 181.

60   35 D.L.R. 4th 338.

61   53 C.C.C. 3d 161.

62   95 D.L.R. 4th 202 (1992).

63   *US v. Schwimmer*, 279 U.S. 644 (1929).

64   *R. v. Hoaglin*, (1907) 12 C.C.C. 226.

65   (1951) 104 C.C.C. 75.

66   (1970) 1 C.C.C. 2d 286.

67   The dissenters also relied on Matsuda, 'Public Response to Racist Speech' 87 *Mich. L. Rev.* 2320 (1989).

68   See *Irwin Toy*, (1989) 58 D.L.R. 4th 577 at p. 625; *Slaight Communications* v. *Davidson*, (1989) 59 D.L.R. 4th 416, at p. 423; *R. v. Wholesale Travel Group*, (1991) 84 D.L.R. 4th 161 at p. 216.

69   P. 241, referring to *Garrison* v. *Louisiana*, 379 U.S. 64, 75 (1964).

70   The dissenters cited Gill Seidel, *The Holocaust Denial: Anti-Semitism, Racism and the New Right* (1986).

71   Ackerman suggests that one might endorse the liberal principle of neutrality because of moral scepticism, in *Social Justice in a Liberal State*. However,

others who agree with liberalism as neutrality, reject this idea. See Dworkin, *A Matter of Principle*, p. 203.

72 From a 1984 report of the Ontario Advisory Council on the Status of Women, *Pornography and Prostitution*, cited in *Prostitution Reference*, [1990] 1 S.C.R. 1123, 1193.

73 *Westendorp v. R.*, [1983] 1 S.C.R. 43.

74 (1987) 38 C.C.C. 3d 408.

75 *Reference re: ss. 193 and 195 of the Criminal Code (Prostitution Reference)*, [1990] 1 S.C.R. 1123. Section 7's guarantee of 'fundamental justice' was also considered, with the majority finding no violation, but see Wilson J.'s dissent.

76 Dworkin, *A Matter of Principle*, pp. 354 -359.

77 See *Butler*, 89 D.L.R. (4th) 449 (1992), discussed in the next section.

78 See MacKinnon, *Only Words*, for a powerful attack on pornography.

79 *R. v. Ramsingh*, (1984) 14 C.C.C. 3d 230, 239, per Ferg J.

80 89 D.L.R. 4th 449 (1992). See also *R. v. Towne Cinema Theatres*, (1985) 18 D.L.R. 4th 1; *Prostitution Reference*, (1990) 56 C.C.C. 3d 65, [1990] 1 S.C.R. 1123.

81 At one point s. 163 was called s. 159, but I shall refer to it only as s. 163.

82 50 C.C.C. 3d 97.

83 60 C.C.C. 3d 219.

84 89 D.L.R. 4th 449 (1992).

85 Pp. 461 - 463. The test was expounded in *R. v. Hicklin*, (1868) L.R. 3 Q.B. 360, 371:
    ... whether the tendency of the matter charged as obscenity is to deprave
    and corrupt those whose minds are open to such immoral influences, and
    into whose hands a publication of this sort may fall.

86 *R. v. Brodie*, (1962) 32 D.L.R. 2d 507; *R. v. Towne Cinema Theatres*, (1985) 18 D.L.R. 4th 1.

87 [1948] V.L.R. 445, cited in *Brodie*, 32 D.L.R. 2d 507, 182, and in *Butler*, at p. 464.

88 P. 465. *R. v. Towne Cinema*, 18 D.L.R. 4th 1, per Dickson C.J.C.

89 Sopinka J. relied on Dyzenhaus, 'Obscenity and the Charter: Autonomy and Equality' (1991) 1 C.R. 4th 367.

90 See *Prostitution Reference*, [1990] 1 S.C.R. 1123, per Dickson C.J.C.

91 [1990] 3 S.C.R. 697.

92 (1989) 58 D.L.R. 4th 577.

93 He also referred to *Paris Adult Theatre I v. Slaton*, 413 U.S. 49, 60, per Burger C.J.

94 'In a marketplace of ideas, ... pornographic imagery is there for the taking, and it finds without any doubt many takers.' (p. 491)

95 He referred to *Big M Drug Mart*, 18 D.L.R. 4th 321; Art. 10 of the European Convention; the ECHR cases of *Handyside* and *Muller*.

96 He referred to Dworkin, *Taking Rights Seriously*, p. 255.

97 P. 498. He invoked S. Gardbaum, 'Why the Liberal State Can Promote Moral Ideals After All', 104 *Harv. L. Rev.* 1350 (1991).

98   It even more closely resembles a perfectionist scheme outlined (though not recommended) by Raz in *The Morality of Freedom* (p. 128), whereby people in a Rawlsian Original Position would endorse a procedure to decide on the best possible conception of the good.

99   Or 'dialogue' as some would prefer: Hogg and Bushell, 'The Charter Dialogue between Courts and Legislatures' (1997) 35 *Osgoode Hall Law Journal* 75.

100 For a consideration of the incoherences in free expression jurisprudence, see Cameron, 'The Past, Present and Future of Expressive Freedom under the Charter' (1997) 35 *Osgoode Hall Law Journal* 1.

5   The Private is Political

Introduction

In the last Chapter, I showed the use of political beliefs in constitutional decision-making in free expression cases in Canada. Now we switch attention across the Atlantic, and look at the constitutional treatment of sexual morality and privacy. In Ireland also, the interrelation between political morality and constitutional law is often of dramatic importance. There is also a somewhat unusual twist: the right to privacy is nowhere mentioned in the Irish Constitution. The State's regulation of sexual privacy has played a fundamental role in Irish politics for decades.[1]

First, I will introduce the political and legal system. Then I provide a basic discussion of constitutional law, especially constitutional interpretation. After this, the reader encounters the privacy cases, dealing with sensitive issues involving the right to use contraceptives, the criminalisation of homosexual intercourse and abortion.

Political System

Irish political life is a parochial Westminster model with republican rhetoric.[2] A directly elected President performs the ceremonial functions of a Head of State in a Parliamentary regime. The President performs most of her official acts 'on the advice of' the Government, i.e. she does what she is told. The Parliament (*Oireachtas*) has two houses. The House of Representatives (*Dáil*) is elected by universal adult suffrage, using the system of proportional representation by the single transferable vote. The politically unimportant Senate (*Seanad*) is composed of eleven persons nominated by the Prime Minister, forty-three elected by local councillors and members of the *Dáil*, and six elected by citizens with university degrees.

The Prime Minister (*Taoiseach*) is elected by the *Dáil*. He names the Government (Cabinet) which is then collectively responsible to the *Dáil* (Art. 28). The Prime Minister may dissolve Parliament at any time, (unless he has lost Parliament's confidence), and directs the policy of the state.

The Judges

The Government appoints all judges. Judges or barristers with 12 years experience are eligible for appointment to the High and Supreme Courts. Once appointed they sit until the age of 70 (High Court) or 72 (Supreme Court). Judges can only be removed by a vote of impeachment for stated misbehaviour, approved by each house of Parliament.

The Supreme Court is the highest court in the state. Today, eight judges sit on this court, presided by the Chief Justice. However, all the cases I examine took place when the Court had only five members. The Government appoints the judges and the Chief Justice. The President of the High Court is also a member of the Supreme Court. In the event of temporary vacancy, the Chief Justice may ask a High Court judge to take the place of the missing Supreme Court judge. When the Supreme Court is considering the constitutionality of a bill or statute dating from after 1937, then it may issue only one opinion (Art. 26.2, Art. 34.4.5). In all other cases, dissenting and concurring opinions are allowed.

The High Court is the highest court of first instance. The High Court and Supreme Court deal with the vast majority of constitutional cases. Allegations of unconstitutionality of post 1937 statutes may only be made in these courts, and one may only seek declarations of unconstitutionality in these courts.

Ireland has a common law legal system. Therefore, the case law of superior courts is a source of law. Judges are bound by the *ratio decidendi* in the relevant decisions of courts superior to themselves. However High Court judges are not obliged to follow the decisions of other High Court judges, and the Supreme Court may depart from its own precedents if it has a good reason.[3] The decisions are found principally in the Irish Reports, Irish Law Reports Monthly, and Irish Law Times Reports.

The 1937 Constitution and Fundamental Rights

The 1937 Constitution, consolidating Irish independence, was adopted by a referendum. The only procedure to alter it is for a bill to be approved by Parliament and then by the people in a referendum (Art. 46).

The Constitution is a mélange of different traditions. There are many religious flourishes. The right to property (Art. 43) is expressed in Aquinian terms. The judicially unenforceable Directive Principles of Social Policy (Art. 45), are influenced by Catholic social doctrine. The Constitution also speaks of the 'dignity and freedom of the individual' (Preamble) and guarantees the classic liberal freedoms. Article 6 neatly combines theocracy with popular sovereignty: the three powers of state are held to 'derive, under God, from the People'. Article 44 contains an apparently remarkable contradiction: it recognises that public worship is due to Almighty God, but then goes on to guarantee freedom of religion, prohibit religious discrimination and forbid endowments of religion.

One of the Constitution's striking departures from the British tradition is the protection of basic rights.[4] These include the rights to: a fair trial (Art. 38.1, equality (Art. 40.1), life, person, good name, property (all in Art. 40.3.2), life of the unborn (Art. 40.3.3), travel (Art. 40.3.3), receive information about services lawfully available abroad (Art. 40.3.3), liberty (Art. 40.4), inviolability of dwelling (Art. 40.5), expression, assembly, association, unionisation (all in Art. 40.6), primary education (Art. 42), and freedom of conscience and religion (Art. 44.2). The rights of the family are also recognised (Art. 41).

The litigant who cannot invoke any of these rights need not despair. In 1965, a woman asserted that the introduction of fluoride into the water system violated her right to bodily integrity, a right which is not in the text of the Constitution.[5] However, Kenny J. of the High Court, after a detailed textual analysis, concluded that Art. 40.3.1 guaranteed the protection of *all* personal rights. Accordingly every personal right, explicit, implicit or unenumerated is protected by Art. 40.3.1. He concluded that the right to bodily integrity was protected by the Constitution, but that it was not violated in this case.

The unenumerated rights so recognised include (so far) the right to earn a livelihood, the right of access to the courts, the right to communicate, the right to marry, the right to procreate, the right to leave

151 The Private is Political

the state, the right to fair procedures, the right to protection of health, the right to an independent legal status, and the right to privacy.[6]

How does one recognise an unenumerated constitutional right? The courts have given myriad answers to this question. Kenny J. thought that certain rights are implicit in the 'democratic and Christian' nature of the state. Other answers include 'the natural law', 'the dignity and freedom of the individual', 'nature of the person', 'justice', 'essential to the human condition and personal dignity'.

The Directives of Social Policy follow the section on rights. Art. 45 lists certain non-justiciable principles for the guidance of Parliament. It stresses that charity and justice must inform all the areas of life, especially the economic one.

Judicial Review

The Constitution provides for judicial review of legislation. This can occur in three ways. When the President is presented with a bill for promulgation, she may, in her discretion, refer it to the Supreme Court for a binding opinion as to its constitutionality (Art. 26). Second, one may invoke the Constitution in the midst of any ordinary court case. Finally, one can go directly before the High Court seeking a declaration of invalidity of any statute which adversely affects one's interests.

In principle the High Court and Supreme Court can review the constitutionality of any official act, subject to certain exceptions.[7] The courts have held that once a violation of the Constitution or of personal rights has been disclosed, their powers are as 'ample as the defence of the Constitution requires'[8] and include the use of injunctions, damages, contempt of court, as well as the traditional remedies against the State. Also, the courts have developed a tort of violation of constitutional rights, which may be invoked against the state, individuals or groups.

Constitutional Interpretation

The debate on constitutional interpretation in Ireland has only recently become heated. This is not to say that there has been a significant consensus on an accepted methodology in the courts or among commentators. Jurists have identified at least five principal interpretative approaches, and a number of ancillary ones.9 The main approaches are usually styled the literalist, historical, purposive, harmonious and 'natural law' approaches. Regrettably, there is little judicial discussion of the reasons for selecting one or other methodology, and one might cynically suppose that judges select the approach which leads to the result they like.

The literalist approach is (supposedly) straightforward: the Constitution means what its 'plain words' say and nothing else.10 There are disadvantages with this approach, not least of which is that it only applies when the text is unambiguous. Of course, it is precisely when the text is ambiguous that we most need a theory of interpretation rather than a dictionary! In any event it is not always evident that a provision is unambiguous.11 Also it seems wrong to subject the broad generalities and fundamental principles of the Constitution to the literalist line by line parsing appropriate for a detailed, easily changeable statute.12 Such an approach may lead to an unworkable or unacceptable result which judges have sought to avoid by using other techniques.13 Even worse, it may involve dogmatic and pedantic distinctions based on subjecting the Constitution to an unnecessarily intense process of parsing and analysis.14

The second approach is the historical one. A historical approach has been endorsed by some academic commentators, in at least some cases.15 Certain writers have suggested that it is particularly useful in the field of educational rights.16 One version of the historical approach involves ascertaining the meaning of the Constitution from the laws in force at the time of the adoption of the Constitution.17 In *McGee* v. *Ireland,* the High Court noted that the law prohibiting the importation of contraceptives was enacted in 1935, two years before Parliament approved the new Constitution. Accordingly, Parliament must have believed that the provisions of the law were valid public policy under the new Constitution.18 A second variant involves using the opinions and morals of the people in 1937 to determine the meaning of the Constitution.19 In *Norris,* (homosexual rights) the majority judgement relied almost exclusively on this approach, saying that something which would not have been acceptable to the people in 1937, could not now be deemed to be required by the Constitution.20

These versions of the historical approach are open to several criticisms. First, the Courts have usually endorsed a 'present tense' interpretation, refusing to cabin the constitutional order by reference to practices of decades before.21 Second, it is odd to use the state of affairs existing in 1937 to interpret the Constitution, since the latter is the benchmark of legality.[22] Third, there is the difficulty of knowing what precisely was the state of affairs in 1937.[23] Fourth, historical analysis can throw up contradictory indications, as history is rarely straightforward.

The next approach to interpretation is the purposive or broad approach, that is the Constitution must be given an interpretation which makes it an effective tool to achieve its purposes.[24] It is inappropriate therefore to rely too much on a literal or historical interpretation as the Constitution is a political document, not a precisely drafted statute, and its broad purposes must be effectuated. In particular the fundamental rights protected by the Constitution are not to be confined by an unnecessarily literalist perspective.[25]

The fourth interpretative approach, a coherentist, is usually called the harmonious approach. This was set out by Henchy J. dissenting, in *O'Shea*:

> Any single constitutional right or power is but a component in an ensemble of inter-connected and interacting provisions which must be brought into play as part of a larger composition, and which must be given such an integrated interpretation as will fit it harmoniously into the general constitutional order and modulation. ... No single constitutional provision (particularly one designed to safeguard personal liberty or the social order) may be isolated and construed with undeviating literalness.[26]

Generally, judges at least mention harmonious interpretation as important,[27] or pay it the tribute of using it reflexively without mentioning it by name,[28] and the leading work on the Constitution describes this approach as 'in logic ... the first canon of interpretation'.[29]

The fifth approach is the natural law, reference to extra-textual values or 'evolving moral standards' approach. Reference to moral (or political) standards is very common.[30] The Supreme Court has unambiguously endorsed reference to evolving moral standards as a legitimate tool in construing the Constitution.[31] The legitimacy of reference to extra-textual values is the justification for the reference to foreign and international law. Once one accepts that moral standards are of relevance in interpretation, then one must acknowledge that such standards might well be found outside of Irish sources.[32]

The above are the five main interpretative approaches, but one other approach should also be considered important. Although it is often not mentioned in this context, Ireland is a common law country and so courts are bound by the relevant judicial precedents of superior courts. A court may of course overrule a decision made by itself, but until it does so it should follow the previous decision.[33]

Finally, there are various ancillary sources of inspiration. These include foreign and international law, and legal and other writers.[34] Judges have relied on foreign case law and legal provisions in deciding what meaning should be given to similar provisions in the Irish context. The references to US case law are so numerous that listing them would exhaust the reader's patience,[35] and judges have referred to other jurisdictions.[36] Treaties do not have normative force in Ireland unless incorporated by statute, but they are legitimate guides to interpretation.[37] Reference to writers and theorists is more unusual.[38] Recently judicial reference to Irish academics has become noticeably more frequent.[39]

The Birth of Constitutional Privacy: *McGee*[40]

Privacy acquired constitutional status in the early 1970s in a case involving the importation of contraceptives. Two years before the referendum on the Constitution, Parliament had passed the Criminal Law Amendment Act, 1935. This made it unlawful for any one to 'sell, or expose, offer, advertise, or keep for sale or to import or attempt to import' contraceptives. Given that no one manufactured contraceptives in Ireland, this was an effective way to ban them. The law was never changed, and under the Constitution, pre-1937 laws remain in force, provided they are consistent with the Constitution (Art. 50). The law was criticised in the 1960s and 1970s, and Senator Robinson introduced a bill to eliminate the restrictive procedures, but her bill suffered an obscure end in Parliament. The Act's demise took place elsewhere.

Mary McGee was a 29 year old married woman with four children. At least one of those births had been a complicated one, and her doctor advised her that any further pregnancies would endanger her health and possibly her life. She and her husband decided that they should use some form of contraception, rather than abstain from sex. She sought to import spermicidal jelly. Customs officers seized it under section 17 of the 1935 Act.

Mrs. McGee brought an action against the Attorney General and the Revenue Commissioners, seeking a declaration that s. 17 of the Act was not carried over into the 1937 State as it was unconstitutional.[41] The plaintiff invoked almost every right in the Constitution, and the Directive Principles of Social Policy for good measure.

At first instance, O'Keefe P. heard the case. The High Court President curtly dismissed the argument based on the non-justiciable directive principles (p. 291). He held that freedom of conscience in Art. 44 (Religion), referred only to religious freedom (p. 291). He regarded the Art. 41 (Family) argument as devoid of any value (p. 292).

He then considered the claim that Art. 40.3 protected an unenumerated right of privacy. He claimed that one must look to *public opinion* in 1937, to determine whether the Constitution implicitly contained such a right. He appealed to the legislative debate on s. 17 in 1935, only two years before the adoption of the Constitution. The section was passed without any vote, so large was the support for it - surely evidence that it was not contrary to public opinion at the time (p. 293). Accordingly, the section did not violate the Constitution.

The Supreme Court Majority

Mrs. McGee appealed to the Supreme Court, where human rights activist Sean MacBride pleaded her case before Fitzgerald C.J., Budd, Walsh, Henchy, Griffin JJ. All the judges delivered opinions, those of Budd, and Griffin JJ. endorsing the approach of Henchy J., with Walsh J. reaching the same conclusion by a different route. The Chief Justice dissented.[42]

Henchy J. stressed that the purpose of s. 17 was to protect the communal notion of sexual morality (p. 324). It did this by, *in effect*, forbidding the use of contraceptives. Although it did not do this explicitly, 'the totality of the prohibition aims at nothing less', given the absence of any manufacturer of contraceptives in Ireland (p. 324).

Henchy J. then set out the unenumerated rights doctrine. Someone claiming that a particular right had constitutional status needed to show that it 'inheres' in the citizen 'by virtue of his human personality' (p. 325). This must be done considering the Constitution as a whole, and in light of the constitutional social order, and the concrete conditions of the person involved. It was not possible to list exhaustively these rights.

The section not merely interfered with an important decision of the couple, it subjected them to the criminal law (p. 326). It condemned them 'to a way of life ... fraught with worry, tension, and uncertainty' (p. 326):

> And this in the context of a Constitution which in its preamble proclaims as one of its aims the dignity and freedom of the individual; which in sub. s. 2 of s. 3 of Article 40 casts on the State a duty to protect as best it may from unjust attack and in the case of injustice done to vindicate the life and person of every citizen; which in Article 41 ... guarantees to protect it [the family] in its constitution and authority as the necessary basis of social order and as indispensable to the welfare of the nation and the State; and which also in Article 41, pledges the State to guard with special care the institution of marriage, ... (p. 326)

The objection to s. 17 is that 'the law, by prosecuting her, will reach into the privacy of her marital life in seeking to prove her guilt' (p. 326). The section violated both Art. 40.3's guarantee of privacy in marriage,[43] and Art. 41's protection of the family (p. 328).

Budd J. reached a characteristically swift decision. After reciting the facts, and the text of Art. 40.3.1, he asked:

> What more important personal right could there be in a citizen than the right to determine in marriage his attitude and resolve his mode of life concerning the procreation of children? (p. 322)

Griffin J. also held that Art. 40.3.1 protected the right of marital privacy (p. 333). However, he rejected the notion that all sexual matters belong to the private realm, quoting Harlan J. in *Poe* v. *Ullman*, that the State may punish 'adultery, homosexuality, fornication and incest'[44] for:

> ... in any ordered society the protection of morals through the deterrence of fornication and promiscuity is a legitimate legislative aim and a matter not of private but of public morality. (p. 336)

Section 17 went beyond that, and invaded the realm of marital privacy.

Walsh J. and Constitutional Philosophy

This case was one of many important ones in which Walsh J. played a role during his 29 year career as a Supreme Court judge. Walsh J. thought that the regulation of the sale or importation of contraceptives might sometimes be justified. The key issue was whether making contraceptives absolutely unavailable violated a fundamental right. Walsh J. expounded his view of the philosophy of Arts. 41 - 43:

> [They] emphatically reject the theory that there are no rights without laws, no rights contrary to the law and no rights anterior to the law. They indicate that justice is placed above the law and acknowledge that natural rights, or human rights, are not created by law but that the Constitution confirms their existence and gives them protection. (p. 310)

The State has a duty to secure the common good, and individuals have a duty to uphold the common good. However, the legislature's determination of the common good is subject to judicial review.

Walsh J. based his decision on Art. 41 which requires the State to protect the family. The couple should be allowed to determine for themselves the number of children to have, if any (p. 311). Only the 'exigencies' of the common good could justify state intrusion into that decision. The religion of the parties, and the moral beliefs of the citizens did not per se amount to such an exigency:

> The private morality of its citizens does not justify intervention by the State into the activities of those citizens unless and until the common good requires it. (p. 312)

There could be no imposition of a code of morality on a married couple (p. 313). Interference could only be justified where necessary to prevent such an effect on public morality that amounted to the subversion of the common good (p. 314). The ban on importation was invalid. However, nothing in his opinion necessarily applied to unmarried persons (p. 320).[45]

Walsh J. discussed the nature of the Constitution and the role of the judiciary. He explained that, although the Constitution envisaged that 'we are a religious people' it also insisted, under Art. 44, that we lived in a pluralist state, where all religions were entitled to the protections of the Constitution (p. 317).

Natural rights were part of the natural law 'of God promulgated by reason [which] ... is the ultimate governor of all the laws of men' (p. 317, referring to the Preamble and Art. 6). However, in a pluralist society, judges cannot turn to religious experts or churches for an explanation of the rights and duties of the natural law. This is a task for the judiciary, guided by the structure of the Constitution, and the virtues of justice, prudence and charity (p. 318 - 319). He added that:

> ... no interpretation of the Constitution is intended to be final for all time. It is given in the light of prevailing ideas and concepts. (p. 319)

Walsh amplified his view on the philosophy of the Constitution in several articles.[46] The Constitution represented the fundamental values of the sovereign people, which they reserved from the political process and entrusted to the judiciary. It was written in the present tense and judges must so interpret it - it was not 'concerned with what has been, but with what may be'.[47] Of course it was a law which included 'social and political objectives ... [and] certain moral concepts' and thus embroiled judges in contemporary 'social, economic, philosophical and political debates'.[48] The judge had to explore questions of justice, rely on 'his own moral sense and his own intelligence'. Both judges and law makers were bound by 'prevailing ideas of justice' with which they were imbued 'by training and experience'.

He regarded the 1937 Constitution as endorsing a natural law approach first seen in *State (Ryan)* v. *Lennon*, where Kennedy C.J., dissenting, argued that a constitutional provision was invalid because the creation of a special military court violated the natural law.[49] Walsh J. noted the disasters of positivism in Nazi Germany and South Africa, and the importance of natural law values in international human rights law. He then stated that the Constitutional version of natural law was theological, but not Catholic.[50] According to Walsh J. all democracies rejected the idea that 'the state is God or that state power is right' - they were committed to defending rights. Given the role of judges as defenders of the Constitution, they could deploy any remedy necessary to defend a fundamental right.

Analysis

What are we to make of the role of moral or political argument in this case? First, the Supreme Court rejected the High Court claim that the Constitution is limited by the morals of 1937, either that embraced by the people who drafted or who adopted it. The Constitution required a present tense interpretation, in the light of today's values. From whence were those values to be derived? Clearly, Parliament's conception of justice was not decisive. Rather:

> The judges must, therefore ... interpret these rights in accordance
> with their ideas of prudence, justice and charity. ... no interpretation
> of the Constitution is intended to be final for all time. It is given in
> the light of prevailing ideas and concepts. (p. 319)

Judges had to interpret the *Constitution's* conception of justice - during which they must rely on their own and others' ideas on the question.[51]

   A second point is whether the right to marital privacy is founded on Art. 40.3.1 or Art. 41. Article 40.3.1 is inspired by secular rationalist thought, and Art. 41 by Aquinian thought.[52] Art. 41 states that the family exists as an institution prior to positive law and has 'inalienable and imprescriptible' rights, which the State must protect. Divorce was forbidden (until 1998). Furthermore, the State recognises the value of woman's work in the home, and guarantees that mothers shall not be forced to work outside the home. Article 40.3.1 requires the State to respect, and in so far as is practicable, defend and vindicate personal rights in general.

   Walsh J. chose Art. 41, and emphasised the value of marriage, whilst the other three members of the majority invoked Art. 40.3.1 which protected all personal rights (Henchy J. agreed that Art. 41 is also violated). Walsh J. specified that the statute violated Art. 41's guarantee of marital privacy, Art. 40.1's guarantee of equality, and Art. 40.3.1's guarantee of a right to health, but not any personal right of privacy in Art. 40.3.1.

   In basing the decision on Art. 41, Walsh J. limited the scope of privacy to marital relations. The majority, by basing the decision on Art. 40.3.1 made it clear that it was a personal right which inhered in every citizen, and left open for consideration whether it extended beyond a right to privacy in marital relations. This difference reflected differing philosophical visions: one an approach centring on individual autonomy, one centring on perfectionist or communitarian beliefs of the importance of the family.

When considering the doctrine of unenumerated rights, the judges rejected several less radical conceptions of rights. They rejected the belief that it was for Parliament to protect rights. They asserted that the state did not merely protect positive rights, whether explicitly mentioned or necessarily implied. The Constitution had outgrown the mindset of its drafters, and embraced the notion that law and state must first pay homage to justice. Walsh J. explicitly stated that the Constitution places justice above the law (p. 310). Henchy J. stressed that the Constitution protected those rights which inhere 'in the citizen in question by virtue of his human personality' (p. 325), not simply because of a constitutional term. The judges pursued a synthesis of justice and the Constitution, required by the Constitution itself, as interpreted (pp. 318, 325).

There is no clear cut technical reason to opt for one or other of these approaches to rights. The soundest argument in favour of each relies on a vision of political morality. Those who believe that the value of the law rests in clear terms being applied by non-political judges worry about the unenumerated rights doctrine, those who believe that some rights are more important than legal certainty endorse the doctrine.[53]

Which view of justice should be relied on in determining personal rights: theological, liberal, perfectionist, communitarian? Did the judges accept Kenny J's assertion that rights were rooted in the 'Christian and democratic nature of the State'[54] and if so what did they mean by it?

Henchy J. believed that personal rights were rooted in the human personality, which gave rise to rights in certain social situations. In this case, a wife and mother made a conscientious decision, about an important area of her life. The State was not entitled to frustrate that decision, even indirectly. Behind this argument is a conception of justice which centres on individual autonomy. The individual may effectuate decisions about intimate matters, even if society disapproves.

Walsh J.'s opinion poses a dilemma for Irish jurists. He asserted that justice is superior to the law, and that 'the individual has natural and human rights over which the State has no authority' (p. 310). On this basis, Art. 41 recognised the right of a married couple to decide whether to have children and how many (p. 311). The State could not interfere with this decision simply because the private morality of some or most people disapproves (p. 312 - 313). This argument would seem more appropriate in the context of an Art. 40 personal right. Why should a right not to have a moral rule imposed on one, be particularly connected with a familial right? In other parts, the emphasis on the family may suggest a communitarian or other perfectionist approach: the marital couple (not the individual) is the most important entity, and so valued is it, that it is exempt from the restrictions which apply outside marriage. However, this seems contrary to the strongly anti-perfectionist streak just referred to.

After disposing of the case, Walsh J. made several comments on religion which might be misinterpreted. He referred to his own statement in *Quinn's Supermarket*,[55] that the Constitution recognised that the people are religious, but also that they lived in a pluralist State (p. 317). However the super constitutional status of rights was founded on their being part of the natural law, whose superiority to positive law was implicit in the Preambular reference to Christianity and the constitutionally recognised authority of God (p. 318). Nevertheless pluralism required that judges determine the contents of these rights in accordance with the virtues of prudence, justice and charity (pp. 318 - 319).

There are two possible interpretations of this. The first is that constitutional rights must be interpreted according to Christian or Judao-Christian conceptions of justice. The second is that the argument recognises that our notions of justice and natural rights have their genesis in religious concepts, but that these concepts have now been bequeathed to the liberal tradition. The concepts of justice and rights are therefore the property of the Constitution, and must be interpreted by judges with respect for the contemporary views of these concepts, with respect for the constitutional text, and the pluralist nature of the State. From the viewpoint of the principles of political moral argument, an argument from Christianity would raise serious difficulties with the criteria of equal respect and explicability. Which of these two views prevailed?

The Demise of Privacy?

One feature of Irish political life is the strange affection that Parliament has for British laws. Often statutes survive in Ireland decades after their

removal from British statute books, and centuries after they should have
been removed. Since the Seventeenth Century, the state has severely
punished certain homosexual acts. In keeping with the other tradition of
Irish political life - letting the courts deal first with contentious issues - the
first serious attempt to eliminate Ireland's anti-homosexual legislation
took place in the judicial arena.

Two statutes singled out homosexual behaviour for
criminalisation. Sections 61 and 62 of the 1861 Offence Against the
Person Act punished sodomy and attempts to commit it (whether between
a man and a man or between a man and a woman), and section 11 of the
1885 Criminal Law (Amendment) Act punished acts of 'gross indecency'
between men. The penalty for the latter crime was a jail sentence of up to
two years. Someone convicted of the first could be jailed for life.

Mr. (later Senator) Norris had not been prosecuted when he
sought a declaration in the High Court that these sections were
unconstitutional.[56] However as a congenital homosexual, and gay rights
activist, he had suffered psychological trauma because of the threat of
their enforcement. He had suffered discrimination at the hands of others.
Also, the trauma made it impossible for him to develop a relationship. At
one stage, he needed medical treatment; his psychiatrist advised him to
emigrate. Instead, he campaigned for an end to the Victorian era in
Ireland. With this aim, he invoked the Constitution in his aid.

Norris argued that the provisions violated six constitutional rights:
equality (Art. 40.1), expression (Art. 40.6), association (Art. 40.6), and
the unenumerated rights to bodily integrity, marital privacy and individual
privacy. The plaintiff called ten witnesses to show that the effects of such
laws on homosexual people were severely negative. All the witnesses
thought the laws violated notions of justice and charity. The State did not
adduce any evidence to show that homosexuality was a threat to society's
morals, health or any other interest. Nevertheless, the State won.

McWilliam J. in the High Court dismissed the equality based
arguments. The anti-sodomy provision punished men and women,
homosexuals and heterosexuals equally, in so far as they committed anal
intercourse (p. 44). Furthermore the gross indecency provisions did not
discriminate against men, because it was reasonably open to the
legislature to conclude that the effects of female indecency were not so
grave as to merit punishment. McWilliam J. did not explain why it would
be reasonable (p. 50). He dismissed the bodily integrity argument on two

grounds. First, that if the plaintiff was harmed by not being able to have anal intercourse, he was unusual in this, and the legislature need not make an exception for him. Second, the statute could not be blamed if other people injured him. The judge also dismissed the expression and association arguments on the same ground, that any limitations on these rights were a consequence of the activities of private persons and not the statute (p. 47). The plaintiff had no standing to plead the right of marital privacy, as he was not, and would never get, married (p. 44).[57]

McWilliam J. then dealt with the issue of privacy. According to him, the courts' role was limited to determining whether reasonable grounds existed for the legislature to believe that principles of morality, order and social policy required a particular legislative provision. If such reasonable grounds existed, then the legislation was valid (pp. 46, 48). McWilliam J. interpreted Walsh J., in *McGee*, as saying that constitutional morality was associated with the morality of the Christian churches in Ireland (p. 48). Regarding the anti-sodomy sections McWilliam commented:

> ... it is not unreasonable for the assumption to be made, whether correctly or incorrectly, that the primary purpose of the sexual organs in all animals, including man, is ... reproduction .... If that is so, it seems to follow that there are some grounds for reasonable people to believe that sexuality outside marriage should be condemned, and that sexuality between people of the same sex is wrong. (p. 45)

He noted that this was the attitude of all Christian churches. This is a stark example of a logical error. One cannot jump from an empirical statement to a normative one. It would be as sensible to say that sex can be enjoyable, therefore sex should only be engaged in for the purposes of enjoyment. It is unclear why reproduction should be limited to marriage, on McWilliam J.'s logic, which is not an institution found among all animals, all of whom reproduce.

From this decision, Norris appealed to a Supreme Court composed of O'Higgins C.J., Finlay P., Henchy, Griffin, McCarthy JJ.[58] The Chief Justice delivered the majority judgement, with which Finlay P. and Griffin JJ. agreed. The other two saved the pride of Irish jurists.

The Supreme Court Majority

O'Higgins C.J. set out the laws and the facts, noting that they concern 'conduct of a kind usually regarded ... as abnormal and unnatural' (p. 51). He forcefully stated that the role of the court was not to reform the law, but merely to interpret it and 'to declare with objectivity and impartiality the result of that interpretation' (p. 53).

O'Higgins C.J. quickly dismissed the less central arguments. Equality was not violated because the anti-sodomy provisions affected men and women, homosexual and heterosexual equally (formally). The gross indecency provision discriminated against men, but not unconstitutionally so as the legislature might form a reasonable opinion that male indecency was different in nature and more serious (p. 60). This argument denuded the equality guarantee of any significant content. If one says that distinctions are justified if Parliament might have a reasonable belief, but then fails to explain why Parliament had that belief or why it was reasonable, equality is meaningless.

The right to bodily integrity was not violated simply because a general law, otherwise valid, imposed greater burdens on some people because of their congenital disposition (p. 61). This ignored what Walsh J. said in *McGee*, that the state must take care not to impose severe physical danger on some people who are in a different category, medically, from others. Freedom of expression and of association could be subject to exceptions, and if the measures did not violate the right to privacy, then they constituted a reasonable restriction on those other rights (p. 61).

The key issue was privacy. O'Higgins C.J. considered the development of the law in the UK. He described as 'understandable' the reluctance of the legislature there to change the law on a matter involving 'deep religious and moral beliefs'. The Chief Justice emphasised that organised religions have despised homosexuality as 'a perversion of the biological functions of the sexual organs and an affront both to society and to God'. The State has also severely punished it (p. 61).

The Chief Justice then cited a book by a Prof. West, to describe the experiences of homosexuals. He described a homosexual lifestyle as being 'sad, lonely, and harrowing', promiscuous, frustrating, unstable, depressing and leading to a high incidence of suicide attempts (p. 62). O'Higgins C.J. did not mention that Prof. West was called as a witness by Mr. Norris, and had said that the *statutes* had these 'prejudicial effects' for homosexuals, without achieving any significant social interest (p. 74, per Henchy J.). O'Higgins C.J. also said that the book mentioned that the effects of decriminalisation were an increase in homosexual behaviour and an increase in sexually transmitted diseases among both homosexual and heterosexual persons (p. 62). He ignored Prof. West's comment on oath, that decriminalisation in England had not produced an increase in homosexual behaviour, or threats to public health (p. 74).

O'Higgins C.J. considered the effect of decriminalisation of homosexual behaviour on marriage. He noted that the 1957 Wolfenden Committee, which recommended decriminalisation in England and Wales, thought that there might be adverse effects for marriage, given known incidents of homosexual behaviour by the husband leading to marital breakdown. The report also thought that decriminalisation might discourage moderately inclined homosexual people from marrying. So 'homosexual behaviour and its encouragement may not be consistent with respect and regard for marriage' and it was reasonable to assume that permitting such behaviour harmed marriage (p. 63).

O'Higgins rejected as unreasonable the idea, that the people, when adopting the Constitution, thought they were sweeping away anti-homosexual laws which had enforced Christian morality for centuries. In 1937, such conduct was prohibited in all parts of the UK and Ireland. He referred to the Preamble and explained:

> It cannot be doubted that the people, so asserting and acknowledging their obligations to our Divine Lord Jesus Christ, were proclaiming a deep religious conviction and faith and an intention to adopt a Constitution consistent with that conviction and faith and with Christian beliefs. (p. 64)

As a matter of principle, the State was not precluded from interfering in private conduct. The State had an 'interest in the general moral well-being of the community' and had the right:

> ... where it is practicable to do so, to discourage conduct which is morally wrong and harmful to a way of life and to values which the State wishes to protect. (p. 64)

Among the immoral acts which the State could forbid, even when done in private, were abortion, incest, suicide pacts, suicide attempts, mercy killing. These could be prohibited even when no harm was done to anyone else.

In fact, homosexual practices might cause harm, at least to oneself, for they might lead one into a homosexual existence, the horrors of which O'Higgins C.J. earlier described. Such conduct lead to an increase in venereal disease, threatening public health. Furthermore homosexual practices harmed marriage, or at least potentially did so and the state was sworn to uphold marriage (Art. 41) (p. 65). For all these reasons, the State could punish homosexual practices.[59]

The Supreme Court Dissenters

Henchy and McCarthy JJ. dissented. Henchy J. agreed that the role of the courts was not to reform the law, but simply to interpret the Constitution. He also rejected the equality argument (p. 70). However, on the question of individual privacy, he held that the Constitution protected certain rights which were not mentioned in its text, including the right to privacy. After referring to the 'Christian' nature of the state, the reference to 'prudence, justice and charity', 'dignity and freedom of the individual' 'democratic State' in the Preamble and Art 5, he explained:

> ... there is necessarily given to the citizen, within the required social, political and moral framework, such a range of personal freedoms or immunities as are necessary to ensure his dignity and freedom as an individual in the type of society envisaged. The essence of those rights is that they inhere in the individual personality of the citizen in his capacity as a vital human component of the social, political and moral order posited by the Constitution. (p. 71)

These rights included a complex of rights which created a zone of privacy:

> ... a secluded area of activity or non-activity which may be claimed as necessary for the expression of an individual personality, for purposes not always necessarily moral or commendable, but meriting protection in circumstances which do not engender

considerations such as State security, public order or morality, or other essential components of the common good. (p. 72)

McGee demonstrated that the condemnation of the activity by religious groups was constitutionally irrelevant.

Therefore, the court had to decide whether there were reasons of public order and morality which required the intrusion into the zone of privacy with such disastrous effects for the plaintiff, who could not adopt any other sexual orientation. Since these statutes indiscriminatingly punished all homosexual acts between males (including those without physical contact, and those with consent), and were passed by a Parliament unaware of the requirements of the Constitution, there was a heavy onus on the State to justify that intervention.

This it completely failed to do. The State called no witnesses; it introduced no evidence from any country, which had decriminalised homosexuality showing that it had had unfortunate effects for social interests. Furthermore, all the testimony was to the effect that: criminalisation severely hurt gay men; that there was no harm to society by decriminalisation; that decriminalisation would benefit gay men and society generally. Henchy J. spent five pages examining the testimony of eminent Irish, British and US psychiatrists, sociologists, theologians (pp. 72 - 76).

Henchy J. observed that the case turned on a factual dispute: were the harmful effects to society of decriminalising homosexual behaviour less significant than the harmful effects to homosexuals of maintaining the Victorian statutes? If the latter harms were significant, and the former harms negligible, then the plaintiff should win (p. 77). Since 'the unrebutted consensus of the evidence was against' any justification of the laws, the trial judge could not disregard it, but was bound to give judgement for Norris. In particular he could not rely on suggestions without evidence, or his own 'intuition' to justify such a serious infringement of the plaintiff's right. Henchy J. described the trial judge as 'substituting his own conclusions on the personal and social effects' of homosexuality (p. 77).

The trial judge went astray in not relying on the evidence, but on the attitude of the Irish Christian Churches in determining the constitutionality of the law. Henchy J. admitted that acts condemned by religious bodies might at times undermine the common good, and so merit punishment. However, even then the State could not seek to eliminate them by the criminal law. Why not?

> To do so would upset the necessary balance which the Constitution posits between the common good and the dignity and freedom of the individual. What is deemed necessary to his dignity and freedom by one man may be abhorred by another as an exercise in immorality. The pluralism necessary for the preservation of constitutional requirements in the Christian democratic State envisaged by the Constitution means that sanctions of the criminal law may be attached to immoral acts only when the common good requires their proscription as a crime. (p. 78)

Decriminalisation was not approval: it only meant that the common good did not require such a severe and drastic encroachment upon the liberty of the citizens in private conduct. At the very least, to be constitutional, the law would have to make an exception for gay men.

Concluding, he noted that the European Court of Human Rights' decision in *Dudgeon* seemed to signal an end at some stage for the law.[60] Also he commented that the legislature would be obliged to punish certain homosexual acts, e.g. involving minors, rape, etc. (p. 79)

McCarthy J. also rejected the majority's sanctioning of a violation of the plaintiff's rights. McCarthy J. commented on the historicist interpretation, which appears in part of the Chief Justice's argument. He referred to Walsh J. in *McGee*, and O'Higgins C.J. in *State (Healy)* v. *O'Donoghue*,[61] and concluded:

> I find it philosophically impossible to carry out the necessary exercise of applying what I might believe to be the thinking of 1937 to the demands of 1983. ... it would plainly be impossible to identify with the necessary degree of accuracy of description the standards or mores of the Irish people in 1937 - indeed, it is no easy task to do so today. (p. 96)

If one accepted the historicist approach, then one would have to accept that even 145 years after 1937, one would have to try to determine the intent of the people in 1937. Such an approach was inconsistent with decided law.

... the Constitution is a living document, its life depends not merely upon itself but upon the people from whom it came and to whom it gives varying rights and duties. (p. 96)

McGee and other cases caused immense surprise in their day as well.

McCarthy J. then examined several unenumerated rights cases.[62] He rejected the view expressed in *Ryan*, which suggested that fundamental rights were based on Christian theology. Rights were certainly related to Christ's 'great doctrine of charity' which the Irish Constitution had inherited (p. 99). Rights were rooted in the human personality, and the State had to treat those rights 'with due observance of prudence, justice and charity, so that the dignity and freedom of the individual may be assured' (Preamble). This dignity and freedom were not in conflict with the common good but formed a key part of it (p. 100).

McGee upheld the right to privacy - the 'right to be let alone'[63], according to McCarthy J. The Constitution protected many aspects of privacy (e.g. secrecy of ballot, use of property, inviolability of dwelling, secrecy of certain court cases, p. 100). However, these were but aspects of the general right to privacy, protected by Art. 40.3.1. In *McGee*, the three judge majority upheld the *personal* right of privacy *in marriage*, not simply the right of a married couple to privacy. Their decision was based on Art. 40.3.1 (personal rights) not Art. 41 (Family).

That right was infringed by a law which said that one man may masturbate in private, a man and a woman may masturbate in private, a woman may masturbate in private, a society of women may masturbate in private - but two men may not (p. 101). Unlike questions of protecting minors and others, or of maintaining military discipline, there was no compelling state interest involved in preventing two consenting men from masturbating in private. McCarthy J. condemned the total failure to justify the 'state interference of a most grievous kind (the policeman in the bedroom)' (p. 102).

McCarthy J. added several comments. He emphasised that his opinion did not justify abortion (p. 103). He ignored the issue of equality, it not being necessary to decide that issue (p. 104). He approved of Henchy J.'s comment that certain homosexual activity (involving minors, etc.) had to be punished (p. 104). He concluded that it was irrelevant that modern theology was for (or against) the decriminalisation of homosexual acts - 'I am content to hold that it is contrary to one of the fundamental rights guaranteed by the Constitution'.

Analysis

I start with the majority opinion of the Chief Justice. He thought that anal intercourse and other homosexual practices were not protected by the Constitution. Of course, he needed a more general reason than this to justify his conclusion. What general reason could be offered? There are several rationales which might justify his decision, but only two serious attention.

The first argument is a historicist / communitarian one. If the 1937 community regarded certain activities as so abhorrent that it punished them with life imprisonment, and if, in its communal charter it included references to philosophies which condemned those practices, then judges could not extend the protection of the Constitution to them.

There is a significant flaw with this approach. The majority did not state that *McGee* was overruled. *McGee* was one of many cases where judges gave the Constitution a 'present tense interpretation'. It must not be shackled to the consciences of an earlier generation. The 1937 generation accepted laws banning the importation or sale of contraceptives. They accepted that accused persons could be subject to preventive detention,[64] that a special criminal status could be created for homeless persons,[65] that women could be exempted from jury service.[66] All these provisions had been declared unconstitutional. Such an approach in *Norris* would have required the judges to explain why they were departing from the principle of a present tense interpretation.

The more likely argument is a perfectionist one asserting the natural inferiority of homosexuality. O'Higgins C.J. referred to homosexual acts as 'abnormal and unnatural'. He noted that organised Christian religion has condemned homosexual acts consistently through history. He examined the alleged harms caused by homosexual behaviour. There was no evidence of these harms, and the majority's willingness to accept their reality underscores their attitude to the worth of homosexuals.

O'Higgins C.J. explained that homosexual acts were not covered by the right to privacy. Why not? First, because the Constitution acknowledged the supremacy of Christian values. Second, the State could protect the 'general moral well-being of the community' and punish what

NB

was 'morally wrong'. Thus, homosexual acts were the same as other victimless acts such as abortion, incest, suicide, mercy killing, which the State could punish because they were wrong. Other than the reference to traditional condemnation as a 'perversion of the biological functions' and an insult to God and society, O'Higgins C.J. did not give concrete substantiated examples of the harms caused by homosexuality.

The majority said that homosexual acts were to be condemned even if they took place in private, and harmed no one. They could be condemned even though that had seriously harmful effects on gay men, without achieving any benefit for society. The majority accepted the sectarian interpretation of Walsh J.'s *McGee* decision, and repudiated his comments on pluralism.

NB

The majority argument is similar to Finnis' natural law approach. Homosexuality, like masturbation, is a form of sexuality which cannot substantiate two basic goods (friendship and procreation). This choice to use oneself for purposes not related to these goods is 'disintegrative manipulation' of oneself, and has been condemned by all reasonable societies.[67] The choice is always wrong regardless of its concrete effects on health or marriage. The choice to do something immoral can be punished regardless of the absence of a concrete harm to the common good.

NB

The dissenters were loyal to the vision of constitutional morality in *McGee*. They insisted that the Constitution had to be interpreted in the present tense; that respect for individual autonomy precluded invading the bedroom because of a conventional social morality; that the beliefs of no church formed any part of constitutional law. Christianity was only the historical tradition which bequeathed to modern liberalism certain core values (p. 99).

NB

There are three elements to the dissenting opinions. First, there is the close attention to the concrete facts, which is tied into the second element, the emphasis that the individual counts. The minority said that *the State, through means direct and indirect, had seriously hurt the plaintiff; it must now justify its actions to him.* The focus on the reality of a situation is a key element of post 1970s liberal thought.[68]

The dissenters believed that the individual, as a 'vital human' in a democratic society, had to be accorded a zone of non-interference where she can develop: 'Each person possesses an *inviolability* founded on justice that even the welfare of society as a whole cannot override'.69 The State could not interfere in this zone, even though what took place within was immoral. To interfere on this ground would violate the pluralism envisaged by the Constitution, endorsed by the Supreme Court in *McGee* and *Quinn's Supermarket*.70 The State could only interfere if it could prove that there was a sufficiently weighty requirement of State security, public order or public morality which required such intervention, and that such weighty requirement counterbalanced the serious harm caused to gay men.

The third element is an anti-perfectionist approach (neutrality), rooted in human equality. Each person is an equal; to respect this the State may not regard some conceptions of the good as superior or inferior to others.71 This is what the dissenters insisted upon, when they denied the power of the State to interfere simply because it objected strongly to the individual's practices within the confines of her constitutionally protected domain. It is also found in earlier decisions of the Supreme Court, most notably in *Quinn's Supermarket*,72 and *McGee*.73 The dissenters' view respected more thoroughly the principles of equal respect which is one of the criteria of political moral argument.

The Irish State did come to endorse the constitutional values of pluralism and privacy, but only after the European Court of Human Rights reminded it of its duty.74 The 1993 debate on the amendment of the laws included contributions from some conservative groups who explicitly relied on the perfectionist vision proposed by the *Norris* majority in their opposition to the reform. The then Prime Minister argued for reform, insisting, as had Henchy and McCarthy JJ., that the principle of equal respect demanded toleration for the orientation of the gay minority. So the competing visions of the Court found their way into the political dialogue, with the dissenting view winning out.

The visionary conflict continued in other areas. *Norris* did not establish a particular vision even in the courts of the 1980s. Three years after *Norris*, the High Court decision in *Kennedy* v. *Ireland*, seemed to resurrect the liberal opinions of the dissenters.75 A Government minister had ordered the illegal interception of telephone calls made by three journalists. The High Court awarded them compensation for this violation of their fundamental rights. Hamilton P. (since elevated to the Chief Justiceship) held that the right to privacy was a constitutional right, founded on the duty to assure the dignity and freedom of the individual in a democratic state. He referred approvingly to the *dissenting* opinions in *Norris*. His opinion suggested that the anti-perfectionist liberal vision of *McGee* and the *Norris* dissenters was not buried. However, he himself gave us grounds to think otherwise.

The Abortion Tragedy

The *McGee* vision provoked public debate on the right to privacy. Some activists were concerned that a judge, relying on US precedent,[76] might discover a right to an abortion lying within the right to privacy and invalidate sections 58, 59 of the 1861 Offences Against the Person Act, which prohibit abortion. This fear led to a divisive political debate on the amendment of the Constitution.

Following this debate,[77] the people approved the Eighth Amendment of the Constitution in 1983. This inserted Art. 40.3.3 immediately after Art. 40.3. 2 (Personal Rights):

> The State acknowledges the right to life of the unborn and, with due regard to the equal right to life of the mother, guarantees in its laws to respect, and as far as practicable, by its laws to defend and vindicate that right.

In the 12 years which followed, Parliament ignored its constitutional duty to legislate on this topic and instead the judges strove to elaborate the meaning of that sub-section in practice.

In 1986, a private organisation, the Society for the Protection of the Unborn Child (SPUC), tried to prevent two agencies assisting women who wished to go to England for an abortion.[78] SPUC sought three remedies: a declaration that the activities of the defendants were unlawful; a declaration that the defendants were engaged in a conspiracy to corrupt public morals; and an injunction prohibiting the defendants from assisting pregnant women to obtain an abortion.

The case went before Hamilton P. He noted that the right to life of the unborn was one of the rights of the natural law. The Constitution did not create the right; it recognised it and guaranteed to protect it (p. 481). The courts had to protect it, whether the threat came from the state or a private individual (p. 483). Courts could protect such rights even if the legislature had not given them a statutory form (pp. 488 - 489). Should no procedure exist to protect adequately a right, then the courts would create one (p. 489). Although the courts could go to great lengths to protect rights, Hamilton P. decided not to create what might amount to a new crime, that of assisting someone to commit an abortion abroad.

Hamilton P. considered a 'crime' allegedly existing at common law: conspiracy to corrupt public morals. A conspiracy is a simple agreement by two or more people to do something; one may be guilty of conspiracy even if one has done nothing. In fact, the English House of Lords invented this 'crime' in the 1960s. Further, the House of Lords held that people may be convicted of conspiracy to corrupt public morals, *even where the conduct they were promoting was not itself a crime.*[79]

Hamilton P. accepted that conspiracy to corrupt public morals was a crime in Irish law (p. 494), though without giving any reason for this incorporation. Furthermore, it was not necessary that the conduct promoted itself be criminal (p. 495). However, he refused to grant a declaration saying that the defendants were guilty of the crime. That would usurp the function of a criminal court sitting with a jury (p. 497).

Hamilton P. then considered whether the plaintiff was entitled to a declaration that the activities were unlawful, as a violation of the right to life. He observed that the defendant agencies were assisting women in obtaining an abortion in England (p. 499). This was a violation of a right, and was not rendered constitutional by committing it abroad (p. 493). Every citizen had to obey the law and respect constitutional rights (p. 496). The right to life must be protected, and no other lesser right (to privacy, to expression or to information) could interfere with it (p. 500). He granted an injunction, prohibiting the defendants from assisting women to obtain an abortion. There was an unsuccessful appeal to the Supreme Court.[80]

Consider Hamilton P.'s recognition of the crime of conspiracy to corrupt public morals. When discussing *Norris*, I argued that the dissenters were moved by a belief that the individual was important, and that there was a heavy onus on the State to justify its interventions into her zone of autonomy. In *Kennedy*, Hamilton P. apparently accepted this. Yet when importing the crime of conspiracy he attached no weight to the rights of privacy or expression. Consider this novel crime. Hamilton P. suggested that it applied to a private conversation between a pregnant woman and her medical counsellor. The justification for this intrusion was that they might be discussing the promotion of immorality. The crime was not limited to conspiracy to attack fundamental rights. It was not limited to conspiracy to do something unlawful. It was not limited to conspiracy to do something immoral. It applied to conspiracies to *promote* immorality. This was a blunt rejection of the proposition in *McGee* and the dissent in *Norris*, that something could not be punished simply because it was perceived as immoral. If Hamilton P. meant that one could punish conspiracy to do or promote something immoral, he was saying that *McGee* should be overruled. For in *McGee*, the court said that Parliament could not criminalise the intention of Mrs McGee and her husband to do something perhaps immoral. Indeed *McGee* goes further: Parliament could not, even by indirect means, punish the effectuation of that intention. This new crime is far more extensive in scope than the law in *McGee*: it covered the joint intention to advocate something, not only the doing of something.

Furthermore, the invasion of the private sphere was done in a very vague manner. It was, and is, unconstitutional for any crime to be so vague that someone did not know whether she was within its terms or not. This applied with even greater force when the activity punished could well be the exercise of a right.[81] The phrase 'conspiracy to corrupt public morals' gave no indication as to what sort of conduct or expression was covered. It thus violated the proscription of vague criminal laws. Suppose that two people admit in public that they are homosexual lovers. Is this conspiracy to corrupt public morals? Suppose that two men hold hands in public. Is this conspiracy to corrupt public morals?

There was no precision as to where this offence, never considered by an Irish legislature or executive, or judge prior to this case, invaded the zone of privacy upheld in *McGee* and *Kennedy*. It was an arbitrary criminalisation of potentially large areas of expression and private conduct. The recognition of this crime was support for the perfectionist element of *Norris*.

In other cases in the 1980s, the courts confirmed these rules: counselling groups and student unions were prohibited from giving information which would assist a woman to obtain an abortion abroad.[82] The right to life could not be defeated by any lesser right, such as privacy, or expression. However, debate on the merits of abortion was permitted. And, apparently, travel abroad was also permitted. By 1990, the judges

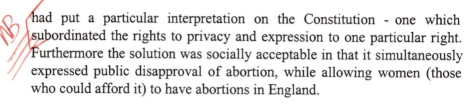

had put a particular interpretation on the Constitution - one which subordinated the rights to privacy and expression to one particular right. Furthermore the solution was socially acceptable in that it simultaneously expressed public disapproval of abortion, while allowing women (those who could afford it) to have abortions in England.

The X case

In a case combining a tragic personal situation, and abstract constitutional principles, a different evaluation emerged. In *Attorney General v. X*, the Government's legal adviser sought an injunction restraining a fourteen year old rape victim from leaving the State to have an abortion.[83] The girl was inclined towards suicide due to the pressures of pregnancy.

Costello J. in the High Court, granted the injunction. He reiterated that constitutional rights were judicially enforceable even if not regulated by statute (p. 10). He held that the threat to the life of the foetus was more serious than the threat to the life of the girl, which Art. 40.3.3 declared to be equal to the life of the foetus. There was evidence that the girl would commit suicide if the abortion did not take place. Costello J. considered that this threat was different from the threat to the life of the foetus. If an abortion took place, the foetus would certainly die, whereas if it did not, it was not certain the young girl would kill herself (p. 12).

Costello J. rejected an argument rooted in the constitutional right against preventative detention.[84] He also rejected a challenge based on the EC right to travel abroad to receive services.[85] He argued that the injunction was justified by a public policy exception to that right, which he derived from an analogy with free movement of workers.[86] The judge also considered that such an injunction would be a proportionate limit on rights under the European Convention on Human Rights. The High Court prohibited the girl or her family from arranging an abortion, and prohibited the girl from leaving the state for nine months. Costello J. provided a reasoned explanation of what the constitutional principles required in the case. In affirming those principles, he also laid down a challenge to those who stood by them.

Seven days later, the Supreme Court heard an appeal. After two days, amidst the greatest publicity ever to attach to any case, the Court granted the appeal. A week later the judges explained why.

Finlay C.J. spoke first. He reviewed the facts, and referred to the judicial duty to protect fundamental rights even in the absence of legislation (pp. 50 - 51). He referred to the statements of Walsh J. in *McGee*, about the superiority of justice, and to remarks of O'Higgins C.J.[87] on the duty to judge according to developing notions of prudence, justice and charity (pp. 52 - 53). He emphasised that judges had to construe the Constitution harmoniously, striving to avoid inconsistent interpretations of constitutional rights. He said that the appropriate test to apply in this case was:

> ... if it is established as a matter of probability that there is a real and substantial risk to the life, as distinct from the health, of the mother, which can only be avoided by the termination of her pregnancy, such termination is permissible, ... (p. 54)

The young girl was suicidal. Since suicide was difficult to prevent, this constituted such a real and substantial risk. The girl was entitled to an abortion, and to leave the State to obtain one. Egan and O'Flaherty JJ. concurred with most of the Chief Justice's reasoning on the right to life.

Finlay C.J. then considered the unenumerated right to travel abroad. He observed that, if the protection of fundamental rights could not be reconciled one with the other, then the courts must protect the most important right (p. 57). The right to life clearly prevailed over the right to travel abroad, and the courts could suspend the right to travel abroad, to protect the right to life. Egan J. agreed (ambiguously) with Finlay C.J. on this issue (p. 92).

McCarthy J. also granted the appeal. He disliked the notion of a hierarchy of rights (p. 78). Even the right to life was not absolute: the Constitution apparently allowed the death penalty. He rejected a hierarchical approach: the real question was how to defend and vindicate the two rights *as far as practicable* (Art. 40.3.3). In his opinion, where there was a real and substantial risk to the life of the mother, then defending the right of the unborn might not be practicable (p. 80).

McCarthy J. then considered the right to travel. He rejected the balancing exercise. One should not balance rights but ascertain whether citizens had them. If they do, then they may exercise them, regardless of their purpose (p. 84). The mere fact that someone intended to do something when abroad (even murder) could not be invoked to curtail the right to travel. Only McCarthy J. defended the position of Henchy J. in *Norris*, that persons may exercise rights even though for an immoral purpose.

Hederman J. delivered a powerful dissent. The State had a far-ranging duty to protect life, the 'essential value of every legal order and essential to the enjoyment of all other rights'. This included positive duties: for instance, the right to life could be invoked to require the State to deal with life-threatening pollution. Indeed, Hederman J. said that not only may all persons invoke the right to life, but also people may invoke it on others' behalf (p. 71).

Art. 40.3.3 of the Constitution made it clear that the foetus was entitled to live. Hederman J. would allow one exception. An operation, 'the sole purpose of which' was 'to save the life of the mother' was not 'a direct killing of the foetus' even if the inevitable consequence of the operation was the death of the foetus. However the mother could not invoke her right to privacy in abortion cases, for 'the unborn life is an autonomous human being protected by the Constitution' (p. 72). The right to self-determination did not include the right to end life.

In this case, the State's duties extended to restricting the right to travel of the young girl. Such a restriction, though offensive to the Constitution, was not so offensive as the 'irrevocable step of the destruction of life' (p. 73). Before an abortion could be permitted to save the life of a pregnant woman, it must be shown, by weighty, cogent evidence, that it was the only way to save her life. In this case, the threat to the girl's life was the threat of suicide. The appropriate response was to put the girl under supervision. It was not acceptable to destroy one life to dissuade someone else from taking her own (p. 76).

Analysis

This case carries forward themes from earlier cases. I draw your attention to the dissent of Hederman J., with its emphasis on the value of life as overriding other concerns, and the overall role of perfectionist - sectarian reasoning in the opinions.

Hederman J.'s dissenting opinion is interesting for its reliance on what appears to be some form of secularised Catholic beliefs, rather similar to the approach promoted by Finnis.[88] He described life as primarily a value to which the Constitution was dedicated. This recalls

Finnis' theory which is a value not a rights based theory. For Finnis (and
apparently Hederman J.) rights and duties flow from the supreme values.
Secondly, Hederman J. was clearly of the opinion that one may never destroy life, echoing Finnis who insists that one has a duty never to act
against a basic value. Third, Hederman J., like Finnis, relied on the
Catholic doctrine of 'double effect' to describe some actions which result
in the death of the foetus as not being an abortion even though the death is
the natural and probable consequence. And, of course, like Finnis, he
believed that the foetus was entitled to the protection of the right to life. In
drawing these comparisons, I do not suggest that Hederman's J. library includes the collected works of the Oxford scholar. Rather I note that he
relied on certain contested moral theories, which happen to have been
expressed by Finnis. In considering the acceptability of Hederman J.'s
opinion, we are surely allowed to consider the debate surrounding the
most sophisticated defender of that view.

The second point is more important. In *Norris*, there were strong
suggestions of a perfectionist, even sectarian, underpinning to the judicial
reasoning. *Open Door* seemed to confirm that vision (although *Kennedy*
disputed it). The most striking feature of the *X* case, is that the reasoning
of the judges was secular; even the dissent did not rely on religious arguments. Reliance on religious arguments would have raised serious
problems with the criterion of explicability discussed earlier, and the
judicial evolution can be seen as a new mark of respect for that principle.
Furthermore, the majority judges did not rely on any perfectionist theory
(or at least not any perfectionist theory with a strong conception of the
good). They relied on a discussion of the rights involved. No one suggested that abortion may be prohibited because it was immoral or
unpopular, or violated God's law. Rather it was prohibited because it
violated the right to life of the unborn. Indeed the majority upheld a *right*
to an abortion, that is a right to do something perceived as immoral.
Again, the argument of some of the judges that the right to life could be
limited to protect the right to life, did not rely on any perfectionist theory.

The Supreme Court provided a controversial concretisation of the
moral legal principles of Irish abortion law. They did not simply say (as
many would have said) that the girl was free to go, although abortion
violated a human right. Nor did they say, as Finnis and the Catholic
Church, that the termination of a pregnancy to save the life of the girl, was

not an abortion. Either (inconsistent) view would have played mere lip service to the constitutional doctrine of a hierarchy of rights, the constitutional right to life of the foetus, and the constitutional supremacy of life.

The decision posed many questions which Parliament tried to avoid answering by proposing three referenda to the People. These amendments provided that Art. 40.3.3 did not limit either the right to travel or the right to receive information about services lawfully available abroad, and provided that an abortion was not justified to prevent a suicide. If all these had been accepted, it would mean that a judge in an *X* type case would have to say to a suicidal woman - 'you have no right to an abortion - but you may go to have one anyway'. This solution the people rejected; rather they voted in favour of the first two proposals, and against the third. The right to abortion in limited cases remained, but now judges and legislators had to reconsider the abortion rules developed in *Open Door*.[89]

The *Abortion Information* case

Parliament passed the Regulation of Information (Services outside the State for Termination of Pregnancies) Bill to implement the Fourteenth Amendment's guarantee of the freedom to receive information about services lawfully available abroad. The Bill did not refer to abortion services within the State which, for the most part, remained unlawful. The Bill referred to information about abortion services outside the State as 'Act information'. Under sections 3 and 4, provided certain conditions are met, one could publish abortion services information, except by a public notice posted in a public place or by unsolicited distribution of publications. Such information could only refer to services which were lawfully available in the foreign State, had to be 'truthful and objective', and could not advocate abortion.

Section 5 of the Bill dealt with people who provided pregnancy counselling. They were not allowed to advocate an abortion. They were obliged to provide information about all the options, in addition to abortion, available to a pregnant woman. Sections 6 and 7 required such counsellors not to have any financial or other personal interest in abortion services, nor to receive any benefit from persons providing abortion services, nor to receive any benefit from pregnant women regarding the provision of abortion information. Section 8 precluded such counsellors from making an appointment or any other arrangement for a pregnant woman with a foreign abortion service. They could however turn medical records over to the pregnant woman. Persons who violated the provisions faced a £1,500 fine.

The Bill avoided certain matters, most notably whether the parents of a minor, or the husband of a pregnant woman, had any right to be informed about her activities and request for abortion information. Also, the duties of pregnancy counsellors, doctors, etc. were left unclear.

When Parliament passed the Bill, President Robinson referred it to the Supreme Court under Art. 26 of the Constitution for a determination as to its validity. The Court appointed two sets of lawyers to argue against the Bill, one set invoking the right to life of the pregnant woman, one set invoking the right to life of the foetus. The Court handed down a single opinion (as required by Art. 26), read by Hamilton C.J. (the first instance judge in *Open Door*) confirming the Bill's validity, and so precluding it from ever being challenged again in a court action.[90]

There are five key elements to the decision: the treatment of natural law; the role of constitutional interpretation; the proper interpretation of the Fourteenth Amendment; the duties of counsellors; and the claims of third parties to be notified where a woman seeks abortion information.

Counsel arguing the position of the foetus argued that the Fourteenth Amendment was itself unconstitutional. They argued that the Constitution was founded on the natural law and anything which assisted an abortion violated the natural law. The provision of abortion information was such a violation and so could not be rendered constitutional by a referendum. In making this argument the lawyers were relying on some of the more extreme statements made by Irish lawyers about the natural law underpinnings of the Constitution.[91]

The Supreme Court dismissed this claim (p. 102). This argument assumed, wrongly, that the natural law was the foundational law of the State. Art. 5 of the Constitution identified Ireland as a 'sovereign, independent democratic state'. Art. 6 of the Constitution said that all powers of government derive 'under God, from the people, whose right it is ... to decide all questions of national policy ....'. The people were the supreme authority and the Constitution their creature.[92] Those powers of government could only be exercised in the manner prescribed by the Constitution which created those powers, and 'limits, confines and restricts' them (p. 103). The Constitution was supreme, and any measure which violated it was unlawful (p. 104). Each organ of government was required to act 'subject to the provisions of this Constitution', and, in addition, judges swore an oath to uphold the Constitution. There was no power to review the substance of a constitutional amendment, (provided it was adopted in a procedurally correct manner).

Counsel's argument was based on what the Court identified as a misreading of several cases. The cases which referred to unenumerated personal rights and extra-textual values did not recognise the natural law as superior to the Constitution (pp. 105 -107).[93] In particular, the Court reiterated what Walsh J. said in *McGee*, that in a 'pluralist society', courts could not choose between the philosophies of different theologians and different denominations (p. 107). What counsel saw as reference to natural law was actually the interpretation of the Constitution which involved reference to extra-textual values. In particular the unenumerated personal rights cases did not establish the superiority of natural law. Rather in each case the court had:

> ... satisfied itself that such personal right was one which could be reasonably implied from and was guaranteed by the provisions of the Constitution, *interpreted in accordance with its ideas of prudence, justice and charity*. (p. 107, italics added)

The Fourteenth Amendment was valid, and had to be interpreted in accord with the Court's ideas of prudence, justice and charity.

These comments are of the greatest importance. First, they emphasised that it was legitimate for courts to refer to extra-textual values to interpret the Constitution. The courts had to pursue a synthesis between the constitutional text and fundamental values (p. 107). Second, these fundamental values did not override the Constitution. That would fail to do justice to the sovereignty of the people, the supreme authority. To put it in more theoretical terms, the natural law argument sought to vindicate natural rights, such as the right to life of the unborn, and put them on a higher plane than procedural rights, expressed in exercises of popular sovereignty. The Supreme Court rejected this position, and rather tried to find a synthesis which did justice both to popular sovereignty and fundamental rights. Third, the Supreme Court vindicated the non-sectarian approach of the *Norris* dissenters, an approach which had re-emerged in the *X case*. [94] The Court rejected the sectarian and perfectionist overtones of cases like *Ryan*, *Norris* and *Open Door*. It repeated Walsh J.'s stalwart defence of pluralism. It dismissed the suggestions in various cases and articles that theological, Christian perhaps even Catholic, teachings on the natural law had a role to play in interpreting the Constitution, and dismissed those arguments as illegitimate in the most powerful way: it ignored them.[95]

Having dealt with these broad issues, the Court turned to other matters. The Court rejected an attempt to narrow the interpretation of the Fourteenth Amendment. Counsel had suggested that the Fourteenth Amendment only permitted the distribution of 'information of a general nature' and did not permit the distribution of information about specific abortion services (p. 101). The Court dismissed this argument. The Fourteenth Amendment provided that the first sentence of Art. 40.3.3 should not limit the freedom to provide such information. So, the Court could not refer to it in determining the freedom of information. The Fourteenth Amendment covered information relating to services (p. 102).

The Court here is motivated by a commitment to freedom of information which is not explicitly announced. This interpretation of the Fourteenth Amendment is only compelling if one assumes that prior to its enactment, the distribution of general information about abortion, was already constitutionally protected, presumably as an aspect of the freedom of expression. This would explain why cases such as *Open Door* only prevented the distribution of specific information about specific abortion services in specific circumstances, i.e. where it was likely to facilitate an abortion. The general right to information being protected already, the Fourteenth Amendment must be given a wider interpretation, or else it is rendered meaningless. The interpretation the Court accepts is that it overturns *Open Door* and its progeny.

The next issue was the scope of the duties affecting counsellors, under the Bill. Counsel arguing for the right to life of the pregnant woman argued that the prohibition on a counsellor not to advise an abortion, and the prohibition against making an appointment or other arrangements for an abortion, posed a threat to the life of pregnant women. The Court disagreed. It explains that a very narrow interpretation must be given to these provisions. Sections 5 - 8 do not prevent a counsellor:

> ... once such appointment is made from communicating in the normal way with such other doctor with regard to the condition of his patient .... (p. 112)

He or she must not advocate or promote an abortion however. This did not mean that giving a pregnant woman information that would encourage her to have an abortion was prohibited:

> ... he is not in any way precluded from giving full information to a woman with regard to her state of health, the effect of the pregnancy thereon and the consequences to her health and life if the pregnancy continues and leaving to the mother the decision whether in all the circumstances the pregnancy should be terminated.

These interpretations are very interesting. In both cases the Bill's language was ambiguous - prohibiting counsellors from 'making an appointment or *any other arrangement*' could easily cover any communication between doctors relating to a pregnant woman seeking an abortion. The prohibition on the 'promotion' of an abortion could also cover the giving even of objectively truthful information. Parliament left both these sections ambiguous precisely so that it could avoid a public stance on the controversial issue of how far a doctor could facilitate an abortion. The Supreme Court decided for it.

The Supreme Court read both of these sections narrowly, to give the greatest scope for the respect of several personal rights. A doctor could not say 'You really should have an abortion', nor could she phone a foreign abortion clinic and make an appointment for a patient. She could however point out the effects or possible effects of continuing with a pregnancy, give a patient the addresses and phone numbers of foreign clinics, and consult with the doctors at such a clinic about her patient's condition. Reading the bill's provisions in this way involved a rejection of the privileged position of the foetus' right to life as identified in *Open Door*, and gave greater emphasis to the freedoms of expression, communication and information, the rights to life and health of the pregnant woman, and her right to privacy. The Court reduced the restrictions on freedom of expression, information and communication to the narrowest possible extent - advocacy of abortion, and making an appointment for an abortion. Its reason to do so is obvious - the life and health of the pregnant woman could possibly be endangered if doctors could not communicate with foreign medical agents about the medical condition of the patients. However, the Court is also here evincing a concern for the privacy of the pregnant woman - interpreted as a right to make decisions about certain intimate matters and to implement those conditions. The Court did not limit the doctor's freedom in these cases to instances where (e.g.) she believed her patient's life was in danger, or to instances where she has ascertained that her patient believed her life to be in danger. The freedom of communication covered all instances, forms and contents of communications, (except for narrowly defined exceptions), where the pregnant woman had made 'the decision whether in all the circumstances the pregnancy should be terminated' in the words of the Court.

This concern for the right to privacy - unprecedented in any of the abortion decisions - is further seen in another clarification of the bill. Parliament did not deal with two further matters: when the pregnant woman is a minor, must the parents be informed about her request for information? if the woman is married must her husband be informed? Must this be done, implicitly under the Bill, or did the failure to provide for it amount to a violation of the rights of parents and husbands? The Supreme Court reiterated the 'presumption of constitutionality' doctrine which has two important features.[96] First, where there is a choice between an interpretation of a statute which violates the Constitution and an interpretation which does not, the courts must choose the latter. Second, where a statute provides for a discretion or power to be exercised, but does not expressly mention that it should be exercised fairly, then it must be presumed that such a discretion will be exercised in accordance with the concept of constitutional fairness or justice (an amorphous phrase which covers a wide range of principles, including certain duties to give notice). If the discretion is not so exercised then the courts will correct that without invalidating the statute.

The Court accordingly ruled that the bill did not violate any constitutional rights of parents or husbands. Counsellors were required to give comprehensive information about all options to pregnant women, and it must be presumed that the counsellor will 'have regard to and give advice in accordance with the principles of constitutional justice' (p. 115). Does this mean the bill implicitly requires such notification? The answer to this question seems to be 'no', for the Court continued:

> Constitutional justice requires that in the giving of such information, counselling and advice regard be had to the rights of persons likely to be affected by such information, counselling or advice. (p. 115)

This seems to require counsellors to discuss the issue of notification with the pregnant woman, but does not require or authorise them to notify such third parties themselves. The 'information, counselling and advice' referred to is that given to the pregnant woman. The decision to notify third parties was left to the woman. The Court did not explain precisely why this should be so. One can easily imagine a Court holding that a minor may not have an abortion without her guardians' consent, nor a wife without at least notifying her husband. The Court's reason not to require notification must rest on a commitment (not expressed) to the right of privacy. It seeks to respect the fact that pregnancy and abortion concern a matter of the most fundamental intimacy for a pregnant woman. Information about a woman's pregnancy is *her* information, relating to a matter covered by the right to privacy. The decision about who else should be informed is one only she can make. A counsellor may only advise her.

In conclusion, the *Abortion Information case* makes several important decisions. The natural law is not the supreme law of the State – the Constitution is. This is the only way to respect the sovereignty of the people who are the supreme authority and who create the Constitution which creates and limits all powers of government. In interpreting the Constitution, judges must however rely on extra-textual values, most particularly their conceptions of 'prudence, justice and charity'. The Fourteenth Amendment does not just cover information of a general nature about abortion, but also specific information. The Information Bill must be interpreted narrowly where it seeks to restrict the freedom of information. In particular it must be read so as to respect the rights to life, health and privacy of pregnant women. Read in the light of these fundamental rights, the Bill,

> ... represents a fair and reasonable balancing by the *Oireachtas* [Parliament] of the conflicting rights herein and is not so contrary to reason and fairness as to constitute an unjust attack on the constitutional rights of the unborn or any other person. (p. 115)

Conclusion

This Chapter has discussed the constitutional position of sexual morality in Ireland during the last three decades. In the early 1960s contraception was legally unavailable in the State, abortion was illegal, and homosexual conduct was illegal. Now, in 2000, contraception is freely available, abortion is legal in very limited circumstances, and gay men and lesbians benefit from anti-discrimination legislation.[97]

This evolution in society was the product of many social and economic changes which I cannot discuss here. The judiciary played a major role in this evolution, at some moments, even the defining role. The judges who, inspired by their US colleagues, took part in the constitutional revolution developed several doctrines which fanned the winds of legal, social and cultural change. Specifically the judges stressed that the Constitution must not be shackled by historical interpretations; that it must be interpreted in accord with evolving notions of prudence, justice and charity; that it protects all personal rights, not just those mentioned in the text; and that the judges should act as constitutional guardians.

This judicial attitude accelerated the public debate on sexual morality. In decisive legal pronouncements in the early 1970s, the Supreme Court declared Ireland to be a 'pluralist society'.[98] While Parliament declined to remove the ban on the sale or manufacture of contraceptives, the Court decided that Irish conditions of the 1970s required the State to recognise a zone of intimacy where it could not interfere with autonomously made decisions. With the *McGee* decision, sexual privacy became a publicly and legally recognised value.

Yet *McGee*, and more specifically Walsh J.'s opinion in it, contained an ambiguity, for it might speak to either a liberal or a conservative interpretation of the Constitution. It might be read as upholding the values of pluralism, tolerance and autonomy; or it might be read as emphasising the Christian natural law inheritance of the Constitution. The latter interpretation would have offended the criteria of equal respect and explicability that we discussed in Chapter Three. The next 25 years were taken up with deciding which interpretation was correct.

The *McGee* decision provoked even greater public debate on other sexual issues, like homosexuality and abortion. In the 1970s judges made it clear that abortion would be perceived as a violation of the right to life. In the early 1980s, conservative groups successfully pushed their agenda and a more perfectionist, indeed sectarian, vision of political morality became prominent. Conservatives succeeded in obtaining an amendment to the Constitution which recognised the equal rights to life of the foetus and the pregnant woman (defeating a Government proposal which would merely have legitimated anti-abortion laws). While the Government in the 1980s sought to liberalise Ireland's contraceptive and divorce laws, the two competing political moralities were powerfully articulated in *Norris*.[99] The majority read the Constitution in the light of perfectionist values emphasised in part of the constitutional text, values which refer to the specifically Christian nature of Irish society. The minority upheld the pluralist vision of the early 1970s, arguing for a zone of privacy in which the individual may develop his personality without State interference.

The rest of the 1980s saw the apparent triumph of perfectionist values. This was emphasised in the *Open Door* case.[100] Here the High Court whipped out of a legal wig, like a juridical conjuror, a 'crime' novel to Irish law, conspiracy to corrupt public morals, a crime likely to strike without warning into the private sphere, likely to hinder the rights of privacy, expression and communication, a crime without any statutory or precedential basis in Irish law.

However, this was not the end of the debate on political morality, for this public debate does not end. The European Court of Human Rights sided with the *Norris* dissenters and Ireland was required to alter its laws. Within the space of a few years, the ban on homosexual conduct was lifted, and it was made a crime to discriminate against gay men and lesbians in employment matters,[101] or to incite hatred against them on the basis of their sexual orientation.[102] The Prime Minister of the day publicly affirmed the value of equal respect in defending these changes, thus vindicating the *Norris* dissent.

Meanwhile a human tragedy brought the issue of sectarianism, perfectionism and liberalism once more to the courts. The Courts ultimately decided that the very wording of the 1983 anti-abortion amendment actually guaranteed a right to an abortion where the life of the pregnant woman was in danger. Otherwise the right to life of the foetus 'trumped' the rights of the woman. What is notable about the *X case* however is the absence of any of the sectarian references invoked by the *Norris* majority. Constitutional law became a matter of balancing constitutional rights, not upholding specifically Christian values.

This commitment to pluralism is even more pronounced in the *Abortion Information Bill* reference.[103] The court refuse to hear the testimony of moral theologians, and dismissed the sectarian perfectionist interpretation of the *Norris* majority. Indeed, in the 1995 case the Supreme Court did not even refer to the religious flourishes of the Constitution. Rather it adopted interpretations of both the Fourteenth Amendment and the Abortion Information Bill, which respected the rights of expression, health and privacy.

By tracing the undisclosed assumptions about political morality, I have tried to make these cases appear as they are, the narrative of a debate on the meaning of the right to privacy, and more generally, on the meaning of constitutional rights. Thus we see how judges have both concretised the political moral choices of the political authorities, but also proposed new and competing visions of constitutional legitimacy.

Other advantages are gained by such an analysis, namely clarity, coherence, legal and moral justification. Clarity is obtained by looking at decisions and exposing all the political moral beliefs on which they are based. See, for instance, Walsh J. in the *McGee* decision. He adopted a strongly anti-perfectionist, and initially secular reasoning to justify a right of marital privacy located in the bounds of Art. 41. However surely such an anti-perfectionist reasoning was inappropriate in the context of the theologically inspired Art. 41. Article 40.3.1, with its individualist secular cast, was a more sensible textual base for an anti-perfectionist right. Furthermore, the initially secular mode of reasoning was possibly in tension with some of the later comments on religion.

Consider the opinion of Hamilton P. in *Open Door*. His approach at one stage emphasised the overriding value of personal rights - judges may do anything to protect them. However, he also accepted, without any qualification, the existence of such a crime as conspiracy to corrupt public morals. Such a crime posed a serious threat to the rights he wished to protect. The essential inconsistency between these two parts of his opinion are exposed only by a political analysis.

By exposing the political moral reasoning behind the decisions we can also examine their coherence with the principles of other decisions. Thus, in *Norris*, we see that the dissenters adopt a political approach which cannot be reconciled with the majority's. It is not merely different. It would be utterly incoherent to attempt to follow both approaches. Yet in *Kennedy*, Hamilton P. follows the approach of the *Norris* dissenters. Why should he opt for an approach which is so at variance with that of a clear cut majority's? This is significant: the Supreme Court majority offered a particular decision, implicitly resting on a particular political argument, and Hamilton P. essentially ignores it.

Even earlier, we can see complete incoherence as regards the *Norris* and *McGee* decisions. *McGee* clearly avoided religious rhetoric, except in some comments of Walsh J.; *Norris* contained several religiously inspired comments. *McGee* unequivocally rested on an interpretation of present day conceptions of justice; *Norris* seemed to suggest a return via time machine to an earlier age. The *McGee* majority endorsed an anti-perfectionist morality, whereas *Norris* was clearly perfectionist in its orientations.

Furthermore, by exposing these underlying assumptions, we draw out all the links in the chain which lead the judges from constitutional text to individual decision. Consider the opinion of Henchy J. in *McGee*. Nowhere did he state bluntly the principle that an individual was entitled to make decisions as regards sexual morality, and the State, as a mark of respect for her autonomy, was obliged to give her reasonable opportunity to implement that decision. He came close to identifying it as the core of his reasoning, but doesn't quite. Yet this was the point that does much of the work in the opinion. Other solutions were possible, which Henchy J. did not consider. In particular he did not justify his choice for this approach over a choice for a more perfectionist approach, or an approach such as FitzGerald C.J.'s which imposed a less significant duty on the State.

Again consider *Norris*. The crux of that case was that homosexuals are inferior to heterosexuals. Yet nowhere was this seriously defended, except by reference to tradition and Christianity. Yet, this assumption is not obviously true. Why should we accept the traditional Christian approach? Is there some communitarian or other perfectionist belief behind it and if so, what is it?

This last question brings us to a final advantage of such an approach. By now the reader appreciates that I believe political moral arguments plays a major role in constitutional adjudication, and that I believe such a role is legitimate. By consciously striving to make explicit that link, we obtain several other advantages. Not least of these is that the question of the moral (or political) critique of law, which everyone agrees is important, is brought quickly to the centre. Why should anyone be allowed to do that which the majority, and Parliament, believes to be immoral? The *McGee* majority does not justify its somewhat activist approach. Why should the State be permitted to intrude into the bedrooms of gay men, and unmarried people, but not into the bedrooms of married heterosexuals? *Norris* gives no answer. Why should any woman even a suicidal one be allowed to destroy the foetal life within her? Why should the State prevent any woman from ending a pregnancy which has become distressful?

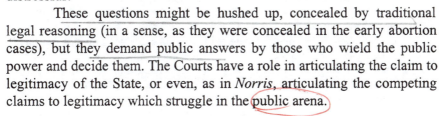

These questions might be hushed up, concealed by traditional legal reasoning (in a sense, as they were concealed in the early abortion cases), but they demand public answers by those who wield the public power and decide them. The Courts have a role in articulating the claim to legitimacy of the State, or even, as in *Norris*, articulating the competing claims to legitimacy which struggle in the public arena.

Notes

1   See Hug, *The Politics of Sexual Morality in Ireland* for a penetrating account of these political, social and legal controversies.

2   See Kelly, Hogan and Whyte, *The Irish Constitution*; Chubb, *The Government and Politics of Ireland*; Twomey, *Ireland's Evolving Constitution*.

3   Departure from precedent has increased of late: see Kelly, *The Irish Constitution* p. xciii.

4   Although these rights are usually phrased in favour of citizens, no court has ever denied non-citizens their protection. See Kelly, *The Irish Constitution*, p. 785.

5   *Ryan* v. *Attorney General*, [1965] I.R. 294.

6   Kelly, *The Irish Constitution*, pp. 755 - 789.

7 The discretionary powers of the President are immune from review (Art. 18.3, as is the Prime Minister's discretion to dissolve Parliament (*O'Malley* v. *An Taoiseach*, [1990] I.L.R.M. 460). Laws passed to resolve a constitutional emergency are immune from review (Art. 28.3.3), as are laws which had been referred as bills to the Supreme Court by the President and declared by the Court to be constitutional (Art. 26).

8 *State (Quinn)* v. *Ryan*, [1965] I.R. 70.

9 See Kelly, Hogan and Whyte *The Irish Constitution* p. xcviii - cxxii for a general overview. For a recent critical assessment, see A. Kavanagh 'The Quest for Legitimacy in Constitutional Interpretation' (1997) 32 *Ir. Jur.* 195 and S. Mullally 'Searching for Foundations in Irish Constitutional Law' (1998) 33 *Ir. Jur.* 333. See also D. Gwynn-Morgan, 'Constitutional Interpretation: Three Cautionary Tales' (1988) 10 *D.U.L.J.* 24; G. Hogan, 'Unenumerated Personal Rights: Ryan's case re-evaluated' (1990 - 92) 25 - 27 *Ir. Jur.* 95; R. Humphreys, 'Constitutional Law - Bonjour Tristesse: reasons and results in constitutional adjudication' (1992) 14 *D.U.L.J.* 105; R. Humphreys, 'Constitutional Interpretation' (1993) 15 *D.U.L.J.* 59; R. Humphreys, 'Interpreting Natural Rights' (1993 - 95) 28-30 *Ir. Jur.* 221; and the various articles in D. Curtin and D. O'Keefe (eds.) *Constitutional Adjudication in European Community and National Law* (Dublin: Butterworths, 1992); F. Litton (ed.), *The Constitution of Ireland* (Dublin: Institute of Public Administration, 1987).

10 So when the Supreme Court had to decide whether the basic common law rule that there can be no appeal against an acquittal in a criminal case was constitutional, O'Higgins C.J. referred to Art. 34.4.3 which provides that there shall be an appeal from *all* decisions of the High Court to the Supreme Court. Simply, 'plain words must ... be given their plain meaning'. 'All decisions' meant all decisions, and so there could be an appeal: *People (DPP)* v. *O'Shea*, [1983] I.L.R.M. 549, 583.

11 Indeed, in *O'Shea* the Supreme Court divided three to two on the meaning of the clause!

12 A Constitution is not a Finance Act, as Gavan Duffy J. quipped: *NUR* v. *Sullivan*, [1947] I.R. 77. Dixon J. thought that a 'unique, fundamental document, concerned primarily with the statement of broad principles in general language' should not be 'parsed with the particularity appropriate to ordinary legislation, and that the intention, if it can reasonably be gathered, should prevail', *O'Byrne* v. *Minister for Finance*, [1959] I.R. 1.
Sometimes, the Irish text is used to clarify the meaning of the English one: *O'Donoghue* v. *Minister for Education*, (right to education) [1996] 2 I.R. 20.

13 In *Tormey* v. *Ireland* the Supreme Court relied on a harmonious technique to avoid overturning the court structure established by law; [1985] I.R. 289.

14 Kelly, Hogan and Whyte, *The Irish Constitution*, p. xcii, xcix.

15 See J. Kelly, 'Law and Manifesto' in F. Litton ed., *The Constitution of Ireland*.

16 Kenny J. observed in *Crowley* v. *Ireland* [1980] I.R. 102, 126:

The *Constitution* must not be interpreted without reference to our history and to the conditions and intellectual climate of 1937....

17   The Supreme Court indicated in 1940 that this would be a consideration, when it held that the Constitution allowed internment without trial. It explained that internment was a measure so widely used in the pre-1937 Irish State, that one would have expected an explicit prohibition on internment, if it was to be prohibited at all: *Offences Against the State (Amendment) Bill,* [1940] I.R. 470.

18   [1974] I.R. 284, 292; see also *Melling* v. *Ó Mathghamhna,* [1962] I.R. 1; *Ryan* v. *Att. Gen.,* [1965] I.R. 294.

19   Sometimes, as in the first instance judgement of O'Keefe P. in *McGee,* it is confused with the previous variant: [1974] I.R. 285, 292.

20   [1984] I.R. 36.

21   The Supreme Court has often rejected this version - in *McGee* the Supreme Court reversed O'Keefe P. There are many other cases where historical institutions existing in 1937 have been swept away by a literalist, harmonious, purposive or moral standards analysis. For instance, the 'royal prerogative' has been eliminated from the constitutional order despite being mentioned in the text itself (Article 49). See *Byrne* v. *Ireland* [1972] I.R. 241; *Howard* v. *Commissioners for Public Works* [1993] I.L.R.M. 665. See also *State (Healy)* v. *O'Donoghue,* [1976] I.R. 325, 347 (criminal legal aid).

22   For, as O'Higgins C.J. said in *O'Shea:* '... the very existence of an inconsistency between what was formerly the law and ... the words of the Constitution ... repeals and abrogates what had been the law'. [1983] I.L.R.M. 549, 553 - 4.

23   Records detailing the secret drafting of the Constitution have only been available since 1987; the Parliamentary debates are unenlightening, and the views of the people difficult to ascertain.

24   The point behind this approach in summed up by Costello J. in a case dealing with whether the right to earn a livelihood was invaded when the State established a monopoly. Costello J. (as he then was) says: '... the courts should bear in mind that this document is a political one as well as a legal one and, whilst not ignoring the express text of the *Constitution,* a purposive approach ... is often a desirable one'. *Paperlink* v. *Attorney General,* [1984] I.L.R.M. 373, 385.

See *Murray* v. *Ireland,* [1985] I.R. 532, 539, rejecting a claim by a married couple, in jail, to be allowed to conceive children; *Quinn's Supermarket,* [1972] I.R. 14, 34, per Kenny J. explicitly preferring a purposive to a literalist approach, and *McGrath and O Ruairc v. Trustees of Maynooth College,* [1979] I.L.R.M. 166, 187.

Sometimes the purposive argument has been taken very far indeed; see *Attorney General* v. *Hamilton (No. 1),* [1993] 2 I.R. 250; *Meagher* v. *Minister for Agriculture* [1994] 1 I.L.R.M. 1, 27.

25   *State (Quinn)* v. *Ryan,* [1965] I.R. 70, at 123, per Ó Dálaigh C.J.

26   *People (DPP)* v. *O'Shea*, [1982] I.R. 384, 426. See his majority opinion in *Tormey* v. *Ireland*, [1985] I.R. 289, 295-6; *McGee* [1974] I.R. 284, 325; and O'Higgins C.J. in *State (DPP)* v. *Walsh*, [1981] I.R. 412, 424.

27   *Attorney General v. X*, [1992] 1 I.R. 1, 53, 71, 86.

28   See for instance *McKenna v. An Taoiseach* (No. 2) [1995] 2 I.R. 10.

29   Kelly, Hogan and Whyte, *The Irish Constitution*, p. ci.

30   In 1976, O'Higgins C.J. explained: '... rights given by the Constitution must be considered in accordance with the concepts of prudence, justice and charity which may gradually change or develop as society changes or develops, and which fall to be interpreted from time to time in accordance with prevailing ideas. ... the Constitution did not seek to impose for all time the ideas prevalent or accepted with regard to those virtues at the time of its enactment.' *State (Healy)* v. *Donoghue,* (criminal legal aid) [1976] I.R. 325, 347.

31   *Abortion Information case*, [1995] 2 I.L.R.M. 81, 102, 107. See *F. v. F.* [1994] 2 I.L.R.M. 401, 408; *Attorney General v. X*, [1992] 1 I.R. 1, 52 - 53.
For discussion of the relationship of the 'natural law' to constitutional law, see: *State (Ryan)* v. *Lennon*, [1935] I.R. 170, per Kennedy C.J. diss.; Grogan, 'The Constitution and the Natural Law' (1954) 8 *Christus Rex* 201; D. Clarke, *Church and State: Essays in Political Philosophy* (Cork: Cork University Press, 1984); Walsh, 'The Constitution and constitutional Rights' in Litton, ed. *the Constitution of Ireland*; O'Hanlon, 'Natural Rights and the *Irish Constitution*', (1993) *Irish Law Times* 8; O'Hanlon, 'The Judiciary and the Moral Law', (1993) ILT 129; Twomey, 'The Death of the Natural Law?' (1995) *ILT* 270; Clarke, 'The Constitution and Natural Law' (1993) *ILT* 177; Murphy, 'Democracy, Natural Law and the *Irish Constitution*' (1993) *ILT* 81; Whyte, 'Natural Law and the Constitution' (1996) *ILT* 8; De Blacam, 'Justice and Natural Law' (1997) 32 *Ir. Jur.* 323.

32   *O'Leary*, per Costello J., [1991] I.L.R.M. 454, 459.

33   Kelly, Hogan and Whyte, *The Irish Constitution*, p. xciii, pp. 532-538.

34   On occasion courts have relied on custom, i.e. what political actors such as Parliament and the Government do, determine the meaning of the *Constitution* to be. However this is quite rare, and open to the obvious criticisms that the political branches should obey the *Constitution*, not determine its content. See *Attorney General* v. *Hamilton (No.1)* for a controversial example: [1993] I.L.R.M. 81, 99, 125.

35   See for instance the lengthy discussion of Church-State case law in *Quinn's Supermarket* [1972] I.R. 1, 17 - 23; discussion of the right to use contraceptives in *McGee* [1974] I.R. 284, 326 - 328, 335; discussion of the right to die in *In re A Ward of Court*, [1996] 2 I.R. 79, 129 - 133; analysis of discrimination and bills of attainder in *An Blascaod Mor Teoranta v Commissioners of Public Works*, unrep. High Court, 27 February 1998. In *Norris*, [1984] I.R. 36, McCarthy J. observed that there were many similarities between the US and Irish Constitutions.

36   See *Byrne*, [1972] I.R. 241, 267; *Murphy* v. *Attorney General*, [1982] I.R. 241;
       Att. Gen. v. *Hamilton, (No.1)*, [1993] I.L.R.M. 81, 88; *Heaney v. Ireland* [1994]
       3 I.R. 593, 607; *M'Kenna v. An Taoiseach* (No. 2) [1995] 2 I.R. 10, 54.

37   In *O'Leary* v. *Attorney General*, Costello J. decided that the right to a fair trial
       included the right to a presumption of innocence. In making this interpretation,
       he referred to the European Convention on Human Rights, the UN Universal
       Declaration, the American Charter of Human Rights and the African Charter on
       Human and Peoples' Rights: [1991] I.L.R.M. 454, 459. In *Heaney v. Ireland*
       [1994] 3 I.R. 593, 605-606 Costello J. found guidance in the case law of the
       European Court of Human Rights. See also *O'Donoghue* [1996] 2 I.R. 20;
       Desmond v. Glackin, [1993] 3 I.R. 67.
       Humphreys has identified the use of international instruments as being of
       particular importance : 'Constitutional Interpretation' (1993) 15 *D.U.L.J.* 59.

38   There have been isolated references to Aristotle (*McGee* [1974] I.R. 284, 318,
       per Walsh J), Hohfeld (*Att. Gen.*v. *Paperlink*, [1984] I.L.R.M. 373; *Murray* v.
       Ireland, [1985] I.R. 532, 540, per Costello J.), Cardozo (*M'Kinley* v. *Minister
       for Defence*, [1992] 2 I.R. 333, 348, per Hederman J.) in case law and judges
       have referred approvingly to Aquinas (Walsh, 'The Constitution and
       Constitutional Rights', in Litton, ed. *The Constitution of Ireland*, p. 94; Costello
       J., 'Limiting Rights Constitutionally' in O'Reilly ed. *Human Rights and
       Constitutional Law*, p. 178, 180), Finnis (O'Hanlon, 'Natural Rights and the
       Irish Constitution' (1993) *I.L.T.* 8.), and Dworkin (Keane J.'s Book Review of
       Law's Empire, (1987) 22 *Ir. Jur.* 125.) when writing extra-judicially. The Pope
       has done much better, with several judges appealing to papal encyclicals (Kenny
       J. in *Ryan* v. *Attorney General*, [1965] I.R. 294; O'Hanlon J. in *O'Donoghue* v.
       Minister for Health and others, [1996] 2 I.R. 20).

39   See the references to Prof. Kelly's work in *Employment Equality Bill 1996*,
       Supreme Court, 15 May 1997; *People (DPP) v Pringle*, Supreme Court, 4
       March 1997. Prof. Casey's work has also been referred to in *An Blascaod Mor
       Teoranta and Others v Commissioners of Public Works*, unrep. High Court, 27
       February 1998; *Eastern Health Board v Fitness to Practice Committee of the
       Medical Council*, unrep. High Court, 3 April 1998.

40   Subsequent portions of this Chapter are modified versions of a piece which
       appeared in (1996) 9 *Ratio Juris* 258 under the title 'Natural Law: Alive and
       Kicking?'. I am very grateful to Basil Blackwell for permission to use material
       from that article.

41   [1974] I.R. 284. References in brackets are to this report.

42   The Chief Justice, after noting the facts, said that s. 17 permitted one to obtain
       contraceptives, or to manufacture them, provided no one engaged in the specific
       prohibited activities (p. 300). Since this *formal* possibility existed there was no
       interference by the State. If the section had prohibited the use of contraceptives
       then it might well violate the fundamental (unenumerated) right of marital
       intimacy under Art. 40.3 (p. 301).

43   He referred to *Griswold* v. *Connecticut* as a similar case, 381 U.S. 479 (1965). The US Supreme Court struck down a statute which made it a crime to use contraceptives. The court divided in its reasoning. Douglas J., speaking for the plurality, held that there was a right of privacy found in the 'penumbras' of various different amendments (p. 483).

44   P. 335, referring to 367 U.S. 497, 552 (1961).

45   Walsh J. also held that the provision violated the right to the protection of one's health, which includes the right to positive assistance from the state in the provision of materials necessary for the protection of health (p. 315).

46   'The Constitution and Constitutional Rights' in Litton ed. *The Constitution of Ireland*, (Dublin, IPA, 1987); Walsh, B., 'The Constitution: A View from the Bench' in Farrell ed., *DeValera's Constitution and Ours*, (Dublin, Gill and MacMillan, 1987); Walsh in O'Keefe, Curtin, eds., *Constitutional Adjudication in Community and National Law*.

47   'The Constitution: A View from the Bench', p. 195.

48   'The Constitution: A View from the Bench', p. 192.

49   Pp. 89 - 91; [1935] I.R. 370.

50   'The Constitution and Constitutional Rights', p. 94.

51   Cf. Dworkin, *Law's Empire*, pp. 254 - 258.

52   Costello, 'The Natural Law and the Constitution' (1956) 45 *Studies* 403; and a Book Review (1962) 51 *Studies* 201.

53   Kelly, *Fundamental Rights in the Irish Law and Constitution* Introduction; Chubb, *The Politics of the Irish Constitution*, Ch. 6.

54   [1965] I.R. 294.

55   [1972] I.R. 1, a religious freedom case.

56   [1984] I.R. 36. Page references are to this report.

57   The issue of standing is one on which Irish judges have wavered from one extreme to another. See *Cahill* v. *Sutton*, [1980] I.R. 269; *SPUC* v. *Coogan*, [1989] I.R. 394; *Crotty* v. *An Taoiseach*, [1987] I.R. 713 and *Norris*, per McCarthy J.

58   McCarthy had been counsel for the State in the *McGee* decision. Henchy and Griffin JJ. had been part of the majority in *McGee*. The reference to Disneyland is derived from a comment of an Irish lawyer, referring to the unpredictability of the Supreme Court: 'Having lost in the High Court, we'll appeal to Disneyland'. See Chubb, *The Politics of the Irish Constitution*.

59   O'Higgins C.J. and Henchy J. rejected the appeal to the European Convention on Human Rights: the matter was one of Irish law, and the Convention was not part of Irish law (pp. 66, 68). McCarthy J. declined to decide this issue (p. 104).

60   (1981) 4 E.H.R.R. 149.

61   [1976] I.R. 325.

62   *Ryan*, [1965] I.R. 294, where Kenny J. describes unenumerated rights as being justified by the 'Christian and democratic nature of the State'.

In *McGee*, [1974] I.R. 284, Walsh J. describes persons as having basic rights that the state may not limit except in the interests of the common good. Judges, not theologians, must determine the extent of those rights in a pluralist society.

In *G.* v. *An Bord Uchtála*, [1980] I.R. 32, which concerned the rights of unmarried mothers, and children born outside marriage, Walsh J. cites approvingly Henchy J.'s *McGee* opinion that unenumerated rights vest in people by virtue of their human personality.

In *State (C.)* v. *Frawley*, [1976] I.R. 365 (the right not to be subject to inhuman and degrading treatment) and *State (M.)* v. *Attorney General*, [1979] I.R. 73 (the right to leave the State) Finlay P. referred to the phrase of Kenny J. in *Ryan* about the Christian ethos of the state.

63   Referring to the definition of Brandeis J. of the US Supreme Court. McCarthy J. also referred to *Stanley* v. *Georgia*, 394 U.S. 557 (1969); *Griswold* v. *Connecticut*, 381 U.S. 479 (1965); *Terry* v. *Ohio*, 392 U.S. 1 (1968); *Meyer* v. *Nebraska*, 262 U.S. 390 (1923).

64   Declared unconstitutional in *People* v. *O'Callaghan*, [1966] I.R. 501.

65   Declared unconstitutional in *King* v. *Attorney General*, [1981] I.R. 223.

66   Declared unconstitutional in *De Búrca* v. *Attorney General*, [1976] I.R. 38.

67   Finnis 'Personal Integrity, Sexual Morality and Responsible Parenthood' (1985) 1 *Anthropos* 43; 'Is Homosexual Conduct Wrong: Disintegrity' (1993) *The New Republic* Nov. 15th.

68   Dworkin, *A Matter of Principle*, pp. 353-9; *Life's Dominion*.

69   Rawls, *A Theory of Justice*, p. 3 italics added.

70   [1972] I.R. 1.

71   Dworkin, *A Matter of Principle*, pp. 181 - 213.

72   [1972] I.R. 1, 13 - 14, per Walsh J: '... this provision [Art. 40.1] ... is a guarantee related to their dignity as human beings and a guarantee against any inequalities grounded upon an assumption, or indeed a belief, that some individual or individuals or class of individuals, by reason of their human attributes or their ethnic or racial, social or religious background, are to be treated as the inferior or superior of other individuals in the community.'

73   [1974] I.R. 284, 312, per Walsh J: 'The private morality of its citizens does not justify intervention by the State into the activities of those citizens unless and until the common good requires it.'

74   1993 Criminal Law (Sexual Offences) Act; *Norris* v. *Ireland*, (1991) 13 E.H.R.R. 186; Walsh J. dissented in this case.

75   [1987] I.R. 587.

76   *Roe* v. *Wade*, (1973) 410 US 113.

77   The High Court rejected an attempt to stop the referendum procedure: *Finn*, [1983] I.R. 154.

78   *Att. Gen. (SPUC)* v. *Open Door*, [1987] I.R. 477. The English 1967 Abortion Act is more liberal than the Irish law.

79   *Shaw* v. *DPP*, [1962] Appeal Cases 220; *Knuller*, [1973] A.C. 446.

80   *Open Door*, [1988] I.L.R.M. 18, p. 27.

81   *King*, [1981] I.R. 223.

82   *Coogan*, [1989] I.R. 734; *Grogan* [1989] I.R. 753.

83   [1992] 1 I.R. 1.

84   *People v. O'Callaghan*, [1966] I.R. 510.

85   *Luisi and Carbone*, [1984] 1 E.C.R. 377, case 286/82.

86   *R. v. Bouchereau*, [1977] 2 E.C.R. 1999, case 30/77.

87   *State (Healy) v. O'Donoghue*, [1976] I.R. 325.

88   *Natural Law and Natural Rights*.

89   The Supreme Court rejected the opportunity to do so in *Att. Gen. (SPUC) v. Open Door*, [1994] I.L.R.M. 256, for procedural reasons. In 1995 Parliament finally enacted the Regulation of Information Act, which the Supreme upheld as valid: *Abortion Information*.

90   *Abortion Information case*, [1995] 2 I.L.R.M. 81. Page references are to this report.

91   This extreme position can be found in *State (Ryan) v. Lennon*, [1935] I.R. 170, per Kennedy C.J. diss.; Grogan, 'The Constitution and the Natural Law' (1954) 8 *Christus Rex* 201; Walsh, 'The Constitution and Constitutional Rights' in Litton, ed. *the Constitution of Ireland*; O'Hanlon, 'Natural Rights and the Irish Constitution', (1993) *ILT* 8; O'Hanlon, 'The Judiciary and the Moral Law', (1993) ILT 129.

92   Referring to Budd J. in *Byrne v. Ireland*, [1972] I.R. 241, 295.

93   *Ryan v. Att. Gen.*, [1965] I.R. 294; *McGee v. Ireland*, [1974] I.R. 284; *State (Healy) v. Donoghue*, [1976] I.R. 325; the *X case*, [1992] 1 I.R. 1.

94   And also in *F. v. F.* which insisted that it was for judges, not religious experts, to determine the meaning of the Constitution, in the light of evolving values, [1994] 2 I.L.R.M. 401, [1995] 2 I.L.R.M. 321.

95   An aspect severely criticised in Twomey, 'The Death of the Natural Law?' (1995) *ILT* 270. See *Corway v. Independent Newspapers* unrep. Sup. Crt., 30 July 1999 for a recent affirmation of pluralism.

96   *East Donegal Co-op Livestock Marts v. Att. Gen.* [1970] I.R. 317, 341.

97   This progression is intimately involved with the fall and rise of a leading Irish liberal and feminist, Mary Robinson from a Senator to a political outcast to President of Ireland. Mrs. Robinson had been involved in many of these cases: she had proposed a bill to abolish the anti-contraception provisions of the 1935 Criminal Law (Amdt.) Act; she had represented Senator Norris in the *Norris* case, and the students in the *Grogan* case; as President she made a delicately worded but moving statement about the *X* case; as President she referred the Abortion Information Bill to the Supreme Court.

98   *Quinn's Supermarket v. Ireland*, [1972] I.R. 1; *McGee v. Ireland* [1974] I.R. 274.

99   [1984] I.R. 36.

100   [1987] I.L.R.M. 477.

101   1993 Unfair Dismissals (Amdt.) Act, 1998 Employment Equality Act. Note also the 1999 Equal Status Bill.

102   1989 Prohibition of Incitement to Hatred Act.

103   [1995] 2 I.L.R.M. 81, see also *F.* v. *F.* [1994] 2 I.L.R.M. 401; [1995] 2 I.L.R.M. 321.

6   The Two Romes

Introduction

In this Chapter, we change the focus to a jurisdiction within the civilian legal tradition, where legal formalism is still an important force: Italy. I look at a particular topic in Italy for the same reason as in other countries: its importance to a central feature of the country's polity. That topic is the constitutional regulation of religion in Italy, and more particularly the relationship between the State and the Roman Catholic Church, whose capital is located within the former's.

The relationship has often been a tense one, most notably when Italian troops breached the walls of the Eternal City.[1] Whilst such State - Church disputes are no longer decided at bayonet point, they have often provoked controversy. It could not be otherwise in a democratic state, which has an overwhelming Catholic majority, but also a strong secularist and pluralist tradition. The 1947 Constitution reflects this tension. Art. 3 guarantees religious non-discrimination, Art. 8 protects the equal religious freedom of churches, and Art. 19 enshrines the individual right of religious freedom. Amidst these comprehensive guarantees of freedom and equality for all religions, there lies Art. 7:

> .1 The State and the Catholic Church are, each within its own ambit, independent and sovereign. .2 Their relations are regulated by the Lateran Pacts. Such amendments to these Pacts as are accepted by both parties do not require any procedure of Constitutional revision.

If the reader detects a certain inconsistency between the other provisions and Art. 7, she should suspend judgement until reading the 1929 Lateran Concordat which states, by reference to earlier texts, that the Catholic religion is the sole official religion of the State.

Of course the 1929 Concordat has been altered, and the 1984 Concordat abolishes this principle.[2] However, note well that 1984 *did not* mark a sudden rupture in the Italian legal order, and the reason for this was the case law of the Constitutional Court. To this legal order we now turn, briefly. Then I shall return to the evolution of the politics of religion in Italy.

Italy's Legal System

The legal inheritance of the Italian Republic is the civilian legal tradition, legal formalism, and the remnants of the fascist nightmare. The Italian system is one of Europe's civilian ones: here Parliament (*Camera dei deputati* and the *Senato*) make the laws, and the judges merely apply the laws impartially. The ordinary judges are recruited by competition and then given serious guarantees of independence (Arts. 101-110).

Typical of civilian jurisdictions, there are several court systems, with four 'supreme courts'. First, there are the ordinary civil courts which deal with civil and criminal law. The supreme civil court is the *Corte di Cassazione*, (Court of Cassation), which only reviews the legal basis of lower court decisions. If a decision is faulty on legal grounds, the *Corte di Cassazione* annuls it and returns it for a decision in accordance with its ruling. There is a separate administrative court system which deals with disputes involving the public administration. Here the *Consiglio di Stato* (Council of State) is the ultimate court of appeal, hearing appeals from the *Tribunali amministrativi regionali* (Regional Administrative Courts, TAR). The third Italian 'supreme' court is the *Corte dei conti* (Court of Auditors), which deals with matters of the state's budget. The fourth 'supreme court' is the *Corte costituzionale*.[3]

Italian dogmatics, legal theory and philosophy are still largely dominated by formalist models and traditional conceptions. Italian jurists are reluctant to deal with the 'game of interpretation' in which the judge mediates social conflicts through individual conflicts.[4] Baldassare writes of an inexplicable 'dogmatic' continuity, from the end of the 19th Century to the present day, of a dominant legal theory which is hostile to the incorporation of moral values into legal theories.[5]

As well as these elements the Italian Republic received a darker bequest from its past - the remnants of fascism. For many years, repressive fascist legislation persisted. Only in 1989 did Italy replace the fascist code of criminal procedure (*c.p.p., codice di procedura penale*); the 1931 code of penal law is still in force. The Italian Parliament never repealed Art. 113 of the Fascist law on Public Security which limited the right to spread information and thoughts - this was abrogated by the *Corte costituzionale* in its first decision.[6] It was left to the *Corte costituzionale* to actualise the Republican Constitution by cleansing the pre-Republican provisions.[7]

Many of these fascist bequests related to religion. The fascist era was a crucial one in church - state relations.[8] Before Mussolini's dictatorship, the liberal state was seen as the natural enemy of the Catholic Church.[9] In the first two decades of this century, the situation improved, and then Mussolini had his own reasons to end the dispute: the Catholic Church had too much influence in Catholic Italy and was thus a threat to Fascist authoritarianism. Also, he hoped to take advantage of the prestige that the Church offered Italy and its imperialist adventures.[10] The resultant compromise was the Lateran Concordat of 1929.

The agreement contains several provisions of interest. First, it resolved the Roman question: the Church renounced all temporal and territorial claims, notably to Rome. The state recognised the independence of the Church, and its remaining properties. As already noted it affirmed the principle, rejected by the liberal state, that the Roman Catholic religion was the sole official religion of the state; other religious groups were tolerated.

This was the inheritance of the Italian Republic - civilian legal system, academic legal formalism, and fascist elements. Into this was born a squabbling baby of post-World War II constitutionalism.[11] The Italian Constitution of 1947 is typical of the basic laws adapted in the aftermath of the cataclysm. Its first Article describes Italy as a democratic republic. Then follow the fundamental principles of inviolable human rights, human equality of dignity and non-discrimination. The Fundamental Principles section of the Constitution also contains the Articles on the Catholic Church and the other religious groups (Arts. 7, 8). This first section is followed by Arts. 13 - 28, which establish the fundamental rights of persons. These include the right to religious freedom (Arts. 19, 20) and the right to freedom of expression (Art. 21). Given the experience of the previous decades, these are expressed in quite strong terms,[12] and include relatively detailed guarantees.[13]

The Constitution also contains many provisions on social justice, and social matters generally. Article 1 describes the democratic republic as being founded on labour; Art. 3 includes an imperative to create a material equality in which workers have an effective political participation. Articles 35 - 46 contain egalitarian commitments on economic institutions, notably the position of workers and the right to property. The Constitution recognises the importance of education (Art. 47). The right to health is guaranteed (Art. 32). The family, founded on marriage, has a particular importance, and is based on the moral and legal equality of the spouses (Art. 29). Article 30 recognises the duties and rights of family members to each other.

The Constitution establishes a parliamentary democracy, where the executive (the *Consiglio dei Ministri*) is politically responsible to the two houses of parliament (*Senato, Camera dei deputati*) each of which is directly elected by the people (Arts. 55 - 82). There is a Head of State, the President of the Republic, who is elected by the Parliament, sitting in joint session. The Head of State's role is largely ceremonial (Art. 89), though the Italian President has several significant powers. He presides over the *Consiglio superiore della magistratura* (the body which safeguards judicial independence), and nominates 5 constitutional judges.

The Constitution can be altered by a bill approved by both houses of Parliament, twice. The second approval must take place at least three months after the first, and must be approved by votes at absolute majority. The proposal must be submitted to a referendum if one-fifth of the members of one house, or 500,000 voters, or 5 Regional Councils, request it. However it need not be submitted if approved by a two-thirds majority in each house (Art. 138). The republican form of the Constitution is unamendable (Art. 139).

Unusually in western democracies, Italy makes provisions for popular referenda on ordinary pieces of legislation. There is provision both for popular initiative of legislation, and popular abrogation (Arts. 71, 75), each time at the request of 500,000 voters.

The Constitutional Court

One of the more striking innovations of the 1947 Constitution is the creation of the *Corte costituzionale*, created in Title VI, on Constitutional

Guarantees (Arts. 134 - 138).[14] In the liberal and fascist regimes, no one could argue (in principle) that a statute was unconstitutional and invalid. As in traditional European legal theory, no judge was competent to review the decisions of Parliament. However, after the end of the dictatorship, absolute popular sovereignty no longer had a good name, and a form of judicial control was envisaged. The *Corte costituzionale* began operating in 1956, when Parliament finally enacted the laws regulating its activities.[15]

Only the *Corte* can decide whether a statute (or act having the force of a statute) is valid.[16] A less centralised system, where any judge could decide, would have eliminated legal certainty given the large number of judges, the multiplicity of legal systems (civil, administrative, fiscal), and the absence of a doctrine of precedent.[17] Also, in 1947, the legal system was impregnated with fascist influences which made it inadvisable to trust the ordinary judges with the power of constitutional review.

The *Corte* has 15 judges, five of whom are elected by the ordinary supreme courts, five by Parliament (sitting in joint session and acting by a super-majority), and five are nominated by the President of the Republic. Each judge sits for a term of nine years which is not renewable. The *Corte* is presided over by a President who is elected by the constitutional judges themselves. The *Corte* has significant guarantees of independence; members can only be removed for serious misbehaviour or incapacity, and then only by a vote of the *Corte* itself, approved by a two-thirds majority.[18] The judges are chosen from among three categories; the ordinary judges of the civil and administrative courts, university law lecturers, advocates having 20 years of experience. In practice, the academics, who include some of Italy's best known constitutionalists, play the significant role in the court.

The selection process for the *Corte* is noteworthy, in comparison with the other two states discussed, as it rejects the outright dominance of the political executive, and tries to balance the requirements of democratic legitimacy with judicial impartiality, by requiring special majorities, and several different bodies to choose the judges.

The *Corte* has four main tasks. It decides upon the criminal responsibility of the President of the Republic (Arts. 90, 134), it judges the admissibility of referendum petitions, it decides upon conflicts of attributions when asked to do so by a political body,[19] and it judges the validity of statutes on preliminary references from judges.

This last activity, called judgement *in via incidentale*, is the predominant one of the Court.[20] This comes about when an ordinary judge (the judge *a quo*), in the course of a case, believes that a decision on the validity of a statute is needed to resolve it. She may refer it to the *Corte costituzionale*, either on her own motion or that of a party, provided she certifies that it is relevant to her decision and that the challenge is not manifestly unfounded.

Once referred to the *Corte costituzionale*, a member of the Court is appointed as *rapporteur* (*giudice relatore*) to prepare the discussion. The parties to the case, as well as the Prime Minister (*Presidente del Consiglio dei Ministri*) (who is represented by an *Avvocato dello Stato*), and the premier of any regional government involved, are invited to present arguments on the question. After argument, the *Corte costituzionale* decides whether to accept or reject the challenge. In the former case, normally the statutory provision ceases to have effect from the day following the publication of the decision,[21] - decisions usually have prospective effect only.[22]

A decision of the *Corte costituzionale* has three parts - the consideration of the facts, the consideration of the law, and the disposition. Only one judgement is released - there are no dissenting or concurring opinions. In the disposition, the *Corte costituzionale* holds the law valid or otherwise. This is the only part of the judgement that has *erga omnes* effect - it is valid for everyone, and not just the parties to the case. Once the Court reaches its decision, then the matter goes back to the referring judge, who applies the Court's decision to the facts before her.[23]

The Catholic Compromise

Fascism and Catholicism were not united during the Mussolini regime - there were often disagreements between the forces spiritual and temporal.[24] However, Mussolini carried to its apex a process which for two decades had seen the convergence of the 'two parallel lines which should never meet'.[25] The Lateran Pacts (a treaty, Concordat, and four protocols) constituted this apex. All the agreements begin 'In the name of the Holy Trinity'. In its first Article, the Treaty affirmed that the Roman

Catholic Apostolic religion was the sole religion of the State. It recognised the sovereignty of the Vatican State, thus resolving the vexed Roman question. The Treaty regulated the proprietary privileges of the Vatican, the status of people working there, etc.

The Concordat regulates the position of the Church in Italy. The first few Articles guarantee the freedom of action of the Church.[26] Article 11 begins the process of entrenching Catholic elements in the State, recognising religious holidays as State holidays.

Article 34 is particularly important. Here, Italy, recognised marriage as the basis of the family, and guaranteed to recognise the civil effects of a canonical marriage celebrated according to the rites of the Catholic Church. Further, questions of the nullity of such marriages were reserved to the ecclesiastical tribunals. Decisions of the ecclesiastical tribunals were to be made effective by a decree of the State's Court of Appeal in the relevant territory.

Article 36 of the Concordat dealt with religious education. The State recognised the overwhelming importance of teaching religion according to Catholic doctrine. The people who taught religious education had to be approved by the ecclesiastical authority. Also the professors of two Catholic universities had to have, in effect, a certificate of moral health from the Vatican (Art. 38).

These were the main terms of the Lateran Pacts. After the death of Fascism, and during the conception of the First Republic, the Constituent Assembly had to consider their position. In 1947 the Constituent Assembly voted to approve the wording of Art. 7 of the Constitution, rejecting the proposals of some republican and socialist deputies for a more secular wording (and also rejecting the more extreme fringes of Christian deputies). The Christian Democrat leader, De Gasperi, argued that the Article assured the world that Italy was a free republic, at peace with the Catholic Church whose head was located in Rome. The Republic was not hostile to minorities - he assured the Assembly that his party would vote to end the provisions of the criminal code hostile to non-Catholic groups (they did not). Article 7 served merely as the basis of the relationship between the two sovereign entities, the Catholic Church and the Italian State. Importantly, he stated that Art. 7 did not 'arrest history' - it left open the possibility of evolution, without the necessity of constitutional amendment. The Article was approved by 350 votes to 149 (thanks to the Communist Party).[27] Article 7 recognised that both the Church and State were independent, but that their relations were regulated in accordance with the Lateran Pacts, taking into account such modifications which may be made to these. Nevertheless, the Constitution also contained generous guarantees of religious non-discrimination, and freedom.

Although not apparently required by the Pacts, the fascist State provided a special position for the Catholic Church as regards certain crimes, specifically blasphemy (*bestemmia*) and outraging (*vilipendio*) the Church. In the case of *vilipendio*, the penalty for outraging religions other than the Catholic one was diminished. Blasphemy against non-Catholic religions was not punished at all.

These were not the only Fascist regulations on religion which survived into the Republic. The royal decree n. 1731 of 30th Oct., 1930, must also be considered. This regulated the position of the Union of the Jewish Community, whose purpose was to look after the religious needs of the Jewish community, in accordance with the law, and Jewish traditions. The decree specified that all Jewish residents of Italy belonged to this organisation. It further specified the various duties (e.g. contributions) of those members, their rights within the organisation, and some of its organisational features. If this does not sound terribly ominous it should. Precisely such Jewish organisations were essential in the process of the Holocaust.[28] (Of course, the persecution in Italy was quantitatively and qualitatively different from that in other Nazi dominated countries.[29])

And now the *Corte costituzionale* ....

The Christian Democrat leader was correct when saying that the Concordat and Article 7 were merely the starting points for an evolution, but he probably did not envisage the forum in which that evolution would occur. One of the main innovations of the 1947 Constitution, was the creation of the *Corte costituzionale*, charged with supervising Parliament's observance of the Constitution. How did it interpret these provisions?

In a series of decisions spanning five decades, the *Corte costituzionale* adopted three approaches, which evolved in a particular direction, as legal text and political morality interacted in constitutional interpretation. The first stage involved the rejection of an openly sectarian interpretation, and the favouring of a communitarian interpretation, slightly tinged with sectarianism. The second stage was an evolution of this communitarian interpretation in a more secular direction, as the scope and status of the Lateran Pacts were reduced. The third stage, with the co-operation of the political branches, moved on to the proclamation of the principle of the 'laicity' of the State. With these evolutions, the *Corte costituzionale* both responded to, and contributed to, the ongoing debate on the place of religion in Italy.

Community or Sect?

The first series of cases saw Court rejecting attempts to bypass or ignore Art. 7 of the Constitution, and eliminate the special position[30] of the Catholic Church. Here I present the reasoning in five decisions, and then make two points concerning them.

The first case is 125/1957.[31] Here Art. 404 of the *codice penale* (c.p. - criminal code) was under review. Article 404 (enacted in 1930) was a 'crime against religious sentiment' and punished *offese alla Religione dello Stato mediante vilipendio di cose* - outraging the state religion (the Catholic religion). Article 406 c.p. prohibited outraging the other churches, but the punishment was not as severe. Did this inequality violate the Constitution? The judge *a quo* thought the provision violated Arts. 7, 8 of the Constitution as the Constitution did not have a special regard for any particular religion. The *Avvocato Generale dello Stato* disagreed, arguing that Art. 8 guaranteed the liberty of the different churches, but did not require absolute equality. The crime was justified by the need to protect the ethical social value of religious sentiment (p.1211).

The *Corte costituzionale* noted that the legislator, in 1930, sought to protect the religious collective interest, recognising that it transcended the mere exercise of an individual right (p. 1213). The 1930 legislature introduced the diverse treatment for the Catholic Church. The Court explained that this difference was based on the social position of the Catholic Church, its long and uninterrupted tradition in Italy, and the fact that most Italians belong to it (pp. 1213 - 1214).

The Court then explained that unequal punishment of *vilipendio* did not violate the principle that all religions are equally free before the law (Art. 8). There was no infringement of liberty - every person was still free to practise her religion and no one's legal status was altered on the basis of her religion (p. 1214). The Constitution did not require absolute equality of treatment - it provided a special position for the Catholic Church in Art. 7. What the Constitution required was equal liberty, not identical regulation (p. 1215). The Court concludes that there was no contradiction between the two Articles, whatever the judge *a quo* may have thought.

Our second case involves a prosecution for blasphemy against the Cross. Article 724 c.p. punishes *bestemmia con invettive contro la divinità o simboli o persone della religione dello Stato* (blasphemy with invective against the divinity, symbols, persons of the religion of the State).[32] The referring judge asked for a decision on Art. 724's compatibility with Arts. 7, 8 of the Constitution.

One assumes that the *Corte costituzionale* considered the answer self-evident (the consideration of law lasts 25 lines). It referred to its decision 125/1957, quoting the reason for the special position of the Catholic Church. The special position was not based on the Church's identity, but rather on the fact that it was professed by most Italians. So it merited special protection, in view of the greater extent and intensity of the natural social reactions caused by such blasphemy (p. 992).

The next case (case 39/1965), combined a comprehensive discussion of the constitutional principles with a *tour de force* of legal reasoning.[33] During a prosecution under Art. 402 of the *codice penale,* which punished outraging the State religion, (*vilipendio*) the trial court requested a ruling on its validity. A veritable battery of constitutional provisions were thrown against its constitutional legitimacy (including Arts. 3, 8, 19, and 20 of the Constitution). The State argued for the provision's validity, stressing that the special position of the Catholic Church was something for the legislature in its own margin of appreciation to decide. Any discrimination against other religions was justified by Arts. 7 and 8 of the Constitution which recognised the unique position of the Catholic Church.

The *Corte costituzionale* dealt with the claims article by article. Against the apparently iron clad argument that Art. 3 of the Constitution forbids any distinction on the basis of religion, the Court responded with a piece of virtuoso reasoning. The *Corte costituzionale* explained that the fundamental principle of Art. 3 provides for the equality of citizens and prohibits making any distinctions based on religion among those citizens. It then noted that Art. 402 *does not* make any distinction among citizens on the basis of religion. It applied in the same way to all persons irrespective of their religion, who commit *vilipendio* against the Catholic religion. The religion of the accused, in the Court's words, had no relevance. No Catholic citizen was put in a position superior to that of her compatriots (pp. 608 - 609). Whichever of them commits *vilipendio* against the Catholic religion of the State was punished to the same extent.

Whilst the remainder of the judgement lacks this intricacy of reasoning, it is not without flair. The Court turned to Art. 8 of the Constitution, with its guarantee of equal liberty for all religions. It reiterated its previous reasoning that there was a difference between the equal freedom of religions and the equal treatment of religions. The first was a constitutional imperative rooted in Art. 8; the second was not constitutionally required. The state could make distinctions based on religion, in accordance with the different social significance of the different religions in the Italian society. This interpretation, according to the court, was confirmed by the text of Arts. 7 and 8 (p. 609). So the equal freedom of religions did not require their equal treatment and permitted the special protection of the religious sentiments endorsed by the (large) majority of Italians (p. 610). The peculiar extent and intensity of such feelings justified such special protection, so long as it did not limit the right to religious freedom of other religions (p. 611).

The Court's reasoning on the matter of Art. 19 (right to profess one's own faith) was also straightforward. The Court accepted that the right to religious expression includes the right to comment on others' religions (p. 612), but it did not include the right to cause grave offence to others' religion. This also applied to Art. 20 (general freedom of thought and expression). Thus, Article 403 was valid.

The the questions of *bestemmia* and *vilipendio* were raised again during the 1970s.[34] Case 14/1973 upheld Art. 724 *c.p.* (blasphemy against the Catholic religion). The *Corte costituzionale* explained that Art. 724 protected religious sentiment which meant that, far from being unconstitutional, it actually had its basis in the Constitution. The limiting of this protection to the Catholic religion was a choice within the legislator's free evaluation of policy, taking into account the various social facts stemming from the fact that most Italians adhere to the Catholic religion. So, even without considering Art. 7 of the Constitution, the distinction was valid (p. 76 - 78).

Case 188/1975 reiterated the point that the protection of religious sentiment is a constitutional good, explicitly and implicitly protected by Arts. 2, 3.1, 8, 19, 20. Accordingly, the protection of this sentiment, provided it was done within the constitutional limits, was necessary. Expression which constitutes holding someone's religion up to intense hatred and disrespect falls outside of the scope of expressing one's own opinion, and becomes an attack on the protected interests of others (p. 1513). *Vilipendio* was not free discussion, nor polemical criticism; rather it involved making a mockery of another, and was not protected by a Constitution which respects the religious sentiments of citizens.

However one should not get the impression that the *Corte costituzionale* simply upheld fascist laws which discriminated against non-Catholic religions. Far from it - one of the most important activities undertaken by the Court was the elimination of the fascist anti-liberal legislation on many topics - trying to wrong foot Martin Clark's assessment that 'Italy had a liberal Constitution, a Catholic government and Fascist laws' or at least prove the last clause wrong.[35] The Court acted to protect other religions.

In one of its first cases - 45/1957, the Court faced a fascist law which required all persons wishing to engage in worship in a place open to the public, to notify the State authority. The requirement of notification did not apply to worship in traditional places of worship, and it did not apply to Catholic worship at all.[36] The Court considered the Article in the light of the right to free assembly (Art. 17). The Court indicated that this was the most appropriate Article since the act of religious freedom (covered by Art. 8) was, in this case, manifested as an act of assembly (p. 585). According to the Court, the right of assembly was so important that such special regimes cannot be tolerated - there must be a law of general effect on the matter. The Court rejected the State's argument that Art. 19 of the Constitution (religious expression) implicitly authorised a pre-emptive control by the executive of religious (non-Catholic) activities.[37]

All Religions are Equal, But ....

So we see several interesting tenets in the Court's doctrine on religious equality. The text of the 1947 Italian Constitution was a compromise (although some may call it a self-contradiction). The Constitution dropped the coffin of fascism into its grave, but did not cover it with earth. The Constitution magnificently proclaimed the inviolable rights of the human person, specifically the rights of religious activity and expression (Arts. 19, 20), religious non-discrimination (Art. 3) and equality of religious freedom (Art. 8). There however, lurking in the fundamental principles section, was Art. 7. This recognised that relations between the State and Catholic Church are governed by the Lateran Treaty. And section 1 of the Lateran Treaty recognised the Catholic religion as the sole official religion of the state. Furthermore the first Parliaments did not repeal (although they sometimes modified) the sectarian pro-Catholic laws of the fascist era.

Given this background, in what direction could the *Corte costituzionale* have interpreted the various provisions? At least three interpretations were open to the Court.

First, it could have adopted an egalitarian approach, by at least two methods. It could have argued that, even though the Constitution mentioned the special position of the Catholic Church, it was clearly pluralistic in its nature. This could be confirmed by reference to the principles of religious freedom and equality strongly endorsed by the same Constitution. Accordingly the reference to the Catholic Church simply recognised a social fact, and did not justify any norms benefiting that, or any other religion. This reasoning is further confirmed by the first sentence of Art. 7 which recognises the independence of the two orders.[38] A second method would have been to follow the suggestion of the judge *a quo* in case 30/1971.[39] In this case, the judge *a quo* suggested that the Lateran Pacts only had force in so far as they were compatible with the rest of the Constitution. This reasoning reads as follows: the Constitution says that State - Church relations are based on a Treaty, that is on the valid provisions of a Treaty. However, a Treaty is not necessarily superior to the Constitution in the order of legal hierarchy. A Treaty, like a statute, may well be inferior to the Constitution. In that case, any Treaty provision in conflict with a Constitutional provision was invalid and so not applicable.

The second alternative open was a sectarian one. Article 7 provided that the relations between Church and State were regulated by the Lateran Pacts. The very first article of the Lateran Treaty confirmed the Catholic religion as the sole official religion of the State. Most of the Pacts were concerned with protecting the special place of the Catholic Church. Many pro-Catholic measures had been adopted which discriminated against other religions. The Court could have simply accepted the validity of all these without question, arguing that the equal freedom of other religions implied only that they will be tolerated, not given a position equal to the sole official religion of the State.

Clearly the Court adopted the third approach open to them - Italy as, what I will call, a confessional State. The State does immerse itself in religion. Indeed, the *Corte costituzionale* argued that the Constitution recognises the importance of religious sentiment, and it is this that permits the punishment of *vilipendio* and *bestemmia*. Further, it accepts the right to equal religious freedom - see case 45/1957. However, it bluntly rejected the claim that this requires equality of treatment, of legislative protection.

So the Court adopts a confessional approach, although at least two other approaches - the egalitarian and sectarian - were open to it on a reading of the text. Each of the three readings attributes some significance to each of the textual provisions, and it may even be argued that the egalitarian reading was slightly more faithful than the confessional one. Of the various textual provisions only one (Art. 7) is the basis for a confessional interpretation, whilst the text and tenor of the others favour the egalitarian one. Nevertheless, the Court concluded that all religions are equal - but some are more equal than others.

So, the Court selected a particular reading of the Constitutional text, among those readings open to it on a textual and systematic interpretation. In such cases, I search for a motive rooted in political morality. There are two political positions which might lead one to adopt a confessional state. It is clear which one moves the court, and the choice is particularly important.

The first reason that one might have to approve of a confessional state is a religious one. One may believe that one particular religion is a true religion, and thus merits special protection. Nevertheless, among the tenets of this religion one may believe that some notion of tolerance plays a role. Accordingly, one will recognise the right to religious freedom of other religions. However, one will not recognise to them the same status as is recognised to the one true religion. Such a motive would fit in with the proclamation in the Lateran Treaty that the Catholic religion is the sole official religion of the State.

This interpretation the *Corte costituzionale* rejects. It selects a communitarian basis for its decision. Briefly, a communitarian believes that there are certain beliefs in a community which are constitutive of that community and the persons within it. Those beliefs (or values) are essential to the community's health, and the health of those within it. Among those beliefs may well be religious beliefs, specifically those beliefs associated with a majority within the community and associated with the community throughout its history.

This motive is clear from the first case examined, 125/1957. The *Corte costituzionale* stresses that the purpose of the crime of *vilipendio* is to protect the value of religious sentiment.[40] The special protection accorded to the Catholic Church is based on the fact of its uninterrupted historical tradition of being the religion of the great majority of Italians. This recognition is the real reason behind the 1929 Pacts. Religious sentiment is universally valued, but not to the same extent, and so there exists no contradiction between the right to equal religious freedom and the right of the Catholic religion to certain special privileges.

Case 79/1958 amplifies this communitarian reasoning. The Court explains that the State is entitled to punish *bestemmia* against the Catholic religion and need not punish *bestemmia* against other religions, by view of the greater extent and intensity of the effects of the former. The effects of anti-Catholic *bestemmia* are more extensive than that of other types of *bestemmia* (simply because there are more Italian Catholics) but they cannot be of greater intensity. Given the postulates of Arts. 2, 3, 8, 19 we must assume that every person values her religion equally. So the intensity of the effects must be meant in terms, not of how it affects particular persons, but rather the community. The damages of anti-Catholic *bestemmia* are certainly more intensive to a community which identifies itself with the Catholic religion. Such a community has a very good reason to punish anti-Catholic *bestemmia*, and none at all to punish other types, since those are not values constitutive of the community. This is precisely the system we find in the laws under consideration, and endorsed by the *Corte costituzionale*.

Two important considerations flow from the choice of a communitarian basis for the Court's decisions. First, the communitarian position in effect reduces the particular importance of the Church and its tenets. The Catholic privileges are not important simply because of what they are in themselves, they are not important because they are the true religion. Rather they are important in so far as they reflect the tenets of the community.[41]

Second, the communitarian interpretation allows for development. If the Court had accepted the religious interpretation, it would have been relying on the following premise 'the Catholic religion, as recognised by Art. 7 and the 1929 Pacts, is the one true religion'. From this premise, little can develop - the Church is supreme, and that's it. However a community is not something so static. It develops and its values can mutate. A religiously oriented community can evolve into a more egalitarian or even secular one. The communitarian interpretation therefore allows for development.

This communitarian justification, during the first phase, is strongly paternalistic. There is a double denial of autonomy. It suggests that persons need to be protected in their religious faith from the strong words of others. It does not trust the soul of each person to that person's own protection, nor does it trust the discretion of people discussing religion. The victims of the blasphemy need to be protected against those who would assail their religious sentiment - the State does not trust them to their own reason and conscience. Nor does the State trust their would be 'assailants' not to abuse their freedom of expression.

These two considerations are vital, as they allow for the Court to move its jurisprudence along in accordance with the development of values in the Italian community. In the second phase of the case law, we see the Court diminishing the importance of Art. 7 and the Catholic Church, and reducing the scope of Art. 7.

This reduction of Art. 7 and the Catholic Church, we already find in two cases discussed above. In case 188/1975, the Court, while discussing Art. 21 of the Constitution (freedom of expression), explained that *vilipendio* was punished because of its extreme appeal to negative feelings. This reasoning, under Art. 21, was separate from any consideration of Art. 7, or the role of religion within the state.

Case 14/1973 saw the Court upholding the crime of *bestemmia*. The Court explained that freedom of religion was implicitly one of the inviolable rights of the person.[42] These rights included the protection of religious sentiment and thus permitted the punishment of *bestemmia*. The decision to punish only anti-Catholic *bestemmia* fell within the discretionary margin of appreciation of the legislature. Thus the discriminatory regulation was legitimate and rational 'legitimate entirely independently of the position attributed to the Catholic Church in Arts. 7 and 8' (p. 78). In deciding such an issue without even considering those Articles, the Court was sidelining those Articles. We will return to this case.

Until Death Does Us Part - Or Until Death Us Do Part?

The second stage of the *Corte costituzionale*'s case law involved cases from several areas - free expression,[43] abortion,[44] but most notably from the area of marriage law. In these cases, the *Corte costituzionale* weakened the links between State and church, though it did not abolish them.

Case 30/1971 was the first in which the Court directly considered the Concordat and the laws implementing it.[45] The judge *a quo*, in a case on familial obligations, had questioned the validity of Arts. 34.4, 5, 6 of the Concordat. Those sections regulated the law of marital nullity - in what circumstances is a marriage deemed never to have taken place. The Concordat reserved this question to the exclusive competence of the ecclesiastical courts. The State's courts were simply to implement their decisions. The judge *a quo* contrasted this with Art. 102.2 of the Constitution which precludes special courts not otherwise foreseen by the Constitution. He suggested that the Concordat provisions were not valid because the Concordat was only valid in so far as it did not violate the Constitution (p. 152).

The State disagreed. The *Presidente del Consiglio* suggested, first, that Art. 102.2 had no reference to ecclesiastical courts. Second, the reservation was a norm of the Concordat, and the State had renounced its jurisdiction in such matters. Such a renunciation was protected by Art. 7 of the Constitution.

The *Corte costituzionale* rejected the judge *a quo*'s reasoning. The Constitution itself referred to the Concordat, and so had made law of its provisions (p. 153).

The next point is the crucial one. The *Corte* continued that Art. 7, as well as making law of the Concordat, also recognised the 'independence and sovereignty' positions of both the State and the Church, each in its own sphere. Accordingly, the terms of the Concordat, although prevailing against the ordinary terms of the Constitution, *must* respect the 'supreme principles of the State's constitutional order'.

Here are a concept and a doctrine, neither of which finds explicit mention in the constitutional text. The concept is that of the 'supreme principles' - what are these? The Court did not indicate either what constitutes the supreme principles, nor what criteria it would use in determining those principles. The Constitution itself does refer to the 'fundamental principles' - this is the heading for the first part of the Constitution. The Court's choice of a markedly distinct wording indicates that the two concepts do not coincide. Evidently the Court chose for itself the role of arbiter, case by case, of what constitutes the supreme principles of the Constitutional order.[46]

The doctrine is the idea that these principles take precedence over the terms of the Concordat. This doctrine, although it contradicts nothing in the text, is also unsupported by any textual reference. The Court justified this doctrine by doing no more than referring to the notions of independence and sovereignty found in Art. 7 of the Constitution. We are left to assume that it flows naturally from these concepts that there are certain basic principles in a sovereign independent order, such that may not be violated without rejecting those concepts themselves. This doctrine will be one of the crucial elements in this story.

Two further techniques also appear in this decision. The Court, in effect, sidelined Art. 7 of the Constitution, and identified the Catholic institutions as being quite distinct, indeed foreign, to the Italian legal order. The Court explained that Art. 102.2 seeks only to ensure the unity of the legal power of the State. It had nothing to do with relations with foreign tribunals. This was a double pronged emasculation of Art. 7. First, Art. 7 was made redundant for the decision of the case - the Court can resolve the matter by looking only at Art. 102. Second, the Court explains that the ecclesiastical courts are foreign courts ('del tutto estranei').

Ecclesiastical judgements on nullity cases are effective in the same way as other foreign judgements. So, the Court emphasised that the courts were foreign, and the process of recognising their decisions perfectly ordinary. There was nothing special about the relationship between the Catholic courts and the State courts. It was regulated in the same way as all other external jurisdictions. The Court drew a comparison between the recognition of ecclesiastical judgements and the recognition of European Court of Justice judgements, concluding that the decisions of such foreign courts were only effective in so far as the Italian courts had an obligation not to ignore their effects in the Italian system (p.153).[47]

Since the Concordat merely recognises that the decisions of ecclesiastical courts are foreign decisions whose legal effects must not be ignored, it did not violate Art. 102.

On the same day as decision 30/1971, two others were handed down. The next case was 31/1971, where the Court considered a challenge to Art. 7 of the matrimonial law of 27th May 1929, n. 847.[48] The judge *a quo* suggested that the provision was unconstitutional as it violated the principle of equality, discriminating between those citizens who contracted a canonical marriage, and those who underwent a marriage according to the civil law only. In the latter case, the marriage was null if the spouses were related in the first degree (*affinità di primo grado fra i nubendi*), however this principle was not accepted by the ecclesiastical authorities. The judge argued that the impugned provision should have explicitly prohibited registration of a canonical marriage where such a relationship existed.

The *Presidente del Consiglio* defended the law for a variety of reasons. First, he suggested that it was perfectly legitimate to recognise the social fact of disparity among many different religions, and to provide different rules for weddings in different churches. Furthermore the law on marriage applied to everyone without distinction as to religion, and each citizen was free to choose either the canonical or the civil rite. Finally, any inequality was a product of the Lateran Concordat, which was rendered constitutionally impenetrable by Art. 7 of the Constitution.

The Court reiterated its opinion that Art. 7 of the Constitution did not protect violations of the supreme principles of the constitutional order. The inequality at issue did not harm these supreme principles.

The implicit assumption in this decision was that, although equality was a supreme principle, in this instance the deviation from it is not so severe as to amount to a violation. Given the prominence of the principle of equality in the Constitution, indeed the egalitarian flavour which marks so many of its provisions, it was inconceivable that equality could not be a supreme principle. Therefore, we have an evolution (already!) of the doctrine that day proclaimed - the Concordat may not violate supreme principles, but those principles do not have an absolute character. Deviations from them will be tolerated.

The third of this trinity is case 32/1971, where *l.* 847 of the 27th May 1929, Art. 16, was at issue.[49] The law did not say that the natural incapacity of one of the spouses was a ground for refusing registration (*trascrizione*) of the canonical marriage. In a civil marriage, such incapacity was explicitly a ground for nullity under Art. 120 of the civil code. The judge *a quo* wanted a decision as to whether this constituted an illegitimate distinction between citizens.

The *Avvocatura dello Stato* defended the law. Specifically he reasoned that what was at issue was not the validity of the registration of the canonical marriage, but rather the validity of the marriage itself. One could not distinguish the registration of the marriage, or the negotiation of the marriage from the marriage itself. And the marriage itself benefited from the clear protection of the Concordat, and Art. 7. Any inequality was, therefore, constitutionally acceptable (pp. 159 - 160).

The *Corte costituzionale* noted that the Concordat required the State to confer civil law effects on marriages conducted according to the rites of the Catholic Church (p. 162). The Concordat also reserved for the ecclesiastical courts the competence to hear nullity suits in such cases. This regime undoubtedly created a distinction, however it did not amount to a violation of the principle of equality, because the distinction was expressly permitted in another constitutional norm (p. 162).

Stop and consider this reasoning a moment. The Court could have said that the different matrimonial regimes constituted a *violation* of the principle of equality, which was nevertheless justified by Art. 7. Such reasoning would imply that Concordatarian norms could *override* a fundamental principle of justice, that of equality. Instead, the Court held that the distinction did not violate the principle of equality, because the very definition of equality precluded that a distinction founded on a constitutional norm violated that principle. The Court thus avoided saying that Art. 7 is hierarchically superior to Art. 3 (equality).

The Court did not let the matter rest there however, but followed it up with a piece of subtle reasoning. The Court clarified that the Concordat did not, and could not regulate situations before the actual act of matrimony itself - all prior stages were regulated according to the general laws of the State (p. 163). Italy's highest Court rejected the argument of the State (also sustained by the majority of jurists) that there was no distinction possible between the marriage and the time when one decides to marry and which type of marriage to enter. This distinction is crucial, for the exception to the principle of equality was only permitted if it fulfilled a double condition: it must be sanctioned by Art. 7 of the Constitution, and it must ensure that the parties to the marriage are possessed of the full capacity to decide freely and autonomously on the ceremony. The Court concluded that the failure of Art. 16 to provide that natural incapacity was a bar to the registration of a canonical marriage was constitutionally illegitimate. The entire scheme of the parallel rites, civil and canonical, depended on the guarantee of personal autonomy (pp. 163- 164).

There are three key features to this decision. First, the Court narrowed the scope of Art. 7 and the Concordat. The Concordat regulated the position of canonical marriage in Italy. The Court said that the Concordat only covered the actual act of marriage itself. It did not cover matters which happen before the marriage, no matter how intimately linked. The range of areas in life over which Art. 7 of the Constitution guaranteed the Catholic Church a special position was thus reduced.

Second, the Court affirmed that the validity of the marriage regime did not depend solely on being mentioned in the Concordat. Given the bald wording of Art. 7 one might have thought that this would suffice. However the Court added a significant rider - the marriage regime must, in addition, respect the supreme principle of the constitution (the Court did not actually use this phrase, but the doctrine seems to be implicit in its reasoning).

The third point is the supreme constitutional principle which the marriage regime must satisfy. Regard the contrast: the marriage regime was established by a fascist government to implement some elements of a confessional state. The ideas of confessionalism, and more especially, of fascism, totally reject the ideals of individualism and autonomy. What principle must this anti-individualist, anti-autonomy institution satisfy?

The principle of individual autonomy. The regime must protect - upon pain of invalidity - the free and conscientious choice of the individual.

The 'nullity trinity' were handed down by the *Corte costituzionale* on the 1st of March, 1971. They mark an important, indeed decisive, step in the alteration of Italian constitutional morality from a confessional to an egalitarian model. Although the Court played a huge role in this transformation, it could not have carried it through unaided. Indeed the nullity trinity's reasoning may have been encouraged by a statute of the 1st of December 1970. The Italian Parliament has often been chided for not implementing the Constitution, for not advancing the Constitutional ideals, and even for not respecting the Constitution. In the area of religion, the Parliament has acted, after the social upheavals of the late 1960s. Yet the Parliament also could not act alone, in defiance of the Constitution. Court without Parliament, Parliament without Court, neither an evolution make.[50]

On the 1st of December 1970 the Italian Parliament enacted law no. 898. For the first time, Italian courts were given the authority to dissolve civil marriages - including those marriages which had been performed according to the rites of the Catholic Church. A Siennese court referred Art. 2 of this statute to the *Corte costituzionale* on the 20th April 1971. Two and a half months later, the *Corte costituzionale* pronounced judgement on Italy's new divorce law.[51]

The *Corte di cassazione* had delivered an interpretation of the Concordat with great relevance for this case. The *Corte di cassazione* had said that Art. 34 of the Concordat intended to secure the recognition, in Italian law, of marriages celebrated according to Catholic rites, including its indissoluble sacramental nature.[52] Such an interpretation would nullify the new divorce law. The judge *a quo* wanted to know whether Art. 2 of *l.* 898 violated a duty, imposed by Art. 7 Const. and the Concordat, to recognise the permanent civil law effects of a canonical marriage. Was the law in any sense an illegitimate attempt to amend the Concordat, or violate Art. 7?

The Court rejected the argument with a display of delicate legal surgery. The Court claimed that the challenge is based on a misinterpretation of the Concordat. The Concordat did not oblige the Italian State not to introduce divorce. The Court referred to the drafting history of the Concordat. At one stage it had indeed been suggested that the Concordat should require the State to recognise the indissolubility of marriage. This idea was not implemented - instead Art. 34 of the Concordat simply required the State to accord to canonical marriages civil legal effects. The Concordat did not require the State to recognise, in civil law, the canonical marriage, including all the canonical features of that marriage. It simply required the State to accord to a canonical marriage the effects of a civil marriage, whatever those civil law effects may be (p. 1789).

The Court went on to affirm a very important principle, that the canonical marriage is actually a double marriage (p. 1789). It was a marriage under both canonical and civil law, each (to echo Art. 7 Const.) independent and sovereign in their own spheres. The State had to recognise the canonical marriage, properly registered, as a marriage possessed of all the effects of a civil marriage - but it could determine for itself what those effects were. The Court relied on the wording of Art. 5 of *l.* 847 of the 27th May 1929 which said that the marriage, celebrated before a minister of the Catholic Church, according to the norms of canonical law, produces, from the day of the celebration, the same effects as a civil marriage, once registered according to the dispositions of Arts. 9 and following. Two distinct legal orders were involved and the indissolubility of the civil legal effects was a matter for the State (p. 1790). Such an interpretation was confirmed by Art. 7 of the Constitution and by the international law principle that limits on the sovereignty of a state must be given a restrictive interpretation.

In this case, the *Corte costituzionale* confirmed the secular activity of the Parliament, and emphasised the separation of the two spheres, State and Church. The decision to stress an element of separation is the key to the decision, not the court's discussion of the drafting of the Concordat. The wording of the provision of the Concordat was ambiguous - the State will recognise to canonical marriages, the effects of civil law. This was susceptible of two meanings - that the effects of a canonical marriage are binding in civil law, thus precluding divorce; or that whatever are the civil law effects of civil marriage, they exist also for canonical marriage. The drafters of the Concordat may have declined to include a specific provision in it precluding divorce. However, this may just as well have been because they assumed that the phrase adopted already had that effect, and did not want to reduce its significance by including an unnecessary clarification. An interpretative technique concentrating only on the intentions of the drafters does not give a decisive reason to choose between these two interpretations. If however the choice between the two interpretations is framed by a value commitment to the separation of the two spheres, then the correct interpretation becomes clear.

Five times over the course of the next few years, the *Corte costituzionale* rejected challenges to the law on divorce. Most brusquely, in Orders 127 and 169 of 1974, the *Corte* rejected challenges to the divorce law as being manifestly ill founded and not presenting any new features for discussion.[53]

This did not burst the dams of secularism and strict separation into Italian constitutional law. Art. 7 remained, the Concordat remained, and even certain sectarian elements remained. The communitarian basis had shifted from a quite conservative, paternalistic approach to a more individual, autonomy centred approach, which saw the community (State) as having interests quite distinct from the Church. However, the transformation was not complete.

1973 saw yet another attack on the nullity jurisdiction of the ecclesiastical courts,[54] contained in Art. 1 of *l.* 810, of 1929. The judge *a quo* evidently had serious doubts as to the reservation's validity, in the light of the supreme principles of the constitutional order. He suggested that the reservation violated the sovereignty of the State, and involved an illegitimate delegation of the sovereign judicial power, which, under Arts. 101, 102 was reserved to the Italian judiciary. Also, the reservation, argued the judge, violated the right to legal action and defence, the right to one's 'natural' judge,[55] and the right to equality. The judge denied that any inequality was justified by the free choice to enter either a civil or canonical marriage, as the canonical marriage was open only to Catholics.

The *Corte costituzionale* accepted that the judicial power of the State was one of the elements of sovereignty, which was constitutive of the State itself. However, the Constitution did not absolutely prohibit delegation of judicial power. The Court accepted the State's argument that Art. 80 sanctioned precisely such a delegation. A derogation or delegation was valid if rationally and politically justifiable (p. 2336). The Court also dismissed the challenges based on equality and the prohibition of special judges (pp. 2337 - 2338).

The next case came before the Court in a manner we have not encountered before.[56] In 1977, a petition for an abrogative referendum (i.e., a referendum to end the legal effects of specific laws) was submitted, directed against Art. 1 of *l.* of the 27th May 1929, no. 810, in so far as it implemented Arts. 1, 10, 17, 23 of the Lateran Treaty, and the Concordat. A petition for a referendum must be approved, first by the central office for referenda, and then by the *Corte costituzionale*. The central office had approved this proposal for presentation to the people.

The *Corte costituzionale* vetoed the proposal. The Court explained that there were several cases where referenda were not permitted. Art. 75 of the Constitution specified some of these. However, the Court explained that there were other instances where referenda were impermissible. Art. 75.2 could not be interpreted in isolation from other constitutional provisions (p. 88). To maintain the integrity of the constitutional scheme, there were four exclusions: where the proposal contained references to many heterogeneous matters, lacking a rational link; where the proposal touched a constitutional provision, or constitutional law; where the proposal sought to invalidate a law required by the Constitution; where the proposal was forbidden by the text of Art. 75.

The *Corte costituzionale* explained that the 1929 law could not be challenged by referendum. The law implemented an accord of international law, and so was explicitly protected by Art. 75.2. Moreover, the law was given constitutional protection by Art. 7 of the Constitution. Citing its earlier cases, the Court held that the law had a 'copertura costituzionale'. Whilst the Pacts, and laws enacted under them did not negate the supreme principles of the constitutional order, they did themselves have a constitutional status. Accordingly, they were immune to a challenge by referendum.

The obligations of Art. 7 could only be changed by a new agreement between the Holy See and the Italian State (under the terms of Art. 7 itself) *or by a constitutional amendment.* Here, the Court casually dropped into the argument a disappointment for advocates of confessionalism: the 'copertura costituzionale' could be altered by a *unilateral* constitutional revision (p. 91).

This conclusion was not self-evident. The Court said that an international agreement could be removed from the Constitution and unilaterally disposed of. There are several arguments which might contradict this. First, there is the issue of international law. It is not certain that a State can, simply by following constitutional procedures, 'violate or alter' its obligations assumed under international law.

A second argument is that Art. 7 provided for a specific manner of changing its requirements - a new Concordat. This could well be interpreted as excluding unilateral revision.

A final argument is suggested by the *Corte costituzionale* itself. The Court accepts that there is a hierarchy of constitutional norms. From this it is but two steps to negating the Court's conclusion in this case. The Court could have held that the supreme principles cannot themselves be altered by constitutional amendments.[57] One supreme principle, that Italy is a republic, is explicitly declared to be immune from revision, and the Court has already shown that it is not above clarifying the gaps in the text's lists of exceptions. The second step is also straightforward - Art. 7 itself may be considered a supreme principle. After all it is mentioned in the fundamental principles section of the Constitution, it does deal with the religious faith of the quasi - totality of Italians, it does protect the pacts which are often reputed to have secured the religious peace in Italy.[58]

Exit(ing) ... Stage Left ... Confessionalism

There are three dominant trends to the second phase of the case law, rooted in the same view of political morality. The 1970s saw the Court moving towards a more egalitarian and autonomy centred understanding of the Constitution.

The first trend was the reduction of the scope of Art. 7 of the Constitution and the 1929 Pacts. Although the Court recognised a 'copertura costituzionale', it also narrowed its scope. In the first nullity case (30/1971) the Court discussed the status of decisions of ecclesiastical judges. It dealt with this matter primarily by considering the principles of the unity of the State's legal power, and the recognition of foreign judicial decrees. The 'copertura' was almost irrelevant to the decision, since the decisions of the ecclesiastical courts were dealt with in the same way as the decisions of other foreign courts. In case 32/1971 the Court further reduced the 'copertura' - it did not cover all matters pertaining to a canonical marriage, but only the act of marriage itself. So the protection of Art. 7 did not extend even to acts which were closely connected to, but distinct from the act of marriage - such as the decision to marry. The First Divorce case (169/1971) gave the Court an opportunity to reduce significantly the constitutional covering offered to the canonical marriage. The Court gave the narrowest possible interpretation to the phrase 'recognise civil effects to marriages conducted according to Catholic rules'. It did not mean that the canonical effects of such a marriage are recognised by the civil law - it meant that the civil law effects alone were recognised.[59] The clear message of all these cases, is that litigants should not invoke Art. 7 for too many purposes.

The second trend is also important, indeed dramatic. The text of the Constitution recognised the legitimacy of the 1929 Pacts. The Court identified two circumstances where the provisions of those pacts may nevertheless be unconstitutional. First, it noted that the terms of Art. 7 could be altered, unilaterally, by a constitutional amendment (Referendum case, 16/1978). This was not so surprising a doctrine as the other exception. Notwithstanding the express terms of Art. 7, a Concordatarian norm could not violate one of the supreme principles of the constitutional order.[60] This doctrine had (and has) no firm textual basis, other than a brief reference to the proclamation in Art. 7 that the State is independent and sovereign. Nevertheless, the Court said that it will decide what principles are so fundamental that they take priority over the wording of Art. 7.

The third trend is the most important, for it explains why the Court was so ready to narrow the scope of Art. 7 and develop the supreme principles doctrine. Consider the supreme principles - they clearly reflect a move away from the paternalistic approach of the first phase, towards a political morality which takes autonomy and equality much more seriously.

This is quite clear in case 32/1971 (Natural Incapacity case). Here the Court said that the very validity of the entire Concordatarian marriage system depended on the system respecting the autonomy of the individual. This autonomous choice was put at the very base of the legal order, determining the legitimacy even of constitutional provisions such as Art. 7. Furthermore, the free choice which the court upheld was not an empty one. The person exercising it must be fully competent. The State still had a protective role to play, and a very important protective role. However, it was not a paternalistic one. The State had to ensure that people were in a proper position to make an autonomous decision. The State could not review the actual decision, only the effective capacity of the individual to reach it autonomously.

Concerns about equality and pluralism animated several of these cases. In the blasphemy case (14/1973) the Court clearly had serious misgivings about its earlier decision on the matter, and called on the State to eliminate the privileged position of the Catholic Church on this matter. Furthermore, the Court embraced a pluralistic approach, which recognised the importance of religion for those who chose one, and also the importance of not having one for those who reject any. This pluralism had to be a realistic pluralism - there must actually be real choices to adhere to one or another or no religion. This could only be achieved by protecting the independence and ideological character of religious schools (195/1972).

Replacing Confessionalism

We have seen the jurisprudence of the *Corte costituzionale* move through two phases, in its reconciliation of the tensions in the Constitution. The first involved a paternalistic communitarian defence of a certain special consideration for the Catholic Church, in the area of the criminal protection of religious sentiment. However then the 1970s and the second stage arrived. Here the Court, though not reneging on its commitment to the importance of religious liberty, emphasised more individualist and egalitarian principles, and started to whittle away the privileges of the Catholic Church. The 1980s and 1990s saw an increase in this last activity.

During this phase, the politicians also played a role in the development of Church / State relations. In this section I first present two key *Corte costituzionale* cases of 1982, and then follow it up with a brief discussion of the process of agreement making between the State and religious authorities. Then I move on to later decisions of the *Corte costituzionale*. What is noticeable is how there are developments, without sharp breaks in our story, how the 1982 cases follow from the preceding case law, and how the State - Church agreements follow from these, to be 'fulfilled' by the later cases.

It is no surprise that the two 1982 cases both involved questions of marriage, and specifically of nullity. The first involved marriage between minors.[61] Articles 12 and 16 of the law of the 27th May 1929, n. 847 were in question. They specified the grounds which precluded the registration of a canonical marriage as a civil marriage; they did not include a reference to the possibility that one or both of the marriage partners might be under age.

The judges who referred the case suggested that this was contrary to Art. 3 of the Constitution (equality) considered in the light of Art. 84 of the *codice civile*.[62] Art. 84 *c.c.* provided for the nullity of a marriage where one of the partners was under the age of 16, or where one was over the age of 16 but had not been admitted to the state of marriage.

The *Corte costituzionale* reviewed the history of the laws on minors and marriage. It noted that Art. 55 of the *c.c.* approved by a decree of the 25th of June 1865, n. 2358, provided that no man under the age of 18, nor woman under the age of 15, could contract a civil marriage. Art. 68 of the civil code provided that, in grave cases, exceptions could be made for men over the age of 14 and women over the age of 12. To implement the Lateran Pacts, Art. 1 of the law n. 847 reduced the age for marriage to 16 for men and 14 for women, altering Art. 55 of the *c.c.* This harmonised the marriage age in civil and canonical law, precluding the possibility that people might chose between the two on the basis of the different legal effects. Later Arts. 55 and 68 became Art. 84 with the 1942 civil code.

The family law reform act, n. 151 of 1975 changed Art. 84 of the civil code. Now no minor could contract a marriage, and the age of competence was raised to the normal age, 18. Further, Art. 84 now provided that a minor who had reached the age of 16, might, for serious reasons, be allowed to marry.

The *Corte costituzionale* examined the motives behind the change in the law. The parliamentary debates emphasised the need for people entering marriage to realise fully its importance. Given the importance of educating people to an age higher than before, the fact that married couples now had a greater level of autonomy in their social settings, the very nature of marriage as a major assumption of responsibilities, and the precariousness of young teenage marriages, Parliament considered it important to raise the age of majority to 18. Parliament also specified that a court could only permit persons under 18, but over 16, to get married, if there were serious reasons justifying it, and if the applicant had reached a satisfactory level of psychological and physical maturity.

The Court held that Art. 12 of the 1929 law was an illegitimate violation of the principle of equality. A simple difference between the civil and canonical regimes would not, by itself, justify such a holding. That would be covered by the 'copertura costituzionale' (p. 131). However here, the Court found itself in a situation similar to case 32/1971 - the marriage parties were being held to a choice which they had made without being fully conscious of the seriousness of that choice (pp. 131 - 132). The possession of the full capacity to choose between the civil and canonical rites was a pre-condition to the legitimacy of the double system itself.[63]

To be capable of a fully free choice, one had to attain a certain level of maturity and consciousness of the consequences of one's actions. The legislator had recognised that such maturity and consciousness only came with age, after a personal development which is physical, sexual and psychological. The legislator had settled on the age of 18, and in exceptional cases, 16, as the age by which such maturity was generally acquired (p. 132). Accordingly, since Art. 12 of the 1929 law did not recognise the nullity of marriages for lack of maturity on the same terms as Art. 84 of the civil code, it was constitutionally illegitimate.

This case continued the trends noted in the previous stage - reduction in the importance of the Lateran Pacts and Art. 7 of the Constitution, and the increase in the importance of the value of personal autonomy. The decision confirmed what 32/1971 said - the Concordat only applied to the act of matrimony itself and not to the events preceding it. Further, the Court reiterated that the choice of rite had to be a fully free one.

The Court added two important points. First it developed the notion of autonomy. Autonomy was not merely a formally free choice, nor was it satisfied by an independent decision. The decision had to be made by someone with all the capacities for a fully informed decision on matrimony, which required a certain level of maturity, not merely physical, but also psychological. The Court insisted that persons be guaranteed a real and practical autonomy.

Of course, this posed an old legal problem - regulating such matters requires a degree of arbitrariness because one needs, practically, to draw a line at a particular age. In this case, the court accepted the line drawn by Parliament - 18. This was important, not merely because it indicated the correct degree of deference to legislative decision making, but because of the way it redrew the powers of Parliament *vis-à-vis* the Concordat. The Constitutional Court had already established that elements of the Concordat could cease to have effect in three circumstances: where the State and Church so agreed by a new accord; where the *Corte costituzionale* declared a Concordatarian provision to violate a supreme principle; and where a unilateral constitutional amendment altered Art. 7. Now a fourth possibility appeared. Parliament could end an obligation under the Concordat, by regulating either matters pertaining to the supreme principles of the Constitution, or matters connected with the Concordat, but not directly covered by it. Note that only one of these four possibilities was stated in the text of the Constitution - the other three's existence were recognised by the *Corte costituzionale* itself.

The second nullity case concerned the rights to legal protection, and to act and defend oneself in justice.[64] The case dealt with Art. 1 of the *l.* 27th May 1929, *n.* 810, (in so far as it refers to Art. 34.4, 5, 6 of the Concordat) and Art. 17.2 of the *l. n.* 847 of the same date - surely the two laws most often challenged in any constitutional democracy! These provisions concerned the entry into force, in State civil law, of ecclesiastical nullity decrees. Under these provisions, a State Court of Appeal simply registered the decision of the ecclesiastical courts without examining the ecclesiastical decision.[65] The judges who posed the question to the *Corte costituzionale* suggested that the procedure violated the right to legal protection, the right to act in justice, and the right to defend oneself in justice. In addition, the judges suggested that certain types of nullity decisions of the ecclesiastical courts, might be contrary to Italian public order.

The Court decided that the Concordatarian regime did not violate the right to 'tutela giurisdizione' since persons who sought a nullity from an ecclesiastical court, were going before a judge and a legal order, whose legal nature had been guaranteed by a 'long tradition' (p. 176). Although there might well be differences between features of the two legal systems, the mere fact that there were some differences did not justify a finding of illegitimacy (p. 176). The right to 'tutela giurisdizionale' was a supreme principle only as regards its essential requirements - differences of detail did not touch that nucleus. Accordingly, the different regime was protected by the 'copertura costituzionale'.[66]

The Court turned to the second challenge to the laws - that they violated the right to act and defend oneself in justice. The judges who referred the cases suggested that the Court of Appeals' 'automatic' role in registering the decisions of the canonical courts, violated this right. Specifically the Court of Appeal did not verify the effectiveness of the rights of defence and the adversarial process,[67] the definitiveness of the decision, the implementation of the guarantees in Art. 34.5 of the Concordat, and the compatibility of the canonical decisions with Italian public policy. The Court accepted this complaint - the failure to require the Court of Appeal to confirm the respect of these principles violated a supreme principle of the Constitution. The right to act and defend oneself in justice was a right protected in Art. 24 of the Constitution. Respect for Italian public policy was an element of sovereignty - an Italian court could not give effect to a decision contrary to the state's public policy (pp. 179 - 180).

The Court also accepted the third complaint. Among one of the causes of nullity in canonical law, was nullity in cases of a marriage that was not consummated (*matrimonio rato et non consummato*). According to the Court, this actually consisted of the canonical courts *ending* a marriage valid in State law. The decision on the termination of a marriage validly made was one for the State courts to decide under *l. n.* 898 of the 1st Dec. 1970. The divorce law provided for divorce in the case of an unconsummated marriage. The canonical courts could not issue a nullity order for what Italian law considered a divorce.

Here again the Court put the Concordat in its place, and by no means a dominant place. First, the Court established the priority of a crucial right over the terms of the Concordat - the right to fair legal procedures. The right to defend oneself was (and is) an inviolable right (Art. 24 Const.) and the laws implementing the Concordat must expressly provide for its protection.

Secondly, the principle of sovereignty was also reaffirmed. The sovereign Italian State had its own conceptions of what constituted public policy. The servants of that State, including the judges, must not harm that public policy. Accordingly, the State had to provide in its enactments implementing the Concordat, that ecclesiastical nullity decisions must not be enforced if they go against the policy of the State.

The third point is that the court once more limited the scope of the Concordat. The Concordat reserved the question of the civil nullity of canonical marriages to the ecclesiastical courts. One might think that this implicitly referred to the grounds of nullity recognised in canonical law, thus providing them with a 'copertura costituzionale'. Not so. The *Corte costituzionale* examined those grounds in canonical law, to ensure that they amounted to what the State considered as grounds for nullity. If those canonical grounds were not strictly speaking nullity grounds, then they were not given a privileged position by Art. 7 of the Constitution.

The Politicians Take a Hand

At various stages in this story politicians contributed to the development of State - Church relations, rejecting the confessional interpretation and furthering a more egalitarian one (e.g. the 1970 divorce law). During the 1970s, the issue of altering the Concordat was on the agenda, and this debate culminated in a new agreement between the Holy See and Italy in 1984.

During the period 1971 - 1984, the *Corte costituzionale* had been eroding the privileges of the Catholic Church, limiting the scope of the Concordat and Art. 7, and asserting the superiority of certain constitutional values over the Concordat, generally moving the State along a more egalitarian path. The 1984 Accord spoke to this concern. It, and its additional protocol, abrogated all provisions of the 1929 Concordat not expressly saved. Specifically, the new agreement repudiated the assertion that the Catholic religion was the sole official religion of the State.[68]

Of particular interest is Art. 8 of the Accord, dealing with marriage. This did not revolutionise the law on marriage - rather it recognised the position already reached in the development of the *Corte costituzionale*'s case law. It recognised that a canonical marriage could not be registered as a civil marriage where one of the parties is below the civil law age of majority,[69] or where there is a non-derogable impediment in civil law.[70] As regards the recognition of nullity decrees of the ecclesiastical authorities, the Accord provided that the Court of Appeal, before giving effect to the judgement, must ensure that the ecclesiastical judge was competent, that the right to act and defend oneself in justice was protected 'in a way not different from the fundamental principles of the Italian legal system',[71] that other civil law conditions for recognition of foreign judgements had also been complied with.[72]

The 1984 agreements also dealt with the issue of education, again confirming the case law of the *Corte costituzionale*.[73] Article 9 of the Agreement endorsed the principles of freedom and equality in education. The 1929 principle that the Catholic religion was the very basis of education was rejected, replaced with a recognition of the historical and cultural relevance of the Catholic religion. Further, the State guaranteed to recognise the value of religious culture.[74] Article 9 emphasised that students and their parents had the right to choose to have religious instruction, or not.

The 1980s were important for another activity that the political branches finally got around to. Article 8 of the Constitution says that relations between the different non-Catholic Churches and the State are regulated by agreements between them. There were two points about this provision. First, Art. 8 does not entrench any specific accord, as does Art. 7. Second, for most of the First Republic, the State entered into no agreements with any other religion. Finally in the 1980s, such agreements were signed, with the Valdesian community,[75] the church of the Seventh Day Adventists,[76] the Pentecostal Church of the People of God,[77] and the Union of the Italian Jewish Community.[78] These accords recognised a degree of freedom to these Churches similar to that provided for the Catholic Church. Thus, these accords signal a double move towards an egalitarian regime. First, the other Churches are formally on the same footing as the Catholic one. Second, the contents of those agreements favour the fully free practice of those religions.

The Return of the *Corte costituzionale* and the Principle of Laicity

The activity of Government and Parliament during the 1980s did not end the role of the Court. On the contrary, the third phase of the case law has seen the Court deal with five different religious issues. It would have been a pleasing end to this story, to report that the Court has completed the development it itself began in the 1970s, and encouraged by the 1984 agreements, to transform Italian constitutional law from a communitarian confessional basis to a more autonomy-centred (though perhaps still communitarian) egalitarian basis. In most of the case law, this seems to be the case, but there are exceptions. The Court accepts that equality and respect for individual autonomy play a major role in the Italian community, but seems to feel that the Catholic heritage cannot be entirely ignored.

The first group of cases are the INVIM cases.[79] These are the last vestiges of the slightly confessional taint endorsed by the *Corte costituzionale*, before the 1989 adoption of the supreme principle of laicity of the State. Case 86/1985 considered the legitimacy of Art. 8.3 of the *l.* 16th Dec. 1977, *n.* 904 concerning the *imposta incremento valore immobili* (INVIM). The law provided an exemption from this tax, for the benefit of ecclesiastical (Catholic) bodies. The judge *a quo* sought to have this extended to other religious bodies. For one of the last times, the Court upheld, without demur, an exception exclusively for the benefit of the Catholic Church, simply repeating its words from case 125/1957. Once again 'equal freedom' did not require 'identical treatment' (p. 584).

The second group of cases (dealing with education) though signifies a major development - the appearance of a new supreme principle of the constitutional order: the principle of the laicity of the State. Since 1984, the *Corte costituzionale* has decided three core cases on religious education. The first of these was decision 203/1989.[80] Here Art. 9.2 of *l.* 25th March 1985, *n.* 121, (implementing the 1984 Agreement and Additional Protocol)[81] and Art. 5 b) 2) of the Protocol[82] were under attack. The concrete issue raised by the referring judge was the legitimacy of the teaching of Catholicism in State schools where those students who chose not to avail themselves of that teaching, were required to study certain other topics. The judge *a quo* considered that this violated Arts. 2 (inviolable rights), 3 (equality) and 19 (religious liberty).

The Court first reaffirmed the doctrine that the supreme principles of the constitutional order take precedence over every other norm, including the Concordat, and other constitutional norms.[83] The Court then identified one of these supreme principles, (which it derived from Arts. 2, 3, 7, 8, 19, 20), the principle of laicity of the State. This was quite a radical statement - after all Art. 7 of the Constitution still gave a particular place to the Catholic Church. Interestingly, this interpretation depended in no way on the 1984 agreements. The Constitution itself embodied this principle - which sits uneasily the privileged position of the Catholic Church prior to 1984.

The Court continued to provide an unusual definition of laicity however. The principle of laicity did not entail the State's indifference to religion, but required the State to protect religious freedom in a regime of religious and cultural pluralism. Thus, the Court chose very clearly an egalitarian position on State - religion questions. It rejected the US separation model, and also its own earlier confessionalist stance. This was a choice - the Court itself had already shown how the same Articles could yield a confessionalist interpretation, and if the Court could wring this egalitarian meaning out of them, a separationist was also possible.

The Court began with a firm declaration: the State embraces the principle of laicity. It then examined the 1984 and 1985 texts, giving these an interpretation in strict conformity to the supreme principle the Court has deduced from the constitutional provisions. The secular State could legitimately commit itself to providing for the teaching of religion in two guises: because of the value of a pluralist religious culture, and because of the historical significance of the Catholic religion in Italy. However, this system of instruction must not be hostile to any particular faith. It must respect the principles of religious equality and freedom (pp. 900 - 901).

Now the agreements had expressly ended the 1929 principle that Catholicism was the basis and aim of education. However, the 1984 agreements specified that the teaching of the Catholic religion must be in the system of aims of the school. This phrase might have been used to reintroduce that Catholic bias. This interpretation the Court rejected. The phrase simply meant that the teaching of Catholicism must be done in a way compatible with the other educational activities of the school.

Article 9.2 of *l.n.* 121 said that parents and pupils exercised the right to chose whether to follow a Catholic education. This protected the rights and principles embodied in Arts. 19 and 30 of the Constitution. The lay State gave to the pupils and parents a free choice on this matter, unlike the fascist State.

The Court continued with its egalitarian interpretation of the texts. It explained that providing alternative education as obligatory for those students who chose not to have religious instruction, would definitely be discriminatory (pp. 902 - 903). To respect adequately religious freedom and equality, the State must not in any sense burden those pupils not availing themselves of Catholic instruction. The decision to accept such education created an obligation to attend it, but persons who reject it were 'in a state of not being obliged to do anything' (p. 903). This means that any religious instruction must be something 'extra', not forming part of the school day, so that one can attend such a school without attending religious instruction, or feeling any pressure or incentive to join it, or otherwise be affected by it.

With this 'sentenza interpretativa di rigetto' the Court rejected the challenge, and returned the case to the judge *a quo* to resolve on the basis of this interpretation. The interpretation is an important one - it is an open rejection of those elements of the Italian legal order - including Art. 7 of the Constitution, Art. 724 c.p., the cases of the first phase - which suggest that Italy favours any particular religion. On the contrary, it respects all religions equally. Therefore, it also rejects the separation model of Church - State relations. A rich religious liberty entails religious and cultural pluralism, which allows the State to provide for religious education, but only in a system with serious and effective guarantees for religious liberty and equality. The Court reaffirmed these principles in subsequent cases.

In 1991 the Court mandated an interpretation of an administrative rule which furthered these principles.[84] The State *must not provide an obligatory alternative activity* for pupils rejecting Catholic instruction, for this would be to apply a condition to what should be the unfettered exercise of a constitutional freedom to choose. Nothing must be decided by the choice to reject other than the actual rejection itself. The question required a 'yes' or 'no', with no conditions attached. The State satisfied this obligation when it permitted pupils to leave the school itself during the period of Catholic instruction (p. 83).[85]

The third group of cases concerned the regulation of the Jewish Union in Italy. The first of these was case 239/1984 and set the stage for the subsequent announcement of the supreme principle of laicity.[86] A Roman judge queried the validity of provisions of the royal decree of the 30th October, 1930, *n.* 1731. These Articles regulated the constitution, membership and powers of the Union of the Jewish Community.[87] The decree made every Jewish resident in Italy a member of the Union irrespective of their personal wishes (Art. 4). (Art. 5 did provide for Jews wishing to leave the Union, but did not permit them to do so simply at their own discretion.)

The Court noted that the decree replaced the various different regimes which preceded it (p. 1746). The decree made the Union a subject of public law, creating it, according it power, and regulating it. The decree obliged all resident Jews to belong to the Union. This norm directly contradicted Art. 3 of the Constitution which insisted that no distinction may be made among citizens on the basis of religion or of race (p. 1747). The fact that one could leave the Union (Art. 5) did not justify this initial distinction, founded on impermissible criteria.

The decree also violated Arts. 2 and 18 of the Constitution. The *Corte costituzionale* explained that Art. 18 (association) must be understood to include a right not to associate. This was one of the inviolable rights of man. Accordingly Art. 4 of the decree was constitutionally illegitimate.

A second case was case 43/1988, dealing with Art. 9 of the same decree in case 43/1988.[88] This Article specified the conditions for being elected to the Council of the Jewish Union. The decree provided that only men, of more than 25 years of age, who had received a specified educational decree, or were rabbis, could become members of the Council. The Union itself had already modified these conditions but the decree remained unmodified. The Court invalidated the decree's provision in a decision little more than a page long. Art. 8.2 of the Constitution did not merely provide a right for religious groups to organise themselves, leaving open the possibility of 'suppletive' state rules. Rather it amounted to an abandonment by the lay State (the *Corte costituzionale* does not actually refer to the principle of laicity which would be recognised next year) of any claim to interfere in the internal order of the religion (p. 116). The State could only interfere with the internal order when the fundamental principles of the State legal order were endangered by the religious order. This was not the case here, and the interference was illegitimate.

This case was the last step before the open pronouncement in 1989 that, among the fundamental principles of the Italian constitutional order, is the principle of State laicity.

Case 259/1990 concerned Arts. 1, 2, 3, 15, 16, 18, 19, 24 to 30, 56, 57 and 58 of the decree.[89] These provisions made a public law subject of the Union. The Constitutional Court rejected an invitation to (in effect) 'misinterpret' the decree as recognising a private law entity, when the dominant practice and academic doctrine was to consider the Union a public law body (pp. 1546 - 1547). The decree regulated the Union in detail: the decree specified the purpose of the Union, its organisation, its powers, its leadership, the rights and responsibilities of members, and relations with state powers. It was thus clearly a public law entity, with the State having a large influence in its activities. This level of interference violated the right of religions to autonomy (Art. 8.2) and the principle of the laicity of the State. The level of State involvement also violated the principle of equality, since other religions were not subject to a similar regime. The decree violated the lay State's commitment to safeguard all religions within a regime of cultural and religious pluralism. A special regime of this nature was impermissible. With this statement, the Court gutted the decree.

The next case (of a fourth type) also demonstrates the Court's commitment to egalitarianism. Case 195/1993 dealt with an important question.[90] Articles 7 and 8 recognise *three* different types of religious groupings - the Catholic Church, those religions with which the State has an agreement, and those religions with which the State does not have such an agreement. Was it acceptable to make distinctions between the third of these groups and the other two? The case concerned a regional law which provided public funds for the construction of places of worship. However, the law only provided funds to religious groups with which the State had an agreement (Art. 1 of *l. reg.* 16th March 1988, *n.* 29 Abruzzo). In the instant case, members of the Jehovah's Witnesses sought such contributions, which the region refused as there was no State agreement with them.

The Court first noted that the provision of such funds was an important element in protecting religious freedom - the State had a duty to make religious worship a real possibility, not merely a theoretical one (p. 1332). However, in fulfilling this task, the State must still respect the principle of State laicity, as declared in case 203/1989. The reason justifying such contributions was that religious worship requires buildings and organisations in which to conduct it. Therefore, the organisations served the important purpose of religious freedom. All religions served this purpose, not merely those with which the State has an agreement.[91] Therefore, the fact of not having such an agreement could not justify such a distinction (p. 1333). Every religion was equally free before the law, with an equal freedom of self-organisation. The option to have an agreement with the State was simply an option. Certain religions might not have such an agreement (perhaps because they did not want one, had not agreed on its terms, or lacked a firm organisation with which to enter agreements), but yet were still entitled to equal freedom before the law. The Court held that, when the State provided such positive assistance to religious activity, then no discrimination between different faiths was permissible (p. 1335). Accordingly Art. 1 of the regional law was invalid, and the Jehovah's Witnesses could receive their funding.

With the fifth group of cases, we return to our beginning. Case 925/1988 concerned *bestemmia* against the religion of the State, the Catholic religion.[92] Article 724 of the penal code still punished this crime even though it seems out of tune with the 1984 agreements, which negated the principle that the Catholic Church was the official State religion. The Court rejected the challenge. First, it noted that the term used was not ambiguous and so complied with the principle of legality whereby criminal provisions must be reasonably precise. Then it recalled its own reasoning in cases 79/1958, 125/1957, 14/1973. These cases held that the legislator could accord to the Catholic religion a special protection not because it was the Catholic religion, but rather because it was the most important religion in Italian society (p. 4302). On this basis the Court rejected the challenge. However it continued. The Court said that after the 1984 agreements with the Catholic Church, it was 'unacceptable' for there to exist discriminations among religions 'based solely on the number of adherents' to the religion (p. 4302). There might be some reason to recognise a difference, but the legislature was obliged to revise the law, extending the law's protection to other religions (p. 4303).

This case contains a rather clear contradiction. The Court felt it could not escape from the central finding, that the punishment only of blasphemy against the Catholic religion was legitimate. Yet it followed this up with a strong condemnation of precisely such a distinction. This condemnation was rooted in a full-blooded commitment to the values the *Corte costituzionale* itself started to emphasise in the 1970s, and which the political branches approved in 1984. It is this more full-blooded respect for equality which now begins to pre-dominate in the third phase.

This commitment to the principle of laicity, interpreted as egalitarianism, was confirmed in a slightly disturbing case decided in Oct. 1995. Case 440/1995 returned to the issue of *bestemmia* once again.[93]

Once again Art. 724 of the *codice penale*, with its special reference to the official religion of the State, i.e. the Catholic one, was challenged as violating Arts. 25, 3 and 8 of the Constitution. This time the Court followed through on the finding of constitutional illegitimacy, though in a worrying fashion.

The Court outlined the development of the legal understanding of Art. 724. In Fascist times, the Catholic religion was perceived as a factor in the moral unity of the nation, a unity the State was obliged to uphold. However case 79/1958 of the *Corte costituzionale* fundamentally altered this understanding. The court recognised the Catholic religion as having a special role in Italian *society*, not specifically in the State. The social fact of its importance justified its special protection by the legislator. As part of a more egalitarian understanding of the Constitution the Court later stressed that Art. 724 could only be justified as a protection of the religious sentiments of the people, and called on the legislator to give this a more comprehensive protection, extending the crime to cover blasphemy against non-Catholic religions (case 14/1973). Nevertheless, it accepted that the Catholic Church's social position still permitted its special protection. However case 925/1988 recognised that this was no longer the case; the justification of Art. 724 could only lie in it being perceived as a protection of the individual right of religion. This being the case, the number of adherents was not relevant, and the norm should be non-discriminatory. The proscription of blasphemy was constitutionally justified but only if the principle of equality was upheld. The Court once more called on the legislator to alter the law.

The legislator failed to act, and so in 1995 the Court acted. It recognised the legitimacy of punishing blasphemy - 'un atto di inciviltà nei rapporti della vita sociale'. However the principle of equality also had to be respected, and so the Court deemed Art. 724 to be unconstitutional. However, it then performed a most remarkable exercise. The Court invalidated the reference in Art. 724 to the 'symbols and persons venerated in the state religion', which left standing the main part of the Article punishing 'blasphemy against the Divinity'. This crime was constitutionally required for the protection of religious sentiment. Removing the condemned portion had the effect of making Art. 724 non-discriminatory in its application, thus implementing the principle of egalitarianism. However, more worryingly, it also amended the crime, enlarging its scope. The judicial expansion of a criminal law provision's scope was an extraordinary exercise in judicial activism, even for a Court renowned for its activism.

The Court, Christ, and Caesar

We have moved through four decades of constitutional case law on religion in Italy. Let's now try and put some of these threads together.

In these cases, the Court had to rely on conceptions of political morality to interpret the constitutional terms. The Court exercised a choice as to which political morality best suited it. However, after its initial choice, it came to regret what it had chosen, and evolved a more adequate justification. It began the long process of altering the doctrine to move it into line with the more acceptable interpretation. In this, it interacted with the political branches, and indeed society, at many points. Eventually it arrived at a doctrine far removed from its original choice, and seriously inconsistent with the remnants of that choice.

When the *Corte costituzionale* started its work in 1956 it found several Articles on religion - Arts. 3, 7, 8, 19, 20. It also found several laws on the statute books that discriminated against the non-Catholic religions. It had to devise an interpretation of the Constitution that would resolve these cases, whilst respecting the textual provisions of the Constitution. Yet those Articles could be read in the light of several different value judgements: an egalitarian, sectarian or confessional reading. The Court rejected the sectarian and the egalitarian interpretations.[94] There are two possible weaknesses - from the point of view of morality - with the other two arguments. First, the egalitarian model (in its full guise) did not perhaps correspond with the very settled convictions of the Italian state and people - a country predominantly Catholic, as the *Corte costituzionale* took pains to point out. As we saw in Chapter Three, it is legitimate to take account of such firmly held convictions. However, these convictions cannot, in moral argument, be given unfettered sway - they are merely 'provisional fixed points'. The *Corte costituzionale* rejected a sectarian doctrine, and also rejected a religious basis for its confessionalist doctrine. Rather it selected a communitarian basis. A communitarian approach has two major advantages, from the moral viewpoint over a sectarian or religious inspired political justification. First, any religious doctrine depends on fundamental claims which are beyond public examination. As such, they cannot be admitted in moral argument. Furthermore, the sectarian interpretation involves a total denial of equality: those not adhering to the dominant religion are deemed to be almost non-persons, whose claims have no merit. Such an approach is ruled out of moral argument by the criterion of universalisability - a moral claim must in some sense treat persons as equals, participating in a dialogue. The sectarian argument just does not do that.

However the communitarian argument also has flaws - as a confessional model, its respect for the principle of universalisability is not as great as it might be; and the *Corte costituzionale* seems to have adopted a moral basis quite distrustful of individual autonomy. These flaws were exposed and exacerbated during the late 1960s and early 1970s, when Italian society went through a significant upheaval in university classrooms and on factory floors, upheavals which dislodged any authoritarian religiosity from the firmly held settled convictions of the Italian community. The communitarian interpretation allowed for the evolution of political morality, an evolution in which the *Corte costituzionale* now began to play a significant role.

The decisions of the 1970s are fundamentally explained by the reworked interpretation of the Constitution. Henceforth equality, autonomy and personal development were the main blocks on which constitutionalism was to be build. The Court did not throw the community element overboard - it recognised the fundamental values of pluralism and religious sentiment, as social elements to be protected.

The Court started to treat Art. 7 of the Constitution as something exceptional - cases were decided without using Art. 7 if possible.[95] Furthermore, it gave quite narrow readings to Art. 7 and the 1929 Pacts.[96] Article 7 was treated as an exceptional provision, as it accorded a privileged position to one religious confession - a privilege incompatible with the greater commitment to equality which the Court now adopted as a more defensible moral position. Exceptions to moral principles had to be strictly and narrowly construed - and so the Court explained that the reservation of the nullity jurisdiction to ecclesiastical courts did not include review of the decision to enter marriage or which marriage to enter, civil or canonical. Nor did the Concordatarian promise to recognise legal effects to canonical marriages mean that the State had to recognise the indissolubility of such marriages in civil law. The Court accordingly confirmed the State's new divorce law.

The Court made it clear that Art. 7 could be derogated from in several circumstances - a constitutional amendment could alter its requirements,[97] and, more stunningly, the Court could identify the 'supreme principles of the constitutional order', which Art. 7 could not violate.[98] The Court designated as such supreme principles, the principles of equality,[99] personal autonomy,[100] sovereignty,[101] the freedom and pluralism of education,[102] and religious freedom.[103]

This process was to continue during the 1980s, with the Executive and Parliament beginning to concur with the Court, that the fundamental basis of the political order must be equality and pluralism, not privilege for one Church. The Court reinforced this with two important decisions on nullity - cases 16 and 18 of 1982.[104] These emphasised the importance of the State's legal order, and the guarantees for personal autonomy and the right to defend oneself before the courts. These principles the State must uphold, and if they conflict with Art. 7 and the Concordat - so much the worse for the latter. The State - and indeed the Church - recognised this new fundamental basis of equality in their negotiations leading up to the 1984 Concordat and Additional Protocol, which in large measure repeated several of the Court's pronouncements.

The Court itself seemed hesitant about carrying its own evolution through to its natural conclusion. This diffidence was particularly apparent in the INVIM cases,[105] and the 1988 *bestemmia* case.[106] However, the logic of the equality and autonomy principles emphasised by the Court lead in a very different direction - as indicated by the Court itself in case 925/1988. This direction was confirmed by the new international treaties with the Vatican, which replaced the Lateran Concordat. No other conclusion was consistent with these materials, and the principle of universalisability (equality) which motivated them, save that the State accepted egalitarianism. And so, the *Corte costituzionale* proclaimed, 30 years after endorsing confessionalism, that one of the supreme principles of the Constitutional order was the principle of laicity.[107]

Notes

1   Aug. 1870 - see Mack Smith, *Italy*, pp. 94 - 97; Jemolo, *Chiesa e Stato in Italia negli ultimi cento anni*, p. 175.

2   See the Concordat of 18 Feb. 1984, as implemented in law n. 121 of 25 March 1985, and also the Additional Protocol which provides an authentic interpretation of the Concordat.

3   There are also other 'special court systems', such as the military tribunal system.

4   Dell'Acqua, 'La Giurisprudenza come Sistema e il 'Gioco' dell'Interpretazione', (1993) *Diritto e Società* 489, 491.

5   Baldassare, 'Costituzione e Teoria dei Valori', (1991) 22 *Politica del Diritto* 639, 640.

6   1/1956, [1956] Giur. Cost. 1.

7   Floridia, 'La Costituzione', in Pasquino (ed.) *La Politica Italiana: Dizionario Critico 1945 - 1995*, p. 15.

8   Milza, Bernstein, *Storia del Fascismo*, p. 303 *et seq.*

9   See Jemolo, *Chiesa e Stato negli Ultimi Cento Anni*, ch. 3; Milza, Bernstein, *ibid.*, 304 - 305. For instance, the 1860s saw the enactment of laws amounting to an Italian *Kulturkampf* (War with the Church). To these Pius IX responded with bitter encyclicals condemning the errant doctrine of liberalism.

10   See Milza, Bernstein, *Storia del Fascismo*, p. 306.

11   On Italian constitutional law, see Barile, *Istituzioni di diritto pubblico*; Zagrebelsky, *La Giustizia costituzionale*; Occhiocupo, (ed.) *La Corte Costituzionale tra norma giuridica e realtà sociale;* Paladin, *Diritto Costituzionale*; Pizzorusso, *Manuale di Diritto Pubblico*.

12   The rights of personal liberty, dwelling, secret communication, are all described as inviolable.

13   Compare Art. 21 of the Italian Constitution (freedom of thought and expression) with Arts. 9 and 10 of the European Convention on Human Rights.

14   See Zagrebelsky, *La Giustizia Costituzionale*, pp. 73 *et seq.*; D'Orazio, *La Genesi della Corte Costituzionale*.

15   Based on Arts. 134 - 7 of the Constitution, these were *legge costituzionale (l.c.)* n.1, 9/Feb./1948; *l.c.* n. 1, 11/March/1953; *legge (l.)* n. 87, 11/March/1953; *Corte costituzionale norme integrative* 16/March/1956, n. 71 (this last was an ordinance of the Court itself). Italian statutes are referred to by their date of adoption, and their number indicating chronological order for that year, e.g. *l.* n. 87, 11/March/1953 is law number 87 of 1953, adopted on the 11th March of that year.

16   See Zagrebelsky, *La Giustizia Costituzionale*, ch. 4, on the notion of acts having the force of law.

17   See Cappelletti, *The Judicial Process in Comparative Perspective*, pp. 136 - 146, 161 - 163. Cf. Brewer-Carias, *Judicial Review in Comparative Perspective*.

18   *L.c.* n. 1, 9/Feb./1948, Art. 3; *l.c.* n. 1, 11/March/1953, Art.7.

19 These take the forms of conflicts between different powers of state, conflicts between the State and the Regions, and conflicts among the Regions. See Art. 127 of the Const., Art. 1 of the *l.c.* 1/1948.

20 In 1990, of 241 *sentenze* (decisions) of the Court, 168 came to it via this route. Of 354 *ordinanze* (orders) 344 originated as preliminary references. See Di Manno, 'L'Activité Contentieuse de la Cour Constitutionelle en 1990: Éléments Statistiques et Techniques de Jugement' (1990) 6 *Ann. Int. Jus. Const.* 769, 771.

21 Actually there are a variety of decisions that the Court uses. Among these are: the *sentenze interpretative di rigetto* (where the court rejects a challenge to the validity of a statute, by giving it a particular meaning; compare the French technique of *rejet sous réserve de l'interpretation*); the *sentenze manipolatrici* (interpretation of a statutory provision in the light of the Constitution); the *sentenze creative* (here the *Corte costituzionale* takes it upon itself to fill in a gap left in the legislation; see the doctoral thesis of S. K. Manolkidis, *Granting Benefits Through Constitutional Adjudication*); the *sentenze sostitutive* (where the *Corte costituzionale* alters the wording of a legislative text).

22 There are some exceptions to this, notably in criminal cases (Art. 30, *l.* 87/1953).

23 The decisions are reported in Giurisprudenza Costituzionale (G.C.), which also contains reports of non *Corte costituzionale* decisions of interest to constitutional law, and articles on constitutional doctrine. Many of the relevant cases (prior to 1985) are found in Carusi, Cerri, et al. (eds.) *Giurisprudenza della Corte Costituzionale Italiana.*

24 See Milza, Berstein, *Storia del Fascismo*, pp. 308 - 322; Clark, *Modern Italy, 1871 - 1982*, pp. 254 et seq.; Cordero (ed.), *L'Autunno del Concordato*, pp. 35 - 38 (texts of the dispute between Mussolini and Pius XI).

25 Giolitti, cited in Clark, *Modern Italy, 1871 - 1982*, pp. 146.

26 When I refer to the 'Church', I am referring to the Roman Catholic Church.

27 Jemolo, *Chiesa e Stato in Italia negli Ultimi Cento Anni*, pp. 533 *et seq.*

28 Hilberg, *The Destruction of the European Jews*; Arendt, *Eichmann in Jerusalem*, p. 117.

29 Arendt, *Eichmann in Jerusalem*, pp. 176 - 180; Milza, Bernstein, *Storia del Fascismo*, pp. 258 - 261.

30 Compare Art. 44.1.1, 2, 3 of the Irish Constitution. Art. 44.1.2 recognised the 'special position' of the Catholic Church, as the religion of the majority of Irish people. Art. 44.1.3 recognised various other churches. Art.44.2 contains a strong guarantee of religious freedom and equality. See also the pluralist interpretation given by the Supreme Court to Art. 44 in *State (Quinn's Supermarket)* v. *Minister for Commerce*, [1972] I.R. 1. Art. 41.1.2, 3 were deleted by a referendum in 1972. Apparently, the Vatican hoped that Art. 44 of the Irish Constitution would inspire the Italian Constituent Assembly in 1947 - it arranged for a special translation into Italian. See Keogh, *Ireland and the Vatican*, p. 226.

31   [1957] G.C. 1209. Italian cases are cited by the number of the case decided that year, i.e. case no. 125 of 1957.

32   Case 79/1958, [1958] G.C. 990.

33   [1965] G.C. 602.

34   Cases 20/1971 (*vilipendio*); 14/1973 (*bestemmia*), [1973] G.C. 69; 188/1975 (*vilipendio*), [1975] G.C. 1508.

35   *Modern Italy, 1871 - 1982*, p. 321.

36   [1957] G.C. 579. The provision was Art. 25 of the single text of laws on the Public Security (*t.u.l. P.S.*), enacted in *l.* 18 June 1931, *l.* 773.

37   See also case 59/1958, [1958] G.C. 885, which invalidated a prior administrative control over the opening of non-Catholic temples.

38   This argument was used by the Irish Supreme Court in *Quinn's supermarket* v. *Minister for Commerce* [1972] I.R. 1.

39   [1971] G.C. 150.

40   [1957] G.C. 1209, 1213.

41   Baldassare criticised the decision for being based based on a mere fact, rather than a constitutional provision. See 'E' costituzionale l'incriminazione della bestemmia?' [1973] G.C. 70, 71.

42   [1973] G.C. 69, 76.

43   49/1971.

44   25/1975.

45   [1971] G.C. 150. The case involved the validity of Art. 34.4, 5, 6 of the Concordat, as implemented in *l.* of the 27th May 1929, n. 810.

46   Lariccia notes that this doctrine does not specify the criteria to determine the supreme principles, and leaves a discretionary power to the *Corte costituzionale* to do so. He describes the distinction between ordinary and supreme norms as 'disputable and dangerous': 'Libertà delle università ideologicamente impegnate e libertà di insegnamento' [1972] 2 G.C. 2177, 2189 - 90.

47   Remember that at this stage, Italian courts had not yet adjusted to the idea that the relationship between the European Community (EC) and national legal orders was a peculiarly intimate one which could not be considered in the light of traditional international law concepts. Therefore the comparison must not be taken to suggest that the strong links which exist now between the Italian and EC legal orders, also exists between the Italian and Catholic legal orders.

48   [1971] G.C. 154.

49   [1971] G.C. 156.

50   Tempestini, 'Laicismo e clericalismo nel parlamento italiano' (1980) *Dir. e Soc.* 407.

51   [1971] G.C. 1784, decision 169/1971.

52   Decision of the 12th March, 1970, n. 635.

53   127/1974, [1974] 1 G.C. 849; 169/1974, [1974] 1 G.C. 994.

54   Decision 175/1973, [1973] 2 G.C. 2321.

55   The right to one's natural judge (art. 25 of the Const.) requires that a judge's competence be specified by a law on the basis of objective criteria, enacted prior to the legal process. The judge must be autonomous, independent, impartial. See case 18/1982, [1982] G.C. 138.

56   16/1978, 7th Feb., [1978] 1 G.C. 79.

57   As eventually it would - see Paladin, *Diritto costitutzionale* pp. 157 - 159. For a
      comparative survey see O'Connell 'Guardians of the Constitution' (1999) 4
      Journal of Civil Liberties 48.

58   A claim often bitterly opposed. See the comments of Calamandrei, cited in
      Jemolo, *Chiesa e Stato in Italia negli Ultimi Cento Anni*, p. 536. He exclaimed,
      during the constituent debates, that it was not the fascist - Church Pacts which
      secured the religious peace, but rather the fact that the Catholic Church was one
      of the few organised opponents of the fascist regime.

59   A further example of this reduction in scope was the University Professor case
      (195/1972) which turned entirely on the interpretation of Arts. 2, 8, 19, 33 and
      not Art. 7. There the Court held that the requirement of religious good character
      for a lecturer in a specific university was legitimate. He had chosen to work
      there, and the religious institution was entitled to defend its own religious
      character.

60   Cases 30/1971, 31/1971, 32/1971, 175/1973.

61   Decision 16/1982, 13th Jan., [1982] 1 G.C. 1 115.

62   Art. 84 inserted by Art. 4.1 of the family reform law of the 19th May 1975, n.
      151.

63   The Court reiterated that the choice of the rite was a matter prior to the marriage
      itself and thus not entitled to the protection of Art. 7 of the Constitution.

64   18/1982, 22nd of January, [1982] 1 G.C. 1 138.

65   The role of the Court of Appeal was essentially a formal one - to verify the
      formal regularity of the decision, and not to examine the actual procedure of the
      ecclesiastical court. The State court did not examine whether the proceedings
      were adversarial, whether legal guarantees were really effective, or whether the
      ecclesiastical decision was compatible with Italian public order.

66   The Court emphasised that the position of ecclesiastical courts *could not* be
      compared with the position of the European Court of Justice (as the *Avvocatura*
      had suggested). Decisions of the ECJ were directly effective in the Italian
      internal legal order, without any Italian judge having to make an order
      incorporating them (p. 177). On the contrary, the decisions of ecclesiastical
      courts were submitted to a special procedure of incorporation. Contrast with
      decision 175/1973.

67   The principle of *contraddittorio*, that the decision cannot be without the
      presence of one of the parties (Art. 101 code of civil procedure, *c.p.c.*).

68   First Article of the Additional Protocol.

69   See case 16/1982.

70   See case 32/1971. See also Art. 4 of the Additional Protocol.

71   Case 18/1982.

72   Case 30/1971.

73   Indeed Art. 6 of the Additional Protocol specifically said that the State will
      follow the requirements of case 195/1972 (the University Professor case).

74   Recall cases recognising the importance of the protection of religious sentiment.

75   11 August, 1984, n. 449.
76   22 Nov. 1988, n. 516.
77   22 Nov. 1988, n. 517.
78   8 March, 1989, n. 101.
79   Decision 86/1985, 27th March, [1985] 1 (1) 576; Ordinance 160/1986, 24th June, [1986] 1 (1) G.C. 1097.
80   203/1989; 11th April, [1989] G.C. 890.
81   Art. 9.2 has three propositions: The State recognises the value of religion and the historical role of Catholicism in Italy, and promises to provide Catholic instruction in non-university schools; Given the freedom of conscience and the educational responisibility of parents, everyone has the right to choose or reject religious instruction; The choice may not give rise to any discrimination.
82   Art. 5 b) 2) says: 'b. By subsequent agreement among responsible school authorities and the Italian Episcopal Conference, the following will be determined: ...
      2. The modalities of organization of such teaching, and also its place in the schedule of the classes;'
      Art. 9 of the 1984 Agreement provides as follows: '1. The Italian Republic, in conformity with the principle of freedom of education and teaching, in the terms set forth by its Constitution, guarantees to the Catholic Church the right to freely establish schools of any order and level and educational institutions. The schools that are granted such equality are assured full freedom, and their students an education equal to that granted to students of State schools and other territorial institutions. Equal treatment shall be granted also for State examinations. 2. The Italian Republic, recognizing the value of religious culture, and taking into account the fact that the principles of Catholicism are part of the historical heritage of the Italian people, will continue to ensure, within the limits of school aims, the teaching of Catholic religion in public schools of any order and level, except universities. In regard to liberty of conscience and the educational responsibility of parents, everyone is guaranteed the right to choose whether or not to avail himself of such teaching. On entry students and their parents will exercise such right, at the request of school authorities, except when their choice could result in any form of discrimination.'
83   See p. 898. The Court refers to cases 30/1971, 12/1972, 175/1973, 1/1977, 18/1982, 183/1973, 170/1984, 1146/1988.
84   13/1991, 11 Jan., [1991] 1 G.C. 77.
85   See also case 290/1992, 4th June, [1992] 2 G.C. 2223.
86   13 July, [1984] 1 (2) G.C. 1727.
87   Article 1 made the Union a legal person, whose role was to look after the religious needs of Jews, in a manner compatible with their traditions and the law. Articles 24 to 30 deal with the Union's power to require contributions from its members. Although a royal decree, the measure had been bestowed with the force of a statute, and so could be referred to the CC.
88   43/1988, 14th January, [1988] 1 (1) G.C. 114.
89   259/1990, 23rd May, [1990] G.C. 1542.
90   195/1993, 19th April, [1993] 1 G.C. 1324.

91   The Court briefly addressed the important question of what is a religious group, declining to give a straightforward or rigid test. It said that a group may be deemed a religious one, either because it had an agreement with the State, under Art. 8, or because of recognised practice, or because its charter clearly set forth its religious purpose (p. 1334).

92   925/1988, 8 July, [1988] 1 (3) G.C. 4294.

93   18 Oct. 1995, case 440/1995. The *giudice relatore* is the distinguished constitutionalist Gustavo Zagrebelsky.

94   Cases 45/1957, [1957] G.C. 579; 59/1958, [1958] G.C. 885 rejected the sectarian interpretation. Those cases which rejected the egalitarian one were 125/1957, [1957] G.C. 1209; 79/1958, [1958] G.C. 1990; 39/1965, [1965] G.C. 602; 14/1973, [1973] G.C. 69; 188/1975, [1975] G.C. 1508.

95   Case 30/1971, [1971] G.C. 150.

96   Case 32/1971, [1971] G.C. 156 (the Concordat does not cover the decision to marry or to marry in which forum); 169/1971, [1971] G.C. 1784 (divorce is constitutionally permissible).

97   16/1978 (Referendum case), [1978] 1 G.C. 79.

98   30/1971 (First Nullity case), [1971] G.C. 150.

99   31/1971 (Second Nullity case), [1971] G.C. 154.

100   32/1971 (Third Nullity case, on natural incapacity).

101   175/1973 (Fourth Nullity case), [1973] 2 G.C. 2321.

102   195/1972 (University Professor case), [1972] 2 G.C. 2173.

103   195/1972.

104   [1982] 1 (1) G.C. 115, 138.

105   Decision 86/1985, [1985] 1 (1) 576; Ordinance 160/1986, [1986] 1 (1) G.C. 1097.

106   925/1988, 8 July, [1988] 1 (3) G.C. 4294.

107   43/1988 (Second Jewish Union case), [1988] 1 (1) G.C. 114; 203/1989 (First School Hours case), [1989] G.C. 890; 259/1990 (Third Jewish Union case), [1990] 1542; 13/1991 (Second School Hours case), [1991] 1 G.C. 77; 195/1993 (Church Buildings case), [1993] 1 G.C. 1324.

7 Constitutional Justice in Post Positivist Legal Systems

> Like the wooden head in Phaedrus' fable, a merely empirical doctrine of Right is a head that may be beautiful but unfortunately it has no brain.

Immanuel Kant, *The Metaphysics of Morals*, p. 55, (p. 230)

> The best forms of positivism lead to conclusions similar in important ways to those derivable from the more credible modes of natural law thought, when we pursue rigorously the matters at hand.

Neil MacCormick, *An Institutional Theory of Law*, p. 141

Introduction

The five chapters preceding this have taken the reader on a journey (an interesting one I hope) from the realm of constitutional law through the sphere of legal theory to the area of political moral argument. Let's begin by picking up some of the threads from the previous three chapters, where I led you through an in depth case study of three constitutional problems as dealt with in the case law of three liberal democracies.

We saw legal arguments that were pitched to resolve complex political moral issues, of fundamental relevance to the countries concerned. Canada's attempt to reconcile its multi cultural pluralist ethos with the exigencies of freedom of expression was played out in the courts in four cases where different views of political morality - running the gamut from Raz style perfectionist liberalism to conservatism - dominated the debate, albeit behind the curtains (or at least judicial robes). In

Keegstra and *Butler*, the issue was most clearly presented - on the one hand the society places great emphasis on freedom of expression. It is a fundamental freedom mentioned in Sect. 2 of the Charter of Rights and Freedoms. It plays a major role in maintaining Canadian democracy, in facilitating the search for truth, in fostering self-fulfilment. However must a society be so committed to these values as to justify no restrictions on speech because of their content? In particular must a society permit the spreading of obnoxious anti-Jewish and anti-woman propaganda? In these two cases the Supreme Court of Canada held that such acts of expression could be prohibited. However the emphasis in each case is different. In *Keegstra* the Court emphasised the extremely narrow reach of the statute, the extreme nature of the expression condemned, and the harm such expression held for the important social values of equality and pluralism. These concerns also appear in *Butler*, but there is also a certain element of deference to the conventional standards of the society. And in the *Prostitution Reference case*, this deference is even more marked. An entirely different reconstructed justification appears in *Zundel*, where McLachlin J. puts forward a remarkably sceptical theory as a defence of free expression.

We then turned to Ireland's long running debate on sexual morality, where the Supreme Court's liberal vision of the 1970s provoked a running battle between progressive and conservative forces in society, a battle which returned to the courts in the 1980s and 1990s. In the 1973 *McGee* decision the Supreme Court endorsed an autonomy based right to make decisions about intimate sexual matters, and to put those decisions into effect. No one was entitled (except in extraordinary circumstances) to interfere with that decision; rights cannot be interfered with on the basis of public morality. Yet in 1983 there were two reversals to this justification of the constitutional order. On the one hand, pro-life activists, seeing in this decision a threat to the life of the foetus, argued for an amendment to prevent an autonomy based interpretation of the Constitution ever leading to such a result. In *Norris*, a majority of the Supreme Court consciously rejected the claim of autonomy, as upheld in *McGee*, in favour of a sectarian interpretation of the Constitution. Late 1980s decisions confirmed this perfectionist stance. Although the waters have not calmed in the 1990s, the Supreme Court and the people, are rethinking this fundamentally conservative stance (as evinced in the *X* case, the *Abortion Information* case, and the amendments to Art. 40.3.3 of the Constitution).

Italy is also a country torn between a traditional Catholicism and a more egalitarian ideal. In its early years the *Corte costituzionale* tended to give a somewhat sectarian tinge in its interpretation of the compromise with Catholicism in Art. 7 of the Constitution and its interpretation of other articles relating to religious freedom. However in the 1970s, it was more open to claims based on an egalitarian interpretation of the Constitution. And this egalitarian interpretation, justification of the State was endorsed in the activities of Parliament, Executive and the people throughout the 1970s and 1980s, resulting in the 1984 modification of the historic compromise. Nor does the story end there, for the *Corte costituzionale* continued that theme of egalitarianism and enhanced it in decisions in the late 1980s and 1990s.

There are certain common traits to these case studies. In all of them the traditional judicial role of 'following the rules laid down' was heavily supplemented by elements (both transparent and obscured) of political moral reasoning. The chain of reasoning was incomplete without the presupposition of further links - links which were most likely those of normative political philosophy. Second there is a very active *debate* going on, or rather a series of such debates. We see the debate between different judges - the dispute between Dickson C.J.C. and McLachlin J. in *Keegstra*, and the flare up between the dissenters and the majority in *Norris*. We also see a debate between the courts and the other political organs - the Italian Government's initiative to amend the Lateran Concordat in 1984 was spurred by the *Corte costituzionale*'s activity in the 1970s, and itself led to further developments by the constitutional tribunal. It is a debate also with the people - either directly through referenda (as in Ireland and Italy) or indirectly through the means of elections and popular pressure in the use of the political process. Further this debate is an ongoing one - the courts pick it up one day from the political arena and hand it back again. Before it returns it may even take a detour (or a straight path) to the people.

In this Chapter I show the underlying unity of these themes, from the point of view of judicial decision-making. The end product is a theory of constitutional interpretation.

The insight is that constitutional law, as practised by the tribunals of constitutional justice, is a legalised form of political morality. Thus legal argument in such cases mirrors argument in cases of political moral reasoning (actually is an instance of it). In this chapter I try to give an overview of the relationship between (constitutional) law and (political) morality. I will outline once more the criteria of rational intersubjective argument, noticing how these are used in the legal arena, with reference to examples drawn from the first three chapters.

This book has been centred within the framework of a debate about the methods of reasoning of judges sitting on tribunals of constitutional justice in 'liberal democracies'. These assumptions are not immune from examination (the very justification of 'constitutional justice' in a liberal democracy is an important problem which cannot be ignored). The comments and conclusions do not necessarily apply to every legal system, nor do they assume that every liberal democracy should have institutions of constitutional justice. Where liberal democracies do have legitimate institutions of constitutional justice then this is how I suggest those institutions interpret the constitutional law entrusted to them.

We start with the position of a constitutional judge, and a legal problem. Consider the position of a judge in *R.* v. *Keegstra*, one of the Canadian cases. As in all cases there are several questions: Dworkin summarises three questions in every case for the judge. The judge must decide what are the facts of the case? what is the law applicable to it? and whether political morality approves of the law and authorises the judge to follow the law in this case?[1] It is the second question that concerns us. How does a judge determine what is the law in this case - what is the correct interpretation of the Constitution? However in approaching the question of interpretation the other issues must not be left aside.

In considering this issue the judge must bear in mind several matters. The two most immediately involved are the fact that she is dealing with an individual case, and the relevant sources of law. Three 'background' concerns must also be born in mind: the claim to legitimacy of law, the notion of fidelity to law, and the celebrated 'counter-majoritarian' problem.

The judge cannot escape the fact that she is dealing with claims and counter-claims of legal subjects who assert that a particular fact situation requires state action. (In *Keegstra* the decision was on whether a schoolteacher had violated a (valid) anti-hate expression statute.) This has two sides to it. First, the decision applies to these particular facts (though it may have effect against all parties). Second, and more importantly the decision has direct practical consequences. The decision on interpretation is not an abstract one, unlike the interpretation of law professors. The decision on interpretation is a crucial step in the process leading to the decision to grant or deny a remedy, to implement or not a sanction. The decision may turn on whether a parent should pay child allowance, whether a contact should be annulled, or whether (as in *Keegstra*) someone should go to jail. The practical effect of an interpretative decision is quite clear in the common law systems I studied, but it is necessary to note that it also applies to the mechanism of constitutional review as practised in, for instance, Italy. It is true that the Italian constitutional judge does not deliver the verdict on the instant case; however she answers an interpretative question only where an ordinary judge has certified that it is necessary for him or her to dispose of a particular fact situation. That factual situation is indicated to the *Corte costituzionale*, and the judges know that their decision is essential to the case's resolution. The practical link between the interpretative decision and the ultimate disposition of the case is maintained.

The individual legal problem is located in a (sometimes turbulent) sea of legal norms. This poses several issues. First, there are often several norms which must be considered. In *Keegstra*, the Supreme Court considered the validity of one provision of the Criminal Code (s. 319), and the correct interpretation of two sections of the Charter (ss. 1 and 2(b)). To do this it considered the meaning of three other provisions of the Criminal Code, two other provisions of the Charter, the Canadian Bill of Rights, various other statutory provisions, several provisions in international law texts, various US and other foreign legal decisions, and a host of Canadian Supreme Court decisions.

These many texts were issued by several different authors at different times. The Charter was enacted by the legislatures of Canada as a constitutional amendment in 1981. The Bill of Rights was adopted by the federal legislature in 1961. Some of the Criminal Code provisions were quite recent enactments, others survivals from the previous century. Of the international law texts, some acquired force of law upon adoption by the United Nations and a sampling of states, and one upon adoption by the Council of Europe. And of course, the judicial decisions were the works of courts in various states.

Whilst the Court referred to all these 'sources', a further problem is that some of them are not considered 'binding' (e.g. international law texts, foreign legal opinions), whilst even those that are binding might not be followed in the instant case for various reasons. They may be pre-empted by a superior source of law (the Criminal Code has a higher legal status than the Bill of Rights, and the Charter takes precedence over both); they may be overturned by a decision of the Court (in the case of its own precedents) and all the norms are subject to interpretation, which may radically alter their perceived meaning and effect.

Further the intentions of the different legal actors, and the socio-political background in which they (en)act(ed), will often indicate more the turbulence of political reality than the certainty of a clear interpretation of the norm. In many cases it will be very difficult to ascertain the subjective intention of the specific human actors involved in enacting a measure, or determine a collective intention ascribable to a collective body. The motives and intentions of the human actors of a legislature will often be extremely mixed - they may be motivated by no more than a desire to finish a debate before lunch, or to garner support in their constituency. Their intention may well be that a law never be enforced, or that it be selectively enforced, and that it means something of which they are not sure, but their party leaders assure them it is a good idea. Even where their motives are sincere and their intentions intelligible, these may conflict with the motives and intentions of other actors, or even the very wording of the measure they adopt. The motives and intentions of state leaders in adopting human rights conventions may be even less obvious or honest. Also the motives and intentions of the judicial actors cannot be immune from suspicion.

All of this does not even get to the problem of the textual meaning of the norms, which is often ambiguous enough. In *Keegstra* the Supreme Court had to consider such ambiguous phrases as 'freedom of expression' and 'reasonable limits prescribed by law as can be demonstrably justified in a free and democratic society'. These were given interpretations ranging from the majority one that expression which is inimical to the fundamental value of equality may be banned by the criminal law, to the minority view that no expression may be banned solely because of the content of the message, however obnoxious. And other views were possible (for instance, that normally the legislature could not ban hate speech, but it could certainly be banned in the case of a school teacher speaking to a class room; or that the legislature could ban speech detrimental to any fundamental value). Furthermore the 'magnificent generalities' of the Charter are not the only ambiguous provisions. Section 319 of the Criminal Code punishes anyone who 'by communicating statements other than in private conversation, wilfully promotes hatred against any identifiable group'. Such phrases as 'private', 'wilfully', and 'hatred', are what guarantee employment to legal dogmaticists.[2]

The above comments relate to what Joseph Raz has called the 'base' of a theory of law, the part concerning itself with the 'concrete reality' of the legal system.[3] That is that the law in many states is:

> ... the result of the rough-and-tumble of politics, which does not exclude the judiciary from its ambit, and reflects the vagaries of pragmatic compromises, or changing fortunes of political forces, and the like. (ibid., p. 283)

The legal sources are quite possibly (though not necessarily) an incoherent collection of norms reflecting different interests at different times. Any acceptable theory of law according to Raz, must not ignore this reality. In particular he is critical of 'coherence' theories which seek to 'transcend the inherent limitations of the workings of human institutions' (*ibid.*, p. 285). However, whilst we must not transcend the limits of humanity, neither should we ignore the possibility of establishing a 'rationalizing element which enables us to view the law as a rational system governing the conduct of affairs in a country' (*ibid.*, p. 273), a system for orientation in constitutional argument.

The judge must also consider three background factors: fidelity to law, the counter-majoritarian difficulty and the problem of law's legitimacy.

The problem of law's claim to legitimacy is a double one: one must be careful not to grant it too much legitimacy, nor reject any claims of legitimacy at all. The first extreme says that whatever is required by legal authorities is legitimate; that it is always wrong to oppose the law. This extreme position is rarely defended today. Ironically it is a position which both positivists and natural lawyers have been accused of maintaining. The stereotype of the former was that the 'law is the law and that is the end of the matter'. In contrast to this natural lawyers are accused of saying that whatever is right is law - which amounts to the same thing more or less.[4]

Some modern positivist writers deal with this problem by distinguishing sharply law and morality. What is law is one thing and what is moral is another. In the event of conflict they argue that one must obey the dictates of conscience. Natural lawyers confound the issues and so deprive the individual of the right to oppose the law: if the decision on what is right has already been made in the process of deciding what is law, and determines the answer to the latter question, then the theorists are saying that what is law is right, and so denying any right to oppose the law on the grounds that it is illegitimate. This is Kelsen, Hart, et al.'s argument that moralistic theories of law are confusing and indeed dangerously confusing ideological stratagems. This is an important problem: a theory of constitutional adjudication must pay tribute to the right of conscience.

There are however problems with the modern positivist solution, in that it goes to the opposite extreme: it makes no sense of law's claim to legitimacy. To be consistent, it must deny it. Yet this runs counter to my experience of what legal language says and implies in practice.[5] Legal language is normative; it deals with what human actors ought to do. It might be argued that legal norms are *constitutive* or *hypothetical* norms in the sense that linguistic norms or (technical) norms of skill are norms. They say, 'A legal contract is where two parties agree about the performance of some promise' or 'Well if you want to do what is lawful, you must act in this way'. Neither constitutive norms nor hypothetical norms raise issues of legitimacy in the sense of morality (obviously they can be called correct or incorrect, but they do not raise a claim to obedience). One can simply say 'Well I do not choose to play the legal language game, so what?'. If this related to technical norms ('I am going to use demarara sugar instead of the caster sugar I should use') the response may simply be 'Okay, but you won't get a nice cake!'. If I decline to speak Italian correctly then (in Italy at any rate) people may regard me as odd (or a tourist) and I may not make many friends. But this is not what is involved in all legal norms.

I am not saying that all legal norms are commands. Hart is surely right that there are secondary rules in legal orders which are constitutive rules - the rules of contractual obligation being an obvious example.

However there are also rules which do prohibit, permit and command (primary rules of obligation). And there is one category of legal norms which go beyond constitutive or technical norms, and demand obedience. And that category is intimately concerned with judicial interpretation: the decision of the judge. The interpretative decision determines (if we accept the concept of fidelity to law) the final disposition of the case. In relation to this there can be no question of saying 'I do not want to play the legal language game'. Neither judge, member of the executive, nor legal subject can say this. They may defy the law, but the law demands obedience. Legal language is normative, and this is most clearly seen in the practical nature of judging.

The judge who hands down her decision expects compliance. She expects the legal subject, or member of the executive or whoever to comply. In the case of defiance, such defiance must be criticised from the legal point of view. Such defiance provides a legal reason for the punishment of the person who so defies.

The law provides certain norms, and a system of adjudication to decide upon the correct application of those norms. The law demands obedience, and insists that one does wrong in not obeying; that legal authorities are entitled to insist on compliance and punish those who do not.[6] This reflects what an important purpose of law is: to provide *authoritative* rules to guide human conduct. It claims the right to provide rules for all legal subjects within its competence, and the right to define its own sphere of competence. The legal authorities may or may not be able to insist on their rules as against the rules of any other group or the beliefs of any legal subject in their territory. However the legal authorities (from the legal viewpoint) claim that in the case of conflict one must follow the legal rules; that one does wrong in not following the legal rules.

This demand does not reflect that of speaking a language, or practising a trade, nor belonging to most types of groups. Nor does it closely resemble the claim of a large scale gangster group (which might argue that it is futile or stupid to defy its rules, but hardly wrong; nor does a gangster group deny the legitimacy of other groups issuing contrary rules). Other than the legal authorities, I can only think of three claims resembling these: the claims of a group which insists it is the legitimate state authority; the claims of a religion; and the claims of morality.

From the point of view of all forms of practical reasoning (including moral as well as legal) the law's demand is not final and unanswerable. Yet the demand is there and is not merely that of a constitutive rule. Positivists such as Raz and Coleman who deny any shred of legitimacy fail to make sense of this demand.[7] What we must do is to make sense of it. However we must not conflate law and morality, for that would convey on law an unanswerable legitimacy.

The judge must also pay attention to the duty of 'fidelity to law'. Judges are expected to base their decisions on legal sources - the casual reference to extra-legal sources raises eyebrows. If we want a decision merely on the basis of the fairness of the case, then we do not turn to a judge, but to a respected member of the community, or a moral casuist, or we engage in private negotiation. From the viewpoint of law, the judge is expected to base her decision in some way on legal sources (statutes, precedents, etc.). Modern theories of law, even those assigning a large element to moral considerations, treat legal sources as important.[8] As Lon Fuller notes, a judge may well provide a wonderful decision, well reasoned, based on principles, in harmony with morality - but if there does not exist a significant link between the judgements and the legal sources, then the citizenry feel cheated.[9] What the judge is doing may be moral, but it is not law. (Unless of course, a legal source expressly leaves something to be decided purely according to the fairness of the case.)

The notion of fidelity has several consequences. First, there is the basic instinct that the judge must somehow link her judgement to the sources available. Second, since these sources are the product of the political process, we expect the sources to provide different answers (or at least guides) in different political communities (e.g. the abortion laws in Ireland are quite different from those in Italy and Canada). Accordingly, we should not be surprised if judges arrive at different conclusions to the same legal problem in different states, as the sources will often differ. The decisions will in some way 'track' the sources. Third, we have seen that the sources of law are not perfectly clear comprehensible linguistic formula edicted by a single legislator who makes her will, motive and intention perfectly evident. The meaning of the legal source is not something which it holds up to the entire world for the sake of transparency. To be faithful to the law means that the judge must perform an act of interpretation, to give the legal source(s) meaning. Unless there is a meaning, the judge's decision cannot be faithful to it. The assigning of a meaning cannot be something arbitrary however, there must be controls on it, or else there is no possibility of fidelity.

The third background factor is particularly important constitutional courts. This is what US scholars call the 'counter-majoritarian problem', the problem of the separation of powers. The problem is this: a constitutional court is empowered to invalidate legislative choices where it decides those legislative choices are unconstitutional. However the appointment procedure of members of a constitutional court and members of a legislature are different. The people elect the legislature, but constitutional judges are usually appointed by various political authorities. The prevailing theories of legitimacy in most liberal democracies stress the legitimating role of election by universal adult suffrage, and confer particular legitimacy on the legislature to make binding political value choices. Accordingly, it is difficult to see why an appointed body should be able to invalidate those value choices.

There is a straightforward rejoinder to this. Advocates of constitutional courts will point out that liberal democracies do not just accept the notion of democratic elections, but also such notions as constitutionalism, the rule of law and legality. The legislature expresses the will of the people, but only within the legal framework created by the constitution. Where the legislatively expressed will of the people violates the constitution the latter must prevail. However this argument immediately runs into two counter-arguments. First, why should a court or tribunal be in charge of protecting the constitution? Can't the legislature also be in charge of protecting it? Second, interpreting any text is not a mechanical operation. This is particularly so where constitutional interpretation is at stake. Constitutional interpretation involves very important value choices (this after all was part of what my first three chapters sought to prove), and such value choices are the provenance of Parliament. Fundamental value choices can be entrusted to common sense, and so to the people and their elected representatives.

This argument has two practical possible consequences. Either someone who holds it is arguing for the abolition of the practice of constitutional review; or one is arguing for a very deferential exercise of the power of constitutional review. 'Deferential' can have several meanings of course: it may mean that the judge usually defers to the will of the legislature, or that she employs various procedural devices to avoid reaching decisions, or that she uses very limited remedies in the event of finding a violation.

The constitutional judge must find a solution to a particular case based on the legal sources, and considering the background factors of fidelity to law, the problem of law's legitimacy, and the counter-majoritarian difficulty. All this just to answer the question, what is the law? What is the way forward?

Practical Reasoning

One of the problems of many great positivist contributions to our understanding of law is precisely this. They offer many insights: Kelsen is right that there are different levels of legal norms; Hart's discussion of secondary rules is invaluable; Raz's discussion of law as providing authoritative reasons for action is very important; MacCormick and Weinberger have done an inestimable service with their analysis of the role of institutional facts in law. However the answers of positivist theories to the question of how to interpret the law are often vague and fail to offer guidance. Hart and Kelsen give the classic answer: within the frame of the legal source the judge must simply choose a solution.[10] Yet this gives the impression that legal theory is a bit like a professional musician who always practises - but never performs.

The answer of positivists to the question of law's legitimacy is similarly elusive: from the insightful but ultimately fruitless discussion of obligation in Hart, to Raz's outright rejection of any duty to obey the law. How can law offer a reason to obey the law, yet not an absolute one?

These two questions are fundamentally interlinked. This is the insight of what I may term 'modern natural law' thinkers, those who pursue the 'third way of law', 'tween the trials of positivism and the tribulations of natural law. Recent legal writing has aimed to come to grips with a 'post-positivist' legal world. In essence I argue that constitutional interpretation is an instance of a moral reconstruction of the legal sources available.

Now these two questions ('How ought I to interpret the law?' 'Ought I to obey the law?') are questions calling for the exercise of practical reason, they try to deal with the practical problem of what to do.[11] Let's keep an eye on the second question (the one of legitimacy) for the moment. Now practical reason is concerned with the issue of 'what to do'?[12] It thus involves a subject, a context and a range of possible actions. It includes several types of practical reason, usually divided into 'instrumental' reason and 'value-oriented' reason.[13]

There is the straightforward, technical type of reason - instrumental reason. For instance I want to drive from Florence to Milan in the shortest possible time, I want to become a legal academic, I want to construct a grammatically correct sentence in Italian, etc. What ought I to do to achieve these goals? This is basic means-end (instrumental or pragmatic) rationality: I have a given goal which I wish to achieve in the current set of circumstances, so how do I do it?

Of course this instrumental reason is not always absolutely straightforward.[14] It is neither a simple nor a trivial exercise. Weber makes it clear that instrumental rationality may also adjudicate among various ends. However it cannot adjudicate among those fundamental value beliefs on which the ends are based.[15] Habermas adds a further gloss; instrumental reason may be divided into instrumental reason proper and strategic reason which comes into play when other actors in society are pursuing their own instrumental reason.[16]

The technical type of practical reasoning simply accepts as given the values of the subject. Some of these goals may simply be explained by other goals ('Why go to Milan?' 'I want to go to Milan to see my girlfriend.'). However not all goals can be explained as simply instrumental goals to a greater goal, which is itself merely an instrumental goal, etc. (the goal of being in a loving relationship is not something which is a means to a further end). Weber identifies what he calls 'value-rationality' which involves beliefs in values for their own sake, e.g. religion, beauty, ethics and morality. In this book, we are concerned with what is broadly called 'morality', and more specifically political morality. In this book I do not come to any conclusion on the debate raging over two alleged sub-categories of general morality, generally called the good and the right,[17] or teleology and deontology, or ethics and morality.[18] This debate is rather complicated since: first, some writers deny that there is any fundamental distinction;[19] second, when a distinction is identified it often differs from one writer to another;[20] third, even where the distinction is the same the relation between the two categories may differ depending on the author.[21]

Now there is a great deal of debate about these types of practical reason, and particularly the relationship between the last two. Both are concerned with different areas of what is broadly called morality. There are those who deny that there is any distinction between the two; others insist that they are different and one or the other is superior. Myself, I wish to note that the two may be conflated in a way: one may be defined in terms of the other. Thus one can have a deontological theory of the good: one is virtuous if one acts from the motive of, and in accordance with, duty. The utilitarian theory defines the right in terms of the good: the right act is the one which promotes the greatest good. I suspect that most theories of the right and the good held by the same subject tend to reinforce the other and are really complementary (it would be bizarre if one held contradictory theories of the right and the good), though it may be more natural to speak in the phrases of one rather than another in a given case. When I am referring to political moralities I do not mean to exclude either type of reasoning, the 'ethical' or the 'intersubjective', nor to exclude political moralities which deny any difference.

Another point to note is that there are *conventional* and *critical* visions of the good and the right. In any given society, there is (or are) *accepted* theories of the good and the right. However this is not the same as an *acceptable* theory of either. We may observe that someone or some society has a particular conception of the good, but it is still possible to ask whether it has the correct (true, most reasonable) conception. There is a difference between what someone believes and what she ought to believe. What she believes is her conventional morality, but she ought to believe in critical morality. Hitler undoubtedly endorsed a racist ideology - but he was wrong.

Again take the question 'How ought intersubjective relations to be regulated?'. This may be asked from the viewpoints of different subjects. I (as an individual person) have certain beliefs about how I ought to behave if someone confides in me, asks for a favour, lends me his car, tries to punch me, insults someone else in my presence, etc. There is another potential subject however: how ought the political community to interact with other subjects? What should the state do when Mr. Jones steals from Ms. Smith, Ms. De Luccia has sex with her husband, Fr. O'Brien goes to Church? Should the state recognise certain contracts, provide for restitution of property in what cases, support what charitable causes? Persons expressing a view on these questions are expressing views on political morality. They are expressing a view on when the political authorities are entitled to invoke that authority to regulate conduct; that is when such and such a political action is legitimate or illegitimate. Note that this is a two stage process: political morality must, first, define whether a particular topic falls within its scope, and second, what should its stance be.

Perhaps the most important ways the political authorities may act is by law. Now when the law is questioned, how will a politician justify obedience to it?[22] A special supertax is imposed on all persons earning above a particular income. A person says 'Look, I do not want to obey this particular law. Why should I?' There are it seems to me, two possible answers. The first is that this law is justified by a correct view of political morality. The second answer is that the bulk of the political system corresponds to the proper set-up of a political system from the point of view of political morality. The problem with the first answer is twofold. First I am not convinced that theories of political morality offer answers to all possible legal issues. Second, even if they do, I am not convinced that lawmakers or judges always adopt those answers. So the more reasonable answer seems to be the second. The legitimacy of a law is fundamentally related to the system which adopted it.

The second answer says that 'Look, the laws of a particular political system are legitimate when that political system corresponds to the requirements of political morality'.[23] A law enacted (or however adopted) by a legitimate political system is itself presumed to be legitimate. How would a political morality designate which political institutions are legitimate? Political moralities generally propose criteria of substance, or procedural criteria, or a mixture, to determine whether a political system is legitimate. Substantive criteria are varied. A utilitarian will say that the system which promotes the greatest possible amount of happiness is legitimate; a communitarian will say that the system which achieves the development of the community *Geist* is legitimate; a liberal may say whichever state observes the rules of the Universal Declaration of Human Rights is legitimate. A proceduralist (e.g. some advocates of discourse ethics) assert that whenever a state acts through a particular procedure (democratic discourse) then its enactments are legitimate. Finally there are mixed theories, typically popular with US style liberals and some proponents of discourse ethics, who try, as Rawls would have it, to reconcile the liberties of the ancients with the liberties of the moderns. Typically they propose a mixture of procedural criteria (the trappings of modern democracy), and certain substantive criteria (recognition of certain basic rights, basic economic fairness). What is the best political morality is something which must be argued using the criteria that I outlined in the previous chapter.

This does not directly help our constitutional judge, nor solve the problem of law's legitimacy. A politician (or whoever) saying that a political system corresponds to the best conception of political morality is invoking that section of practical reason called political morality. Someone speaking from such a position is relatively unencumbered: she is bound by the criteria of political moral argument, but that is all. It is open to such a person to say that a political system is perfectly legitimate, or not legitimate at all. Such a person can say that a political system ought to be overthrown. The person speaking from such a position does not have to accept as given (even as merely prima facie given) any of the institutions and rules of the political system. This is a relatively unrestricted exercise of practical reason.

Not so the position of a judge, or someone else interpreting a law from the legal point of view. Such a person cannot ask the question 'whether to obey the political system?' in such an unrestricted manner - as a participant within it, she has already accepted, at least for the purpose of participating in the legal enterprise. From within the legal viewpoint we cannot pose the ultimate question so bluntly. The question facing us is, how can the legal system claim legitimacy, what is the nature of the legal system's claim? If the system does correspond to the requirements of political morality, then well and good, but this is not the legal question. Furthermore, given the realities of the political situation, it is unlikely that all legal rules fit into a coherent, acceptable political morality.

We cannot simply say that the legal system is the society's expression of political morality. This is no doubt true, but trivial. In a sense any society's legal system contains the norms the society accepts as part of its conventional political morality.24 Legislators enact what they consider to be the most just rules. However this does not answer the problem of legitimacy, for *conventional* morality cannot ground a claim to legitimacy. That some people (let us assume everyone else bar Mr. Bean) *believes* that Mr. Bean ought to act in a certain way does not mean that

Mr. Bean ought to act in that way. The first matter is a fact, a question of conventional morality. The second is an aspect of critical morality, a question for practical reason. That the legal system expresses society's conventional morality is not enough.

There is an answer to this conundrum. Before presenting it however, I want to turn to the second of the questions facing the constitutional judge.

How is the judge to interpret the law? What are the deliberative steps in determining the meaning of the relevant legal norms? Now it may seem that this is a question for cognitive rather than practical reason. However, this ignores the basic fact that meaning does not lie within words or phrases or texts, waiting to be unlocked. Rather it must be constructed; meaning must be assigned. So it may seem to call for the technical exercise of practical reason: to arrive at the most appropriate construction of a legal text what deliberative steps should we take? We need a theory of interpretation.

Now a theory of interpretation must fulfil certain requirements. First of all, it must provide criteria to judge whether an interpretation is acceptable or not. Second, it must obey the concept of fidelity to law - meaning must not be simply invented. So a legal theory of interpretation must pay attention to the sources before it, and must provide criteria which allow us to say that certain interpretations are acceptable or unacceptable (a theory of interpretation which would permit anything is ruled out). Thirdly it must do justice to our experience of law and legal systems. So it must not contradict in any way certain basic assumptions (that sources play a role in law, that law is normative, that there are different legal institutions, etc.) about law.

Now the answer to the conundrum is a joint answer, for we attempt to provide criteria of interpretation and explain law's claim to legitimacy at one stroke. The answer is not particular novel.[25] Law cannot claim simply to be legitimate. However, the judge can offer a reason to accept the legitimacy of law, if we construe one of the elements of legal theory as being a feature which we noted time and time again in the first three chapters. Let us perceive one of the elements of law as being a public dialogue (Rawls uses the phrase 'omnilogue' at one point[26]) on the justification of public authority, with the actors including courts, legislators, other officials and citizens. Each of these plays its own role in an on-going dialogue of justification. The legislator and constitutional legislator must provide rules which they claim justify the political system. Citizens debate, criticise, agitate, protest, litigate and provide the ultimate touchstone of justification. The political debate produces a variety of legal rules for judges to interpret. The judge offers justification of the law, in effect she says that 'The decision I offer is the most legitimate justification of the sources before me, given the requirements of political morality'. This justification is offered up once more for the public debate.

Rawls provides a typically clear discussion of this process from the point of view of his particular conception of political morality. The constitutional judge must offer a reconstruction of the legal materials before her, to offer the best possible construction of the constitution, viewed from the viewpoint of political morality:

> ... it is the task of the justices to try to develop and express in their reasoned opinion the best interpretation of the constitution they can, using their knowledge of what the constitution and constitutional precedents require. Here the best interpretation is the one that best fits the relevant body of those constitutional materials, and justifies it in terms of the public conception of justice or a reasonable variant thereof. (p. 236)

In doing this the judges must:

> ... appeal to the political values which they think belong to the most reasonable understanding of the public conception and its political values of justice and public reason. (p. 236)

The crucial points are these: judges must interpret the legal materials before them in accordance with the criteria of critical political moral argument, as brought within the legal sphere. Please note that I am saying the judges must invoke the criteria of *critical* morality when interpreting provisions. It is not acceptable to interpret the legal materials in the light of the conventional morality of society, for that conventional morality cannot ground a claim of legitimacy.

Please also note that I said the criteria of critical political moral argument *within the legal sphere*. The judge still faces the duty of speaking from the legal point of view. As we shall see shortly, the judge invoking legalised political moral argument is constrained in certain ways the individual simply involved in political argument is not.

Rawls concentrates on constitutional justice, as have I, but there is a clear reason for this. If we see law as involving (inter alia) a debate on the justification of public authority (and there is no other way to accommodate law's peculiar claim to legitimacy), then we see judges asserting that, given the legal materials before them, this particular solution is the best, as it fits into the most legitimate reconstruction of the legal materials. Clearly constitutional law plays a particular role here - see my brief discussion of political legitimacy. The proffered justification cannot be that every legal norm corresponds to the requirements of political morality. The basic claim must be that it was adopted by a political system which respects the claims of political morality. Hence legitimacy will be heavily concerned with those basic criteria of legitimacy: fundamental rights, basic economic fairness, and democratic procedures. And those basic elements, although involved in many areas of law, are first and foremost involved in the area of constitutional law: constitutional rights, constitutional guarantees of economic justice, constitutional guarantees of democratic procedures. That legalised political morality is particularly evident in constitutional law is therefore to be expected. For constitutional law provides the peg on which the legal system's claim to legitimacy is mainly based.

The Legalised Criteria of Political Moral Argument

In Chapter Five, I outlined nine criteria to determine the validity of claims about political morality. The basic idea was that the validity of moral claims must be founded on a claim that one can offer as a reason to another party to accept. An acceptable theory of political morality should be supported by reasons, consistent, non-individualising, general, capable of solving problems, factually accurate, explicable, held by a reflective equilibrium, and universalisable.

In this section I wish to explore how these criteria adjust themselves in the context of constitutional interpretation, where a constitutional judge is bound from the legal point of view, not merely the moral. Judges must provide a political moral reconstruction of the legal order. In doing this an element of a coherentist approach comes in (under the headings of consistency and reflective equilibrium). However the coherence sought is a principled one - explications are to be rejected if they violate other criteria of rational intersubjective argument, such as explicability or universalisability. In this way I hope to avoid at least some of the pitfalls of coherence based theories as identified by Raz.[27] Specifically: political morality is not treated as a simple tie-breaker among coherent theories; and evil but coherent explications are ruled out.

As I discuss each criterion I shall try to explain its requirements. I shall then identify some instances of its use from the first three chapters. This is important, for the perception of law as involving a debate on the legitimacy of public authority, a debate where judges reconstruct the legal elements into the most legitimate construction possible, stems from an overview of the constitutional practice in those states. If now, consciously considering the requirements of political morality, we find that they have been used in constitutional argument, then this strengthens the case for regarding this on-going debate as one of the elements of law. Furthermore, I will also try to identify instances where these criteria have been ignored. A theory of interpretation must be able to show where an interpreter puts her foot wrong.

Two objections may be raised to the foregoing comments: that they are circular and contradictory. It might be said that it is circular to derive from the case studies the perception that law concerns such a dialogue, then to develop the criteria of the dialogue and invoke the fact that one finds the criteria in concrete instances of constitutional interpretation to justify the insight. I do not find this circular, rather I see it as mutually supporting. I have two starting points - constitutional practice in three liberal democracies (Chs. 1 - 3), and the criteria of political moral argument (Ch. 5). The first starting point suggests that constitutional interpretation involves this dialogue on legitimacy. I confirm that by leaving the domain of constitutional practice, and then discussing the criteria of legitimacy in political moral argument. I now go looking again in constitutional practice to see if those criteria are to be found. If they are, then I conclude that the original insight was correct. This is a question of mutual support, not circularity.

It might be objected though that I look for instances of where constitutional judges have followed and have violated these criteria: is this not contradictory? I do not believe so. The criteria of argument would not have much value if they resembled the constitutional practice not in the slightest. However they would have even less value if they justified every single interpretative step in every single decision in those case studies. After all there were changes of mind, evolutions of case law, dissents and outright contradictions in those studies. If the criteria of argument held that all those steps were valid, then it would be useless.

In discussing these criteria, it must be born in mind that they are to be applied by a judge in a modern legal system - that is a system of norms and institutions providing guidance for the behaviour of legal subjects, and claiming a right to be obeyed. The judiciary in these states (and generally in liberal democratic states) as an organ of adjudication and interpretation has a special duty of fidelity to law. That the legislator does not like a law is enough of a reason for the legislator to change it. For a judge to dislike a law is irrelevant, her duty is to interpret and apply it. Interpretation (particularly constitutional interpretation) is not a mechanical task, but often involves values, and this embroils the judiciary in the counter-majoritarian problem. One of the ways out of this problem is to provide criteria by which to guide judicial interpretation, and perhaps more importantly by which to criticise judicial interpretation. The specification of the criteria of argument is one important limit on judicial power.

It is important to note that in any case, there are two sets of norms which the judge interprets explicitly or implicitly. The first set comprises the norms needed to solve the case (the rules of contract in a contract case, the rules of criminal law in a murder case). The second set reflects on the position of the judge herself. A judicial decision is also based on the rules creating the position of the judge, establishing the judicial procedures, the correct interpretative method, etc. The judge must apply the criteria of political argument not just to the substantive rules governing the fact situation before her, but also to the rules which establish her competence and by which she may reach an authoritative decision. Not just the judicial decision but the judicial power must be interpreted according to the criteria of political argument. Implicit in the exercise of the constitutional justice, is a decision on the limits of judicial power - the counter-majoritarian problem. What those limits are in a particular state depends not merely on arguments of political morality, but on the how those arguments interpret the legal materials in that state (constitutional, statutory, common law) on the exercise of judicial power. Accordingly those limits may differ from state to state - I assume that fidelity to law requires some exercise of constitutional justice (the

Canadian, Irish and Italian constitutions all explicitly recognise the power after all) and that political argument prohibits that constitutional tribunals function as super-legislatures. Where in between is a trickier question.[28]

So in discussing these criteria, I wear a variety of hats (and wigs). I move from the realm of unrestricted political argument, to the realm of legalised political argument, and often dip into the area of legalised political argument in a liberal democracy (typified by the three case studies), and sometimes into the specific arena of legalised political argument in a specific state. The last two moves may be quite controversial, but I do so for two reasons. First, it is only fair to the reader to show what sort of results might follow from this theoretical approach. Second, it confirms the reading of the first three chapters, that law involves a debate on the legitimacy of public authority.

Reasons

The basic insight was that the criteria of validity of political moral argument were based on the concept of offering a reason that someone could accept. Most of those criteria concerned what such a reason would look like. An important criterion is that one gives a reason.

In practical debate, one person may propose a particular norm to resolve a conflict. This she may do without necessarily offering a reason for it. However once challenged she must offer a reason, which the other party may accept. Or he may reject it, offering a counter-reason. A conflict of reasons may then develop. One party offers a reason, another a counter-reason. A counter-reason may either assert that the initial reason violates a criterion of political moral argument; or it may be a reason in favour of another norm where such a reason better complies with the criteria. The criteria of validity determine whether the reasons and counter-reasons are valid.

In a case, there may or may not be a dispute as to the proper interpretation of the law. If there is a dispute, then lawyers, parties, advocates-general and judges offer competing interpretations backed up by competing reasons. The judge, to dispose of the case, must act upon an interpretation of the law. In the case of ambiguity she must determine the correct (or if you like best possible, or most appropriate) or at any rate the better interpretation of the law. Must the judge give a reason for her interpretation?

Raz comments that judicial decisions must be capable of being explained, but that judges need not necessarily provide an explanation. This seems correct - if there is no dispute among the parties or judge as to what the correct interpretation is then there is no reason to offer a reason for an uncontested interpretation. It would be grossly impractical if a judge had to justify the interpretation of every single rule which was involved in a legal case. However in certain cases we can insist that a reason be given.

Where an interpretation is contested, then the judge must offer a reason for the interpretation she accepts. This reason can then be criticised invoking the criteria here described. Furthermore where an advocate has proffered a reason in favour of a competing interpretation, then the judge's decision must deal with it, i.e. it must offer a compelling counter-reason. The reasoning process must be rendered transparent in full, with each link in the chain of reasoning made apparent. This of course means that those links which are political moral in nature, rather than one of the conventionally designated legal sources, must also be exposed to public light.

It is almost embarrassing quoting examples of this criterion from the case law, since as some may point out, it is rather obvious: we expect constitutional courts to provide reasons in cases of dispute. Consider an Italian case, the First Blasphemy case,[29] where the *Corte costituzionale* decided whether art. 724 of the criminal code (punishing the crime of blasphemy against the religion of the state, the Catholic religion, but not other religions) violated arts. 7 and 8 of the Constitution on the position of religions. The interpretation of the constitutional provisions was contested, and the Court settled on one interpretation: the constitutional provisions did not require absolute equal treatment of all religions. And it offered a reason for this: the different position of different religions in Italian society may require different regulation. Whether this is a convincing reason is another question - but at last the first stage of providing a reason has been reached.

Not so in the case of *Open Door*.[30] Here Hamilton P. incorporates the English common law crime of 'conspiracy to corrupt public morals' into Irish law. This is, to put it mildly, a controversial interpretation of Irish law. It is therefore disappointing that he does not give a reason for this incorporation. This constitutes a failure of interpretation, and a rather severe one - not giving a reason for a contested interpretation.

Consistency

The next requirement is consistency. Consistency requires that we do not give interpretations to norms which contradict each other. Contradictions might be found in a single norm or between two norms of the same level, or between two norms of different levels. Judges must avoid contradictions and so pursue consistency when constructing a justification of the Constitution.

It would be plainly absurd for a judge to say 'You are and are not to pay compensation to the plaintiff'. This problem is one we are unlikely to find. However we may well find two other types of contradiction. The first is between a higher and a lower norm. For instance, in *Zundel*, the Canadian Supreme Court held that s. 2, in combination with s. 1 of the Charter, properly interpreted, permitted persons to tell what are commonly called lies, if the only objection to them was that they harmed some unspecified public interest.[31] Section 181 of the Criminal Code prohibits persons from publishing lies which injure the public interest. Here you have a norm which permits certain conduct and a norm which prohibits it.

The second type of inconsistency is between two norms of the same level - for instance two constitutional provisions. Consider the possible interpretations of s. 2 (free expression) of the Charter and s. 15 (equality rights) in *Zundel* and *Keegstra*.[32] It is perfectly possible to look at these provisions separately and give the following interpretations: that s. 2 of the Charter prohibits Parliament to enact incitement to hatred laws, and that s. 15 permits (or even requires) Parliament to enact incitement to hatred laws. Or consider the cases of *McGee* and *Norris* in Ireland.[33] If we interpret *McGee* as saying that the State may not prohibit consensual activity between two persons in the privacy of their bedroom, and *Norris* as saying that the State may prohibit consensual activity between two persons in the privacy of their bedroom, then we have a contradiction.

When we have such contradictions, then the judge must resolve them. This she does by one of two techniques. She may interpret one or both of the provisions to eliminate the inconsistency,[34] or she may deem one of the provisions to be invalid.

Consider the case of a constitutional provision and a statute, as in *Zundel*. Here the judge may decide to give an interpretation to s. 2 of the Charter different to the one actually adopted in the case. She may decide that free expression does permit the state to punish the publicising of lies. Or she may reinterpret the statutory provision (for instance, interpreting 'harming the public interest' as meaning not some vaguely defined matter, but a specified special constitutional value, like equality).

Now suppose that the judge has decided that it is not possible to determine an interpretation of the two provisions which would eliminate the contradiction. Then she must choose to invalidate one provision, to eliminate the contradiction. Here we come across an important difference between political argument and political argument from the legal point of view. In political argument, a participant may choose to drop either norm in the event of contradiction. Not so a judge. Our experience of law includes - as Kelsen so aptly demonstrates - the notion of a hierarchy of legal norms. Individual acts are based on statutory or common law rules, which are based on constitutional provisions. If there is a conflict between a constitutional norm and a statutory norm, then the judge must hold for the invalidity of the latter - as did the Supreme Court in *Zundel*.

Now suppose that upon interpreting the statute there are two fair interpretations of the statute - one of which does not contradict the interpretation of the constitutional norm, and one of which does. Is there any reason for the judge to opt for one interpretation rather than another? Normally in political argument I would say not. In our particular context though the answer is more difficult. I assume any acceptable reconstruction of the constitutional order (certainly in Canada, Ireland and Italy), would include two elements (though assigning varying weights to those elements). First, great importance would be attached to the decisions of a democratically elected parliament, acting through democratic procedures. Second, the judicial invalidation of such a democratic decision (and therefore conflict with the parliament) should be undertaken with reluctance. It should not be lightly assumed that parliament will violate the Constitution. Given these considerations, facing a situation where a statute is susceptible of two interpretations, one compatible with the Constitution and one incompatible, the Court should be reluctant to choose the incompatible interpretation, which would imply that parliament had violated the code of constitutional legality. This is the approach of the Canadian Supreme Court in *Butler*,[35] and the *Corte costituzionale* in the *Divorce case*.[36] (Please note the evolution here. From the viewpoint of political argument, one must avoid contradictions. Within a legal context, this means one must not invalidate a constitutional provision which collides with a statutory provision. In the legal context of a liberal democracy this leads to the principle that one should only invalidate a statutory provision where it cannot be given an interpretation compatible with the Constitution.)

Consider now the inverse case: the statute has a particular meaning, but the Constitutional provisions are capable of two meanings. That is, considering all of the criteria here discussed, there are two reconstructions which are equally attractive. However one of them validates the statute and the other one is incompatible with it. Is this factor a reason to adopt one or other interpretation of the Constitution? In ordinary political argument, and even in legalised political argument, there does not seem to be any preference.

However, in a liberal democracy, such as the cases studied, any reconstruction of the legal system will include respect for the democratic process and most particularly, the democratic decision-making of parliament. If the Supreme Court considers there to be two equally legitimate reconstructions of the Constitution, and a statute reflects the judgement of parliament as to which is the valid one, then, all other things being equal, the Court should accept that judgement.[37] This is the position, I believe, in *Keegstra*. Here the judiciary join a public debate on the issue of hate speech. The majority and dissenters offer two competing reconstructions of the Charter, one based on the notion of a mild liberal perfectionism, one based on the notion of liberal neutrality. Assuming that there is no other ground to choose between (as I think may well be the case), should the fact that parliament has adopted a statute (indeed a comprehensive statutory policy) favouring a mild liberal perfectionism be a decisive point? If, (as I assume) the overall reconstruction of the legal system makes a significant place for the role of the legislature, then here its decision should tip the scales. And indeed, this is how the majority ruled.[38]

So far I have discussed possible contradictions between norms of different levels - constitutional and sub-constitutional. Consider possible contradictions of norms on the same constitutional level. In political argument, where there exists an inconsistency between two norms of the same level, the arguer may either re-interpret them to ensure harmony, or reject one of them. In legalised political argument in typical liberal democracies there are very strong arguments in favour of re-interpretation rather than holding constitutional provisions invalid. First, there is the fact that a constitutional order may well authorise a court to invalidate a statutory provision; none expressly authorises a court to invalidate a constitutional provision. Second, judges are generally appointed to uphold the laws and to uphold the Constitution. Since this is interpreted in the sense that judges must give priority to the Constitution in case of conflict, it is clear that their primary duty is to the Constitution. In this case judicial invalidation of the Constitutional provision seems out of place. Thirdly, the adoption of a Constitution is usually considered to be a matter of 'higher politics', as Ackerman terms it.[39] It is enacted by a special, solemn process, usually after serious deliberation. It represents the considered judgement of the Constituent Authority on the fundamental rules to govern a political system. This means two things: judicial invalidation of the decision of a Constituent Authority is a particularly serious matter; it is not natural to assume that the Authority would include inconsistencies in the basic law.[40] (Incoherence is much more likely, but not inconsistency; for instance the Italian Constitution contains incoherent provisions: the special position of the Catholic Church in art. 7, and the guarantees of religious equality and freedom in arts. 3, 8, 19. Similarly the Irish Constitution is incoherent in containing both Thomistic and Rational Natural Law inspired elements: compare art. 40 and 44 with arts. 41 - 43. However none of these incoherences necessarily imply inconsistency.)

For these reasons, there is a strong onus on the Court to eliminate any inconsistency through re-interpretation rather than holding a provision invalid, or declining to apply it when it conflicts with another provision. So, as in the *X* case, a court should seek to harmonise two apparently inconsistent provisions, rather than refuse to apply, or declare invalid, one of them.[41] There the inconsistency was between the provisions guaranteeing the right to life of the foetus, and the right to life generally (in the case the pregnant woman's life). The Supreme Court eliminated the inconsistency by holding that the right to life of the foetus meant that the foetus had a right not to be aborted, except where an abortion was the only way to protect the life of the pregnant woman.

Whilst the *X* case majority eliminated the inconsistency in that aspect of the decision, the judgement of Finlay C.J. seemed to contemplate a constitutional contradiction when speaking hypothetically about other abortion cases. He suggested that there was a straightforward conflict between the right to life of the foetus and the rights to receive information and to travel abroad. Should such a case come up for discussion, the above considerations suggest that the Court should look to eliminate any such contradiction through interpretation, rather than simply declining to apply a constitutional provision.

Non-Individualising

One feature of political argument is that someone's identity cannot be part of the reason justifying action in his or her regard. That I am 'Rory O'Connell' does not justify the State in enriching me or jailing me. Of course, this does not mean that it is wrong ever to mention identities in political argument. If one believes that the eldest son is entitled to inherit all of his parents' estate, then someone is justified in saying 'You, Rory O'Connell (being an eldest son) are entitled to inherit your parents' estate'. But my identity cannot be a reason for that.

In legalised political argument we come across norms which identify persons all the time: the individual norm issued by a judge or official charged with applying the law to a particular case. If these individual norms did not mention names, then the administration of law would be impossible, or at any rate rather crowded with red tape. However here the identity does not function as a reason for the decision: the reason for the decision is (presumably) a more general norm.

This dislike of individualising norms (other than in cases of specific application to concrete cases) is widely reflected in the legal experience of liberal democracies. It is this which leads to the Anglo-American dislike of 'Bills of Attainder'. A bill of attainder is what is apparently a statute, enacted by Parliament, in which a person is named, and deemed guilty of a crime (usually treason). The 'statute' then goes on to specify punishment (usually death and seizure of property). Such bills of attainder are now out of fashion. A similar dislike of individualising measures is reflected in the celebrated provision of the French

Déclaration des droits de l'homme et du citoyen: a statute must be the same for everyone, whether it protects or punishes.

There was one norm which I discussed at length in the case studies, which was an individualising norm. This was art. 7 of the Italian Constitution, which specifies the Catholic Church by name (the Catholic Church is, after all, a legal subject). Consider the *Corte costituzionale*'s reconstruction of the constitutional provisions. It could have said that the Constitution accepted a sectarian principle whereby the Catholic Church was the one true church of Christ on earth, and so merited special consideration. The reconstruction actually adopted, rejected any special position for the Catholic Church simply because it was the Catholic Church. Special legislative regard for the Catholic Church was not based on the Catholic church being named in art. 7. Rather it was justified because the Catholic church was the one to which most Italians belonged, and had a particular social and historical importance in Italy.[42] Whilst the Court's reconstruction in this regard was criticised by Baldassarre, as not being based on a constitutional value, but rather on a 'mere fact', I think the criticism was misplaced.[43] The Court was paying tribute to the criterion that an individualising norm cannot serve as a justificatory reason. In that it was absolutely correct.

Generality

Suppose that the *Corte costituzionale* had simply said that the legislature was entitled to give special protection to the Catholic Church as it was the faith adhered to by the quasi-majority of Italians. Such a reason would not contradict the principle of non-individualisation. However there is a further flaw with it - it is not *general*. It is not enough to say 'The Catholic Church is entitled to special benefits', nor is it satisfactory to say 'The Church with the largest number of adherents is entitled to special benefits'. In its reconstruction, the Court must offer something more.

The situation is similar to one discussed by Cass Sunstein.[44] The bare desire to benefit or harm some class or another is not justification for conferring such benefit, nor inflicting some harm. Legal provisions always divide persons into categories and assign benefits and burdens accordingly: between citizens and non-citizens, adults and minors, farmers and workers, etc. Sunstein's point is that the mere fact of a difference does not justify the different treatment itself. To say that a difference in treatment is justified by some (whatever) difference does not add anything to the knowledge that there is a difference in treatment.

Consider also the *Norris* case.[45] If the Supreme Court had simply said that homosexual and heterosexual sexual acts are different, and so one can treat them differently, the legal public would have been left gagging (I hope). A reason more general than 'The single largest church merits special protection', 'Homosexual acts can be punished' is needed.

Both those courts offered more general reasons. The *Corte costituzionale* stressed the communitarian justification of the Italian laws, and the legislature's desire to protect the ethical social value of religion in that community. The *Norris* majority referred to various justifying reasons (the alleged harm that homosexual conduct posed to various values).

Factually Accurate

Where a decision is justified in the light of a political reconstruction which refers to certain facts, then it must be shown that the ascertainment of those facts is accurate. This requires the court to examine its factual assumptions carefully. It may seem remarkable to deal with this criterion at all, but human reasoning is fallible, and often assumes what is false is true. Alas judges are not immune from ordinary human errors.

A good example of this is *Norris*. One possible interpretation of that case is that the Supreme Court ruled that where private sexual conduct is likely to cause harms to important social goods, (in this case marriage and public health) then the legislature is entitled to prohibit such private conduct. The Supreme Court held the anti-sodomy legislation to be valid because of its threat to those values. Now there is a serious flaw with this argument. In the *Norris* case no evidence was adduced to show that there were any such harms. On the contrary Senator Norris adduced a significant amount of evidence to show there was no such harm. Despite this the High Court ruled against him. Even more surprising is the decision of the Supreme Court majority. The Chief Justice quotes a book by one expert suggesting that there may be harms, despite the fact that the expert himself had testified to the contrary in *Norris*. He invokes a 20 year old comment of a committee in a foreign country to the effect that there might be such harms, to assert that today there are such harms justifying the legislature's decision. As the dissent of Henchy J. made clear, the majority's opinion was factually flawed.

The facts in the *Norris* case were rather clear. However it is easy to envisage cases where the facts are not so clear. For instance, it is uncertain whether there is a causal relationship between pornography and sexual violence. If the Supreme Court of a country has determined that expression may only be curtailed where it is likely to promote sexual violence, then, faced with an obscenity statute, it must determine whether there is proof of such a causal relationship. Now in a country where the reconstruction of the legal system includes respect for the democratically elected body, then it seems that, in cases of doubt, the Court should defer to the legislative judgement.

Capable of Solving Problems

One criterion that we use in political argument is the ability to solve a problem. This is crucially important in legalised political argument, which is one of the classic examples of problem solving. Court cases usually begin with a problem.

So the interpretation proposed by the judge must provide a solution. It must not be irrelevant or too vague to guide anyone. Now it is rather unusual for a court to propose an interpretation which is irrelevant to the problem. However it is quite common for judges to provide vague standards. In Ch. 5 I gave the example of someone who proposes as a reason for action that 'good is to be done and evil avoided'. Regrettably this gives us no criteria by which to judge whether something is good or bad - it gives no practical guidance. We need criteria by which to decide whether this doctrine has been correctly applied. There are two instances in the case studies where the courts failed to provide a constitutional doctrine with adequate criteria by which to apply it.

Consider the Italian *First Nullity case*, where the *Corte costituzionale* had to decide whether the Concordat was to be regarded as valid, even where it violated a constitutional norm.[46] The Court held that, even in that event, the Concordat was valid - up to a point. The Court held that the Concordat could not violate the 'supreme principles of the State's constitutional order'. The Court did not enumerate the supreme values entitled to such special status, nor did it identify any criteria by which it would recognise a supreme principle.[47] Among such supreme principles we find the principle of equality, unity of the State's jurisdiction,[48] State sovereignty,[49] rights to legal protection and to defend oneself in justice.[50] I have no special grievance with any of these principles, however my trouble is with the jump between 'supreme principles of the State's constitutional order' and the enumeration of the specific values. Some further step is necessary to make clear how the Court determines what is a supreme principle.

A similar problem appears in the Irish case law. Irish constitutional law recognises the concept of 'unenumerated rights', that is, rights which are considered constitutional rights, entitled to the full protection of the courts, although they are nowhere mentioned in the text of the Constitution. Since 1965 the courts have recognised the following unenumerated rights: to health, to marriage,[51] to leave the state,[52] to freedom from inhuman and degrading treatment,[53] to independent legal personality,[54] to communicate,[55] to work,[56] the right of access to the courts,[57] to fair procedures,[58] and of course to privacy.[59] Now these rights are all very admirable and should (I think) be protected. However I have a problem with the manner in which judges identify these unenumerated rights. The argument made in *Ryan* and *McGee* that the Constitution protects certain rights not mentioned in the text, seems a strong one. The weak point (the failure to provide adequate criteria) comes when one has to decide whether a right is entitled to this status. Most judges identify rather vague standards: 'justice', 'natural law', 'the democratic and Christian nature of the state'. In *McGee* Walsh J. states that unenumerated rights are based on the 'natural law', (which in extra-judicial writings he identifies as Thomistic natural law). Without more explanations, this is too vague a standard to reach decisions. Walsh J. invokes it to uphold the right to use contraceptives, but without a greater specification of the requirements of the natural law, it could just as easily be invoked to deny any right to use contraceptives.[60]

The only serious effort to provide criteria is made by Henchy J., in *Norris*, where he relies on a liberal reconstruction of the constitution. He holds that persons are entitled to such rights as secure their dignity in a democratic pluralist society. This includes a complex of rights which secure a zone of non-interference where this 'vital human' can develop and express his or her personality, even when this conduct would be criticised by others as immoral. Such principles of individual autonomy and pluralism lead to a right to sexual privacy.

The Canadian Supreme Court is particularly sensitive to this criterion. In Ch. One we saw how it was faced with the interpretation of rather vague standards: 'freedom of expression' (s. 2(b)), 'such reasonable limits as can be demonstrably justified in a free and democratic society' (s. 1). It has not been satisfied with simply leaving these criteria undeveloped. In *Irwin Toy*, the Supreme Court explained that anything that can have meaning is considered expression.[61] The content of a meaning can never be a reason to consider it something other than expression, though sometimes the form can. Public action is considered to be a restriction on freedom of expression if its purpose is to control the publication of messages, or if its effect adversely impacts on the fundamental values protected by free expression. If public action does violate s. 2(b)'s guarantee of free expression, then it must satisfy the requirements of s. 1. The Court has not left this provision bereft of more specific criteria either: *R. v. Oakes* provides certain criteria (though these have been subject to re-interpretation).[62] To be acceptable a limitation must be for a legitimate purpose, it must be provided for by law, and it must be proportional to the legitimate aim (the Court also provided three sub-criteria under this last heading).

The criterion of ability to solve problems means that judges may not simply rely on vague standards in constitutional law. They must flesh out the requirements of such provisions. This goes some way to redress the fears expressed by Kelsen about vague constitutional provisions.[63] It also casts some doubt on several constitutional doctrines, particularly those like the constitutional doctrine of formal equality or reasonableness imposed by some court decisions in some jurisdictions.

Explicability: Publicity, Teachability, Transparency

One criteria which I identified in Ch. Five is explicability: a reason must be such that another person can be expected to understand it. A reason may fail this criterion if it is secret, self-frustrating, illogical, irrelevant or opaque.

The principle that reasoning must not be secret harks back to the first criterion, the duty to give reasons. Each step in the reasoning process must be made apparent. The reliance on unspoken assumptions justifies the criticism of a judicial decision. For instance, in the *Prostitution Reference* the majority relied on an unspoken denigration of prostitution to uphold a statute restricting freedom of expression in cases of soliciting. The implicit assumptions about the value of prostitution in the majority decision in the *Prostitution Reference* case, should not have been left under the judicial bench, but should have been discussed. The dissenters did discuss them and came to the opposite conclusion.[64]

The principle that decisions should not rest on reasons that are secret or self-frustrating reasons has an interesting effect. It means that crude forms of judicial 'pragmatism' or critical legal studies style 'realism' are ruled out. Such extreme critics of the legal system argue that judges make decisions in basically the following way: 'Well I favour this particular result (irrespective of the law), and I am going to achieve it by invoking whatever legal doctrine permits me to reach that decision.' Such a 'principle' simply cannot work if made public. In this sense the requirement of publicity supports the notion of 'fidelity to law'.

Now whatever else a decision should do or not do, it seems a minor enough requirement that it should not violate the formal rules of logic. One example of this is the formal principle of equality: where a court cannot point to any relevant difference between one case and another case, then it ought to decide them in the same way. This is not a requirement for a strict common law doctrine of precedent. It is a requirement of consistency which underpins the common law doctrine but is also found in civil law jurisdictions. Consider the train of cases on *bestemmia* and *vilipendio* before the *Corte costituzionale*. For so long as the Court was not prepared to review its interpretations in the first cases, and there were no other changes, then it would have been arbitrary to start invalidating the statutory provisions. The Court did alter its interpretation of the Constitution, but this decision was not arbitrary (and was entailed by later criteria).

An example of a possible failure in formal equality is found in *Zundel*. McLachlin J. explained at one stage that part of her objections to the statutory provision, which related to telling lies injuring a public interest, was that there were extreme epistemological difficulties in determining the truth of such historical facts as the Holocaust. She noted that courts often had to determine what was the truth when deciding questions of fact, e.g. in libel cases. Since both situations require a Court to determine the truth in contests over facts, how can she distinguish the two cases? Her blunt assertion that the difficulties are simply greater when discussing such historical phenomenon is a remarkable claim. Without a substantial justification for it I think we can accuse McLachlin J. of failing to distinguish between the two comparable situations.

It might be surprising to find failures of formal logic in many court cases, but nevertheless they can be found. One classic violation of the principles of formal logic is the so-called 'naturalistic fallacy'. This is the fallacy by which someone derives an 'ought' from an 'is', that is jumps from a descriptive to a normative statement. We find this violation in *Norris*, in the first instance judgement. Regarding the anti-sodomy laws McWilliam J. makes the following comment:

> ... it is not unreasonable for the assumption to be made, whether correctly or incorrectly, that the primary purpose of the sexual organs in all animals, including man, is ... reproduction .... If that is so, it seems to follow that there are some grounds for reasonable people to believe that sexuality outside marriage should be condemned, and that sexuality between people of the same sex is wrong.[65]

The function of the reproductive organs is a matter of fact, and cannot lead to any normative conclusions about which particular acts involving those organs are morally right or wrong.

Similarly a reason must not be based on irrelevant factors, or ignore relevant ones. What is or is not a relevant factor is an independent question. Our legal practices generally provide standards by which to form a prima facie judgement whether something is relevant or irrelevant. When these are challenged, judges must be prepared to offer reasons defending them, or choose to abandon them. In particular where a judge goes against these conventional standards, she must explain herself. There are several instances of problems of relevance in the case studies.

In Decision 79/1958, the *Corte costituzionale* justified the special treatment of the Catholic Church by referring to certain social facts. This was criticised by Baldassarre, who asserted that mere facts were an irrelevant consideration, the Court should have relied simply on the words and values of the Constitution.[66] If this reflects a convention of the Italian legal system, and if such an objection had been raised during the case, then we would have to insist that the Court answer it.

A more dramatic example of the inverse failure is found (again) in *Norris*. It seems a perfectly reasonable supposition that uncontested evidence tendered by credible witnesses should be considered a relevant factor by judges. Yet the majority of the Supreme Court ignored this relevant evidence. This despite the fact that all the testimony was unanimous, consistent and uncontested and to the effect that homosexuality did not harm any social value, but that punishing homosexual acts harmed individuals and possibly social values. To have dismissed this as irrelevant without a reason is extraordinary.

A further (double-sided) aspect of explicability is opaqueness - a reason must not be opaque. A reason may be opaque in two ways: it may be something incomprehensible for others, or it may not fully explain all its steps. Judges may not rely on reasons which others cannot understand, and must fully explain their reasoning.

A very clear example of the first aspect is found in the early Italian cases I discussed. As I explained there were two possible reconstructions of the Constitution which would enable the Court to uphold the *bestemmia* and *vilipendio* rules giving special protection to the Catholic Church. The Court could have adopted a sectarian interpretation, recognising the special position of that Church as being in some sense a true religion. Or it could have adopted a communitarian interpretation giving special recognition to the dominant religion in the community. The Court, in its reconstruction, adopted the latter interpretation, faithful to the criterion of explicability. Discussions of communal values are open to public analysis, argument and verification. Matters of religious truth are not open to argument in the same manner. This is not to say that religious claims are incapable of being true or false, merely that there is no public way to verify them. If I say the Catholic Church is the one true Church, and someone else prefers the Church of Druidical Science, what criteria can be offered to choose between them? Judges must eschew reasoning on matters where public reasons are not available.

A similar issue appears in the Irish case law. In the first case on unenumerated rights, Kenny J. bases his decision on the '*Christian* and democratic nature' of the state.[67] References to Christianity are made in other cases. In *Norris*, the majority judgement makes prominent rhetorical use of Christian references. The dissenters embrace the pluralistic vision of *Quinn's Supermarket* and *McGee*, and give a 'harmless interpretation' to the religious references. This is the correct approach from the viewpoint of political morality, and becomes the dominant one in later cases.[68]

The other aspect of opaqueness is that a judge might leave the elements of her thought, the steps in her reasoning, unclear. If a judge says that a statute which punishes the spreading of lies harmful to the public interest is invalid because it violates the constitutionally guaranteed freedom of expression, she still has some explaining to do. Freedom of expression is capable of many different interpretations,[69] as is demonstrated by the different interpretations in the *Zundel* case. The judge must give us a reason to favour one rather than the other interpretation.

This criterion, avoiding gaps in the reasoning, is clearly related to avoiding vague standards, and I refer to my comments in that category. More generally this book has been about exposing gaps in reasoning and the first three chapters contain sufficient examples both of the observance and violation of this criterion.

This aspect of legalised political argument has a particular significance in a state where the principle of respect for the democratic legislature is considered important. Requiring a judge to provide a full explication of her opinion is an important limit on the judicial power, likely to discourage arbitrariness.

The duty to provide reasons, and more specifically, to provide a full explication, is of particular relevance where one sees constitutional law as a public debate, between different officials and citizens, on the legitimacy of public authority. Constitutional courts, by trying to provide complete explications, help to transform what might be merely an exercise in power and strategic rationality into a proper debate on matters of political morality. In a democracy, the judiciary are not to be valued because they provide the right answers always. They are to be valued because they play a role in keeping political debate away from a mere power play, and within the 'forum of principle'.[70]

Reflective Equilibrium - A Principled Coherence

An important criterion is that a reason fits into our considered judgements held in reflective equilibrium.[71] Reflective equilibrium functions when we test our considered and firmly held beliefs against a moral theory which purports to provide a reasonable and acceptable explanation of them. This is a two way process where we seek to find an equilibrium between our firmly held judgements and our reasoned beliefs - a principled explication of our beliefs.

In political argument this is a two way process. We can begin with our judgements and judge our theory in the light of them, or we can relinquish our attachments to certain judgements in deference to our justificatory theory. In this process we try to find a position where judgements and principles coincide.

Furthermore it need not be a permanent equilibrium. We may be called to re-examine the principles, and come to conclude either that they do not any longer reflect our judgements, or violate principles of political moral argument. Or we may re-examine the judgements themselves, when confronted with a particular case which challenges them.

In legalised political argument, a judge must give a decision which fits into such a principles explication of 'our beliefs'. The constraints of the legal viewpoint appear at this point. It is not enough or even in point for a judge to demonstrate that a particular decision fits into her principled explication of her own beliefs. This would be a claim that from the viewpoint of critical political morality, the decision was just, right, etc. This is obviously a very important claim. However it answers the third type of question 'Is this decision right? Should I obey it?' rather than the second type of question 'What is the law? How do I decide this case according to law?' which is our concern. Similarly, fitting the decision into the community's reflective equilibrium, deals with the question 'What is the community's political morality?' rather than 'What is the law?'.

Both those approaches have two flaws. First, they deal with the wrong question. Two, they are failures of fidelity to law. Judges are not supposed to hand down decisions based on their view of political morality, nor what the community wants. They are expected to decide according to law, and if this is not what either they themselves, or the community wants, then that is not a legal problem. I note two points here. First, such factors may well enter into the question what is the law. Indeed I argue that our beliefs about critical political morality do shape our interpretations of constitutional law. However they do not replace the question 'What is the law?' Second, I do not mean to suggest that the legal viewpoint is always the better or best one. It does not provide the ultimate answer whether to obey or change the law. It may well be right to change a legal position, even retrospectively, or break the law.

Back however to legalised political argument. The principled explication of beliefs which a judge must offer must not be based on the considered judgements of the judge's personal views. It must contribute to providing the legal system with the best claim to legitimacy that it can make, and this it can do only by taking as 'provisional fixed points', legal judgements. The legal system presents a judge with various fixed points: constitutional norms, statutory norms, case law, etc. These are the legal sources on which a decision must be based. The judge must be prepared to fit her decision into a principled explication of these legal norms. More particularly, the constitutional judge must offer a principled explication of the constitutional norms which she is called on to defend.

A constitution contains various norms on different matters, and of different levels of generality. The judge must be prepared to offer a principled justification of these which demonstrates how they fit together. This process may result in some provisions being given an expanded interpretation, and others being given a curtailed one, to fit them into the overall justification. This principled justification allows the judge to accord a more precise meaning to the constitutional provisions in question, and to decide whether there is an inconsistency between a constitutional and sub-constitutional norm. The process is eloquently described by Henchy J.:

> Any single constitutional right or power is but a component in an ensemble of inter-connected and interacting provisions which must be brought into play as part of a larger composition, and which must be given such an integrated interpretation as will fit it harmoniously into the general constitutional order and modulation. It may be said of a constitution, more than of any other legal in-strument, that 'the letter killeth, but the spirit giveth life.' No single constitutional provision (particularly one designed to safeguard personal liberty or the social order) may be isolated and construed with undeviating literalness.[72]

Whilst these words are admirable, they leave some factors in the dark. Henchy J. is right to look for coherence, but should stress that it is a *principled* coherence. A coherent explanation which involves violations of criteria like explicability, universalisability, generality, etc., must be rejected as unprincipled.[73]

Furthermore even principled coherence is not enough, if this implies that there could be a coherent interpretation of the constitutional order without some point. The coherence of the interpretation can only be judged in the light of a normative theory which has some sort of point. An interpretation of a constitution which says that freedom of expression includes the right to criticise government policies and that elections must be democratic in the sense of involving secrecy of voting, equality of voting power, etc. is certainly coherent - when ones sees such interpretations as furthering the principles of liberal democracy.

Accordingly it counts in favour of a judicial interpretation that it fits into a principled explication of the constitutional order. An interpretation that involves incoherence is open to criticism on that account - at least where a more coherent principled explication is forthcoming.

Let's look again at *Keegstra*.[74] The majority judgement of Dickson C.J.C. is concerned to provide an interpretation of s. 2(b) and s. 1 of the Charter in a case of hate speech. He ultimately gives these a strongly egalitarian interpretation, which allows the legislature to punish speech injurious to egalitarian values. This interpretation fits into an egalitarian justification of the legal order, endorsing a mild liberal perfectionism. In doing this he looks at many other legal provisions in support of this interpretation. He notes that Court decisions have emphasised such values as the search for truth, social and political democratic participation and self-fulfilment. He singles out s. 15 (equality) and s. 27 (multi-culturalism) of the Charter as being of particular relevance. The link between this normative justification and the Canadian legal norms is further strengthened by reference to provisions of the Race Discrimination Convention and the International Covenant on Civil and Political Rights, which Canada has signed. The constitutional reflective equilibrium of Canada is best understood by assigning it a strongly egalitarian point, which recognises the need for a liberal democracy to dissuade, discourage and punish those who invoke fundamental freedoms to attack the very values on which those freedoms are based.

Such a reflective equilibrium can evolve of course. A very powerful example is seen in Italy. In the first phase of its jurisprudence on religious matters, the *Corte costituzionale* adopted a principled explication of the constitutional order which had strong communitarian overtones. (At this point Parliament had done little to remove the fascist anti-liberal elements, and the Constitutional Court itself had only just started.) This lead it to recognise (in line with Art. 7 of the Constitution) a special position for the Catholic Church. It interpreted the Constitution as recognising the equal freedom of all religions, but as not guaranteeing identical legal protection. (This principled explication was adopted in preference to a more avowedly sectarian one.) Yet in the 1990s, this principled explication no longer holds: the Court has adopted a more egalitarian and pro-individual autonomy justification, which has even lead it to announce the supreme principle of the secular nature of the State. This shift is justified by several factors (among them I would argue the principle of universalisability, and perhaps explicability). An important factor was the change in some of the legal materials on which the original justification was based. Given the many changes wrought by the 1984 Concordat and Additional Protocol, the pro-equality, pro-autonomy justification started to make a lot more sense of a lot more of the Constitution than the original explication.

However the *Corte costituzionale* has also sometimes failed to pay attention to this criteria. Consider decision 440/1995, which finally pronounced the unconstitutionality of the art. 724 of the Criminal Code, though only in part. In accordance with the egalitarian reading of the Constitution, the Court held that Parliament could prohibit blasphemy against God, provided it did not give a special position to any one religious faith. Parliament could protect the religious sentiments of all citizens, but not just those of Catholic citizens. So far this seems a reasonable interpretation in accord with a principled explication of the Italian constitutional order (though from the viewpoint of critical political morality I think the State has no business punishing people for blasphemy). However the failure comes with the precise remedy: the Court only pronounced the invalidity of the part which referred specifically to the religion of the State, the Catholic religion. The effect of this decision was that the Court broadened the crime of blasphemy. Now this may seem in accordance with the egalitarian interpretation of the constitutional order, but there is a failure of coherence. The Court's principled explication must include not just the substantive legal question, but also its own competencies and powers. Now the Italian Constitution, in revulsion from its fascist past, contains strong guarantees of legality.[75] For the judiciary to broaden a criminal offence seems to violate any credible theory of legality in Italian constitutional law. It is difficult for me to see how the Constitutional Court could provide a principled explication which provides for the principles of legality, and yet justifies the specific ruling in decision 440.

Universalisability as Equal Respect

The final criterion is universalisability. In political argument, one may not offer as a reason, that someone or some group is simply inferior to another, and for that reason may be discriminated against. Any reason must, in some way accept the equality of different parties. The very process of intersubjective reasoning demands this minimal respect for the principle of equality.[76]

This principle is often considered fundamental in liberal democracies, and even exalted into its most important principle. Section 15 of the Canadian Charter provides compendiously:

> Every individual is equal before and under the law and has the right to the equal protection and equal benefit of the law without discrimination and, in particular, without discrimination based on race, national or ethnic origin, colour, religion, sex, age or mental or physical disability.

Article 3 of the Italian Constitution also gives expression to this principle:

> Tutti i cittadini hanno pari dignità sociale e sono eguale davanti alle legge, senza distinzione di sesso, di razza, di lingua, di religione, di opinioni politiche, di condizione personali e sociali.

The first phrase in the Irish Constitutional chapter on fundamental rights begins:

> All citizens shall, as human persons, be held equal before the law.

These are very general and extreme expressions of the principle of equality. They go far beyond the basic requirement of universalisability which is best stated by Walsh J.:

> ... this provision [Art. 40.1] ... is a guarantee related to their dignity as human beings and a guarantee against any inequalities grounded upon an assumption, or indeed a belief, that some individual or individuals or class of individuals, by reason of their human attributes or their ethnic or racial, social or religious background, are to be treated as the inferior or superior of other individuals in the community.[77]

The principle of universalisability does not relate to the doctrine of reasonableness or rationality review often adopted under the guise of equality review. Nor does it express precisely the content of anti-discrimination rules with which the citizens of Twentieth Century liberal democracies are familiar. It is not necessarily incompatible with universalisability to deny voting rights to Afro-Americans, or sexual privacy to gay men, or equal legal protection to minority religions. It might be possible to offer a reason which respects universalisability to justify these norms. The principle does rule out one type of reason however: a reason which simply asserts the inferiority of certain people. It would not be acceptable to offer as a reason 'But they are simply blacks', 'Gay men are just perverts', 'No one not belonging to the majority church is a worthwhile person'. The principle rules out such reasons, and also gives us a reason to prefer justifications which display a greater degree of universalisability than a lesser one.

The importance of this criterion can be seen in cases in all chapters. *Keegstra* offers two possible reconstructions of the constitutional order of Canada, both of them seeking to respect this principle as far as possible. The majority interprets it as guaranteeing everyone an extensive right to free expression, provided only that they do not use it to undermine the value of equality on which this freedom, and liberal democracy are based. The minority view argues that everyone (no matter how odious their views) is entitled to express their beliefs. Both of these incorporate respect for the principle of universalisability though in different ways. I find it difficult to see how either of these views fulfils that principle better. However that is not the most important point here.

What is significant is that the *only two interpretations considered credible* by the Supreme Court incorporated respect for this principle.

Just as the *Keegstra* case demonstrates profound respect for the principle of universalisability, trying to fulfil it to the highest possible extent, the *Norris* case involves a remarkable attack on this criterion. The majority judgement in that case is rather unclear, and might be based on one of several grounds. However, given the extreme weaknesses in most of those arguments, the only explanation of the case (unless the Court overturned *McGee*) was a commitment to the bare inferiority of gay men. Such a commitment is ruled out by the criteria of rational intersubjective political argument. The minority opinion in that case does respect that principle and even proposes an extreme protection of it.

The *Corte costituzionale* has also chosen between more and less universalisable principled explications of the constitutional order. In the first phase of its case law, it rejected a sectarian interpretation of the Constitution, and preferred a communitarian one. A sectarian interpretation would simply have involved disregarding the religious rights of the minority. The communitarian interpretation does not involve such a bare rejection. A communitarian may well argue that it is in the interests even of minorities for the communal values to be protected. However in the 1970s and 1980s the *Corte costituzionale* started to consider a different reconstruction of the constitutional order. The egalitarian justification still attaches great importance to the communal significance of religious-ethical values, but it attaches such significance to religious views of all the citizens, which is what leads it to the decision on blasphemy in 1995.

Conclusion

This book attempts to get to grips with the institutions of constitutional justice, where they exist. More particularly it is concerned with the criteria of validity of the reasoning used in constitutional interpretation. The conclusions argued for are based on a starting point in three case studies of constitutional justice, with detours through the fields of legal theory and political moral argument.

The key point emerging from the case studies is that constitutional law is a dialogue on the justification of public authority.

There are several participants in that dialogue: citizens, legislators, officials and judges. Participants who act in this dialogue from the legal point of view may not simply vote their own conception of political morality. Politicians, citizens, the constituent legislator are permitted to do this - if they do not like a law, they may change it. If they object on principle to a law, they may disobey it, or even invoke the right to revolt. Persons looking from the legal viewpoint cannot simply do this.

This takes us on a detour through legal theory. This establishes that the case for a conceptual separation of law and political morality is not water-tight. More importantly it indicates the problem posed by law's claim to legitimacy. How do we make sense of this apparent claim to legitimacy, without conferring too much legitimacy on the legal system? I try to provide an answer to this by reclaiming for legal theory one important task sometimes abandoned by legal positivists: providing criteria by which to evaluate judicial interpretation.

The dilemma of legitimacy can be resolved, I think, if we see judges as trying to make the legal order into the most legitimate that it can be, given its constraints, through the process of interpretation. This process of *reconstructing* the legal order is most clearly seen in the arena of constitutional law for it is here that political morality is most apparent. In constitutional decisions judges must offer a *principled explication (and justification) of the constitutional legal order*. This involves the judge in a reflective engagement with three sets of norms, an engagement where the interpretation and validity of those norms are always potentially in play. These three sets of norms are: those norms conventionally labelled 'legal' by positivists; the norms of various theories of contrasting political moralities; the criteria of political moral argument understood in a legal guise.

Those criteria are various. I have discussed the following:

1. Where an interpretation is contested, then the judge must offer a reason for the interpretation she accepts.
2. Furthermore where an advocate has proffered a reason in favour of a competing interpretation, then the judge's decision must deal with it, i.e. it must offer a compelling counter-reason.
3. The judge must not commit herself to norms which are contradictory (inconsistent in a strict sense); such inconsistencies

must be eliminated through interpretation or declarations of invalidity.

4. The reasons for the judge's ultimate disposal of the case must not refer to an individualising norm.

5. The reasons the judge gives must be based on norms of a general level.

6. The judge's argument must be factually sound.

7. The norms justifying the decision must not be left vague by the judge.

8. The reasons given by the judge must not include formally illogical statements.

9. Where two cases appear identical in all relevant factors, a judge must offer a reason for not reaching the same decision in both.

10. The judge must refer to all relevant and no irrelevant factors. A reference to an apparently irrelevant factor, or failure to refer to an apparently relevant factor, are criticisable and call for explanation.

11. Judges must not offer opaque reasons - reasons which appeal to private methods of knowledge and so are not capable of public debate.

12. The judge must explain all the steps in her reasoning.

13. The judge's explication must provide a principled justification of the norms of the legal order, weaving it into a coherent order. This is the legal equivalent of the 'reflective equilibrium' technique.

14. Judges must not rely on 'reasons' which are based on the simple inferiority of persons or groups.

Bearing in mind these criteria the judge must offer a reconstruction of the legal order: a principled explication which offers a justification of the law's claim to legitimacy. This is a reflective process: a proposed justification is read against both the criteria of political moral argument, and against the norms (the 'provisional fixed points') of the constitutional order. A justification may be rejected or altered because it is out of kilter with the majority of the presumptive constitutional norms; or because it fails the criteria of political moral argument. Or it may be accepted provisionally until a justification which better satisfies the criteria appears. The presumptive legal norms may themselves be interpreted or invalidated, in the light of the principled explication which the judge settles upon as offering the best claim to legitimacy that the legal order can make. The criteria of political moral argument must be applied bearing in mind that it is the *law's* (to be reconstructed) theory of political morality, and not the judge's personal theory of critical political morality which is to be used.

So the judiciary must offer a principled explication of the legal order which attempts to justify its claim to legitimacy. This is what the judges of the Canadian and Irish Supreme Courts, and the *Corte costituzionale*, were implicitly doing in the three case studies. In this chapter I have mentioned examples of how those judges relied on these criteria in making their decisions. I have also noted some of the failures to apply those criteria. I consider that showing what the judicial enterprise in constitutional justice is implicitly about, has also shown where judges may go wrong. Those concerned with issues of constitutional interpretation should more consciously invoke these criteria when discussing constitutional controversies.

So constitutional judges offer such principled explications. They must give reasons for their decisions, and those reasons must expose the complete chain of reasoning, which leads from the principled explication to the concrete decision, tying both into the norms of the legal order. This is a contribution to the public debate on legitimacy (which is a full-blooded debate of political morality, not just the restricted legalised version of it). Articulating the political moral element in law, and relying on the criteria of legalised political argument has four advantages. First, it allows us to judge the validity of the judicial decision, to determine whether it respects fidelity to law. Second, it exposes the legitimacy claim on which the legal exercise of authority is based; that is it makes the basis of legitimacy public. Third, this facilitates the public debate by clarifying it. Fourth, the judicial debate may throw up new justifications, a new proposal for the basis of the legitimacy of the state.[78]

These advantages protect the argumentative game of justification that the political actors, judges and people are playing. By making public the political moral basis of the reconstructed legal order, and clarifying its requirements, the judiciary help themselves and other actors understand the issues involved in the public debate. Further they themselves may make contributions to the public debate, suggesting justifications and proposals which have not yet been articulated in the public forum. At the same time the criteria of reasoning provide standards by which we can assess the legal correctness of judicial decisions, and so verify the observation of fidelity to law. Thus these criteria serve as limits on judicial power, allowing us to criticise (or accept of course) judicial decisions not just on the basis of unrestricted practical reason, but also from the viewpoint of law.

Keegstra exemplifies this process.[79] Dickson C.J.C. demonstrated how the bulk of Canadian constitutional law, statutes, and treaties are best justified by an egalitarian interpretation which permits Parliament to punish hate speech. His decision clearly fulfils many of the criteria I have here discussed, and so we can judge whether it is acceptable or not. Furthermore the *Keegstra* majority publicised the legitimacy claim which justified this statute, and arguably serves to justify Canadian constitutional practice: that it is justified by an egalitarian mildly perfectionist liberalism, which protects autonomy rights for so long as they do not undermine the fundamental basis of equality and autonomy. Third, the *Keegstra* judgements, including the dissenting one, clarified the public debate on legitimacy. In effect the judges made the following statement: 'Looking at the different norms you the people have adopted (through legislation, the Charter, international treaties, case law, etc.) we can see two credible theories which provide a justification of the constitutional order. The minority feels that the best theory attributes special importance to freedom of expression and interprets the notions of autonomy and equality to mean that anyone can say anything, no matter how odious. This rests on a theory of political morality which we can call liberalism as neutrality. The majority finds a different justification more attractive, which we might call mild liberal perfectionism. This attaches great importance to freedom of expression, but sees it as subserving the values of equality and autonomy. Accordingly where the democratic Parliament believes that hate speech is inimical to those values, it may punish such speech.'

Another instance of this can be seen in *Norris*.[80] The criteria enumerated allow us to determine whether it is a correct decision or not. In my opinion the majority's reasoning fails many of these criteria - notably factual accuracy, universalisability as equal respect, generality, explicability, the requirement of a principled coherent explication. The decision, like the *Open Door* case,[81] asserts a particularly perfectionist political theory which makes individual liberty subject to communal values of conventional morality. The legitimacy claim is thus held up in public view, once we study the case from the viewpoint of legalised political morality. Further the terms of the public debate are clarified. The judges make clear that the Irish constitutional order could be based on one of at least two different political moralities - a perfectionist conservatism or a neutrality oriented liberalism. Fourth, the liberal judges make an important new proposal for public debate. That the legitimacy of the State is based on liberalism was implicitly claimed in *McGee*.[82] However the dissenters introduced an important new element. For the first time, a public official, a constitutional officer, asserted that the liberal basis of the State required that gay men should be treated as equals. Nearly a decade later the political authorities accepted this vision.

This is also seen in the Italian cases. The criteria provide standards by which we can confirm or reject a judicial decision as being lawful. For instance decision 440/1995, which expands the crime of blasphemy can be criticised on the grounds that it fails to establish a coherent explication of the constitutional order, since it conflicts with the value of legality. A legalised political moral approach also exposes the legitimacy claims in the different cases, from the rather communitarian stance in the early cases,[83] to the pro-autonomy and equality position in later cases.[84] Furthermore those cases made important suggestions to the political debate, arguing that the State should be based on notions of equality rather than community,[85] and suggesting how such an equality-oriented marriage regime should be organised - suggestions later accepted in the 1984 negotiations with the Catholic Church.

What are citizens, legislators and others to do in the face of this proposed reconstruction? The obvious first answer is to consider it in the light of their own conceptions of critical political morality. A second step is to consider whether the decision is actually a correct (or at any rate an acceptable) interpretation from the legal point of view. The practical response if any, will be shaped by both these answers. It is always possible for a citizen or legislator to ignore the legal debate and simply approve, or rebel against a legal decision. However let's stick to phenomenon within the law for the moment. The response is itself a matter of constitutional law, and so the subject of this reflective dialogue on legitimacy. That a judge must interpret legal materials in the spirit of proposing a principled explication which justifies them, relates to any legal system exhibiting the basic features outlined by traditional legal theory. A judge in a state without a written constitution (e.g. the United Kingdom), or without constitutional review (e.g. the Netherlands), can still take part in this interpretative enterprise. Such a judge provides (or at least may provide) such principled explications. To go further than this requires discussion of particular legal systems.

How does this public debate evolve? The answer depends on whether we discuss a legal system without a written constitution (the UK), without constitutional review (the Netherlands), without a written Bill of Rights (Australia), or one with a written constitution, bill of rights and constitutional review (Italy, Canada, Ireland, the United States, India, etc.). The public debate here is itself regulated by constitutional law, and so its terms are determined by a reflective debate between legal norms, political morality, and the criteria of political moral argument. What those exact terms are differs from system to system. Which is not to say each legal system must develop ignoring others. Since the criteria of argument are universal, and theories of political morality do not necessarily respect boundaries, one can expect to find similarities; especially so since there are common constitutional trends in such countries rooted in their shared past. So it is reasonable to look to other legal systems for suggestions as to the correct interpretation of our own, particularly where the non-positive elements of a legal system play a large role in the legal problem.

However the exact terms of the public debate depend on an interpretation of constitutional law, and so differ from state to state. How the public debate is to take place depends on a principled explication of the constitutional material. Whether the judiciary can invalidate legislative decisions, and in what circumstances; whether the legislature can protect statutes from constitutional scrutiny; how the citizenry can react: these depend on an interpretation of the constitutional material. I think that certain elements of that constitutional debate can be indicated though by looking at our three case studies again.

First, consider the constitutional material. In each case there are some features which stand out both in the legal texts and practices. Each of the states emphasises that it is a democracy, where the will of the people, expressed through Parliament is vitally important. Yet each also includes the institution of constitutional justice, and bills of rights which are considered to express fundamental values. It seems that in at least some cases those rights may be invoked by citizens before courts to override a democratic decision. And in all three systems there are mechanisms for the political branches and citizenry to undo what the constitutional court has done (either through the process of amendment, or the Canadian institution of 'override').

Second, consider the prominent political moralities advanced in those states. Some groups do advocate religious or perfectionist agendas. Others argue for a rediscovery of the community's values, whatever those may be. There are also advocates of human rights who insist that these be protected come what may. There are firm defenders of majoritarian democracy, of communist equality, social democracy, laissez-faire capitalism, etc. Yet few of these political moralities fail to make place for democratic institutions. And most believe in securing some basic forms of human equality and dignity. There are political ideals on which the law (more correctly, judges involved in reconstructing the legal order) may draw.

Third, the criteria of political moral argument. These criteria come from a basic intuition about deliberation 'What does it mean to offer someone a reason which she can accept to regulate a dispute between them?', and so they are not unfair to different theories of political morality (see page 74). Nevertheless, although they start out from that basic intuition, they clearly look forward to the very principles of equality and democracy which constitutional texts and practice in Canada, Italy and Ireland so highly value. Any reconstruction will likely give a very large role to the democratically elected legislature, (and other means of expressing the will of the people,) to decide public policy. This priority of the legislature I have already suggested by stressing the need for judges to provide complete explanations of their chain of reasoning, by prohibiting them from relying on vague standards, by requiring them to defer to the legislature's judgement in cases of doubt, by requiring them not merely to justify their decision on substance but also their implicit decision on their own position in a constitutional democracy, and by insisting that the reasoning pay attention to the positivist legal materials reflecting the political judgements of the other branches of government.

Any reasonable exercise of legalised political argument will provide for respect for the decisions of a democratically elected body. Yet the criteria of argument, and the constitutional texts, as well as many popular theories of politics and law,[86] suggest that there are occasions where the constitutional court may make a reasoned opinion which suspends the decision of the legislature and put a matter previously decided by that body back in the public debate.

The criteria would particularly lend themselves to approving judicial attempts to safeguard the mechanisms of public debate, i.e. those features of the political system which are institutionalised forms of intersubjective political moral argument (democratic elections and freedom of expression being obvious examples). The principle of universalisability also requires judges to be suspicious of any measures which might be motivated by prejudice and convictions of inferiority, rather than proper intersubjectively valid (or at least arguably valid) reasons. The criterion of explicability will lead judges to frown on any mixing of the worlds spiritual and secular, especially when not even handed. Indeed the criteria lead pretty quickly to those pillars of liberal democracy which we are quick to say parliamentary majorities may not touch: democratic principles themselves, non-discrimination, separation of state and church; while requiring judicial deference in most areas; and always requiring that judicial decisions form a fully reasoned contribution to the public debate. There, in that public debate, the result of legalised political argument must itself be judged in the light of unrestricted critical political morality.

Any such decision is a matter for participants in a given legal order to decide. Yet this does not mean that other legal orders are irrelevant. A legal decision must be rooted in the legal materials of its system. Yet probably the theories which debatably justify it, and certainly the criteria by which we argue, appeal across the borders of legal systems. The approach argued for in this book does not follow the particularist lead of legal positivism which emphasises the legal sources of one's own system. Nor does it leap thoughtlessly into the eternity of universal and timeless values suggested by some naive natural law theories. Rather it seeks to unite the particular and the universal; the here and now, with the view from nowhere.

Notes

1   *Law's Empire*, p. 3. He identifies these as questions of fact, law, and a mixture of political morality and fidelity. Wroblewski identifies four different elements: what are the valid rules, what is the proper interpretation of the valid rules, what is the evidence, and what is the legal consequence appropriate to the proven facts, *The Judicial Application of Law*, p. 11. Dworkin's question, 'what is the law' subsumes Wroblewski's first two questions and his fourth.

2   Some people go further in arguing for textual indeterminacy. See Guastini, 'Interprétation et description de normes' in Amselek, ed., *Interprétation et droit*, p. 89; Troper, 'La motivation des décisions constitutionnelles', in Perelman, Fortiers, eds. *La motivation des décisions en justice*; Fish, 'With the Compliments of the Author' *Doing What Comes Naturally*; Hutchinson, 'That's Just the Way it Is' (1989) 39 *McGill Law J.* 145; and more generally works by Critical Legal Scholars, American Legal Realists and some Post-Modernists.

3   *Ethics in The Public Domain*, pp. 272 - 273.

4   Indeed this can be seen in Hobbes, whose conception of natural law lead to the almost absolute duty to obey the sovereign's laws.

5   I do not refer to our feelings of obligation to legal authorities. As my supervisor pointed out to me this is by no means a widespread feeling in some liberal democracies: there are long traditions of alienation from the law in parts of Ireland, Italy and the United States for instance.

6   To clarify: in the event of a conflict, I agree one must follow the dictates of conscience. However the law cannot recognise that a non-legal reason can triumph over a legal reason for acting (though here I understand law in a larger sense than positivists who accept the sources thesis): See Raz, *The Authority of Law*, p. 30; *Ethics in the Public Domain,* Chs. 14 and 15.

7   Raz, *The Authority of Law*, p. 233; Coleman, 'On the Relationship Between Law and Morality', (1989) 2 *Ratio Juris* 66.

8   Raz, *Ethics in the Public Domain*, pp. 194 - 195.

9   Fuller, *The Morality of Law*, p. 38.

10   Hart, *The Concept of Law*, p. 132; Kelsen, *The Pure Theory of Law*, pp. 348 - 357. The two approaches, whilst similar, are not identical. Kelsen believes that there is always scope for discretion (p. 349), while Hart makes allowance for 'the core meaning' which presumably means that there are clear cases where there is no discretion. However both agree that in cases where there is linguistic uncertainty, the jurist has no real advice to offer the judge who must simply choose.

11   The fundamentally practical nature of law makes the question of proper interpretation a practical not a cognitive one.

12   See Habermas, *Justification and Application*, pp. 1 - 17, 'On the Pragmatic, the Ethical, and the Moral Employments of Practical Reason'.

13   Weber offers this basic distinction between 'instrumentally-rational' and 'value-rational' (*zweckrational* and *wertrational*), *Economy and Society*, pp. 24 - 26.

14   It includes for instance what Kant divides into two categories of practical reason, 'rules of skill' (simple technical rules), and also 'counsels of prudence', prudential advice on the pursuit of happiness. See *The Groundwork of the Metaphysics of Morals,* p. 80 (416).

15   Compare Habermas, *A Theory of Communicative Action,* Vol. 1, p. 281, commenting on Weber.

16   *A Theory of Communicative Action,* Vol. 1, p. 285.

17   See Rawls, *A Theory of Justice,* pp. 319 - 416, 446 - 452; *Political Liberalism,* Ch. 5.

18   Habermas, *Justification and Application,* pp. 1- 17; *Between Facts and Norms,* pp. 16, 95 - 102, 108 -109, 159 - 165, 255 - 259.

19   Sandel, *Liberalism and the Limits of Justice.*

20   See Taylor, 'Justice after Virtue', pp. 26 - 27 in Horton and Mendus eds., *After MacIntyre.*

21   To outline very briefly the view of Habermas: Habermas draws a distinction between ethics and morality. Some practical questions concern one's values in a very fundamental way: it implicates one's very identity. They involve consideration of 'what life one would like to lead, and that means what kind of person one is and wants to be'. Ethical questions demand *authentic* answers, which give one's own (self-) understanding of the good life, and what one ought to do. Ethics is teleological and is concerned with values.

However this is distinct from the *moral* exercise of practical reason, which involves cases where intersubjective conflicts must be resolved in an impartial manner. Morality is concerned with a universalistic, intersubjective viewpoint with involves reliance on principles rather than values.

See *Justification and Application,* pp. 1 -17; *Between Facts and Norms,* pp. 254 - 259; 'Reconciliation Through the Public Use of Reason', (1995) *J.Phil.* 109, 114 - 115.

22   I am just sketching a possible, though common answer, I am not attempting to answer the question of political legitimacy and obligation.

23   As Kant notes: 'Thus, no government has so far dared to declare freely and openly: that right and wrong are mere illusions to which it need not pay any attention, and that it is therefore entitled to make its absolute will the law of the land. On the contrary, governments always appeal to the sense of right which their subjects possess as free moral beings ....'

Cited in Reiss, ed. *Kant: Political Writings,* p. 272, Reflection no. 8077. See also Alexy, 'On Necessary Relations Between Law and Morality' (1989) *Ratio Juris* 167, 173.

24   Hart, *The Concept of Law,* p. 199. Aarnio, describes a legal norm as 'an officially ossified section of the moral code of society', *The Rational as Reasonable,* p. 177.

25   Among the writers who have suggested something of the sort (implicitly or otherwise) are: Habermas, *Between Facts and Norms*; Dworkin, *Law's Empire*;

Ackerman, *We the People*; Nino, 'A Philosophical Reconstruction of Judicial Review' (1993) *Cardozo Law Rev. 799*; Alexy, *A Theory of Legal Argumentation*; Wroblewski, *The Judicial Application of Law* (the notion of rational and legal judicial decision-making). Rawls provides a concise discussion in *Political Liberalism*, ch. 6, 'The Idea of Public Reason', p. 231.

26   'Reply to Habermas', (1995) *J. Phil.* 132, 140.

27   *Ethics in the Public Domain*, Ch. 12.

28   The exact parameters have been drawn differently by many different theorists. Ely suggests that judges should stick to representation reinforcing; see *Democracy and Distrust*. Nino recommends that judges protect democratic processes, anti-perfectionist rights, and the preservation of a continuos legal practice 'A Philosophical Reconstruction of Judicial Review' (1993) *Cardozo Law Rev.* 799. Protecting the rationality of the legislative process is Bickel's main concern, *The Least Dangerous Branch*.

29   Case 79/1958, [1958] G.C. 990.

30   [1987] I.L.R.M. 477.

31   95 D.L.R. 4th 202 (1992).

32   [1990] 3 S.C.R. 697.

33   [1974] I.R. 284 and [1984] I.R. 36 respectively.

34   I understand the traditional legal technique of *lex specialis* and *lex generalis* as being a subspecies of this.

35   89 D.L.R. 4th 449 (1992), where the Supreme Court interpreted an anti-obscenity provision in accordance with the requirements of the 1982 Charter.

36   Decision 169/1971, [1971] G.C. 1784, where the Court interpreted the Concordat in accordance with secularised reading of art. 7 of the Constitution.

37   See Nino, 'The Epistemological Moral Relevance of Democracy' 4 *Ratio Juris* 36 - 51 (1991).

38   This notion is also seen, in the Hungarian *Abortion* decision. There the Constitutional Court ruled that the issue of the foetus' right to protection was one where all arguments were carefully balanced, and it was for the legislature to decide; [1993] 1 (1) East.Eur.Case Rep. Const. Law 3

39   Ackerman, *We, The People.*

40   See MacCormick, *Legal Reasoning and Legal Theory*, p. 106 on the difference between consistency and coherence. Two norms are inconsistent when it is simply not possible to follow both. Two norms are incoherent if, even though it is possible to follow both, they are based on values which oppose in some way, if they just 'do not make sense'.

41   [1992] 1 I.R. 1.

42   Decision 125/1957, [1957] G.C. 1209.

43   'E costituzionale l'incriminazione della bestemmia?' [1973] G.C. 70.

44   'Naked Preferences and the Constitution', (1984) *Col. L. Rev.* 1684.

45   [1984] I.R. 36.

46   Decision 30/1971, [1971] G.C. 150.

47   See Lariccia, 'Libertà delle università ideologicamente impegnate e libertà di insegnamento'[1972] 2 G.C. 2177. Furthermore, as made clear in Decision

31/1971, a Concordatarian norm may infringe on a supreme principle without being considered to have violated it, [1971] G.C. 154.

48   Decision 30/1971.

49   Decision 175/ 1973.

50   Decision 18/1982, [1982] 1 G.C. 138.

51   *Ryan*, mentions both health and marriage, [1965] I.R. 294.

52   *State (M.)* v. *Attorney General*, [1979] I.R. 73.

53   *State (C.)* v. *Frawley*.

54   *M.* v. *M.*, [1991] I.L.R.M. 268.

55   *Kearney*, [1986] I.R. 116.

56   *Attorney General* v. *Paperlink*, [1984] I.L.R.M. 373.

57   *MacAuley* v. *Minister for Posts and Telegraphs*, [1966] I.R. 345.

58   *Haughey*, [1971] I.R. 217.

59   *McGee*, [1974] I.R. 284; *Kennedy*, [1987] I.R. 587.

60   And has by Finnis and the Catholic Church, see *Natural Law and Natural Rights*, p. 124.

61   58 D.L.R. 4th 577 (1989).

62   26 D.L.R. 4th 200 (1986).

63   'La garantie juridictionnelle' (1928) *R.D.P.* 197.

64   *Reference re: ss. 193 and 195 of the Criminal Code (Prostitution Reference)*, [1990] 1 S.C.R. 1123.

65   [1984] I.R. 36, 45.

66   'E costituzionale l'incriminazione della bestemmia?' [1973] G.C. 70, 71.

67   *Ryan*, [1965] I.R.

68   *Attorney General* v. *X*, [1992] 1 I.R. 1; *F.* v. *F.* [1994] 2 I.L.R.M. 401.

69   To use phraseology popularised by Gallie, Rawls and Dworkin, it is a concept capable of several different conceptions.

70   See Dworkin, *A Matter of Principle.*

71   Rawls, *A Theory of Justice*, p. 20, 48 - 51; Dworkin, *Taking Rights Seriously*, Ch. 6, pp. 159 - 168.

72   *State (DPP)* v. *O'Shea*, [1982] I.R. 384, 426. See also Henchy's majority opinion in *Tormey* v. *Ireland*, [1985] I.R. 289, 295-6, and O'Higgins C.J. in *State (DPP)* v. *Walsh*, [1981] I.R. 412, 424.

73   See Raz, Ch. 12 'The Relevance of Coherence' in *Ethics in the Public Domain*. I hope that this avoids certain criticisms that he directs at legal theories using coherence. I treat coherence - as an aspect of reflective equilibrium - as a part of moral argument. I do not rely mainly on a coherentist theory which then calls in morality as a tie-breaker (p. 287 in *Ethics in the Public Domain*). Secondly, I exclude the possibility of relying on an unprincipled coherent interpretation. So I would not agree with Raz that such a Dworkinian approach requires a judge to 'respect and extend the [conventional] political morality' of a legal order (*ibid.*, p. 207).

74   [1990] 3 S.C.R. 697.

75   See arts. 13 - 27, arts. 101 - 113. See in particular art. 25, which bluntly prohibits retrospective penal legislation.

76   Minnow gives excellent advice on how to achieve universalisability - 'Engendering Justice', in Smith ed., *Feminist Jurisprudence*.

77   Walsh J., *Quinn*, [1972] I.R. 1, 13 - 14, italics added.

78   See Rawls, *Political Liberalism*, pp. 233 - 240.

79   61 C.C.C. 3d 1, [1990] 3 S.C.R. 697; 1 C.R. 4th 129; [1991] L.R.C. (Const.) 333.

80   [1984] I.R. 36.

81   [1987] I.L.R.M. 477.

82   [1974] I.R. 284.

83   See decisions 125/1957, 39/1965.

84   See decisions 203/1989, 16/1982, 18/1982.

85   Starting with the nullity trinity of 1971 - cases 30, 31, 32.

86   See Nino, 'A Philosophical Reconstruction of Judicial Review'; Ely, *Democracy and Distrust*; Habermas, *Between Facts and Norms*. Rawls, *Political Liberalism*, pp. 5, 299.

8   Final Thoughts

> [Positivism insists upon] the last-resort sovereignty of the individual moral conscience, the right to criticise established law for its injustice as quite distinct from formal validity and invalidity, the right to weigh up the case for obedience and disobedience, the right and even the duty to disobey iniquity commanded in the name of law.

Neil MacCormick, *An Institutional Theory of Law*, p. 139

> ... a judge cannot justify any decision on the basis of a legal norm, such as a congressional statute, if he does not ground the legitimacy of that norm, either explicitly or implicitly, upon some *moral* principles ....

Carlos Nino, 'A Philosophical Reconstruction of Judicial Review', p. 814

> But how much and how accurately would we *think* if we did not think, so to speak, in community with others to whom we *communicate* our thoughts and who communicate their thoughts to us!

Immanuel Kant, 'What is Orientation in Thinking?' p. 247

Law and Practical Reason

My argument has moved from three bases: a series of case studies showing the role played by political morality[1] in constitutional adjudication in three liberal democracies; a discussion of the weaknesses of positivist accounts of law; and a presentation of the requirements of intersubjective moral argument. The case studies showed how the reasoning of judges relied heavily on visions of political morality. These visions were competing ones however - there was a dialogue between different judges, courts, and political actors over the appropriate conception of political morality to invoke when interpreting the Constitution. Furthermore these visions were not always adequately articulated, but left in the background as unspoken assumptions.

Chapter Two suggested that traditional positivist arguments for the separation of law and political morality, as conceptual matters failed. Furthermore the law's claims of normativity and authority can only be understood by linking law to morality in some fashion. However the positivists do have telling points: law and morality are not identical, and law must not be given an unimpeachable claim to obedience, for that would imperil the sovereignty of conscience. I suggested that this could be done by seeing one element of law as involving a debate on the legitimacy of the exercise of public power. Positivists themselves admit that the law makes a claim to exercise legitimate authority, and introducing this notion of a political moral debate seems to develop this notion, as well as highlighting the strongly argumentative, interpretative nature of modern legal practice.

Chapter Three then offered a presentation of the main elements of what Nino calls 'moral constructivism', an intersubjectivist approach to moral argument developed on the basis of work by several writers. Such an intersubjectivist approach shows the way for rational argumentation in moral matters to proceed through the use of various criteria in a debate. One of those criteria is the notion of explicability or publicity. This itself requires that the reasoning process be made explicit and that each of the steps in the reasoning be apparent.

Chapter Seven tried to bring these together. Constitutional interpretation requires the use of political morality. This infusion of political morality helps give sense to law's normativity, without conferring on it unimpeachable legitimacy. Furthermore it serves to provide criteria for constitutional argumentation since rational criteria of moral argumentation are available. Since constitutional law already involves such a public debate on the legitimacy of public power, it is not surprising that we find many instances where these criteria were relied upon by judges. However since this notion of a debate is not always brought to the foreground there were also cases where these criteria were violated, and I noted some of those cases. There are criteria of validity in political moral argument. One of those (derived from the notions of explicability and giving of reasons) is the requirement to justify publicly the elements in one's reasoning and this requires judges to bring to the fore the political moral beliefs on which they rely and argue them out within the legal context. This involves the judges in putting forward principled coherent explications of the legal order. In doing this, judges must rely on the criteria of legalised political morality, which is a subspecies of practical reason.

In all these areas, the function of *dialogue*, communicative rationality, is stressed. Constitutional law and practical reason are each conceived in terms of an argumentative practice, in which actors make claims and suggestions, testing each according to the force of arguments. The criteria of political argument, and of legalised political argument allow us to assess the merits and demerits of the different claims and suggestions. Legalised political argument is not the same as unrestricted practical debate. Nevertheless it too touches upon the question of legitimacy. For law to make its claim to normativity, it must try to answer that question within the legal viewpoint.

Many of the authors on whom I rely have discussed this connection between the law and practical reason.[2] They have sometimes been over-enthusiastic (in my opinion) about the value of law. Consider the following comments:

> We have an institution that calls some issues from the battleground of power politics to the forum of principle. It holds out the promise that the deepest, most fundamental conflicts between individual and society will once, finally, become questions of justice. I do not call that religion or prophecy. I call it law.[3]

> ... the supreme court is the branch of government that serves as the exemplar of public reason.[4]

> To check whether we are following public reason we might ask: how would our argument strike us presented in the form of a supreme court opinion?[5]

> Moral theory must bequeath this question [on the possibility of the unity of practical reason] to the philosophy of law ....[6]

These seem rather large claims. A more level-headed approach is that of a HLA Hart, which seeks to dispel 'philosophical mists', reject 'moralising myths', and help dissipate the 'excessive veneration' with which the law is sometimes regarded.[7] We would do well to remember too the warning of Kelsen, that the 'historical function of the natural-law doctrine was to preserve the authority of the positive law'.[8] The law has not always been - indeed perhaps has rarely been - a force for good. Furthermore it seems to ask a lot of jurists, that they not merely practise law, nor merely exercise constitutional justice, but also serve as the 'exemplar' of public reason.

Consider *Keegstra*, where the Canadian Supreme Court debated the interpretation of freedom of expression and the reasonable limits on it, under the Charter. The opinions in that case articulated opposing political philosophies - a slightly perfectionist liberalism, and liberalism as neutrality. The majority upheld the anti-hate speech law at issue, holding that Parliament was pursuing the worthwhile goal of making equality a social reality rather than just a nice ideal. The *Zundel* dissenters and the *Butler* majority also confirmed the fundamental principle of a free expression doctrine which takes equality seriously. Two opposing political philosophies were at issue in the Irish case of *Norris*, where a strongly perfectionist majority won out over liberal dissents. The dissenting voices provided a public articulation of the values of autonomy and equality, a political vision which was eventually relied upon by a more liberal Parliament to end discrimination against homosexuals. A more secular vision has now been confirmed by the Supreme Court, most spectacularly in the *Abortion Information* case. The Italian Constitutional Court, in a long series of decisions from 1970 to 1984, upheld the values of autonomy and equality, whittling away at the special position of the Catholic Church, and pointing the way for a move to a more egalitarian regime accomplished with the renegotiation of the Lateran agreements in 1984.

All these seem like valuable achievements. However we should not get over enthusiastic about judicial power, or judicial reason. The *Zundel* decision, where a judge implied there might be legitimate doubt about the fact of the Holocaust, cannot be praised for its moral sensitivity or rigorous reasoning. The *Prostitution Reference* case involved a rather casual assumption about the value of prostitution. *Norris* and *Open Door* involved the validation of strongly perfectionist views, with (e.g.) little reasoning to back up the creation of a crime 'conspiracy to corrupt public morals'. There are disturbing features in many of the earlier Italian cases I discussed. The recent blasphemy decision, 440/1995, is also worrying. Its commitment to equality is praiseworthy, but its failure to consider the principle of legality is unacceptable. The institution of constitutional justice - modern natural law- has its nightmares as well as its noble dreams.[9]

There are different ways of looking at this phenomenon. We can of course look at it all from the viewpoint of political morality. Is constitutional justice a morally defensible institution? We can also look at the phenomenon from a political science point of view. How does constitutional justice function? In the main I have looked at it from a third viewpoint, between the strongly normative discussion and the mainly empirical analysis, a viewpoint between facts and norms, the viewpoint of law.

We must pay attention to the messy, inconsistent, often arbitrary and unfair concrete 'base' of the legal orders in which we live.[10] However we cannot ignore our understanding of the concept of law. That understanding includes a conception of normativity which requires some link to practical reason in its moral exercise to explain it. Law makes a claim to obedience, a claim that can only be understood if law involves a debate on the legitimate exercise of public power. This requires the judiciary to engage in a reconstructive exercise when interpreting the Constitution, mediating between the particularities of the specific legal system, here and now, and the wider claims of normativity, which involves a universal claim. They do not construct an 'ideal constitution' but offer a reconstruction of the Constitution to justify its claim to legitimacy. This involves the exercise of practical reason, (political moral argument), but in a restricted way.

That it is restricted gives us cause to doubt the more grandiose claims of some modern natural lawyers or post-positivists. The restricted exercise of practical reason cannot replace unrestricted practical reason. Law's claim to legitimacy is not unimpeachable, and the sovereignty of conscience must be accepted. As jurists we engage in legal interpretation, trying to apply the criteria of legalised political morality. As citizens and persons we have unrestricted use of practical reason, and can decide what is right and wrong, and whether constitutional review is an appropriate way to secure the just state. As citizens and persons, we must be wary of ceding to jurists the task of establishing justice. As jurists, we have difficulties enough already with the restricted exercise of practical reason in law. Justice is too important to be left to jurists.

Notes

1   Or if you prefer, practical reason in its (political) moral exercise. See Habermas, *Justification and Application*, pp. 1 - 17.

2   See Alexy, *A Theory of Legal Argumentation*, pp. 287 - 295, where he outlines four connections. First, there is the need that practical reason (what he discusses is general practical discourse) has of law to supplement its weaknesses. Second, both involve a claim to correctness. Third, there is a correspondence between the rules and forms of the two discourses. Fourth, legal reasoning must rely on general practical reason at certain points.

3   Dworkin, *A Matter of Principle*, p. 71. In a footnote I have omitted, he notes the writings of Michael Perry who considers law a form of prophecy.

4   Rawls, *Political Liberalism*, p. 231.

5   Rawls, *Political Liberalism*, p. 254.

6   Habermas, *Justification and Application*, p. 17.

7   Raz, *Ethics in the Public Domain*, p. 194.

8   Kelsen, *What is Justice?*, p. 297.

9   Hart, 'American Jurisprudence through English Eyes: The Nightmare and the Noble Dream', in *Essays in Jurisprudence and Philosophy*.

10   Raz, *Ethics in the Public Domain*, p. 273.

Bibliography

Aarnio, Aulis, *The Rational as Reasonable: A Treatise on Legal Justification*. (Dordrecht: Reidel, 1987)

Ackerman, Bruce, *Social Justice in the Liberal State*. (New Haven: Yale UP, 1980)

Ackerman, Bruce, *We The People*. (Cambridge: Harvard UP, 1991)

Aleinikoff, 'Constitutional Law in the Age of Balancing.' (1987) 96 *Yale L. J.* 943

Alexy, Robert, 'A Discourse-Theoretical Conception of Practical Reason.' (1992) 5 *Ratio Juris* no.3, 231

Alexy, Robert, 'A Theory of Practical Discourse.' In Benhabib; Dallmayr, eds., *The Communicative Ethics Controversy*

Alexy, Robert, 'Legal Argumentation as Rational Discourse.' (1993) 70 *Rivista Internazionale di Filosofia del Diritto* no.2, 165

Alexy, Robert, 'On Necessary Relations Between Law and Morality.' (1989) *Ratio Juris* no.2, 167

Alexy, Robert, 'Rights, Legal Reasoning and Rational Discourse.' (1992) 5 *Ratio Juris* no.2, 143

Alexy, Robert, *A Theory of Legal Argumentation; The Theory of Rational Discourse as Theory of Legal Justification*. (English translation of *Theorie der juristischen Argumentation*) Adler; MacCormick, (trans.) (Oxford: Oxford University Press, 1989)

Alexy, Robert; Peczenik, Aleksander, 'The Concept of Coherence and Its Significance for Discursive Rationality.' (1990) 3 *Ratio Juris* no.1, 130

Amselek, Paul, (ed.), *Interprétation et Droit*. (Bruxelles: Bruylant, 1995)

Anderson, Gavin, (ed.), *Rights and Democracy: Essays in UK-Canadian Constitutionalism* (London: Blackstone, 1999)

Antieau, C., *Adjudicating Constitutional Issues*. (London: Oceana, 1985)

Antonelli, Sergio, 'Questione Cattolica e Questione Democristiana.' (1988) *Diritto e Società* no.1, 307

Apel, Karlo-Otto, *Towards a Transformation of Philosophy*. (English translation) Adey; Frisby, (trans.) (London: Routledge & Kegan Paul, 1980)

Arendt, Hannah, *Crises of the Republic*. (New York: Harvest HBJ Book, 1972)

Arendt, Hannah, *Eichmann in Jerusalem: A Report on the Banality of Evil*. (New York: Penguin, 1964)

Arendt, Hannah, *Lectures on Kant's Political Philosophy*. (with an interpretive essay by Ronald Beiner) (Sussex: Harvester Press, 1982)

Augustine, *The City of God*. (New York: Modern Library, 1993)

Avineri, S.; De-Shalit, A., *Communitarianism and Individualism*. (Oxford: OUP, 1992)

Baier, Kurt, *The Moral Point of View: A Rational Basis for Ethics*. (Ithaca: Cornell University Press, 1958)

Baier, Kurt, *The Moral Point of View: A Rational Basis for Ethics*. (Second Edition) (New York: Random House, 1965)

Baldassarre, A., 'Costituzione e Teoria dei Valori.' (1991) 22 *Politica del Dirritto* 639

Baldassarre, A., 'E Costituzionale l' Incriminazione della Bestemmia?' (1973) *Giuris. Cost.* 71

Barile, Paolo, *Istituzioni di Diritto Publicco*. (Padova: CEDAM, 1987)

Barile, Paolo; Cheli, Enzo; Grassi, Stefano, (eds.), *Corte Costituzionale e sviluppo della forma di governo in Italia*. (Bologna: Il Mulino, 1982)

Beard, Charles, *The Supreme Court and the Constitution*. Austin, (ed.), (Englewood Cliffs, N.J.: Prentice-Hall, 1962)

Beatty, David, 'The Canadian Charter of Rights: Lessons and Laments' (1997) 60 *Modern Law Review* 481

Beatty, David, *Constitutional Law in Theory and Practice*. (Toronto: University of Toronto Press, 1995)

Beatty, David, *Human Rights and Judicial Review: A Comparative Perspective*. (Dordrecht: Kluwer Academic Press, 1994)

Beatty, David, *The Canadian Production of Constitutional Review: Talking Heads and the Supremes*. (Toronto: Carswell, 1990)

Beaudoin, G.; Ratushny, E., *Charte Canadienne des Droits et Libertes*. (2nd ed.) (Montreal: Wilson and Lafleur, 1989)

Benhabib, Seyla, 'Afterword: Communicative Ethics and Contemporary Controversies.' In Benhabib; Dallmayr, eds., *The Communicative Ethics Controversy*

Benhabib, Seyla, *Situating the Self*. (Cambridge: Polity Press, 1992)

Benhabib, Seyla; Dallmayr, Fred, (editors), *The Communicative Ethics Controversy*. (Cambridge, Ma.: MIT Press, 1990)

Bickel, Alexander M., *The Least Dangerous Branch: The Supreme Court at the Bar of Politics*. (Indianapolis: Bobbs-Merrill, 1962)

Blair, Lowell, (trans.), *The Essential Rousseau*. (New York: Meridian, 1983)

Bobbio, Noberto, *Il futuro della democrazia*. (Turin: Einaudi, 1995)

Bork, Robert, *The Tempting of America: The Political Seduction of the Law*. (New York: Simon and Schuster, 1990)

Brewer-Carias, A. R., *Judicial Review in Comparative Perspective*. (Cambridge: Cambridge University Press, 1989)

Broglio, Francesco, 'La Rilevanza Costituzionale dei Patti Lateranensi tra Ordinamento Giuridico Fascista e Carta Repubblicana.' (1983) *Rivista Trimestrale di Diritto Pubblico* 1332

Bryden, P.; Davis, S.; Russell, J., *Protecting Rights and Freedoms*. (Toronto: University of Toronto Press, 1994)

Cameron, Jamie, 'The Past, Present and Future of Expressive Freedom under the Charter' (1997) 35 *Osgoode Hall Law Journal* 1

Cappelletti, M., *The Judicial Process in Comparative Perspective*. (Oxford: OUP, 1989)

Carusi, V.; Cerri, A.; D'Orazio, G.; Goldoni, V.; Morelli, M.; Roselli, F., (eds.), *Giurisprudenza della Corte Costituzionale Italiana (1956 - 1984)*. (Milano: Giuffre, 1985)

Cassels, 'Judicial Activism and Public Interest Litigation in India.' (1989) 37 *American Journal of Comparative Law* 495

Cheli, Enzo, *Costituzione e sviluppo delle instituzioni in Italia*. (Bologna: Il Mulino, 1978)

Chubb, Basil, *The Government and Politics of Ireland*. (London: Longman, 1992)

Chubb, Basil, *The Politics of the Irish Constitution*. (Dublin: Institute of Public Administration, 1991)

Clark, Martin, *Modern Italy, 1871 - 1982*. (London and New York: Longman, 1984)

Clarke, D., 'The Constitution and Natural Law.' (1993) *Irish Law Times* 177

Colaianni, N., 'Il Principio Supremo di Laicità dello Stato e l'Isegnamento della Religione Cattolica.' (1989) 1 *Foro It.* 1333

Coleman, Jules, 'On the Relationship Between Law and Morality.' (1989) 2 *Ratio Juris* 66 (Article)

Cordero, Mario, (ed.), *L'Autonno del Concordato - Chiesa cattolica e stato in Italia: i documenti del dibattito politico (1929 - 1977)*. (Torino: Editrice Claudiana, 1977)

Costello, Declan, 'Book Review.' (1962) 51 *Studies* 201

Costello, Declan, 'Limiting Rights Constitutionally.' In O'Reilly, ed., *Human Rights and Constitutional Law*

Costello, Declan, 'The Natural Law and the Constitution.' (1956) 45 *Studies* 403

D'Orazio, G., *La Genesi della Corte Costituzionale*. (Milano: Ed. di Communita, 1981)

Dahrendorf, Ralf, 'A Confusion of Powers: Politics and the Rule of Law.' (1977) 40 *Modern Law Review* no.1, 1

de Franciscis, M.; Zannini, R., 'Judicial Policy Making in Italy: The Constitutional Court.' In Volcansek, ed., (1992) *Judicial Politics and Policy Making in Western Europe*

de Franciscis, Maria Elisabetta, *Italy and the Vatican: The 1984 Concordat Between Church and State*. (Bern: Peter Lang, 1989)

Deleperee, F., 'Crise du Juge et Contentieux Constitutionnels en Droit Belge.' In Lenoble, ed., *La Crise du Juge*

Delgado, P., 'Words that Wound: A Tort Action for Racial Insults, Epithets and Name Calling.' (1982) 17 *Harv. C.R.C.L.L. Rev.* 133

Dell'Acqua, Cesare, 'La Giurisprudenza come Sistema e il 'Gioco' dell'Interpretazione.' (1993) *Diritto e Società* 489

Dhavan, Rajeev, *The Supreme Court of India and Parliamentary Sovereignty*. (New Delhi: 1976)

Di Cosimo, Giovanni, 'La Sentenza n. 195 del 1993 della corte Costituzionale e Sua Incidenza sulla Restante Legislazione Regionale in Materia di Finanziamenti all'Edilizia di Culto.' (1993) 2 *Giuris. Cost.* 2151

Di Manno, Thierry, 'L'Activité Contentieuse de la Cour Constitutionnelle en 1990: Éléments Statistiques et Techniques de Jugement.' (1990) 6 *Annuaire International de Justice Constitutionnelle* 769

Discussion, 'Language as Violence v. Freedom of Expression.' (1988-89) 37 *Buff. L. Rev.* 337

Dworkin, Ronald, (ed.), *The Philosophy of Law*. (New York: OUP, 1977)

Dworkin, Ronald, 'In Defence of Equality.' (1983) 1 *Social Philosophy and Policy* 31

Dworkin, Ronald, *A Matter of Principle*. (Cambridge: Harvard University Press, 1985)

Dworkin, Ronald, *Freedom's Law: The moral reading of the American Constitution*. (Cambridge: Harvard University Press, 1996)

Dworkin, Ronald, *Law's Empire*. (London: Fontana, 1986)

Dworkin, Ronald, *Taking Rights Seriously*. (London: Duckworth, 1978)

Dyzenhaus, David, 'Law and Public Reason.' (1993) 38 *M'Gill Law Review* 366

Dyzenhaus, David, 'Obscenity and the Charter: Autonomy and Equality.' (1991) 1 *C.R.* no.4th, 367

Dyzenhaus, David, 'Pornography and Public Reason.' (1994) 7 *Canadian Journal of Law and Jurisprudence* no.2, 261

Ely, John Hart, *Democracy and Distrust*. (Cambridge: Harvard UP, 1980)

Emerson, T., 'Towards a General Theory of the First Amendment.' (1965) 72 *Yale L. J.* 877

Epp, Charles, *The Rights Revolution* (Chicago: University of Chicago Press, 1998)

Esposito, C., 'La Bestemmia nella Costituzione Italiana.' (1958) *Giur. Cost.* 990

Farrell, Brian, (ed.), *DeValera's Constitution and Ours*. (Dublin: Gill and MacMillan, 1988) Thomas Davis Lecture Series

Favoreau, Louis, *Cours Constitutionnelles Europeenes et Droits Fondamentaux*. (Paris: Economica PUF, 1982).

Favoreau, Louis, *Les Cours Constitutionnelles*. (Paris: PUF, 1992) Que sais-je?

Favoreau, Louis; Loic, Philippe, *Les Grandes Decisions du Conseil Constitutionnel*. (5th edition) (Paris: Sirey, 1989)

Finnis, J.; Boyle, J., and Germain, G., *Nuclear Deterrence, Morality and Realism*. (Oxford: Clarendon Press, 1987)

Finnis, John, 'Is Homosexual Conduct Wrong? Disintegrity.' (1993) *The New Republic* Nov. 15

Finnis, John, 'Personal Integrity, Sexual Morality and Responsible Parenthood.' (1985) 1 *Anthropos* 43

Finnis, John, *Fundamentals of Ethics*. (Oxford: Clarendon, 1983)

Finnis, John, *Natural Law and Natural Rights*. (Oxford: Oxford University Press, 1980) Clarendon Law Series

Fish, Stanley, *Doing What Comes Naturally*. (Oxford: Clarendon Press, 1989)

Floridia, G., 'Dall'Eguaglianza dei Cittadini alla Laicità dello Stato.' (1989) 2 *Giuris. Cost.* 1086

Floridia, G., 'La Costituzione.' In Pasquino, ed., *La Politica Italiana: Dizionario Critico, 1945 - 1995*

Fuller, Lon, 'Positivism and Fidelity to Law - A Reply to Professor Hart.' (1958) 71 *Harvard Law Review* 630

Gallie, W. B., 'Essential Contestable Concepts.' (1956) 56 *Proceedings of the Aristotelian Society* 201

Gardbaum, S., 'Why the Liberal State can Promote Moral Ideals After All.' (1991) 104 *Harv. L. Rev.* 1350

George, R. P., (ed.), *Natural Law Theory: Contemporary Essays*. (Oxford: Clarendon, 1992)

Gewirth, Alan, *Human Rights*. (Chicago: Uni. of Chicago Press, 1982)

Gismondi, Pietro, 'Vilipendio della Religione Cattolica e Disciplina Costituzionale delle Confessioni.' (1965) *Giuris. Cost.* 609

Grasso, Giuseppe, 'Laicismo di Stato e Punizione del Reato di Bestemmia.' (1988) 1 *Giuris. Cost.* no.3, 4304

Greenawalt, Kent, 'Free Speech in the United States and Canada.' (1992) *Law & Cont. Prob.* 5

Grogan, V., 'The Constitution and the Natural Law.' (1954) 8 *Christus Rex* 201

Grzegorczyk, C., Michaud, F., and Troper, M., (eds.), *Le Positivsme Juridique*. (Paris: LGDJ, 1992)

Guastini, R., 'Interprétation et Description de Normes.' In Amselek, ed., *Interprétation et Droit* 89

Guastini, Ricardo, *Le fonti del diritto e l'interpretazione*. (Milano: Giuffre, 1993) cited

Gunther, Klaus, *The Sense of Appropriateness: Application Discourses in Morality and Law*. (English translation of *Der Sinn für Angemessenheit*) Farrell, (trans.), (New York: State University of New York Press, 1993)

Guyer, Paul, (ed.), *The Cambridge Companion to Kant*. (Cambridge: CUP, 1992)

Gwynn-Morgan, D., 'Constitutional Interpretation: Three Cautionary Tales' (1988) 10 *D.U.L.J.* 24

Habermas, Jürgen, 'Reconciliation through the Public Use of Reason: Remarks on John Rawls' Political Liberalism.' (1995) 92 *J. Phil.* no.3, 109

Habermas, Jürgen, 'Towards a Communication Concept of a Rational Collective Will Formation.' (1989) 2 *Ratio Juris* 144

Habermas, Jürgen, 'Law and Morality.' (1988) 8 *Tanner Lectures on Human Values* 217

Habermas, Jürgen, *Between Facts and Norms*. (English translation of *Faktizität und Geltung*) Rehg, W., (trans.), (Cambridge: MIT Press, 1995)

Habermas, Jürgen, *Justification and Application, Remarks on Discourse Ethics*. (English translation *Erläuterungen zur Diskursethik*) Cronin, C., (trans.), (Cambridge: Polity Press, 1993)

Habermas, Jürgen, *Moral Consciousness and Communicative Action*. (English translation of *Moralbewusstein und kommunikatives Handeln*) MacCarthy, (trans.), (Cambridge: Polity Press, 1990)

Habermas, Jürgen, *Theory of Communicative Action*. (English Translation of *Theorie des Kommunikativen Handelns*) (Boston: Beacon Press, 1984)

Hamilton, A.; Madison, J.; Jay J., *The Federalist Papers*. Rossiter, (ed.), (New York: Mentor, 1961)

Hare, Richard, *Freedom and Reason*. (London: Oxford University Press, 1965)

Hart, H.L.A., 'American Jurisprudence Through English Eyes: The Nightmare and the Noble Dream.' In Hart, (1983) *Essays in Jurisprudence and Philosophy* 123

Hart, H.L.A., *The Concept of Law*. (Oxford: Clarendon Press, 1961)

Hart, H.L.A., 'Positivism and the Separation of Law and Morals.' In Hart, (1983) *Essays in Jurisprudence and Philosophy* 49

Hart, H.L.A., 'Problems of the Philosophy of Law.' In Hart, (1983) *Essays in Jurisprudence and Philosophy* 88

Hart, H.L.A., *Essays in Jurisprudence and Philosophy*. (Oxford: Clarendon, 1983)

Hart, H.L.A., *Essays on Bentham*. (Oxford: Clarendon Press, 1982)

Henkin; Rosenthal, (eds.), *Constitutionalism and Rights*. (New York: Columbia University Press, 1990)

Hilberg, Raul, *The Destruction of the European Jews*. (New York: Holmes & Meier, 1985)

Hogg, Peter and Bushell, Allison, 'The Charter Dialogue between Courts and Legislatures' (1997) 35 *Osgoode Hall Law Journal* 75

Hogg, Peter W., *Constitutional Law of Canada*. (2nd) (Toronto: Carswell, 1985)

Holland, Kenneth, *Judicial Activism in Comparative Perspective*. (London: MacMillan, 1991)

Honoré, T., 'The Dependence of Morality on Law.' (1993) 13 *Oxford Journal of Legal Studies* 1

Horowitz; Bramson, 'Skokie, the ACLU and the Endurance of Democratic Theory.' (1979) 43 *Law and Cont. Problems* 328

Horton, John; Mendus, Susan, (eds.), *After MacIntyre: critical perspectives on the Work of Alasdair MacIntyre*. (Oxford: Polity Press, 1994)

Hug, Chrystel, *The Politics of Sexual Morality in Ireland* (London: MacMillan, 1999)

Humphreys, Richard, 'Constitutional Interpretation' (1993) 15 *D.U.L.J.* 59

Humphreys, Richard, 'Constitutional Law - Bonjour Tristesse: reasons and results in constitutional adjudication' (1992) 14 *D.U.L.J.* 105

Humphreys, Richard, 'Interpreting Natural Rights' (1993 - 95) 28-30 *Ir. Jur.* 221

Hutchinson, Allan C., 'That's Just The Way It Is: Langille on Law.' (1989) 34 *McGill Law Journal* 145

Ison, Terence, 'A Constitutional Bill of Rights - the Canadian Experience' (1997) 60 *Modern Law Review* 499

Jemolo, Arturo, *Chiesa e Stato in Italia negli Ultimi Cento Anni*. (Torino: Giulio Einaudi, 1971)

Kant, Immanuel, *An Answer to the Question: What is Enlightenment?* in *Political Writings*. (English translation) Reiss, (ed.), (Cambridge: Cambridge University Press, 1991)

Kant, Immanuel, *Groundwork of the Metaphysic of Morals, The Moral Law*. (English translation) Paton, H. J., (trans.), (London: Hutchinson, 1948)

Kant, Immanuel, *On the Common Saying: This may be true in theory but it does not apply in practice* in *Political Writings*. (English translation) Reiss, (ed.), (Cambridge: Cambridge University Press, 1991)

Kant, Immanuel, *Political Writings*. Reiss, (ed.), (Cambridge: Cambridge University Press, 1991)

Kant, Immanuel, *Religion Within the Limits of Reason Alone*. (English translation) Greene, T.; Hudson, H., (trans.), (New York: Harper & Row, 1960)

Kant, Immanuel, *The Critique of Judgment*. (English translation) Meredith, (trans.), (Oxford: Clarendon Press, 1952)

Kant, Immanuel, *The Metaphysical Elements of Justice*. (English translation) Ladd, J., (trans.), (USA: Bobbs-Merrill Press, 1965)

Kant, Immanuel, *What is Orientation in Thinking?* in *Political Writings*. (English translation) Reiss, (ed.), (Cambridge: Cambridge University Press, 1991)

Kavanagh, A., 'The Quest for Legitimacy in Constitutional Interpretation' (1997) 32 *Ir. Jur.* 195

Keane, Ronan, 'Review of Law's Empire.' (1987) 22 *Irish Jurist* 125

Kelly, J. M., 'The Constitution: Law and Manifesto.' In Litton, Frank, ed., (1987) *The Constitution of Ireland*

Kelly, John, *A Short History of Western Legal Theory*. (Oxford: Clarendon Press, 1992)

Kelly, John, *Fundamental Rights in the Irish Law and Constitution*. (Dublin: Figgis, 1967)

Kelly, John; Hogan, G.; Whyte, G., *The Irish Constitution*. (Dublin: Butterworths, 1994)

Kelly, Michael, (ed.), *Hermeneutics and Critical Theory in Ethics and Politics*. (Cambridge: MIT Press, 1990)

Kelsen, Hans, 'Chi dev'essere il custode della costituzione?' In Kelsen, *La giustizia costituzionale*

Kelsen, Hans, 'La Garantie Jurisdictionnelle de la Constitution.' (1928) 35 *Revue du Droit Public et de la Science Politique* 197

Kelsen, Hans, 'La garanzia giurisdizionale della costituzione.' In Kelsen, *La giustizia costituzionale*

Kelsen, Hans, 'Law and Logic.' In Kelsen, *Essays in Legal and Moral Philosophy*

Kelsen, Hans, 'Law, State and Justice in the Pure Theory of Law.' In Kelsen, *What is Justice?* (originally published in 1948)

Kelsen, Hans, 'On the Concept of Norm.' In Kelsen, *Essays in Legal and Moral Philosophy*

Kelsen, Hans, 'The Pure Theory of Law.' (1934, 1935) *Law Quarterly Review* 474, 517

Kelsen, Hans, *Essays in Moral and Legal Philosophy*. Weinberger, (ed.), (Dordrecht: Reidel, 1973)

Kelsen, Hans, *General Theory of Law and State*. Wedberg, (trans.), (New York: Russell & Russell, 1961)

Kelsen, Hans, *General Theory of Norms*. (English translation) Hartney, M., (trans.), (Oxford: Clarendon Press, 1991)

Kelsen, Hans, *La Giustizia Costitutzionale*. (Italian translation) Ceraci, (ed.), (Milano: Giuffrè, 1981)

Kelsen, Hans, *The Pure Theory of Law*. (Second edition; English translation) Knight, M., (trans.), (Berkeley: University of California Press, 1978)

Kelsen, Hans, *What is Justice? Justice, law and politics in the mirror of science*. (originally published 1957) (Berkeley: Uni. Calif. Press, 1971)

Kenny, Sally, et al. *Constitutional Dialogues in Comparative Perspective* (London: MacMillan, 1999)

Keogh, Dermot, *Ireland and the Vatican: The Politics and Diplomacy of Church-State Relations, 1922 - 1960*. (Cork: Cork University Press, 1995)

Knopff; Morton, *Charter Politics*. (Scarborough: Nelson Canada, 1992)

Kymlicka, William, *Liberalism, Community and Culture*. (Oxford: Clarendon Press, 1983)

La Torre, Massimo, *Linguaggio, norme, istituzioni*. (Florence: EUI, 1995)

Landfried, C., (ed.), *Constitutional Review and Legislation*. (Baden-Baden: Nomos, 1988)

Lariccia, Sergio, 'Libertà delle Università Ideologicamente Impegnate e Libertà di Insegnamento.' (1972) *Giuris. Cost.* 2177

Lariccia, Sergio, 'Limiti Costituzionale alla Libertà delle Confessioni Religiose.' (1988) 1 *Giuris. Cost.* no.1, 120

Lariccia, Sergio, 'Tutela Penale dell''Ex Religione dello Stato' e Principi Costituzionale.' (1988) 1 *Giuris. Cost.* no.3, 4311

Lariccia, Sergio, 'Valori Costituzionali e Sistema Italiano di Diritto Ecclesiastico.' (1983) *Diritto e Società* 252

Larmore, Charles, *Patterns of Moral Complexity*. (Cambridge: Cambridge University Press, 1987)

Lasson, 'Racial Defamation as Free Speech: Abusing the First Amendment.' (1982) 17 *Harv. C.R.C.L.L.Rev.* 11

Lavagna, 'Prime Decisioni della Corte Costituzionale sul Concordato.' (1971) 1 *Giur. It.* 628

Lenoble, J., (ed.), *La Crise du Juge*. (Bruxelles: LGDJ, 1990)

Lenoble, J.; Berten, A., 'Jugement juridique et jugement practique.' (1990) 95 *Revue de Metaphsique et de Morale* 337

Lipstadt, Deborah, *Denying the Holocaust: the growing assault on truth and memory*. (New York: Free Press, 1993)

Litton, F., (ed.), *The Constitution of Ireland*. (Dublin: Institute of Public Administration, 1987)

Llewellyn, Karl, *The Bramble Bush: On Our Law and Its Study*. (New York: Oceana, 1981)

Lloyd, Denis, *The Idea of Law*. (Middlesex: Penguin, 1964)

Locke, D., 'The Trivialisability of Universalisability.' (1968) 77 *Phil Rev.* 25

Locke, John, *Two Treatises of Government*. Laslett, (ed.), (Cambridge: Cambridge University Press, 1967)

Lyons, David, 'Reconstructing Legal Theory.' (1987) 16 *Phil. & Pub. Aff.* no.4, 379

MacCormick, Neil, 'A Moralistic Case for A-Moralistic Law.' 20 *Valparaiso L. Rev.* 1

MacCormick, Neil, 'Natural Law and the Separation of Law and Morals.' In George, ed., *Natural Law Theory: Contemporary Essays*

MacCormick, Neil, 'The Concept of Law and *The Concept of Law*.' (1994) 14 *Oxford Journal of Legal Studies* 1

MacCormick, Neil, *HLA Hart*. (London: Edward Arnold, 1981)

MacCormick, Neil, *Legal Reasoning and Legal Theory*. (Oxford: Clarendon Press, 1978) Clarendon Law Series

MacCormick, Neil; Weinberger, Ota, *An Institutional Theory of Law: New Approaches to Legal Positivism*. (Dordrecht: Reidel, 1986)

Macedo, Philip, *Liberal Virtues: citizenship, virtues and community in liberal constitutionalism*. (Oxford: Clarendon Press, 1990)

Mack Smith, Denis, *Italy: A Modern History*. (Michigan: University of Michigan Press, 1969)

Mackie, John, 'The Third Theory of Law.' (1977) 7 *Philosophy and Public Affairs* no.1, 3

MacKinnon, Catherine, *Only Words*. (Cambridge: Harvard University Press, 1993)

Mahoney, K., 'The Canadian Constitutional Approach to Freedom of Expression in Hate Propaganda.' (1992) 55 *Law and Contemporary Problems* 77

Mandel, Michael, *The Charter of Rights and the Legalization of Politics in Canada*. (Toronto: Thomson Educational, 1994)

Manfredi, Christopher, *Judicial Power and the Charter: Canada and the Paradox of Liberal Constitutionalism*. (Toronto: McClelland & Stewart, 1993)

Manolkidis, S. K., *Granting Benefits Through Constitutional Adjudication: the extension of the most favourable norm in Greece and Italy*. (Florence: European University Institute (Ph.D. Thesis), 1995)

Marini, Giuliano, 'Ancora sulla Legittimità Costituzionale dell' art. 724 comma 1 c.p.' (1988) 1 *Giuris. Cost.* no.3, 4307

Markesinis, Basil, *German Law of Obligations*, Vol. 2, (Oxford: Clarendon Press, 1997)

Matsuda, Mari, 'Public Sanction of Racist Speech: Considering the Victim's Story.' (1989) 87 *Mich. L. Rev.* 2320

Mertl, Steve; Ward, John, *Keegstra: The Issues, The Trial, The Consequences.* (Saskatoon: Western Producer Prarie, 1985)

Michelman, Frank, 'Law's Republic.' (1989) 97 *Yale Law Journal* no.8, 1499

Milza, P.; Berstein, S., *Storia del Fascismo: Da Piazza San Sepolcro a Piazzale Loreto.* (Milano: Biblioteca Universale Rizzoli Supersaggi, 1995)

Minow, Martha, 'Engendering Justice' in Smith, ed. *Feminist Jurisprudence*

Mirabelli, Cesare, 'Problemi e Prospettive in tema di Giurisdizione Ecclesiastica Matrimoniale e di Divorzio.' (1973) 2 *Giur. Cost.* 2323

Modugno, Franco, *I 'nuovi diritti' nella Giurisprudenza Costitutzionale.* (Torino: Giappichelli, 1995)

Monahan, P., *Politics and the Constitution: The Charter: Federalism and the Supreme Court of Canada.* (Toronto: Butterworths, 1987)

Murphy, T., 'Democracy, Natural Law and the Irish Constitution.' (1993) *Irish Law Times* 81

Murphy, W.; Tanenhaus, J., *Comparative Constitutional Law.* (New York: St. Martin's Press, 1977)

Musselli, Luciano 'Insegnamento della Religione Cattolica e tutela della Libertà Religiosa.' (1989) *Giuris. Cost.* 908

Musselli, Luciano, 'Chiesa e Stato all'Assemblea Costituente: L'Articolo 7 della Costituzione Italiana.' (1988) 53 *Il Politico* no.1, 69

Nagel, Thomas, 'Moral Conflict and Political Legitimacy.' 16 *Philosophy and Public Affairs* 215

Nagel, Thomas, *Equality and Partiality.* (New York: OUP, 1991)

Nagel, Thomas, *The View From Nowhere.* (New York: Oxford University Press, 1986)

Nania, R., 'Concordato e 'Principi Supremi' della Costituzione.' (1977) 1 *Giur. Cost.* 251

Nania, Roberto, 'Il Concordato, i Giudici, la Corte.' (1982) 1 *Giur. Cost.* no.1, 147

Narveson, Jan, 'The How and Why of Universalizability.' In Potter, Timmons, eds., *Morality and Universality*

Neumann, Franz, *Behemoth.* (London: Victor Gollanz, 1942)

Nielson, Kai, 'Universalizability and the Commitment to Impartiality.' In Potter; Timmons, eds., *Morality and Universality*

Nino, Carlos S., 'Dworkin and Legal Positivism.' (1980) 89 *Mind* 519

Nino, Carlos S., *The Ethics of Human Rights.* (Oxford: Clarendon Press, 1991)

Nino, Carlos, S. 'A Philosophical Reconstruction of Judicial Review.' (1993) 14 *Cardozo Law Review* 798

Nino, Carlos, S. 'The Epistemological Moral Relevance of Democracy.' (1991) 4 *Ratio Juris* 36

Note, 'Doe v. University of Michigan: First Amendment - Racist and Sexist Expression on Campus.' (1990) 103 *Harv. L. Rev.* 1397

Nozick, R., *Anarchy, State and Utopia.* (Oxford: Blackwell, 1975)

O'Connell, Rory, 'Guardians of the Constitution: Unconstitutional Constitutional Norms', 4 (1999) *Journal of Civil Liberties* 48

O'Connell, Rory, 'Natural Law Alive and Kicking: A look at the constitutional morality of sexual privacy in Ireland' (1996) 9 *Ratio Juris* 258

O'Hanlon, R., 'Natural Rights and the Constitution.' (1993) 11 *Irish Law Times* 8

O'Hanlon, R., 'The Judiciary and the Moral Law.' (1993) *Irish Law Times* 129

O'Keefe, P.; Curtin, D., (eds.), *Constitutional Adjudication in European Community and National Law.* (Dublin: Butterworths, 1992)

O'Neill, O., 'Vindicating Reason.' In Guyer, ed., (1992) *The Cambridge Companion to Kant*

O'Neill, Onora, 'The Public Use of Reason.' (1986) 14 *Pol. Th.* no.4, 523

O'Reilly, J., (ed.), *Human Rights and Constitutional Law: Essays in Honour of Brian Walsh.* (Dublin: Round Hall Press, 1992)

Occhiocupo, Nicola, (ed.), *La Corte Costituzionale tra norma giuridica e realta sociale: Bilancio di vent'anni di attività.* (Padova: CEDAM, 1984)

Paine, Thomas, *The Rights of Man* in Foner, Eric, ed. *Collected Writings: Common Sense and other pamphlets.* (New York: Library of America, 1995)

Paladin, Livio, *Diritto Costituzionale* (CEDAM: Padova, 1995)

Pasquino, Gianfranco, (ed.), *La Politica Italiana: Dizionario Critico, 1945 - 95.* (Roma: Laterza, 1995)

Peczenik, Aleksander, *On Law and Reason.* (Dordrecht: Kluwer, 1989)

Perelman, Chaim, *Ethique et Droit.* (Bruxelles: Editions de l'Universite de Bruxelles, 1990)

Perelman, Chaim, *Justice, Law and Argument.* (Dordrecht: Reidel, 1980)

Perelman, Chaim; Foriers, P., (eds.), *La motivation des décisions en justice.* (Bruxelles: Bruyant, 1978)

Perry, Michael, *Morality, Politics and Law.* (New York: OUP, 1989)

Perry, Michael, *The Constitution, the Courts, and Human Rights.* (New Haven: Yale University Press, 1982)

Pizzorusso, Alessandro, 'L'influence de la constitution italienne sur le droit judiciaire' (1983) *Rev. int. droit comparé* 7

Pizzorusso, Alessandro, *Manuale di Diritto Pubblico*, (Napoli: Jovene Editore, 1997)

Potter, Nelson; Timmons, Mark, (editors), *Morality and Universality, Essays on Ethical Universalizability.* (Dordrecht: Reidel, 1985) Theory and Decision Library

Quint, Peter, 'Free Speech and Private Law in German Constitutional Theory' 48 (1989) *Maryland Law Review* 247;

Quint, Peter, *The Imperfect Union: Constitutional Structures of German Unification.* (Princeton: Princeton University Press, 1997)

Rasmussen, David, (ed.), *Universalism versus Communitarianism: contemporary debates in ethics.* (Cambridge: MIT Press, 1990)

Rawls, John, 'Reply to Habermas: Reconciliation through the public use of reason.' (1995) 92 *J. Phil.* no.3, 132

Rawls, John, *A Theory of Justice.* (Oxford: Oxford University Press, 1972)

Rawls, John, *Political Liberalism*. (New York: Columbia University Press, 1993)

Raz, Joseph, *Ethics in the Public Domain*. (Oxford: Clarendon, 1994)

Raz, Joseph, *Practical Reason and Norms*. (Princeton: Princeton University Press, 1990)

Raz, Joseph, *The Authority of Law*. (Oxford: Clarendon Press, 1979)

Raz, Joseph, *The Morality of Freedom*. (Oxford: Clarendon Press, 1986)

Redor, Marie-Joëlle, *De L'Etat Legal a L'Etat de Droit: L'evolution des conceptions de la doctrine publiciste Francaise 1879 - 1914*. (Paris: Economica, 1992)

Reiss, Hans, (ed.), *Kant: Political Writings*. (Cambridge: Cambridge University Press, 1991)

Richards, David A. J., 'Comment on Alexy's *A Theory of Legal Argumentation*.' (1989) 2 *Ratio Juris* 304 (Book Review)

Richards, David, *A Theory of Reasons for Actions*. (Oxford: Clarendon, 1971)

Rizza, Giovanni, 'Nuovo Concordato, Insegnamento della Religione Cattolica e Costituzione.' (1993) *Diritto e Società* no.1-2, 113

Roermund, Bert van. *Constitutional Review: theoretical and comparative perspectives*. (Deventer: Kluwer, 1993).

Rorty, Richard, 'Human Rights, Rationality and Sentimentality.' In Shute; Hurley, eds., *On Human Rights*

Ross, Alf, *On Law and Justice*. (Berkeley: University of California Press, 1958)

Rousseau, Jean-Jacques, *The Essential Rousseau*. (English translation of *Le Contrat Social* and other writings) Blair, Lowell, (trans), (New York: Meridian, 1983)

Rousseau, Jean-Jacques, *The Social Contract*, in *The Essential Rousseau*. Blair, (ed.)

Russell, Peter, 'The Political Purposes of the Canadian Charter of Rights and Freedoms' (1983) 61 *Can.Bar Rev.* 30

Saccomanno, Albino, 'Insegnamento della Religione Cattolica: Ancora una Interpretativa di Rigetto.' (1991) 1 *Giuris. Cost.* 88

Sandel, Michael, 'Moral Argument and Liberal Toleration: Homosexuality and Abortion.' (1989) 77 *California Law Review* 521

Sandel, Michael, 'The Procedural Republic and the Unencumbered Self.' (1984) 12 *Political Theory* 81; copy in Avineri and DeShalit, *Communitariansim and Individualism*

Sandel, Michael, *Liberalism and the Limits of Justice*. (Cambridge: Cambridge University Press, 1982)

Sartre, Jean-Paul, *L'existentialisme est un humanisme*. (Paris: Nagel, 1970)

Sassi, Paolo, 'Scuola Elementare e Insegnamento della Religione Cattolica nel Giudizio della Corte Costituzionale.' (1992) 2 *Giuris. Cost.* 2229

Scanlon, T., 'A Theory of Freedom of Expression.' In Dworkin, ed., *The Philosophy of Law*

Schauer, Frederick, 'The Aim and Target in Free Speech Methodology.' (1989) 83 *Nw. U.L.Rev.* 562

Schauer, Frederick, *Free Speech: A Philosophical Enquiry*. (Cambridge: Cambridge University Press, 1982)

Scheffler, Samuel, 'Moral Scepticism and the Ideals of a Person.' (1979) 62 *Monist* 288

Schmitt, Carl, *Il custode della Costituzione*. (Italian translation of *Der Hüter der Verfassung*) Caracciolo, A., (trans.), (Milano: Giuffrè, 1981) Civilta del Diritto

Schwartz, Bernard, *A History of the Supreme Court*. (New York: OUP, 1993)

Searle, John, *Speech Acts*. (Cambridge: Cambridge University Press, 1980)

Seidel, Gill, *The Holocaust Denial: Anti-Semitism, Racism and the New Right*. (Leeds: Beyond the Pale Collective, 1986)

Sharpe, Robert, 'Commercial Expression and the Charter.' (1987) 37 *University of Toronto Law Journal* 229

Shute, S.; Hurley, S., (eds.), *On Human Rights*. (New York: Basic Books, 1993)

Singer, Marcus, 'Universalisability and the Generalisation Principle.' In Potter; Timmons, ed., *Morality and Universality*

Singer, Marcus, *Generalisation in Ethics*. (New York: Alfred Knopf, 1961)

Smith, Patricia, *Feminist Jurisprudence*. (Oxford: Oxford University Press, 1993)

Soper, Philip, 'Choosing a Legal Theory on Moral Grounds.' 4 *Social Philosophy and Policy* no.1, 31

Soper, Philip, 'Legal Theory and the Claim of Authority.' (1989) 18 *Philosophy and Public Affairs* no.3, 209

Stone Sweet, Alec. *Governing with Judges: Constitutional Politics in Western Europe* (Oxford: OUP, 2000)

Stone, A., *The Birth of Judicial Politics in France: the constitutional council in comparative perspective*. (Oxford: OUP, 1992)

Summers, Robert, 'Toward a Better General Theory of Legal Validity.' (1985) 16 *Rechtstheorie* 65

Sunstein, C., 'Naked Preferences and the Constitution.' (1984) 84 *Columbia Law Review* 1684

Symposium, 'Constitutional Judicial Review of Legislation.' (1983) 56 *Temple Law Quarterly* 287

Symposium, 'Judicial Review in Comparative Perspective' (1990) 19 *Policy Studies Journal* 76.

Symposium, 'The New Constitutional Politics of Europe.' (1994) 26 *Comparative Political Studies* (4) 397.

Tate, C., and Torbjorn Vallinder. *The Global Expansion of Judicial Power*. (New York: New York Uni. Press, 1995)

Taylor, Charles, 'After Virtue.' In Horton; Mendus, eds., *After MacIntyre*

Tempestini, Attillo, 'Laicismo e Clericalismo nel Parlamento Italiano tra la Legge sul Divorzio e Quella sull'Aborto.' (1980) *Diritto e Società* 407

Toibín, Colm, 'Inside the Supreme Court.' (1984) *Magill*

Toulmin, Stephen, *An Examination of the Place of Reason in Ethics*. (Cambridge: Cambridge University Press, 1950)

Toulmin, Stephen, *The Uses of Argument*. (Cambridge: Cambridge University Press, 1964)

Trakman, Leon, *Reasoning with the Charter*. (Toronto: Butterworths, 1991)

Tribe, L., 'The Puzzling Persistence of Process Based Theories.' (1980) 89 *Yale Law Journal* 1063

Tribe, Lawrence, *Abortion: The Clash of Absolutes*. (New York: Norton, 1990)

Troper, Michel, 'La Liberté d'Interprétation du Juge Constitutionnel.' In Amselek, ed., *Interprétation et Droit* 235

Troper, Michel, 'La Motivation des Décisions Constitutionnelles.' In Perelman; Forier, eds., (1978) *La Motivation des Décisions de Justice* 287

Twomey, Adrian, 'The Death of the Natural Law.' (1995) *Irish Law Times* 270

Twomey, Patrick, *Ireland's Evolving Constitution, 1937 - 1997*. (Oxford: Hart, 1995)

Volcansek, Mary, (ed.), *Judicial Politics and Policy Making in Western Europe*. (London: Frank Cass, 1992)

Von Wright, G.H., 'Is There A Logic of Norms?' (1991) 4 *Ratio Juris* no.3, 265

Waldron, Jeremy, 'A Right-Based Critique of Constitutional Rights.' (1993) 13 *Oxford Journal of Legal Studies* 18

Waldron, Jeremy, *Liberal Rights: Collected Papers, 1981 - 1991*. (Cambridge: Cambridge University Press, 1993)

Walsh, Brian, 'Fundamental Rights.' In O'Keefe; Curtin, eds., *Constitutional Adjudication in European Community and National Law*

Walsh, Brian, 'The Constitution and Constitutional Rights.' In Litton, (1987) *The Constitution of Ireland*

Walsh, Brian, 'The Constitution: A View From the Bench.' In Farrell, (1988) *DeValera's Constitution and Ours*

Walzer, Michael 'Philosophy and Democracy.' (1981) *Political Theory* 379

Walzer, Michael, 'A Critique of Philosophical Conversation.' In Kelly, ed., *Hermeneutics and Critical Theory in Ethics and Politics*

Walzer, Michael, *Spheres of Justice*. (Oxford: Robertson, 1983)

Warnke, George, 'Rawls, Habermas and Real Talk: A reply to Walzer.' In Kelly, ed., *Hermeneutics and Critical Theory in Ethics and Politics*

Weick, G., 'Challenges to the Law of Contract' in Wilson and Rogowski, *Challenges to European Legal Scholarship*

Weimann, Gabriel; Winn, Conrad, *Hate on Trial: The Zundel Affair*. (Oakville: Mosaic Press, 1986)

Weinberger, Ota; MacCormick, Neil, *An Institutional Theory of Law: New Approaches to Legal Positivism*. (Dordrecht: Reidel, 1986)

Wilson, Geoffrey; Rogowski, Ralf, *Challenges to European Legal Scholarship*. (London: Blackstone, 1996)

Wroblewski, Jerzy, *The Judicial Application of Law*. (English translation) Bankowski; MacCormick, (eds.), (Dordrecht: Kluwer, 1992)

Zaccaria, Giuseppe, *L'Arte dell'Interpretazione*. (Padova: CEDAM, 1990)

Zagrebelsky, Gustavo, *Il diritto mite: legge, diritti, giustizia*. (Torino: Einaudi, 1992)

Zagrebelsky, Gustavo, *La Giustizia Costituzionale*. (Milano: Il Mulino, 1988)

Case References

Canadian Cases

Andrews v. *Law Society of British Columbia*; (*Alien Lawyer case*) (S.C.C.); [1989] 56
    (4th) D.L.R. 1

Carrier, R. v. (S.C.C.); [1951] 104 C.C.C. 75

Cherneskey (S.C.C.); [1979] 1 S.C.R. 1067

Committee for the Commonwealth of Canada v. *Canada* (S.C.C.); [1991] 77 (4th) D.L.R.
    385

Edmonton Journal v. *Attorney General for Alberta* (S.C.C.); [1989] 64 (4th) D.L.R. 577

Edward Books v. *R.* (S.C.C.) 35 (4th) D.L.R. 1

Edwards v. *Attorney General of Canada* (Privy Council of the House of Lords); [1930] 1
    D.L.R. 98; [1930] Appeal Cases 124

Ford v. *Quebec*; (*Quebec Language Laws case*) (S.C.C.); [1988] 54 (4th) D.L.R. 577

Fraser v. *Canada* (S.C.C.); [1985] 23 (4) D.L.R. 123; [1985] (2) S.C.R. 455

Hunter et al. v. *Southam Inc.* (S.C.C.); [1984] 11 (4th) D.L.R. 641

Irwin Toy; Attorney General of Quebec v. *Irwin Toy* (S.C.C.); [1989] 58 (4th) D.L.R. 577

Keegstra, R. v. (*Nazi Teacher case*); [1984] 19 (3d) C.C.C. 254 (H.C.); [1988] 43 (3rd)
    C.C.C. 150 (Court of Appeal); (S.C.) [1990] 3 S.C.R. 697

Law Society of Upper Canada v. *Skapinker* (S.C.C.); [1984] 9 (4th) D.L.R. 161

McKinney v. *Board of Governors of the University of Guelph* (S.C.C.); [1990] 76 (4th)
    D.L.R. 545

Motor Vehicle Act (B.C.) Reference, [1985] 2 S.C.R. 486

Morgentaler v. *R.*; (*Abortion case*) (S.C.C.); [1988] 38 (4th) D.L.R. 385

Osborne v. *Canada*, 82 (4th) D.L.R. 321

Police Services Union v. *Port Moody Police Board* (British Colombia Court of Appeal);
    [1991] 78 (4) D.L.R. 79

Prostitution Reference; Reference re: ss. 193 and 195 of the Criminal Code (S.C.C.);
    [1990] 1 S.C.R. 1123 (S.C.); [1987] 38 (3rd) C.C.C. 408 (Court of Appeal) 133

R. v. *Andrews* (S.C. of Canada); [1990] 77 (4th) D.L.R. 128

R. v. *Big M Drug Mart* (S.C.C.); [1985] 18 (4th) D.L.R. 321

R. v. *Boucher* (S.C.C.); [1951] S.C.R. 265

R. v. *Brodie* (S.C.C.); [1962] 32 (2nd) D.L.R. 507

R. v. *Butler*; (*Obscenity case*) 50 (3rd) C.C.C. 97 (Queen's Bench); 60 (3rd) C.C.C. 219
    (Court of Appeal), [1992] 89 (4th) D.L.R. 449

R. v. *Hoaglin*; [1907] 12 C.C.C. 226

R. v. *Keegstra*; (*Nazi Teacher case*); see *Keegstra*

R. v. *Kirby*; [1970] 1 (2nd) C.C.C. 286

R. v. *Oakes* (S.C.C.); [1986] 26 (4th) D.L.R. 200

R. v. *Rahey*, [1987] 1 S.C.R. 588

R. v. *Ramsingh*; [1984] 14 (3rd) Canadian Criminal Cases 230

R. v. *Towne Cinema Theatre Ltd.* (S.C.C.); [1985] 18 (4th) D.L.R. 1

R. v. *Wholesale Travel Group*; [1991] 84 (4th) D.L.R. 161

R. v. *Zundel*; *(Holocaust Denial case)* (S.C.C.) 35 (4th) D.L.R. 338 (H.C.); 53 (3d) C.C.C. 161 (Court of Appeal); (S.C.C.); [1992] 95 (4th) D.L.R. 202

Reference re Electoral Boundaries Commission Act (S.C.C.); [1991] 81 (4th) D.L.R. 16

Reference re Public Service Employees Relation Act, Labour Relations Act, Police Officers Collective Bargaining Act (S.C.C.); [1987] 38 (4th) D.L.R. 161

RJR MacDonald v. *Canada* (S.C.C.); [1993] 102 (4th) D.L.R. 289

Rocket v. *Royal College of Dental Surgeons* (S.C.C.); [1990] 71 (4) D.L.R. 68

RWDSU v. *Dolphin Delivery* (S.C.C.); [1986] 2 S.C.R. 57

Slaight Communications v. *Davidson* (S.C.C.); [1989] 59 (4th) D.L.R. 416

Symes v. *R.* (S.C.); [1993] 110 (4th) D.L.R. 470

Taylor v. *Canadian Human Rights Commission* (S.C.C.); [1991] Law Reports of the Commonwealth (Const.) 445; [1991] 75 (4th) D.L.R. 577

Thomson Newspapers v. *Director of Investigation* (S.C.C.); [1990] 67 (4th) D.L.R. 161

US v. *Costroni* (S.C.C.); [1989] 1 S.C.R. 1469

Westendorp v. *R.* (S.C.C.); [1983] 1 S.C.R. 43

Irish Cases

Abortion Information case; In re Art. 26 and the Regulation of Information (Services Outside the State for the Termination of Pregnancies) Bill (S.C.); [1995] 2 I.L.R.M. 81

Attorney General v. *Hamilton, Sole Chairman of the Tribunal of Inquiry*, (No. 1); *(Cabinet Confidentiality case)* (H.C. and S.C.); [1993] 2 I.R. 250; [1993] I.L.R.M. 81

Attorney General v. *Hamilton, Sole Chairman of the Tribunal of Inquiry*, (No. 2) (H.C. and S.C.); [1993] 3 I.R. 227; [1993] I.L.R.M. 821

Attorney General v. *McBride*; [1928] (I.R.) 541

Attorney General v. *Paperlink* (H.C.); [1984] I.L.R.M. 373

Attorney General (Society for the Protection of the Unborn Child) v. *Open Door Counselling Ltd, Dublin Well Woman Centre* (S.C.); [1994] I.R. 256; [1994] 1 I.L.R.M. 257

Brennan v. *Attorney General*, [1983] I.L.R.M. 449

Byrne v. *Ireland* (S.C.); [1972] I.R. 241

Cahill v. *Sutton* (S.C.); [1980] I.R. 269

Conroy v. *Attorney General of Ireland* (S.C.); [1965] I.R. 411

Open Door; Attorney General (Society for the Protection of the Unborn Child) v. *Open Door Counselling Ltd, Dublin Well Woman Centre* (H.C.); [1987] I.R. 477; (S.C.); [1988] I.L.R.M. 18

People v. *O'Callaghan; (Bail case)* (S.C.); [1966] I.R. 501

People v. *Shaw* (S.C., Court of Criminal Appeal); [1982] I.R. 1

People (Director of Public Prosecutions) v. *O'Shea* (S.C.); [1982] I.R. 384; [1983] I.L.R.M. 549

Quinn's Supermarket v. *Minister for Industry and Commerce* (S.C.); [1972] I.R. 1

Ryan v. *Director of Public Prosecutions; (Bail case)* (S.C.); [1989] I.R. 399

Ryan v. *Ireland, and the Attorney General; (Fluoridation Case)* (H.C., S.C.); [1965] I.R. 294

Society for the Protection of the Unborn Child v. *Coogan; (Abortion Information)* (H.C. and S.C.); [1989] I.R. 734; [1989] I.L.R.M. 526

Society for the Protection of the Unborn Child v. *Grogan; (Abortion Information case)* (H.C. and S.C.); [1989] I.R. 753; [1990] 1 C.M.L.R. 689 (Also [1990] I.L.R.M. 350)

Society for the Protection of the Unborn Child v. *Grogan, (No. 3)* (H.C.); [1992] 2 I.R. 471

Society for the Protection of the Unborn Child v. *Grogan, (No. 4)* (H.C.); [1994] 1 I.R. 46

Society for the Protection of the Unborn Child v. *Union of Students in Ireland*, March 6th, 1997, unrep. Sup. Ct.

State (C.) v. *Frawley* (H.C.); [1976] I.R. 365

State (Director of Public Prosecutions) v. *Walsh and Conneely* (S.C.); [1981] I.R. 412

State (Gilliland) v. *Governor of Mountjoy Jail* (S.C.); [1987] I.R. 201; [1986] I.L.R.M. 381

State (Healy) v. *O'Donoghue; (Healy's case)* (S.C.); [1976] I.R. 325

State (M.) v. *Attorney General and Ireland* (H.C.); [1979] I.R. 73

State (Quinn) v. *Ryan* (S.C.); [1965] I.R. 70

State (Ryan) v. *Lennon* (S.C.); [1935] I.R. 370

State (Trimbole) v. *Governor of Mountjoy Prison; (Trimbole)* (H.C. and S.C.); [1985] I.R. 550; [1985] I.L.R.M. 465

State (Walshe) v. *Lennon* (H.C. and S.C.); [1942] I.R. 112

Tilson (infants), in re (H.C. and S.C.); [1951] I.R. 1

Tormey v. *Ireland* (S.C.); [1985] I.R. 289

W. v. *W.* (S.C.); [1993] 2 I.R. 476; [1993] I.L.R.M. 294

X; Attorney General v. *X; (Abortion case)* (H.C. and S.C.); [1992] 1 I.R. 1; [1992] I.L.R.M. 401

Italian Cases

Before the Constitutional Court unless otherwise stated.

1956, Decision 001 /1956, (*Religious Freedom case*), (14 June 1956), [1956] Giur. Cost. 1 235

1957, Decision 045 /1957, (*Religious Liberty of Assembly case*), (18 March 1957), [1957] Giuris. Cost. 579

1957, Decision 125 /1957, (*First Vilipendio case*), [1957] Giuris. Cost. 1209

1958, Decision 059 /1958, (21 Nov. 1958), [1958] Giur. Cost. 885

1958, Decision 079 /1958, (*First Blasphemy case*), (30 Dec. 1958), [1958] Giur. Cost. 990

1965, Decision 039 /1965, (*Second Vilipendio case*), (13 May 1965), [1965] Giur. Cost. 602

1970, Decision 635/1970 of the *Corte di cassazione*

1971, Decision 030 /1971, (*First Nullity case*), (24 Feb. 1971), [1971] 1 Giur. Cost. 150

1971, Decision 031 /1971, (*Second Nullity case -- First Degree of Relationship*), (1 March 1971), [1971] 1 Giur. Cost. 154

1971, Decision 032 /1971, (*Third Nullity case - Natural Incapacity*), [1971] 1 Giur. Cost. 156

1971, Decision 049 /1971, (*Contraception case*)

1971, Decision 169 /1971, (*First Divorce case*), (5 July 1971), [1971] 2 Giur. Cost. 1784

1972, Decision 012 /1972, (27 Jan. 1972), [1972] 1 Giur. Cost. 451

1972, Decision 195 /1972, (*University Professor case*), (14 Dec. 1972), [1972] 2 Giur. Cost. 2173

1973, Decision 014 /1973, (*Second Blasphemy case*), (27 Feb. 1973), [1973] 2 Giur. Cost. 69

1973, Decision 175 /1973, (*Fourth Nullity case*), (6 Dec. 1973), [1973] 2 Giur. Cost. 2321

1974, Ordinance 169 /1974, (*Fifth Divorce case*), (6 June 1974), [1974] 1 Giur. Cost. 994

1975, Decision 188 /1975, (*Third Vilipendio case*), (27 June 1975), [1975] Giuris. Cost. 1508

1977, Decision 001 /1977, (*Sixth Nullity case*), (4 Jan. 1977), [1977] 1 Giur. Cost. 3

1978, Decision 016 /1978, (*Referendum Admissibility case*), (2 Feb. 1978), [1978] 1 Giuris. Cost. 79 218

1979, Decision 117 /1979, (*Court Oath case*), (2 Oct. 1979), [1979] Giuris. Cost. 816

1982, Decision 016 /1982, (*Marriage for Minors case*), (13 Jan. 1982), [1982] Giuris. Cost. 115

1982, Decision 018 /1982, (*Legal rights and nullity case*), (22 Jan. 1982), [1982] Giuris. Cost. 138

1984, Decision 239 /1984, (*First Jewish Union case*), (13 July 1984), [1984] 1 (2) Giuris. Cost. 1727

1985, Decision 086 /1985, (*First INVIM case*), (27 March 1985), [1985] 1 (1) Giuris. Cost. 576

1986, Ordinance 160 /1986, (*Second INVIM case*), (27 June 1986), [1986] 1 (1) Giuris. Cost. 1097

1988, Decision 043 /1988, (*Second Jewish Union case*), (14 Jan. 1988), [1988] 1 (1) Giuris. Cost. 114

1988, Decision 1146 /1988

1988, Decision 925 /1988, (*Third Blasphemy case*), (8 July 1988), [1988] 1 (3) Giuris. Cost. 4294

1989, Decision 203 /1989, (*First School Hours case*), (11 April 1989), [1989] 1 (1) Giur. Cost. 890

1990, Decision 259 /1990, (23 May 1990), [1990] Giuris. Cost. 1542

1991, Decision 013 /1991, (11 Jan. 1991), [1991] 1 Giuris. Cost. 77

1992, Decision 290 /1992, (4 June 1992), [1992] 2 Giuris. Cost. 2223

1993, Decision 195 /1993, (19 April 1993), [1993] 1 Giuris. Cost. 1324

1995, Decision 440 /1995, (*Fourth Blasphemy case*), (18 Oct. 1995)

United States Cases

Abington School District v. *Schempp* 374 U.S. 203 (1963)

Abrams v. *United States* 250 U.S. 616 (1919)

American Booksellers v. *Hudnut* 771 F.2d 323 (1985)

Anti-Defamation League v. *Federal Communications Commission* 403 F.2d 169 (1968)

Ashton v. *Kentucky* 384 U.S. 195 (1966)

Beauharnais v. *Illinois* 343 U.S. 250 (1952)

Boos v. *Barry* 485 U.S. 312 (1988), 107 S.Ct. 1282 (1987)

Bowers v. *Hardwick* 478 U.S. 186 (1986)

Brandenburg v. *Ohio* 395 U.S. 444 (1969)

Civil Rights Cases 109 U.S. 3 (1883)

Cohen v. *California* 403 U.S. 15 (1971)

Collin v. *Smith* 447 F.Supp. 676 (1978)

Cornelius v. *NAACP Legal Defence and Education Fund* 473 U.S. 788 (1985)

Debs v. *US* 249 U.S. 211 (1919)

Dennis v. *US* 341 U.S. 494 (1951)

Eisenstadt v. *Baird* 405 U.S. 438 (1972)

Engel v. *Vitale* (*School Prayer case*) 370 U.S. 421 (1962)

Garrison v. *Louisiana* 379 U.S. 64 (1964)

Griswold v. *Conneticutt* (*Contraception case*) 381 U.S. 479 (1965)

Korematsu v. *United States* 323 U.S. 314 (1944)

Lochner v. *New York* 198 U.S. 45 (1905)

Marbury v. *Madison* 5 Cranch 137 (1803)

Meyer v. *Nebraska* 262 U.S. 390 (1923)
New York v. *Ferber* 458 U.S. 747 (1982)
New York Times v. *Sullivan* 376 U.S. 254 (1964)
Paris Adult Theatre v. *Slaton* 413 U.S. 49 (1973)
Pasadas de Puerto Rico v. *Tourism Co. of Puerto Rico* 478 U.S. 328 (1986)
Plessy v. *Ferguson* 163 U.S. 537 (1896)
Poe v. *Ullman* 367 U.S. 497 (1961)
Quirin, ex parte 317 U.S. 1 (1942)
Roe v. *Wade* (*Abortion case*) 410 U.S. 113 (1973)
Roth v. *United States* 354 U.S. 476 (1957)
Schenck v. *United States* 249 U.S. 47 (1919)
Stanley v. *Georgia* 394 U.S. 557 (1969)
Terry v. *Ohio* 392 U.S. 1 (1968)
Tollett v. *US* 485 F.2d 1087 (1973)
US v. *Schwimmer* 279 U.S. 644 (1929)
West Coast Hotel v. *Parrish* 300 U.S. 379 (1937)
Whitney v. *California* 274 U.S. 357 (1927)

UK, Australian, Indian, South African and New Zealand Cases

Anisminic v. *Foreign Compensation Commission* (House of Lords); [1969] 2 Appeal
    Cases 147; [1968] 2 Queen's Bench 862 (Court of Appeal)
Australia Capital Television v. *Commonwealth*; [1992] 177 C.L.R. 106
Certification of the Constitution of South Africa; 6 Sept. 1996, (23/96)
Kesavananda Bharati; (*Essential Features case*); [1973] (Supp.) S.C.R. 1; [1973] All
    India Reports (S.C.) 1461
Khatri v. *State of Bihar*; [1981] All India Reports (S.C.) 928
Knuller v. *Director of Public Prosecutions* (House of Lords); [1973] Appeal Cases 446
Liversidge v. *Aldridge* (House of Lords); [1942] Appeal Cases 206
Mukti Mocha v. *India*; [1984] A.I.R. S.C. 802
R. v. *Bourne*; [1939] 1 Kings Bench 687
R. v. *Close*; [1948] V.L.R. 445 126
R. v. *Hicklin*; [1868] L.R. 3 Q.B. 360
RC Cooper v. *India*; (*Bank Nationalisation case*); [1970] 3 S.C.R. 530; [1970] All India
    Reports (S.C.) 1318
Shaw v. *Director of Public Prosecutions* (House of Lords); [1962] Appeal Cases 220

German, Hungarian and French Cases

Art. 117 case 3 BVerfGE 225
German Abortion Reform Law case 39 BVerfGE 1 (1975)
Second Abortion Decision, 88 BVerfGE 283 (1993)
Hungarian Abortion case 1 (no. 1) East European Case Reporter of Constitutional Law 3 (1994); Case no. 64/1991
Incontestabilité de la Loi Référendaire (Decision of the 6th Nov. 1962, 62-20 DC)
Klass (Interception of Communications case) 30 BVerfGE 1 (1970)
Liberté d'Association (Decision of the 16th July 1971, 71-44 DC)
Southwest State case 1 BVerfGE 14

International Tribunals

Att. Gen. of Ireland (Society for the Protection of the Unborn Child) v. *Open Door Counselling, Dublin Well Woman Centre*; [1992] 14 E.H.R.R. 131
Dudgeon v. *United Kingdom*; [1981] 4 E.H.R.R. 149
Felderer v. *Sweden*; [1986] 8 E.H.R.R. 91
Glimmerveen v. *Netherlands*; [1979] D.R. 18
Handyside v. *United Kingdom*; *(Little Red Schoolbook case, 1976 Ser. A, no. 24)*; [1979] 1 E.H.R.R. 737
Lowes v. *UK*; [1988] No. 13214/87, 9/12/1988
Luisi and Carbone v. *Minestero del Tesoro*, (Cases 286/82, 26/83); [1984] 1 E.C.R. 377
Norris v. *Ireland*; [1991] 13 E.H.R.R. 186
R. v. *Bouchereau*, (Case 30/77); [1977] 2 E.C.R. 1999
Society for the Protection of the Unborn Child v. *Grogan*, (No. 2); *(Abortion Information)*; [1991] E.C.R. 4685; [1991] 3 C.M.L.R. 849
Taylor, and the WGP v. *Canada*, (Comm. 104/1981); [1983] 2 Selected Decisions under the Optional Protocol 25; [5] C.H.R.R. D/2907
X v. *Germany*; [1982] D.R. 29

Index